ELECTRIC EDWARDIANS

Electric Edwardians

The Story of the Mitchell & Kenyon Collection

Vanessa Toulmin

Publishing

First published in 2006 by the
BRITISH FILM INSTITUTE
21 Stephen Street, London W1T 1LN

The British Film Institute's purpose is to champion moving image culture in all its richness and diversity across the UK, for the benefit of as wide an audience as possible, and to create and encourage debate.

Cover design: Paul Wright
Front Cover illustration: *Workforce Leaving Alfred Butterworth and Sons, Glebe Mills, Hollinwood* (1901).
Frontispiece: *Leeds Lifeboat Procession* (1902).

Set by Fakenham Photosetting Limited, Fakenham, Norfolk
Layout and design by Ketchup, London
Printed in the UK by Cromwell Press, Trowbridge, Wiltshire

British Library Cataloguing-in-Publication Data
A catalogue record for this book is available from the British Library

ISBN (pbk) 1-84457-145-9
ISBN (hbk) 1-84457-144-0

Contents

Acknowledgments

The research into what is know known as the Peter Worden Mitchell & Kenyon Collection first began in 1995 when I was contacted by Peter Worden at the National Fairground Archive (NFA). Over the following ten years, this original contact has developed into something that has shaped both my life and research and the research community of early film scholarship. The resulting project, which started with a small British Academy Research Grant and then became an AHRC-funded collaboration between the University of Sheffield and the British Film Institute, has resulted in a three-part BBC 2 series, two DVDs, many publications, a book of collected essays, over eighty film shows throughout the world and now this latest publication. None of these would have been possible without the generosity of Peter Worden, who granted access to both the films and also to his own immense knowledge of the company and Blackburn local history. When Peter donated the films to the BFI in 2000, he urged me to take care of them and to make sure that the achievements of this company from Blackburn would never again be forgotten. I hope I have carried out his wishes. The films have been magnificently restored by my colleagues in the National Film and Television Archive (NFTVA) in Berkhamstead and it is their skill and expertise that has enabled the films to be seen once again. In particular, Kevin Patton and Phil Read, 'now in the Archive in the sky', whose substantial initial work with Dr João S. de Oliveira, Ben Thompson and Peter Marshall, can be seen in every restored frame of film. Ann Fleming was the Head of the NFTVA when the BFI acquired the collection; I hope the results have exceeded her expectations. In addition, colleagues at the BFI have been indispensable, and I would like to thank Margaret Deriaz, Christine Whitehouse, Karen Alexander, Patrick Russell, Jan Faull; and Tom Cabot, Claire Milburn, Rebecca Barden and Sophie Contento in publishing for their attention to detail in all aspects of the project. Friends such as Derek, John, Tony, Lulu, Lesley, Nico, Sabine, Frank, Bregtje, Dave and Carolyn have offered their support over the ten long years and reminded me there was life beyond the collection. Particular thanks and gratitude must go to Rebecca Vick, former Research Assistant to the project and now Assistant Curator of Non-Fiction at the BFI. Her love and devotion to the films has gone above and beyond the call of duty and it is largely her efficiency and attention to detail that has enabled the project to run as smoothly as it has.

The research has always been a collaborative process and would not have been possible without the support of colleagues in the film and archival community both nationally and internationally. The local history archives and libraries visited are too numerous to mention, but particular thanks must go to Manchester Central Library, Morecambe Library, Janet McBain at the Scottish Film Archive, Marion Hewitt from the North West Film Archive, Dave Berry at the Welsh Film Archive and Robert Todd of the National Maritime Museum; Dr Melanie Tebbutt from Manchester Metropolitan University, and Jan Hargreaves from the Museum of Science and Industry in Manchester. Colleagues in Blackburn Local Studies Library, Birmingham Central Library, National Library of Ireland, Museum of Science and Industry in Manchester, the National Tramway Museum and the West Yorkshire Archives Service in Bradford also deserve special mention. Certain individuals have given freely of their time and knowledge for the sake of enriching the collection for both the research community and the greater public: my long-term collaborator and friend, Simon Popple, Richard Brown, Martin Loiperdinger, Luke McKernan, Nico de Klerk, Tony Fletcher, Charles Musser, John and Bill Barnes, Mark Fuller, Robert Monks, David Williams, David Robinson, Steve Bottomore and Jon Burrows from the early film community and Ian Wilkinson of the Manchester Wheelers. Martin Humphries and Ronald Grant have also allowed access to the Mitchell & Kenyon films in the Cinema Museum. Special thanks must go the Giornate del Cinema for their promotion of the Mitchell & Kenyon Collection over the past few years – their generous support of the films at the festival have greatly enriched the project and widened public interest in the Collection.

In order to understand the films, I have tried to place them in the context of the society in which they were filmed. Many colleagues who have shared their expertise are acknowledged in the text, but I would particularly like to thank the following historians and specialists from other disciplines who have enabled this approach. These include Dave Russell, Tony Collins, Ian Yearsley, Winston Bond, Kevin Kelly, Chris Wrigley, Robin Whalley, Andrew Prescott, Brian Steptoe, John Barker, Brian Cook and Robert Gate. Rob Mason, Paul Tully, Graham Bell and Alan Candlish; Newcastle, Middlesbrough and Sunderland football clubs. Some of the ideas outlined in this publication were first presented at film shows, research seminars and conferences, in Yale, Chicago, New York, Trier, South Carolina, Preston, Sheffield, Leeds and Exeter, and Le Giornate del Cinema Muto in Pordenone. I would like to express gratitude to all those who have been part of the audience during a Mitchell & Kenyon screening and who made suggestions. Of the many referees both anonymous and known who passed comments in individual chapters, I am greatly indebted to John Walton, whose comments on various drafts of the text saved this author from considerable embarrassment. His generosity in both expanding my reading material with suggestions and his incisive and critical comments have resulted in a stronger and richer manuscript, but all mistakes and omissions are my own. Special thanks must go the Giornate del Cinema for their promotion of the Mitchell & Kenyon Collection over the past few years – their generous support of the films at the festival have greatly enriched the project and widened public interest in the Collection.

Finally, thanks go to my colleagues at the University of Sheffield Library and the School of English, who have allowed me the luxury of spending time on the Mitchell & Kenyon Collection as it grew from an important but slightly obscure research project on early film to one that touched the nation: in particular, Amanda Bernstein, whose close reading of the text and copy-editing skills have resulted in a more enjoyable and accurate read, and Lesley Allen and Ian Trowell, who ran the NFA in my absence. The AHRC funded the original three-year research project but Martin Lewis, University Librarian, and Professor Dominic Shellard from the School of English have enabled time and additional support for the book to be completed.

This book is dedicated to two Lancastrians: first, Peter Worden, for his generosity in sharing the collection and welcoming me into his family; and second, to my late father, Harold Toulmin, a freeman of Lancaster, who died before this book was completed. I will never forget that they were both there on that momentous evening in Blackburn in January 2005 when over a thousand people came to the St George's Hall to see once again, in the words of Sagar Mitchell and James Kenyon, 'Local Films for Local People'.

Foreword

> Periods of history, like place, are thought of by most people as a set of images which, however close or however distant from the reality of these periods, are the basis of all their thoughts about them.[1]

The Mitchell & Kenyon company was a small but pioneering cinematograph firm based in Blackburn in the first decade of the twentieth century. For many years, their memory was kept alive by only a few film historians and dedicated local enthusiasts. Known for only a handful of surviving films, they were merely a footnote in the canon

Street Scenes in an unidentified town in the North of England (c. 1902)

of film history. Since 2001, this picture has changed, with the discovery of 820 rolls of film comprising over twenty-eight hours of footage from the early 1900s. The films that have survived were shot for travelling exhibitors in the days before the emergence of purpose-built cinemas. Shown in town halls, at village fetes or at the local fair and advertised as 'local films for local people', they were a wonder of their age, and audiences flocked to see their neighbours, children, family and themselves on the flickering screen.

This study is an attempt to look more closely at these scenes of everyday life as represented in the collection. The individual fragments of two minutes or so reveal snapshots of the working class at work, play and going about their daily business, watching football, both association and rugby, participating in civic and religious events, and enjoying a range of leisure activities. Individually they can be described as tiny vignettes capturing fragments of larger, more complex events. More importantly, and when studied collectively, the twenty-eight hours of actuality footage that has survived gives us a new perspective on an era that has been written about largely from the viewpoint of politics and privilege.

The book is divided into eight distinct but interlocking sections based on themes and areas of research that are reflected in the contextual subject matter that survives in the filmic record. Although it is an endeavour to view the Edwardian era through the filmic record, the majority of the material relates to the time of transition between the last days of Queen Victoria and the first three years of her son Edward's reign. So in true historical terms, it is both the late-Victorian world and early Edwardian era that is captured on record and analysed in this study. It is not, therefore, an attempt to produce a chronological history of the period leading up to the Great War. Recent studies, such as G. R. Searle's *A New England: Peace and War 1886–1918*, provide the political backdrop for such a story.[2] Instead, it combines the pictorial record that is revealed in the films with recent scholarship in the fields of popular entertainment, leisure and sporting history, urban and transport studies and those of labour and social history,[3] to create a contextual framework that allows us both to enjoy the films as poetic fragments of early film technology and newly discovered historical texts. For, in the words of Giovanni Morelli (1816–91): 'If you would like to understand . . . history . . . you should look carefully at portraits. In people's faces there is always something of the history of their time, if one knows how to read it.'[4]

Notes

1 Earl F. Bargainnier, 'Fog and Decadence: Images of the 1890s', *Journal of Popular Culture*, Vol. 12 No. 1 (1978), pp. 19–29.

2 G. R. Searle, *A New England: Peace and War 1886–1918* (Oxford: Oxford University Press, 2004).

3 For an in-depth study of how the films have already been analysed by subject historians, see Vanessa Toulmin, Simon Popple and Patrick Russell (eds), *The Lost World of Mitchell & Kenyon: Edwardian Britain on Film* (London: BFI, 2004).

4 Cited in Peter Burke, *Eyewitnessing: The Uses of Images as Historical Evidence* (London: Reaktion Press, 2001), p. 21.

1
The Mitchell & Kenyon Film Company

> The mass of actuality films from the first decades of film history in our archives around the world are ripe for rediscovery and re-examination. They constitute a neglected and, indeed, repressed aspect of film history. They present an incredibly rich reserve of information about the foundation of our modern culture . . .[1]

Discovery

What we now know as the Peter Worden Mitchell & Kenyon Collection first became a historical reality when three large drums containing over 800 reels of nitrate film were acquired by the BFI in July 2000. The Collection came to light in June 1994 when Peter Worden, a Blackburn businessman, arranged for two local workmen to bring the films they had found in a local shop to him. Worden recalls the moment thus:

> On 23rd June 1994 my wife and I went to the Pavarotti concert at the Birmingham NEC . . . On our return, there was a message for me from the owner of a local wedding video and film to video transfer company who knew I had an interest in old, especially Blackburn orientated, film. Several specimen rolls of 35mm film had been brought in to him, which he wanted me to look at. On examination, these were all stylus-inscribed at the 'head', were typically 50′ to 100′ in length, and clearly M&K because they had been found in the cellar of 40 Northgate. This building had been unoccupied for about 18 months . . . In the cellar had been found 3 metal drums approximately the size of milk churns minus the conical upper section. All were crammed solid with film, and if I didn't 'rate' them, they were going into the skip! I contacted the foreman of the work-gang and, curbing my excitement, arranged for the drums to be delivered to me.[2]

Operatives of Acme Spinning Co., Pendlebury (1901), including James Kenyon captured at the front of the picture

When the drums were inspected, they were found to contain separate layers of between fifteen and twenty films per layer, with sixteen layers in total. Each roll of film was wrapped with a rubber band and many had scraps of paper attached to them. These pieces of paper invariably contained information pertaining to the location of the film, the name of the exhibitor or a date of filming. In all instances, they corroborated the information on the first two frames of the negatives, which were either inscribed with a stylus or black ink. The scraps measured between one-and-three-quarter inches in length and one-and-a-half inches wide and were either blank pieces of paper cut to size or unused handbills produced by Mitchell & Kenyon in association with a travelling exhibitor.

Over the next three months, each layer of film was carefully taken out of the drums, the dust and debris that had formed between the films carefully vacuumed out, and then placed into small plastic sandwich bags. The paper inscriptions were placed in the bags and the information from the first two frames copied onto a sticky label on the outside of the sandwich bags. The films were numbered and placed in plastic cartons and stored in the unplugged refrigeration unit.[3] The work undertaken nightly over three months by Peter Worden and Robin Whalley produced a working list of the showmen/exhibitors who were associated with Mitchell & Kenyon, a timescale of the film production and the geographical boundaries where the firm operated. The numbering system employed by

Peter and Robin has been retained for the filmography and all film titles in the collection are preceded by the original number that was assigned to them immediately after their discovery.[4]

The discovery was first premiered in Blackburn in November 1994 when Peter Worden presented a selection of newly restored material on 16mm to an audience consisting of local people, predominantly members of the Blackburn Local History Society.[5] Between 1994 and 1999, Peter sent various batches of films to a commercial laboratory to be printed, and showed a selection of this material to local interest groups in the Lancashire region.

Eventually, in July 2000, with the aid of the NFA at the University of Sheffield, 830 camera negative rolls were acquired by the BFI to form the Peter Worden Mitchell & Kenyon Collection. Alongside the discovery of the Peter Worden Collection, two smaller collections of Mitchell & Kenyon material, numbering approximately seventy camera negatives, appeared between 1994 and 1997 and are now held by the Cinema Museum in London and Lobster in Paris.[6] A selection of the fiction films will be considered in the following chapter.

Together with the existing titles held in the NFTA, the Imperial War Museum and the North-West Film Archive, over 900 films relating to the company now survive, making it the third largest film collection associated with one company from the early film period after the Edison Collection in the United States and the Lumière Collection in France.[7] Although the filmic record is immensely rich, one major disappointment was the lack of any contemporary archival material or business records associated with the company, either in Blackburn itself or in the hands of private collectors. The existence of this material was cited in an interview with Sagar Mitchell published in 1951 and in obituaries following his death in 1952.[8] When Sagar's son, John Mitchell, retired from the family business in 1959, according to John's daughter, June Witter, the family offered the films, costumes, studio equipment, cameras and business records to Walter W. Yeates, the Librarian and Curator of the Museum of Blackburn. When the offer was rejected, a local authority refuse wagon was hired and all extant material relating to the company was disposed of by Blackburn Council.[9]

The importance of business records in assessing the wider social and economic significance of early British film companies cannot be underestimated.[10] The absence of any business records for Mitchell & Kenyon means that we have only the films themselves, and the advertisements placed in local, national and trade press in the 1900s, with which to understand their expansion and development as a company. This is in contrast to other companies like the Warwick Trading Company, Pathé, Edison and the American Biograph Company, where the filmic record is balanced by important archival material. Over the course of a decade of research, the only business record found in relation to the company is one memo written to Sydney Carter of New Century Pictures in Bradford, offering their services as a company for the taking of local views.[11] Consequently, any consideration of the importance of Mitchell & Kenyon in relation to their contemporaries must rely mainly on the historical record of the rich visual treasure of films. In order to create an overview of Mitchell & Kenyon as a company, we must view the inscriptions left on the negatives as a record of a business transaction, as they document the company's relationship with the travelling exhibitors. In addition, the advertisements placed by the company in contemporary newspapers of films for sale, or the services they offered to the trade, are a supplementary source of information (see Plate 1).

It is only through studying these sources alongside the films that the company's impact as a business in the rapidly expanding world of Edwardian film-making and exhibition can be examined and evaluated. Finally, it must be understood that although the company produced films from 1899 to 1913, the largest body of material relates from 1900 to 1905, with only 10 per cent of the collection relating to the period 1906–13. This is a major factor in understanding the impact of the company and its relationship with other film-makers in the UK at that time, and it is the first six years of production that provides the evidence for this study.

It is worth noting that when Rachael Low and Roger Manvell, under the auspices of the History Committee of the BFI, were conducting their research on the history of British film in 1948, Mitchell & Kenyon as a company warranted little more than a passing mention.[12] Despite the abundance of contemporary evidence for their film output in local newspapers and the trade press, Mitchell & Kenyon were seen largely as a footnote in film history, one of many regional film companies operating in the UK in the 1900s, and little attention was paid to their impact on early film history.[13] This could have been due partly to the assumption that very few of the films had survived, as only a handful were known to exist, and perhaps also because of the emphasis placed by early film scholars on film production in the south-east of England, in particular the work of James Williamson, Robert Paul and Cecil Hepworth.

This focus on the output of film-makers from the London and Brighton region (the Brighton School) persists today, with little attention being paid to many of the regional companies who operated outside the south-east, for example Bamforth's of Holmfirth and the Sheffield Photo Company.[14] Even though important work on Mitchell & Kenyon and other local film companies was undertaken by regional historians in the 1970s, the true significance of Mitchell & Kenyon and the importance of regional film companies only began to be appreciated in the mid-1990s, with the emergence of the two film collections, one largely consisting of non-fiction and the second relating to their fiction output.[15] This introduction to the work of the company will consider the discovery of the new collections, Mitchell & Kenyon as a business and their contemporaries in the film world, as well as the impact and consequences of this new material for our understanding of early film and the Edwardian era more widely. In Chapter 2, I will investigate in more detail the varying types of material produced by Mitchell & Kenyon, and compare the types of films produced by the company with those of their contemporaries.

(l. ro r.) *Kiss in the Tunnel*, Bamforth & Co., 1899; *The Big Swallow*, James Williamson, 1901; *A Daring Daylight Burglary*, Frank Mottershaw, 1903.

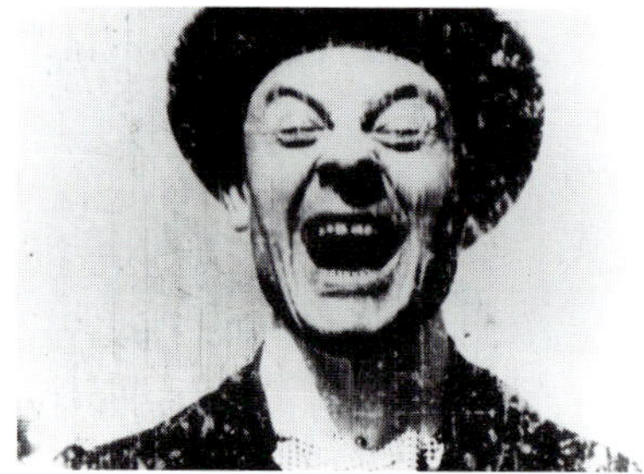

The Company and its Contemporaries

The firm of Mitchell & Kenyon, founded in Blackburn in 1897 by Sagar Mitchell (1866–1952) and James Kenyon (1850–1925), was one of many companies producing cinematograph films in the 1900s.[16] Before their arrival in the world of early film-making, Mitchell ran the family photographic apparatus business with his father and Kenyon had a successful penny-in-the-slot-machine business from the late 1890s onwards that was incorporated into Mitchell & Kenyon's business activities in 1902.[17] They used the trade name Norden to advertise their fiction films, with 'Norden' originally being used by Sagar Mitchell and his father to describe their photographic camera apparatus.[18] In 1938, Mitchell recollected the origins of their innovative enterprise:

> I was (with Mr Jas Kenyon as partner) making cinematograph projectors and accessories. I designed the machine and made the pattern and we got our costumes from Mr Page . . . The first exhibition of the cinematograph in Blackburn . . . was a private show given on my premises at 40, Northgate and the Editor of *The Blackburn Times*, of November 27th, 1897, the late Mr Rostron, was present . . . A few weeks later Mr Page gave me a contract to show pictures for several weeks and we had a very successful run.[19]

The Mr Page in question was Edward Hermann 'Papa' Page, proprietor and licensee of the Lyceum Theatre in Blackburn, who, according to Sagar Mitchell, loaned the fledgling company costumes and props from the theatre for their first fiction films. The first film show was reviewed in the *Blackburn Times* by Rostron, who wrote:

> I have seen the cinematograph in use in a great many places, in the provinces, in London and in Paris, but hitherto always with unpleasant defects which Messrs Mitchell and Kenyon have succeeded in almost entirely remedying . . . the unpleasant, jerky motion of the pictures, and the noise of the machinery.[20]

When Mitchell & Kenyon began producing films in 1897, they were operating within an already crowded field populated by film companies from Britain, Europe and America. John Barnes's pioneering five-volume study of Victorian cinema revealed the myriad of companies and quantities of films produced in Great Britain alone by 1897.[21] No records of Mitchell & Kenyon's activities for 1898 have been traced, although a later recollection from a member of the Green family, a fairground showman from Lancashire, remembers the company filming local films for Blackburn Easter Fair in 1898.[22] However, in September 1899 they reached national prominence with the release of three Norden films – two of them comedies and one a historical costume-type film.[23] By the time of Mitchell & Kenyon's main years of production, the early 1900s, the field had yet again expanded and showmen exhibitors could not only purchase films from Méliès and Pathé in France, or the American and British Biograph Company in London, but also a whole range of film companies in the UK, ranging from Walkers in Aberdeen to Robert Paul, Cecil Hepworth, Charles Urban and others in London.

When Mitchell & Kenyon first started business in 1897, there were very few regional film companies operating in the north of England. Advertisements in the trade press remarked on how the region was ripe for such an opportunity, and, across the Pennines, Yorkshire was becoming a strong area of activity. Pioneers such Jasper Redfern of Sheffield, Bamforths of Holmfirth, Riley Brothers of Bradford and, by the 1900s, the Sheffield Photo Company, were producing a range of fiction and local films for exhibition and distribution purposes.[24]

Despite this, there appeared little competition in the Lancashire region, which is surprising, considering its rich history of entertainment culture and wide variety of venues for the cinematograph, including music halls, seaside venues, travelling fairs and pleasure gardens. As John Walton has argued, Lancashire was the first industrialised region for mass entertainment in the United Kingdom, with the development of association football as a spectator sport, the growth of the seaside resort and the development of music-hall entertainment.[25]

Other cinematograph companies had filmed the north of England: the Lumière cinematograph filmed Liverpool in October 1897, while the Biograph Company and Arthur Cheetham came to Blackburn to film a match between Blackburn Rovers and West Bromwich Albion in October 1898.[26] Unlike Arthur Cheetham, who was based in Rhyl, Mitchell & Kenyon were offering a service that was local, instantaneous and tailored to the needs of the various exhibitors operating in the north of England. The speed with which they could produce local films on demand for the fairground and travelling showmen fraternity is reflected in the filmic and advertising record:

Handbill for the original Lumiérè Cinematograph Show in London in 1895

> If you run a CINEMATOGRAPH SHOW
> See our FILMS – Specially designed for Showmen
> If you value your films, and want to give a perfect
> Show quickly and well, see our New Machine for 1900.
> And if you want Attractions in the way of Special or
> Local Pictures consult us
> WE TAKE THEM AND MAKE THEM.[27]

In 1900 alone, Mitchell & Kenyon had supplied films for over twenty different venues in the Lancashire region, the vast majority of them associated with the annual wakes fairs.[28] Their contacts in the entertainment world proved invaluable and the showmen who used the company in Lancashire asked them to travel further afield to Nottingham Goose Fair, the Yorkshire feasts in Dewsbury and to Hull Fair.[29] Their advert in *The Showman* reflects this dominance of the market – although other companies such as Hepworth and Warwick were offering a similar service, Mitchell & Kenyon's proximity to the showmen gave them a head start. In addition, they had a stock supply of titles already made on towns in the north of England, and they were prepared to visit at short notice any towns or villages in the region that

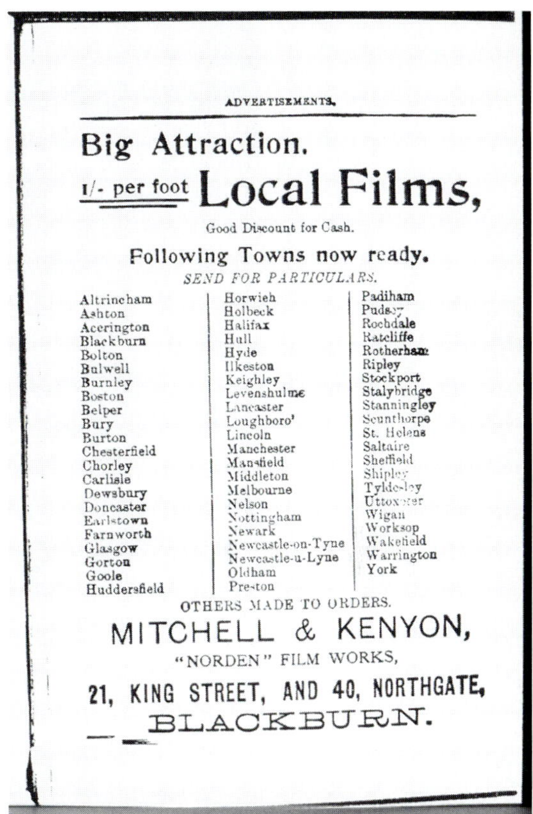

Mitchell & Kenyon adverts from the *Showman's Year Book*: (left) 1900, offering both the film service and the penny in the slot machine business; (right) 1901, illustrating the wide range of locations already filmed (NFA)

the exhibitors wished them to film. The earliest dated titles in the collection are images of workers leaving their place of work, a genre defined by film historians as 'factory gates' films. The earliest inscribed date relates to *Workers Leaving Haslam's Ltd Colne* (1900) and was shown six weeks later at the annual Wake.[30] *The Millhands of Cheetham's Bankwood Mills, Stalybridge* (1900) was filmed on 17 July 1900 and shown eleven days later in Payne's Cinematograph show:

> We make our way to what appears to be the centre of attraction, a cinematograph exhibition announcing a picture of local interest. This we are utterly unable to resist ... After a very good show of pictures . . . the great attraction is announced in stentorian voice by the guide. The mill hands (we are told) at one of the local mills – Mr Cheetham's it was announced – had been photographed specially for this show, and we are enabled to see the employees as they appeared for dinner. Much amusement is caused by the exclamation of the audience as one after another appears on the screen and is recognised. It certainly was a smart idea on the part of the showman to adopt this method of popularising his show, and we have no doubt he has reaped the benefit of his enterprise.[31]

This pattern continues throughout 1900, with Mitchell & Kenyon being commissioned to produce films of factories for wakes fairs in Ordsall, Salford, Chorley, Gorton, Stockport and Oldham, to name but a few.[32] They also followed the showmen into Yorkshire with *Salt's Works in Saltaire* (1900), filmed on 24 July and shown four days later at Shipley Feast.[33]

Advert for Hepworth & Co., from *The Showman* newspaper, December 1900

The fairground circuit in the early 1900s was particularly dominated by showmen based in the north and the Midlands, with upwards of nine cinematograph shows appearing at Nottingham Goose Fair and Hull Fair in 1900 alone. Fairground showmen brought fiction titles from a variety of film-makers – Gaumont, Pathé and Méliès titles all featured in the cinematograph shows.[34] But it was the use of the local film that gave Mitchell & Kenyon an edge over their competitors. Based in Blackburn, they enjoyed easy access to West Yorkshire, Liverpool, Manchester and the rest of Lancashire, the areas where many of the major fairs were held.

The company's relationship with fairground showmen exhibitors was fundamental to its development in these early years and would continue for over ten years. In 1898, George Green commissioned them to film a series of local views for projection on Green's Cinematograph at Blackburn Easter Fair. In 1899, Green advertised further local films of operatives leaving Audley Hall Mills, Blackburn, to be shown at

(Below) *The 'Hands' Leaving work at North-street Mills, Chorley* (1900); (below right) *Green's Cinematograph show at the Annual Whitsundtide Fair at Preston* (1906)

the annual Easter Fair held on Blackburn market.[35] Mitchell & Kenyon continued to be associated with Green until at least 1907, and worked with him when he travelled to Cork and Glasgow.[36] Fairground showmen, including such famous names as Captain Thomas Payne, Pat Collins and President Kemp (the majority of them based in the Lancashire region), commissioned films from Mitchell & Kenyon in the years up to 1908.[37]

The number of local films shot for projection at the Bioscope shows is difficult to estimate. However, over a hundred titles in the collection were made for this purpose, the majority dating to 1900–1. By December 1900, Mitchell & Kenyon were advertising that 'nothing is so great a draw as a local subject' and offering films of over sixty towns to their showmen clients, including views of Lancaster, Belper, Scunthorpe, York, Oldham and Boston.[38]

By 1901, Mitchell & Kenyon were producing three distinct genres of films – non-fiction or 'actualities', fiction films and reconstructions – and were filming extensively outside the Lancashire region, in Yorkshire and the Midlands. The classification of film genres is difficult in the early film period, but, in brief, non-fiction could feature subjects such as films of royalty, town views or factory gates; fiction titles might depict comic incidents or tales of misfortune, with a fairly basic storyline; while reconstructions, or 'fake' films, usually re-enacted or fictionalised contemporary events.

Although they produced three fiction titles in 1899, it was the reconstruction film that first provided the company with a national market for film distribution in 1900. The films Mitchell & Kenyon supplied were similar to those of their competitors in the film world, in one instance employing the same title used by James Williamson, a film-maker from Brighton, for a fake Boxer Rebellion film, *Attack on a China Mission* (1900).[39] As with the local film, Mitchell & Kenyon apparently made a speciality out of the fake war titles, and continued producing them until 1902. The income generated must have been considerable, because in September 1901, Mitchell & Kenyon, who had until this point continued to occupy their respective premises on Northgate and King Street, moved to a location at the rear of Kenyon's property at 22 Clayton Street. They installed a laboratory and studio across the street alongside a chapel, and built an open-air triangular lock-up stage, for the filming of some of their fiction titles.

In addition to the local and Boer War titles, they filmed events of national interest, creating a catalogue of titles that were distributed by other companies, and advertising almost weekly in the trade press. In terms of business relationships, Mitchell & Kenyon were by now receiving commissions from a range of exhibitors, including music-hall showmen and stand-alone companies, and were offering a developing and printing service to all their customers.[40]

By early 1901, they were able to compete on the national stage, and in February of that year, Mitchell successfully obtained permission to film the funeral of Queen Victoria in London and Windsor. On that occasion, he 'was perched on a site near a lamp-post at Hyde Park Corner from four o'clock in the morning until late in the afternoon in order to secure the necessary pictures'.[41] The films were shown in many parts of the country – over 900 feet of film was available at the price of one shilling per foot.[42] With the *Funeral of Queen Victoria* (1901), they produced a film that, like their fiction output, could be advertised nationally and could compete with titles produced by London-

Advert from *The Showman*, March 1901, for the Funeral of Queen Victoria (NFA)

Address: HOWARD THURSTON, Palace Theatre, London.

The Queen's Funeral.

Undoubtedly the best animated picture taken of this important event was photographed by us at Windsor. The entire procession is seen coming down the slope towards the camera thus affording the best view possible of the

Coffin on the Gun Carriage drawn by the ever ready Handymen.

No. 1. Escort of Life Guards, General Pole Carew and Staff, and Lord Roberts. 75 feet.
No. 2. The Massed Bands, 60 feet.
No. 3. Coffin on Gun Carriage drawn by Bluejackets and followed by the King and the other Royal Personages. 75 feet or 125 feet.
No. 4. Officers and Men of the German Army, Yeomen of the Guard, Queen's Pipers and Life Guards. 100 feet.
No. 5. The Crowd after the Procession. 40 feet. Total length 400 feet.

We also took

The London Procession coming along Piccadilly. Total length 500 feet.

Supplied in sections as required.

Just Out! THE SNOW MAN. Roars of Laughter. 65 feet.

Price 1/- per foot. Liberal discounts.

MITCHELL & KENYON, Cinematographers, Blackburn.

To Showmen, Entertainers,

based companies such as the Warwick Trading Company and Robert Paul, who also filmed the event.[43]

If the non-local genres that Mitchell & Kenyon were now producing resulted in national coverage and international distribution possibilities, it was their relationship with the network of new stand-alone film commissioners in the north of England that formed the bedrock of the company. Ranging from former music-hall showmen to magic-lantern exhibitors, the stand-alone or town-hall showmen became the main clients for Mitchell & Kenyon's local titles as, from 1900 onwards, the exhibitors promoted their two-hour film shows around the industrial cities in the north of England and Scotland.

One of the main companies supplied by Mitchell & Kenyon was the North American Animated Photo Company, who, between 1901 and 1907, commissioned a series of local titles within the full range of its exhibition circuit, encompassing Scotland, the south-west, the Midlands and the north-east of England (see Plate 2).[44] Ralph Pringle, the manager of the North American Animated Photo Company, had previously worked for A. D. Thomas, a showman based primarily in the Manchester region who operated as the Thomas-Edison Animated Photo Company. Pringle's decision to leave Thomas and to base his operations in Liverpool created a further business possibility for Mitchell & Kenyon, who were not Thomas's sole suppliers.

The relationship between A. D. Thomas and Mitchell & Kenyon, which dates back to 1900, is complex and difficult to understand. Their arrangement appears to involve more than just the commissioning of titles, as films in the collection reveal that Thomas had his cameraman working for him, and Mitchell & Kenyon were also offering him a developing and printing service.[45] A number of the Manchester titles show Kenyon in the crowd,

Manchester Street Scenes filmed in 1901, showing the crowds of faces that were to become a feature of the company's films

working in conjunction with Thomas.[46] In addition, Albert Wilkinson, a cameraman for Mitchell & Kenyon, also worked for Thomas in Ireland in late 1901 and early 1902, and many of the films commissioned by the fairground showman George Green from Mitchell & Kenyon were also shown by Thomas in Ireland.[47]

Faced with these complexities and the lack of business records, it is difficult to assess the true relationship between Thomas and Mitchell & Kenyon. Understanding this is important, however, as over 130 titles in the collection associated with A. D. Thomas could be classified as a collection of titles by a previously unknown film-maker from the early period, rather than the work of Mitchell & Kenyon; but for the purposes of this book, I will refer to them as part of the Mitchell & Kenyon Collection. What is clear is that a strong business relationship did develop between Mitchell & Kenyon and Ralph Pringle, which resulted in the company supplying a constant flow of local titles for the newly formed North American Animated Photo Company.

Pringle hired Mitchell & Kenyon to film a series of local views or scenes pertaining to the town where he was exhibiting. One incident, at Roker in Sunderland, resulted in hundreds of pounds' worth of equipment being lost in the waves when Pringle and Kenyon were filming local scenes together. The precious ribbons of films where then used by local children to fly their kites the following day.[48] It is possible that Mitchell & Kenyon offered the company either a reduced rate to produce films for all of their shows or an exclusivity clause. As Richard Brown's research has revealed, the stand-alone or town-hall showmen were intensively competitive, as there were only a few suitable venues in each location for their type of exhibition. Not only would showmen try and secure the best dates in advance but also the best and most exclusive pictures, so Mitchell & Kenyon guaranteed the various exhibitors 'sole rights' for each locality.[49] Therefore, the same exclusivity clause that Richard

Programme for Ralph Pringle's Cinematograph Exhibition Company at the Colston Hall Bristol (1908). Pringle was the Manager of the North American Animated Photo Company (NFA)

Brown suggests applied in the hire and use of the venues could also be enforced in the supply of films for the show.

Mitchell & Kenyon travelled extensively with Pringle and, by 1902, had produced local films of Bristol, Nottingham, Sheffield, Birmingham and Hull. Although they were associated with over forty exhibitors, the films commissioned by Pringle represent the largest percentage supplied to any one company. The exclusive nature of the relationship between the two companies was cemented by the film *Arrest of Goudie* (1901), which was produced by Mitchell & Kenyon and sold exclusively through Ralph Pringle. This pioneering title will be covered in further detail in the following chapter, but, in summary, *Arrest of Goudie* was filmed in a realistic mode and advertised as an authentic animated picture reconstructing the arrest of the bank embezzler Thomas Peterson Goudie in Liverpool in December 1901. The film was produced, exhibited and advertised for sale less than three days after Goudie's arrest in Liverpool.

Although Mitchell & Kenyon specialised in the production of local films for showmen, they were not the only film company to be offering this service: Arthur Cheetham, for example, was also 'making a speciality of doing local kinematographic work, and exhibiting it in the neighbourhood in which the same occurred'.[50] Cecil Hepworth, of the Hepworth Film Company, writing in his autobiography *Came the Dawn*, describes filming local events in the Manchester area, where he worked with A. D. Thomas to supply local films:

Wigan Coronation and Street Scenes (1902) reveals the prominent use of posters by the North American Animated Photo Co. – who commissioned the title from Mitchell & Kenyon for Edward's coronation

> He employed me to take particular local films for him. These were generally of workers leaving some large factory in the neighbourhood of places being visited, or about to be visited, by one of his travelling shows. The turn out of the local fire brigade, all smoke and sparks and perspiring horses, was one of his favourite subjects and I must have taken well over fifty of them for him.[51]

The Showman, July 12, 1901

MESMERISM (?)

THE SHOWMAN

An Illustrated Journal for Showmen and all Entertainers.

Vol. II.—No. 32. [All Rights Reserved.] JULY 12, 1901. [Registered at the G.P.O. as a Newspaper.] Twopence.

To Showmen.

The most popular Cinematograph Film in a Travelling Show is ALWAYS A LOCAL PICTURE containing Portraits which can be recognised. A Film showing workers leaving a Factory will gain far greater popularity in the town where it was taken than the most exciting picture ever produced. The workers come in hundreds, with all their friends and relations, and the Film more than pays for itself the first night. In other words this is

The Greatest Draw you can have,

AND IT IS

Our Business to Provide it

for you in Advance, for each Town you visit.

Write, for particulars and prices, to

HEPWORTH & CO.,

Telephone: No. 16, Walton-on-Thames.
Telegrams: "Hepworth," Walton-on-Thames.

Cinematographers, **Walton-on-Thames.**

London Agents—L. GAUMONT & Co., 25 Cecil Court, Charing Cross Road, W.C.

Entered at Stationers' Hall.

(Above left) *Sunday Parade in East Park in Hull* (1904) was commissioned by Ralph Pringle and shown at the Circus building in April that year; (above right) Advert for Hepworth and Co., taken from the *The Showman*, July 1901 (NFA)

The collection shows evidence of a competitive environment in which film operators travelled throughout the country to capture events that were local in nature but could also be sold nationally. Hepworth appears in *Lord Roberts's Visit to Manchester* (1901), filmed on 10 October (the period during which he claims to have worked with Thomas), where two camera crews can be seen filming.[52] Additionally, throughout 1901 and 1902, *The Showman* newspaper is littered with advertisements for Hepworth and Co., promising to make it 'our business to Provide it for you in advance, for each Town you visit'.[53] Although it is not clear if Hepworth was hired by Thomas, or was just another film crew covering the visit, it does demonstrate the spread in popularity of the local subject.

Hepworth also supplied other exhibitors in the north of England and travelled to Bingley in Yorkshire to supply titles to Henry Hibberts for film shows at the New Co-op Hall in 1900, including a number of Boer War items.[54]

Mitchell & Kenyon also offered a same-day service to their exhibitors, which suggests that they had a portable developing and printing unit. Without business records, it is difficult to estimate the charges they applied, the number of their employees or the scale of their operations. However, the reviews from a show in Liverpool reveal that Mitchell & Kenyon certainly owned a portable printing unit, as filming and showing took place within four hours of the event:

> A record in photography or rather cinematography was achieved by Messrs Mitchell and Kenyon of Blackburn, on Saturday last, on the occasion of the homecoming of the Liverpool Volunteers. An animated picture of the arrival of the troops was taken by

> Messrs Mitchell and Kenyon a few minutes before 6 o'clock p.m. and was developed and ready for exhibition between 9 and 10 o'clock the same evening. It was shown to a crowded audience at Hengler's Circus by the North American Animated Photo Co.[55]

Other companies offered this particular service, with the Sheffield Photo Company stating in 1906 that they specialised in local subjects, and had a 'travelling dark room plant always ready for this class of work'.[56]

Mitchell & Kenyon's period of highest activity for local film production occurs between 1901 and 1905. Prices for supplying local films advertised in the trade papers varied between exhibitors, with Mitchell & Kenyon selling local films outright for 25s., or more specialised items at 1s. per foot. Their competitors were charging around 10s. a day for the hire of a cameraman and between 4½d. and 8d. a foot for developing and printing. The Warwick Trading Company reduced their prices in April 1901 to 5d. per foot, and by 1903 the Sheffield Photo Company, a more geographical rival to Mitchell & Kenyon than the London-based companies, was offering to print and develop showmen's films for 4½d.[57]

By 1902, Mitchell & Kenyon were a successful and well-established film company producing hundreds of local films each year for a wide variety of venues, from Bristol to Glasgow. It appears that they had a number of operators working for them, as the collection includes titles that were filmed on the same day but at different locations. *Visit of HRH Princess Louise to Blackburn* (1905) was filmed from different angles by three cameramen, who are signalled to with a white handkerchief, implying that by 1905 Mitchell & Kenyon had at least three camera units working for them.[58]

Pringle continued to use Mitchell & Kenyon despite the availability of other locally based companies. In 1902, Pringle became involved in a battle with Jasper Redfern for local audiences in Hull.[59] Redfern was a Sheffield-based optician who, by 1898, was producing his own film titles. One of the earliest film pioneers in Yorkshire, he not only produced his own films but also exhibited them at a variety of venues, including seaside shows, music halls and town halls. His exhibition programme was very similar to Pringle's, and included fiction films, actualities and local titles.

Redfern travelled around with Sheffield United football club during 1899, photographing at least four major matches, climaxing with the cup final at Crystal Palace, when Sheffield United played Derby (15 April 1899). All this added to the public's fascination for films, and Redfern started to present shows on a regular basis throughout the north of England, including Sheffield, Chesterfield and Manchester. He went on to make a series of films featuring Sheffield United, in a league tie against Liverpool and in cup matches against Nottingham and Bolton. After filming was finished, he exhibited these and other productions at the Central Hall in Sheffield, and subsequently in halls in Manchester and Liverpool.

Following the example of the travelling fairground exhibitors, Redfern went into the exhibition circuit with his 'World Renowned Animated Pictures and Refined Vaudeville Entertainments'. He also invested in a portable exhibition booth, which he opened as a seaside summer show at Westcliffe – 'Jasper Redfern's Palace by the Sea'.

In April 1902, Pringle and Redfern filmed and displayed a series of films recounting the return of the Boer War veteran Clive Wilson to the family home at Tranby Croft.[60]

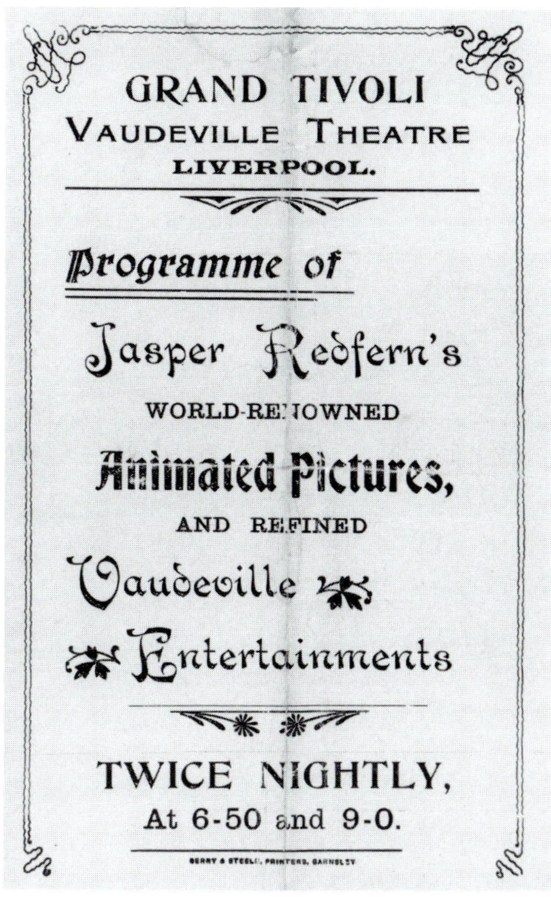

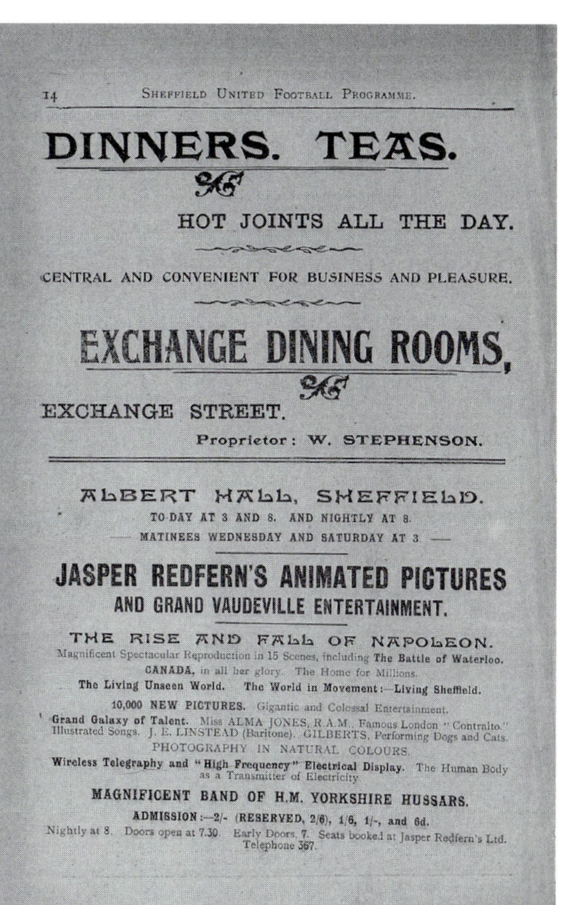

(Above left) Advert for Jasper Redfern's World Renowned Animated Pictures at the Tivoli Theatre, Liverpool (1902) (NMPFT); (above right) Advert for Jasper Redfern's Animated Pictures and Grand Vaudeville Entertainment in Sheffield (1903) (NFA)

The surviving films, *Lieutenant Clive Wilson and Tranby Croft Party* (1902), reveal the existence of Jasper Redfern's camera crew also filming Wilson's homecoming. The presence of Redfern filming in Hull provides an insight into the business practices of Edwardian exhibition companies, and explains why Mitchell & Kenyon were filming outside their usual locality. Although Redfern was one of the earliest film-makers, by 1901 he was also operating as an exhibitor and presumably did not wish to supply film prints to a rival company. Pringle would therefore need to hire another film company in order to secure the latest up-to-date scenes of local events. This could also be a factor in Mitchell & Kenyon's success: although they had presented a few local shows in Blackburn, it was the production and supply of cinematograph films that was the main thrust of the business, unlike, for example, Jasper Redfern, who operated as both supplier and exhibitor.

Mitchell & Kenyon also entered into a business arrangement with New Century Pictures, an exhibition company founded in Bradford in 1902 (see Plate 3). The failure of A. D. Thomas to fulfil an engagement for Sydney Carter at St George's Hall in Bradford resulted in Mitchell & Kenyon supplying local films for Carter in Bradford and in a greater presence into the Yorkshire exhibition circuit. The company also supplied equipment, as revealed in a memo to New Century Pictures from Mitchell & Kenyon, in which they quote £40 for the cost of 'A projector with the best arc lamp as used by

NEW DRILL HALL, GILESGATE.

ENORMOUS SUCCESS OF

THE NEW CENTURY PICTURES.

ENTIRE CHANGE OF PROGRAMME.

SPLENDID REPRESENTATION OF

THE PRODIGAL SON

IN COLORS. The Latest Invention in Animated Photography.

EXCLUSIVE REPRODUCTION OF

SCENERY ON THE RIVER WEAR.

FRAMWELLGATE BRIDGE, THE BANKS, THE WEIR, PREBENDS BRIDGE, THE CATHEDRAL.
A Triumph in Animated Photography. The Most Beautiful Animated Picture Ever Exhibited.

DURHAM SANDS RACES

ON GOOD FRIDAY.

Specially Taken by the New Century Company. Come and See Yourselves as Others See You.

BY SPECIAL REQUEST the Management will Once More Exhibit the Recent Successful Picture,

HOLLOW DRIFT PROCESSION,

IN CELEBRATION OF THE CORONATION.

HUNDREDS OF NEW COMIC PICTURES
Never Before Exhibited in Durham.

TERRIFIC SUCCESS OF

VICTOR RITTER,

THE ORIGINAL GROTESQUE MUSICAL COMEDIAN.
"LESS QUIETNESS PLEASE!"

NIGHTLY AT 8.

Doors Open at 7-30. Early Doors at 7, 3d Extra.
PRICES OF ADMISSION—2s, 1s, and 6d.
MATINEE FOR SCHOLARS ON SATURDAY AT 3.

Newspaper advert for New Century Pictures exhibition at the Drill Hall, Durham (1902)

Mr Wilkinson' (Mitchell & Kenyon's cameraman).[61] Carter's partner, Frank Sunderland, later recalled 'Buying New Century's first Cinematograph projector in Blackburn' on Good Friday 1902.[62] This additional 'contract' with Carter does not appear to have unduly affected their relationship with Pringle, who was based primarily at that time in areas such as Liverpool, where New Century were not yet operating.[63]

New Century Pictures were a different concern from other touring exhibition companies operating at that time. Using St George's Hall, Bradford, as the base for their operations, the company appears to have hired many of the venues and indeed showmen who had managed A. D. Thomas's shows, and formed a company in which the managers were employed on a share of the profits as opposed to a flat wage. Mitchell & Kenyon also provided local films for their shows, not only in Bradford but also in Glasgow, Leeds and Birmingham:

> The Cinematograph Entertainment at Curzon Hall, Birmingham, is also to be brought to a close at the end of this week. The new century pictures are still a source of great attractions, and the films secured by Messrs Mitchell and Kenyon's operators of Mr Chamberlain's home are projected amid considerable applause.[64]

Carter continued to use Mitchell & Kenyon and other companies, including Robert Paul and Hepworth, to supply films for his rapidly expanding exhibition circuit.[65] New Century Pictures developed into a highly successful company, and operated shows throughout the north of England, including Liverpool, Leeds and Morecambe. It diversified into equipment manufacture, film rental, film production and permanent cinema exhibition, until it was sold to the Gaumont Company in 1928.

1902 was a pivotal year for Mitchell & Kenyon in which they produced other non-fiction titles for a national audience, including travelogues and films of royalty, notably the *Coronation of Edward VII*, an event filmed by a number of cinematographers.[66] Further success was gained with the filming of *A Trip to North Wales on the St Elvies* (1902), which was widely shown, as was *The King's Ride in the Isle of Man* (1902).[67]

Mitchell & Kenyon began to concentrate more on their fiction output from 1903 onwards, and the decline in the 'local' film as a major subject of film production is reflected throughout the UK. Although still an active part of their business, the 'local' became just one feature of a exhibition programme as opposed to the main attraction, with fiction, travelogues and more ambitious dramatic titles becoming a staple of exhibition and production. In addition, sporting subjects became popular, with association football matches preferred by exhibitors over factory gate titles. Local subjects declined in popularity partly because the novelty of seeing oneself on screen had worn off.

A Trip to North Wales on the St Elvies (1902) is an example of the travelogue films produced by the company, which were sold nationally

By 1904, Mitchell & Kenyon were seen by the trade press as one of the top six cinematograph companies in the UK, listed alongside Gaumont, Paul, Hepworth and Co., the Warwick Trading Company and the Charles Urban Trading Company.[68] Their fiction output increased and was marked by one of their most ambitious projects to date, a dramatic illustration in sixteen tableaux of a collier's life, filmed on location in the Black Country in 1904.

Their output of 'local' titles rapidly declined after 1905, with fewer than a hundred titles in the collection pertaining to these years, the vast majority restricted to the East Lancashire region. In 1906, James Kenyon retired from his furnishing business and Mitchell resumed possession of his Northgate shop a year later.[69]

Despite their national prominence in 1904 and 1906, by 1907 little evidence for Mitchell & Kenyon's fiction output can be found and they appear to have returned to filming local views. Kenyon's 'retirement' to Southport may be a factor, but wider concerns in the British film industry as a whole were affecting the business. By 1908, the growth in permanent cinema theatres, the decline in popularity of the local film and demise of their core clientele, travelling exhibition shows, resulted in a steady decline in their output. The causes of the apparent decline in their national standing are unclear, but it does appear to be part of a larger picture in which the mode of production under which the

British film companies had operated was being superseded, not only by technically advanced productions but also as a result of changes in rental and distribution practices throughout the UK. Film distribution at that time followed 'the season', with the dark evenings of the winter months from October to March bringing in the largest audiences. Distribution patterns were regionally diverse, with Lancashire and Yorkshire considered to be the strongest counties for film exhibitions.

Mitchell & Kenyon, in line with other companies, were setting the price of films according to production expenses and also subject matter. Fiction titles were generally priced at a higher rate per foot, with companies generally charging 6d. per foot. After 1905, the British film industry struggled to compete with Pathé, who were charging only 5d. a foot. Jon Burrows's ground-breaking work on this period has demonstrated that price-cutting by Pathé resulted in the formation of the first significant cartel in film history, the Kinematograph Manufacturers' Association (KMA), with Robert Paul as its first chairman.[70] The twelve founder members included the Charles Urban Trading Company, the Sheffield Photo Company, Clarendon, Hepworth, Williamson, Walturdaw and Mitchell & Kenyon. One of the resolutions at the meeting held on 19 July 1906 was to maintain the price of selling films at 6d. per foot and to forbid its members from selling films to customers who were also buying titles from Pathé or sources outside the KMA. This strategy failed dismally and by 1907 the KMA was in disarray, as many of its founder members broke the resolution and became engaged in a price war with Pathé that continued up to 1908, with prices falling from 6d. a foot to 4d. By the time of the 1909 Paris Congress, which they were not invited to attend, Mitchell & Kenyon were no longer making films outside the East Lancashire region.

Although their earlier fiction titles were still being offered for sale in Walturdaw's 1907 catalogue, no new titles appear in film catalogues after this date.[71] With British companies facing competition from Pathé and then, from 1909 onwards, American companies, Mitchell & Kenyon appear to have withdrawn from the national market after this period. By 1908, film sales were in decline nationally, as the market was flooded by second-hand titles that were being leased or rented out without any profit going back to the original film companies.[72] From 1909 onwards, American production companies increased their interest in the British exhibition market after being invited to do so by the Cinematograph Trade Protection Society, an organisation set up by renters and exhibitors in response to the resolutions passed at the Paris Congress. When interviewed in 1984, John Mitchell remembers how his father blamed the increase of American titles in 1910 for the company's withdrawal from the film market. By 1913, the company were filming no more than fifteen miles outside Blackburn and once again producing local titles, such as *Whitsuntide Processions at Clitheroe* (1913) and *Mayor's Sunday at St Mary's Church, Clitheroe* (1912).[73]

Although this pioneering partnership was not dissolved officially until 1922, there is no evidence for any film production after 1913. James Kenyon moved to Southport in 1915, to return to Blackburn in around 1921, four years before his death in 1925. Sagar Mitchell, who had continued with his Northgate photographic business, died in 1952, four years after his company, with its prodigious output, had been described as little more than a footnote in film history.[74]

Impact and Consequences

> It is the regional location of companies such as New Century Pictures and Mitchell and Kenyon which is an important factor in encouraging a new and less metropolitan focus in the current re-assessment of early British film history.[75]

Despite the downturn in the firm's fortunes as a result of the factors outlined above, Mitchell & Kenyon were not the only early pioneers affected by the changes in the British film industry, as film-makers like James Williamson and Robert Paul also ceased production before the outbreak of the First World War. What is surprising is that it has taken over a century for their contribution to British film history to be recognised. The collection changed the emphasis of British film history scholarship towards non-fiction by revealing how non-fiction production was a major factor in the development of British film-making and exhibition. While most conventional film histories have identified the Brighton School and London-based companies as the most important contributors in film technique, the Mitchell & Kenyon Collection now reveals the significance of the north of England, in particular Lancashire, as a centre for early film production and exhibition. It also demonstrates the importance of Lancashire in the field of popular entertainment, with its industrial entertainment economy providing a strong bedrock for the development of the company and also early film exhibition. The collection also reveals the importance of the local film in the early period of film-making, a factor that continued in Europe and America well into the 1930s, and demonstrates how British firms produced such titles far earlier than other companies.[76] Early film exhibition was not solely a stage for the presentation of narrative films; it was also the local film that kept the crowds coming, a crucial factor for the development of the cinema audience in the early 1900s. The power of the Mitchell & Kenyon Collection is that it not only reveals the types of material shown but also allows us to view the audience who went to see it.

As outlined in this introductory chapter, Mitchell & Kenyon did not operate within a vacuum, and the films they produced were similar in form and overall style to those made by their contemporaries. Conversely, one could argue that it is not only the scale of the surviving material that finally places them within the recognised canon of film-makers of the Edwardian period but also innovations in style and technique. Writing many years before the discoveries of the last decade of the twentieth century, Rachael Low claimed that the company does 'not seem to have exerted any influence on the development of cinema technique'.[77] In order to evaluate fully their contribution as makers of innovative films that had a formative effect on early film development, as opposed to their success as a business, the next chapter will examine the films themselves, alongside those produced by their contemporaries.

New and Interesting Series of . . Local Pictures.

THE BRADFORD

CYCLE PARADE

ON SATURDAY, JULY 9th.

DAY SCHOOL SPORTS!

AT PARK AVENUE ON TUESDAY, JULY 12th.

Complete Reproduction of the Principal Scenes during

The ROYAL VISIT TO BRADFORD

NEW PICTURES OF THE WAR BETWEEN

JAPAN and RUSSIA.

The Most Varied, Amusing, and Interesting Entertainment in the City!

EVERY AFTERNOON AT 3. EVERY EVENING AT 8.

POPULAR PRICES: Gallery, 6d.; Area, 1s.; Stalls, 2s.

CHILDREN HALF-PRICE TO ALL PARTS.

Reserved Seats at the Box Office. Telephone 1718.

Handbill for New Century Pictures show in Bradford in 1904, but showing the same type of local films produced by Mitchell & Kenyon as early as 1901 and 1902 (West Yorkshire Archive Service)

Notes

1 Tom Gunning, 'Before Documentary', in Daan Hertogs and Nico De Klerk (eds), *Uncharted Territory: Essays on Early Nonfiction Films* (Amsterdam: Nederlands Filmmuseum, 1997), pp. 9–24 (24).

2 An edited version of this account was published in *Le Giornate del Cinema Muto 2001:* 20th Pordenone Silent Film Festival (Sacile, Italy: Conivne di Sacile, 2002) pp. 110–11. However, the text referred to here is taken from the full unedited correspondence between Peter Worden and Patrick Russell, Keeper of Non-Fiction at the NFTVA, after a request to Peter for the account of the full provenance of the collection to be placed on file.

3 Personal communication, Peter Worden to Vanessa Toulmin, 26–30 January 2003.

4 A full version of this account can be found in Vanessa Toulmin, Patrick Russell and Tim Neal, 'The Mitchell and Kenyon Collection: Rewriting Film History', *The Moving Image: The Journal of the Association of Moving Image Archivists,* Vol. 3 No. 2 (Autumn 2003), pp. 1–18.

5 Full details of the films shown can be found on a handout produced by Peter Worden and Robin Whalley that lists six titles relating to Blackburn, including M&K: 256–60: *Princess Louise Unveiling Queen Victoria's statue* (1905), M&K 265: *Blackburn Rovers v. Sheffield United* (1907), and M&K 48: *Workforce Leaving Hornby's Brookhouse Mill, Blackburn* (1900).

6 Precise dates for the discovery of the latter films are hard to estimate. When the collections were auctioned at Christie's in November 1995 and February 1997, the provenance of the material was not stated, but it is reliably reported that this was so. Therefore, it is only a deduction from unsubstantiated secondary evidence that the smaller collections were found in the premises at 40 Northgate. The sixty-five titles now preserved by the Cinema Museum in London were largely fiction, while the remaining small batch of five rolls of films were purchased by Lobster Films (Paris).

7 For information on Edison see Charles Musser, *Edison Motion Pictures, 1890–1900: An Annotated Filmography* (Washington: Smithsonian Institution Press, 1997), For Lumière see Michelle Aubert, Jean-Claude Seguin (eds), *La Production cinématographique des frères Lumière* (Paris: Bibliothèque du film: Editions Mémoires de Cinéma, 1996).

8 *Blackburn Times*, 9 February 1951; *Northern Daily Telegraph*, 2 October 1952 (obituary); *Blackburn Times*, 10 October 1952, p. 5 (obituary).

9 Personal communication with Peter Worden, March 2005. John Mitchell stated in an interview with Robin Whalley that the top floor of the Northgate premises in Blackburn was at that time full of Mitchell & Kenyon material, which was offered to Blackburn Museum. The offer was refused because of budgetary restrictions, so a refuse wagon was ordered and all of the contents were thrown out of a second floor window into the street below. See also Robin Whalley and Peter Worden, 'Forgotten Firm: A Short Chronological Account of Mitchell and Kenyon, Cinematographers', *Film History*, Vol. 10 (1998), pp. 35–51, for the same account.

10 Richard Brown and Barry Anthony's pioneering study of the British Biograph Company has demonstrated the importance of film company business records for the understanding of their wider social and economic significance. See Richard Brown and Barry Anthony, *A Victorian Film Enterprise: The History of the British Mutoscope and Biograph Company, 1897–1915* (Trowbridge: Flicks Books, 1999).

11 Memo from Mitchell & Kenyon to Sydney Carter of St George's Hall Bradford, West Yorkshire Archive Service [WYAS] (Bradford), 17 February 1902.

12 Rachael Low and Roger Manvell, *The History of British Film, 1896–1906* (London: George Allen, 1948), pp. 22–3.

13 For further information see Robin Whalley and Peter Worden, 'Forgotten Firm', pp. 35–51.

14 New research projects are attempting to change this, with Simon Popple at the University of Leeds setting up a research group in association with the Magic Lantern Society and Kirklees Museums on the history of the Bamforth Company.

15 See the work of the late Roland Whiteside on Mitchell & Kenyon, in particular the full-scale exhibition on the company in association with Blackburn Museum and Art Gallery in 1977 and described in Baynham Honri, 'The Blackburn Movies', *The British Journal of Photography*, Vol. 124 No. 6085 (11 March 1977), pp. 205–7.

16 For a full history of Victorian film exhibition see John Barnes, *The Beginnings of the Cinema in England, 1894–1901, Vols 1–5* (Exeter: Exeter University Press, 1996–8).

17 See advertisements for Kenyon and Co., suppliers of automatic amusement machines in the *Showmen's Year Books* for 1900–2 (Manchester: United Kingdom Showmen and Van Dwellings Protection Association, 1900, 1901, 1902). In 1902, the advert stated 'that the well known Kenyon's Penny-in-the-slot Business will from 1 January 1902 be carried out by us and exhibition proprietors may look out for some new money making ideas. Mitchell & Kenyon'.

18 They were advertising the 'Norden' Camera in 1891, although this was clearly a stills camera. This advert for 'The "Norden" Camera, No 8', as well as 'Cameras, Lenses, Slides, Plates, Paper, Chemicals, Compressed Oxygen, Limelight' can be found in *Tom-O'-Dick-O'-Bobs' Blegburn Dickshonary*, Blackburn, 1891.

19 *Blackburn Times*, 6 May 1938. E. H. Page was proprietor of the Lyceum Theatre, Blackburn.

20 *Blackburn Times*, 27 November 1897, p. 6.

21 Barnes, *The Beginnings of the Cinema in England.*

22 Letter from Herbert Green to Henry Simpson, 8 January 1945, Scottish Film Archive.

23 See *The Optician and Photographic Dealer Trade Review*, 29 September 1899, p. 46.

24 For further information on northern film-makers see Geoff Mellor, *Movie Makers and Picture Palaces* (Bradford: Bradford Libraries, 1996).

25 John K. Walton, *The English Seaside Resort: A Social History, 1750–1914* (Leicester: Leicester University Press, 1983); Tony Mason, *Association Football and English Society, 1863–1915* (Brighton: The Harvester Press, 1983); John K. Walton, *Lancashire: A Social History, 1558–1939* (Manchester: Manchester University Press, 1987); Robert Poole, *Popular Leisure and the Music Hall in Nineteenth Century Bolton* (Lancaster: Centre for North West Regional Studies, University of Lancaster, 1982).

26 See Aubert and Seguin (eds), *La Production cinématographique des frères Lumière*, pp. 297–8 for details of the Liverpool titles; Brown and Anthony, *A Victorian Film Enterprise;* and *Photography*, Vol. 10 No. 517 (6 October 1898), p. 656.

27 Reverend Thomas Horne (ed.), *The Showmen's Year Book* (Manchester: UKSVDPA, 1900).

28 For the full list see the Filmography. For details of the Lancashire wakes films see Vanessa Toulmin, 'Local Films for Local People: Travelling Showmen and the Commissioning of Local Films in Great Britain, 1900–1902', *Film History*, Vol. 13. No. 2 (2001), pp. 118–38.

29 The films in question being M&K 31: *Workpeople and Girls Leaving Thos. Adams Factory, Nottingham* (1900), M&K 7: *M. Oldroyd & Sons, Dewsbury* (1900) and M&K 27: *Amos & Smith Boiler Works, Hull* (1900).

30 M&K 5: *Workers Leaving Haslam's Ltd Colne.*

31 *The Herald*, 28 July 1900, p. 8, for details of M&K 8: *Cheetham's Bankwood Mills, Stalybridge.*

32 For example, M&K 12: *Workmen Leaving Platt's Works, Oldham* (1900); M&K 14: *Workmen Leaving Peacock's Works at Meal Time, Gorton* (1900); M&K 15: *The 'Hands' Leaving Work at North-street Mills, Chorley* (1900); M&K 19: *Workers at India Mills, Stockport* (1900).

33 M&K 9: *Salt's Works in Saltaire.*

34 Vanessa Toulmin, 'The Cinematograph at the Goose Fair, 1896–1911', in Alain Burton and Laraine Porter (eds), *The Showman, the Spectacle & the Two-Minute Silence* (Trowbridge: Flicks Books, 2001), pp. 76–86.

35 See *Northern Daily Telegraph*, 1 April 1899, p. 1, for details of the advert for Green's Electric Cinematograph exhibiting 'two splendid living pictures specially taken of the operatives leaving Audley Mill Blackburn, Church Street and Station Road'.

36 For further details see Janet McBain, 'Mitchell & Kenyon's Legacy in Scotland – The Inspiration for a Forgotten Film-making Genre', in Vanessa Toulmin, Simon Popple and Patrick Russell (eds), *The Lost World of Mitchell & Kenyon: Edwardian Britain on Film* (London: BFI, 2004), pp. 113–25. The last film commissioned by George Green was M&K 95: *Blackburn Rovers v. Sheffield United* (1907).

37 For details of Mitchell & Kenyon's relationship with the travelling film exhibitors see Toulmin, 'Local Films for Local People'.

38 *The Showman*, December 1900, p. 3.

39 See Barnes, *The Beginnings of the Cinema in England.*

40 For further information on these travelling films exhibitors see Mellor, *Movie Makers and Picture Palaces.*

41 *Kinematograph Weekly*, 5 March 1925.

42 *The Showman*, 15 February 1901, p. iv; 22 February 1901, p. iv.

43 See *Blackburn Weekly Telegraph*, 9 February 1901, p. 4, for an account of the filming, and see M&K 807, 817: *Funeral of Queen Victoria.*

44 For further details on Pringle and the North American Animated Photo Company see Vanessa Toulmin, 'An Early Crime Film Rediscovered: Mitchell & Kenyon's *Arrest of Goudie* (1901)' *Film History*, Vol. 16. No.1 (2004), pp. 37–53; and also Toulmin *et al.* (eds), *The Lost World of Mitchell & Kenyon.*

45 This is certainly true in the case of A. D. Thomas in Ireland. A memo in the notebook of Louis De Clercq held by the National Library of Ireland notes 'Tram Fair (sic) to Kingstown 7d. – Film from M. & K. 4d'. Kingstown was the port just outside Dublin where the mail boat from Holyhead docked, and the note implies that Mitchell & Kenyon were developing and printing films shot by De Clercq for Thomas-Edison.

46 See M&K 426: *Race for the Muratti Cup* (1901) for a shot of Kenyon directing the crowd in a title that is distinctly associated with A. D. Thomas. For further information see Chapter 5 on the sporting films.

47 For more information see Robert Monks, 'The Irish Films in the Mitchell and Kenyon Collection', in Toulmin *et al.* (eds), *The Lost World of Mitchell & Kenyon*, pp. 93–103.

48 See *The Showman*, 29 November 1901, p. 187, and *Sunderland Echo*, 14 November 1901, for two accounts of the same incident.

49 'Sole operating rights' was a common exhibition practice on the fairground in particular: the showmen would claim sole rights for the showing of a particular show or attraction, or,

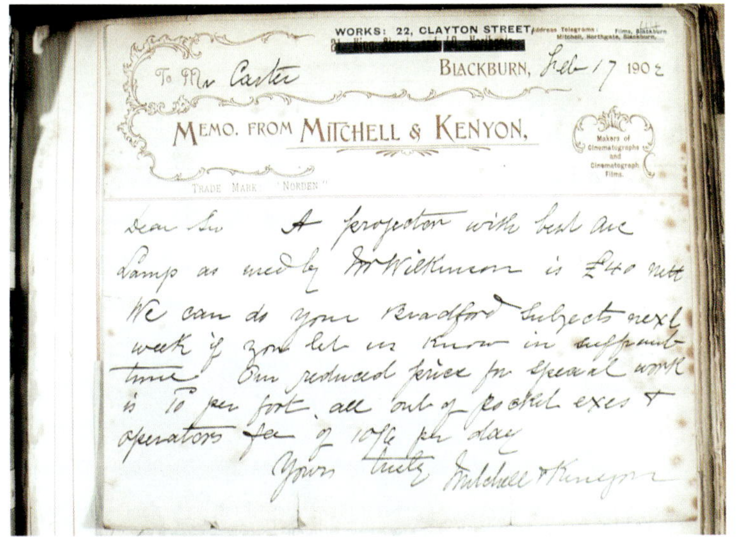

WORKS: 22, CLAYTON STREET

BLACKBURN, Feb 17 1902

To Mr Carter

MEMO. FROM MITCHELL & KENYON,

Makers of Cinematographs and Cinematograph Films.

TRADE MARK "NORDEN"

Dear Sir A projector with best arc lamps as used by Mr Wilkinson is £40 nett. We can do your Bradford subjects next week if you let us know in sufficient time. Our reduced price for special work is 10 per foot all out of pocket exes & operators fee of 10/6 per day

Yours truly Mitchell & Kenyon

Registered at the G.P.O. as a Newspaper.

Searchlight

No. 9. Hull, Thursday, May 16, 1901. One Penny.

WAR IN HULL!!

The Greatest and Most Genuine Show of Animated Pictures ever seen.

DO NOT BE MISLED.

The SIEGE of the ASSEMBLY ROOMS continued Twice Daily, at 3 and 8.

TRIUMPH OF EDISON!

SEE EDISON'S PICTURES.

SEE EDISON'S PICTURES.

SEE EDISON'S PICTURES. AT THE ASSEMBLY ROOMS ONLY.

China and Boer Wars.

EDISON'S LOCAL ANIMATED PICTURES OF HULL & DISTRICT,

Edison's Complete Reproduction of the QUEEN'S FUNERAL, from Cowes to Frogmore. The Sight of a Lifetime.

BARNBY & RUST

15, MARKET PLACE, HULL.

KLEINERT'S SELF FITTING DRESS SHIELDS ARE THE BEST.

MERRYWEATHER'S

GARDEN HOSE

Plate 1: Memo from Messrs Mitchell & Kenyon outlining the terms and rates of their film service to Sydney Carter of New Century Pictures in Bradford, 1902 (West Yorkshire Archive Service).

Plate 2: Full-page advert for the two-hour film show presented by Thomas-Edison in Hull, 1902.

Plate 3: Advertising card for New Century Pictures show in Bradford, c. 1905 (West Yorkshire Archive Service).

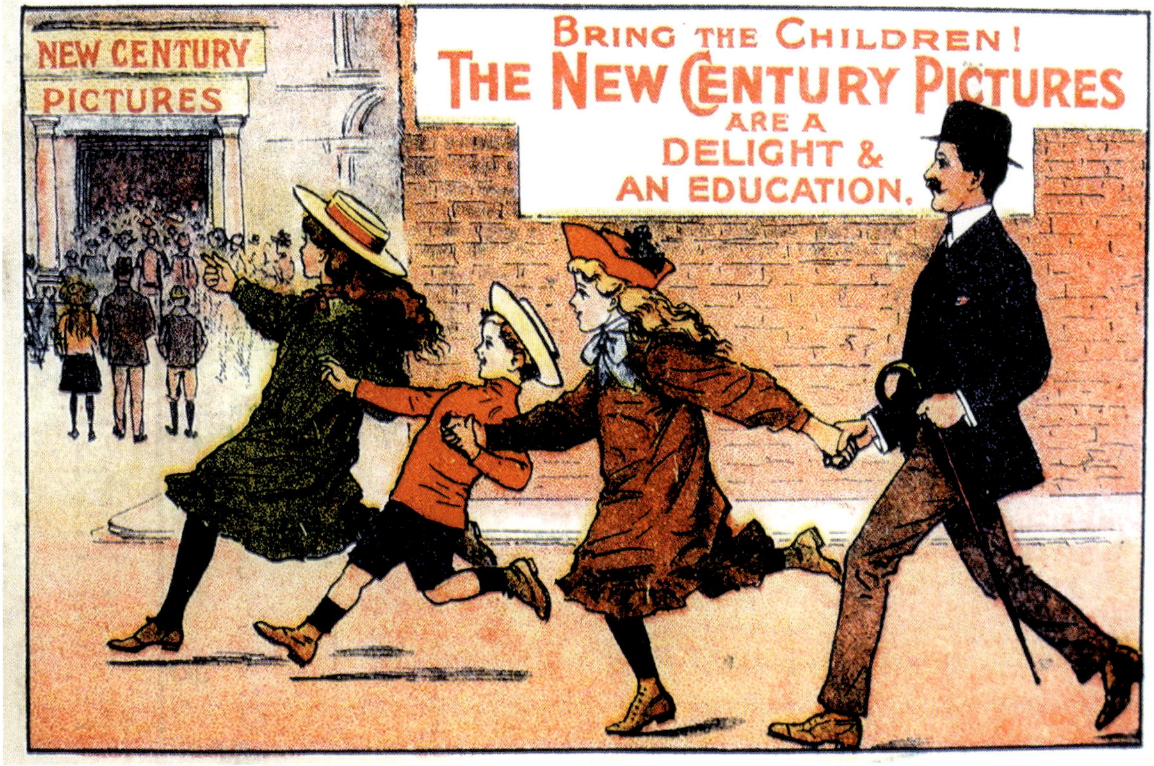

Plate 4: Colour illustrative poster of the Life of Charles Peace showing the major incidents in his life, which formed the basis for the penny dreadful, the stage play and the subsequent films, 1890 (NFA).

Plate 5: Programme for Buffalo Bill's Wild West Show in Huddersfield, 1903 (NFA).

Plate 6: Handbill illustrating 'The Greatest Show on Earth', Barnum and Bailey's Circus produced for visit to London in 1889 (NFA).

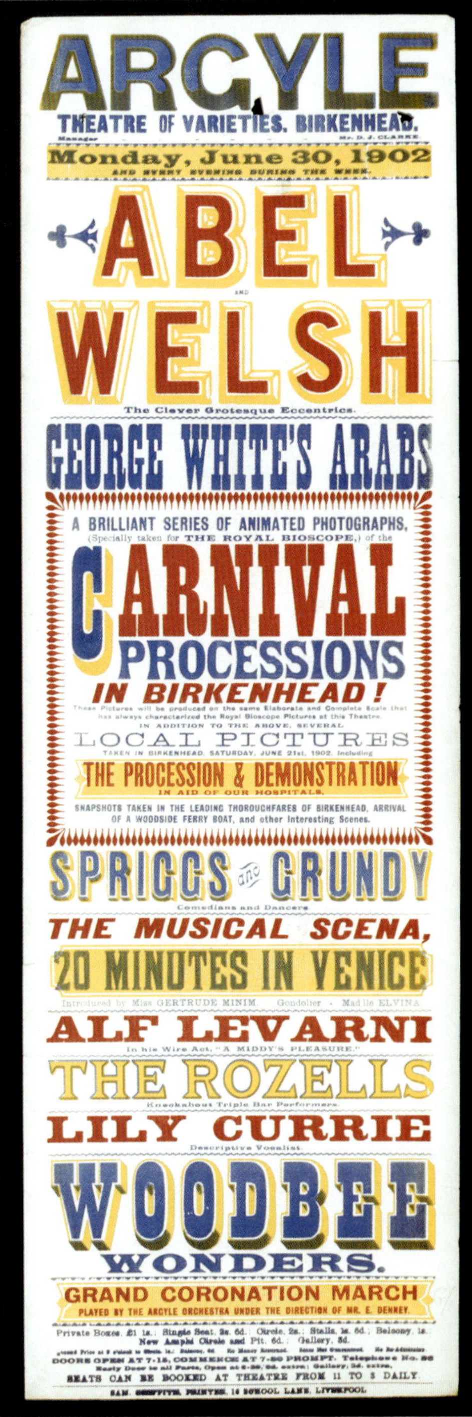

Plate 7: The film of local carnival processions in Birkenhead is the main attraction at the Argyle Theatre, Birkenhead, in the summer of 1902 and shows the growing popularity of the cinematograph (NFA).

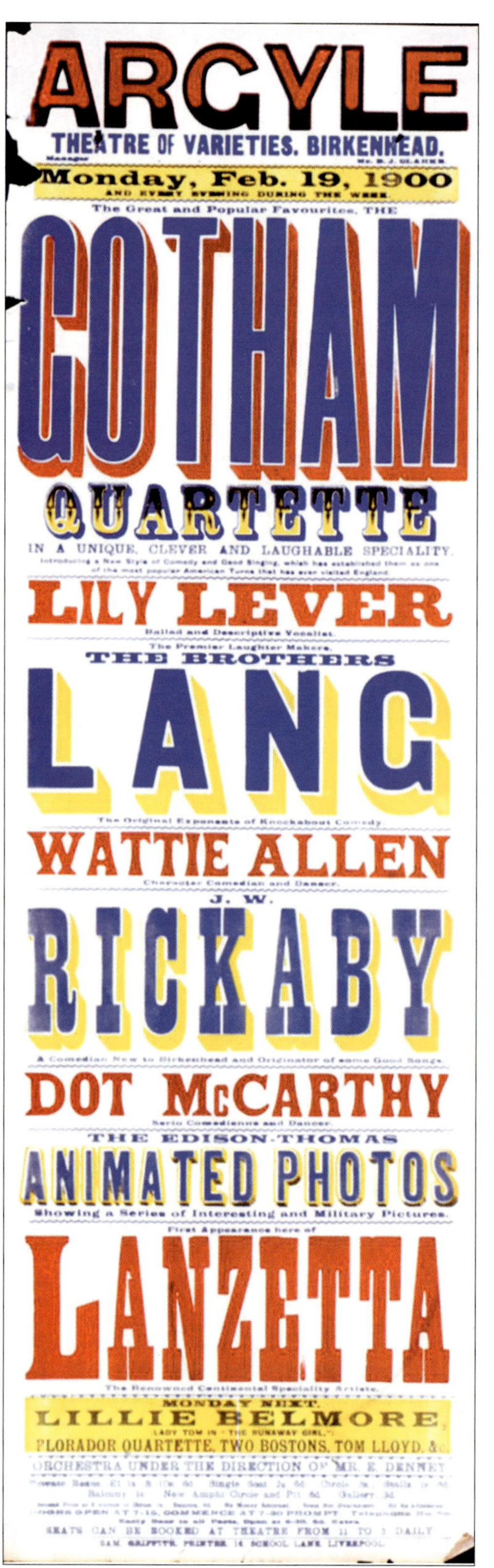

Plate 8 (left): Poster from the Argyle Theatre, Birkenhead, February 1900, with the cinematograph appearing as one-act in the programme of events (NFA).

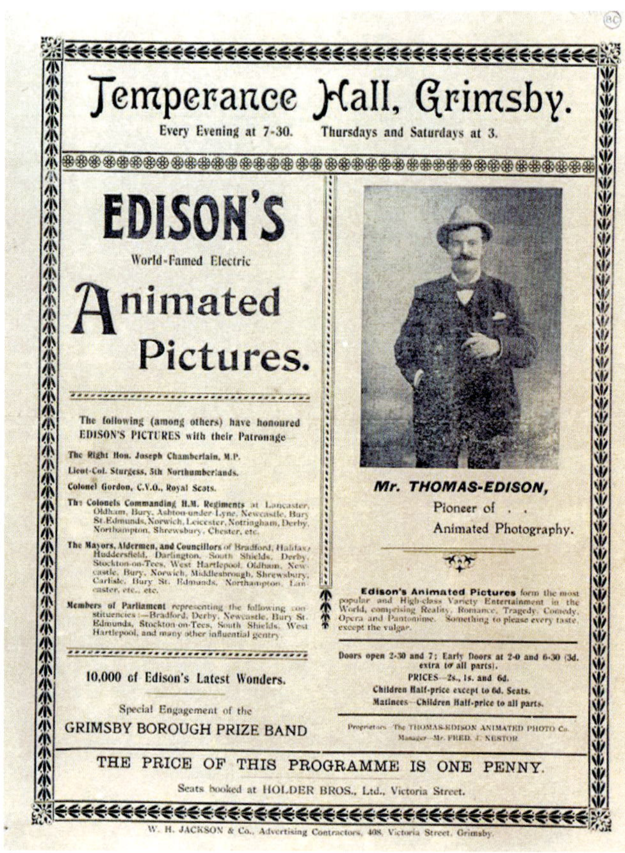

Temperance Hall, Grimsby.

Every Evening at 7-30. Thursdays and Saturdays at 3.

EDISON'S

World-Famed Electric

Animated Pictures.

The following (among others) have honoured EDISON'S PICTURES with their Patronage

The Right Hon. Joseph Chamberlain, M.P.

Lieut-Col. Sturgess, 5th Northumberlands.

Colonel Gordon, C.V.O., Royal Scots.

The Colonels Commanding H.M. Regiments at Lancaster, Oldham, Bury, Ashton-under-Lyne, Newcastle, Bury St. Edmunds, Norwich, Leicester, Nottingham, Derby, Northampton, Shrewsbury, Chester, etc.

The Mayors, Aldermen, and Councillors of Bradford, Halifax, Huddersfield, Darlington, South Shields, Derby, Stockton-on-Tees, West Hartlepool, Oldham, Newcastle, Bury, Norwich, Middlesbrough, Shrewsbury, Carlisle, Bury St. Edmunds, Northampton, Lancaster, etc., etc.

Members of Parliament representing the following constituencies:—Bradford, Derby, Newcastle, Bury St. Edmunds, Stockton-on-Tees, South Shields, West Hartlepool, and many other influential gentry.

10,000 of Edison's Latest Wonders.

Special Engagement of the

GRIMSBY BOROUGH PRIZE BAND

Mr. THOMAS-EDISON,

Pioneer of . .

Animated Photography.

Edison's Animated Pictures form the most popular and High-class Variety Entertainment in the World, comprising Reality, Romance, Tragedy, Comedy, Opera and Pantomime. Something to please every taste, except the vulgar.

Doors open 2-30 and 7; Early Doors at 2-0 and 6-30 (3d. extra to all parts).

PRICES—2s., 1s. and 6d.

Children Half-price except to 6d. Seats.

Matinees—Children Half-price to all parts.

Proprietors—The THOMAS-EDISON ANIMATED PHOTO Co.

Manager—Mr. FRED. J. NESTOR

THE PRICE OF THIS PROGRAMME IS ONE PENNY.

Seats booked at HOLDER BROS., Ltd., Victoria Street.

W. H. JACKSON & Co., Advertising Contractors, 408, Victoria Street, Grimsby.

Plate 9 (above): Thomas-Edison's programme outlining the types of film exhibited during the two-hour film shows he presented to the Temperance Hall, Grimsby, 1901–02 (Barnes Collection).

Plate 10 (above): Another incarnation of A. D. Thomas's exhibition when he advertised as Ediscope and Barnum's Pictures, Kettering, c. 1903 (NFA).

Plate 11 (right): Early handbill for A. D. Thomas which uses the real Thomas Edison's image and advertising style as a means of confusing the public into believing his show was that of the great American inventor, 1899 (NFA).

Plate 12 (below): Poster for Edison's Animated Pictures at the St James's Hall, Manchester, June 1901 (Richard Brown).

Plate 13 (below right): Advert for the A. D. Thomas's Royal Canadian Animated Pictures Co. at the St James's Hall, Manchester, showing the visit of King Edward VII to Manchester, 1905 (NFA).

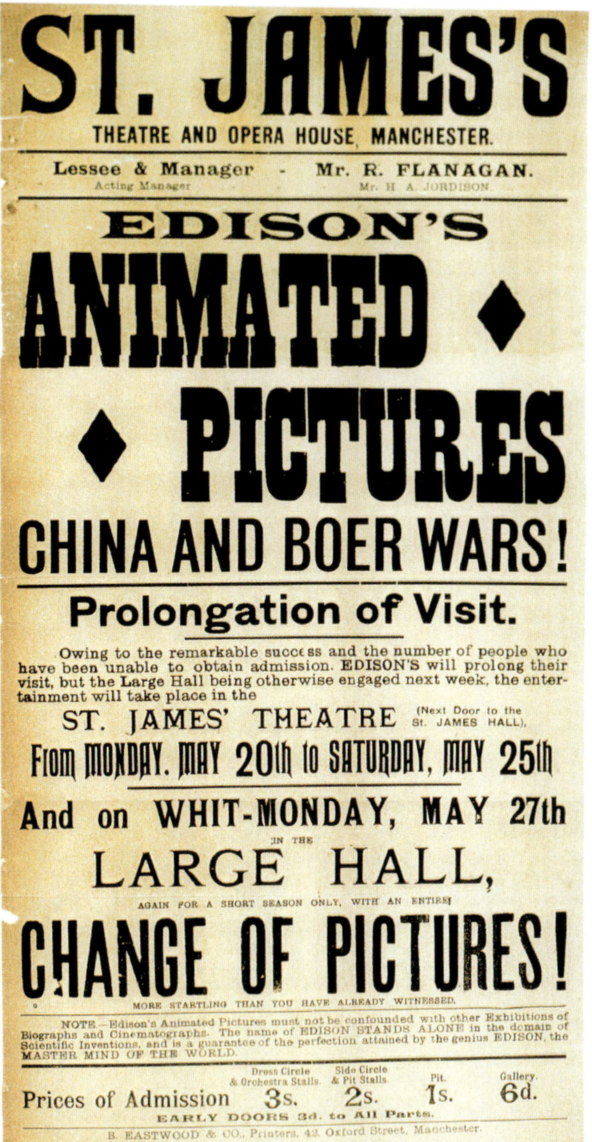

Plate 14 (above): Programme of entertainment for the Kursaal Pleasure Gardens in Harrogate, 1908 (NFA).

Plate 15 (above right): Programme for the Winter Gardens and Victoria Pavilions in Morecambe. This lavish music hall was the venue for Thomas-Edison's show in Morecambe in the summer of 1901 (NFA).

Plate 16 (right): Poster advertising War Pictures at the top of the bill at the New Bedford Palace of Varieties in London, January 1900 (NFA).

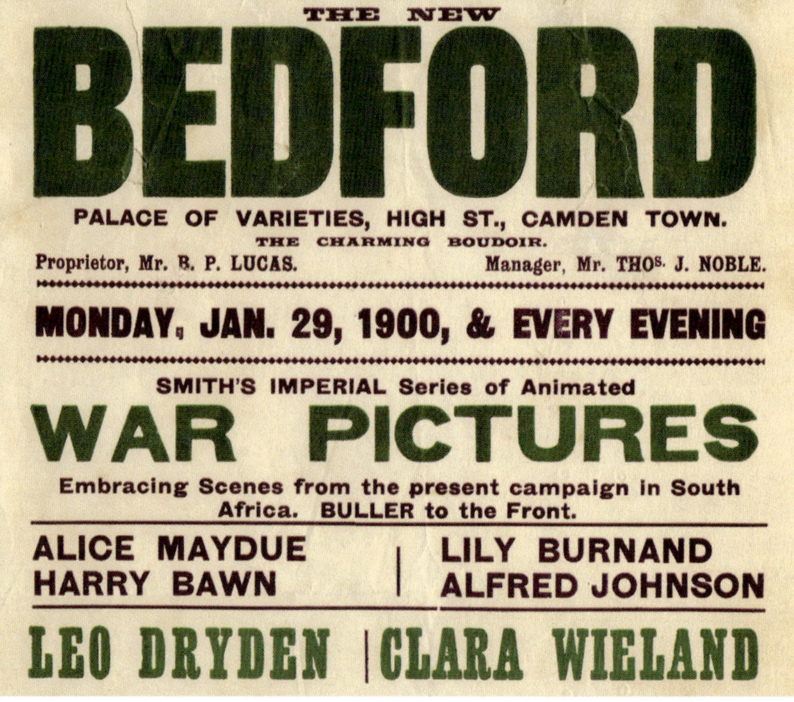

PROGRAMME

Price] MORNING PERFORMANCE [Two-pence.

Wednesday, February 19th, 1890, at 2 p.m.

1. The Four Marvellous Pretty Shetland Ponies, Minuet, Jacob, Turk & Tom Puss, introduced by **M. VICTOR MARIVONT.**
2. **Mons. PERMANÉ** in his pleasing Trick Act. Clown, **HAPPY ASHBY.**
3. The **SISTERS HOFFMANN,** Champion Lady Horizontal Bar Performers.
4. **GOU-GOU,** the Comical, and his well-educated **PIG.**
5. **Miss ELLEN BOORN,** the accomplished Equestrienne, in her flight through Garlands, Hoops and Balloons. Clown, **WHIMSICAL WALKER.**
6. Comic Entrée by **WHIMSICAL WALKER.**
7. **The FEELY FAMILY,** with their Magical Hats.
8. The Astounding Performing **BEARS,** introduced by their trainer, **Sig. PERMANÉ.**
9. **Miss JESSICA** in her marvellous performance on the Telephone Wire.
10. The marvellous School and Menage Act by **M. RANCY,** on a beautiful thoroughbred.
11. **HERR HAGENBECK'S** Marvellous **Equestrian Lion and Royal Dane Boar Hound,** introduced by **Herr W. PHILADELPHIA.**

INTERVAL OF TEN MINUTES.

12.—FOR THE FIRST TIME IN LONDON,

The Grand Military Spectacle,

THE WAR IN ZULULAND;

Or, THE BRITISH IN SOUTH AFRICA.

Produced by Mr. ALBERT HENGLER.

CHARACTERS:

Cetewayo, King of the Zulus .. Mr. ALFRED AUSTIN
Lieut. Melville, 24th Regt. .. Mr. GEORGE PALMER
Lieut. Coghill, 1st 24th Regt. .. Sig. PERMANE
Wungio .. MONS. PASHA
Dabulamanza .. Mr. ASHBY
Zongo .. Mr. LE BARB
Motoli .. Mr. FEELY
Amazulu .. Miss MAUD
Dennis O'Donnybrook (Special Correspondent of the Tipperary Telegraph) .. Mr. DAVID ABBEY SEAL
Lieut. Chard, Royal Engineers .. Mr. LITTLEFIELD
Lieut. Bromhead, Royal Engineers .. Mr. HARVEY
Captain Hope, Royal Buffs .. Mr. A. STYAN
Lieut. Douglas .. Mr. DAN FEELY
Colonel Williams .. Mr. LUDGWHIG

Other Characters, Zulus, Water Carriers, Camp Followers, &c., &c., by the most powerful Company ever concentrated within a Circus Arena.

SYNOPSIS OF SCENERY AND INCIDENTS:

PALM TREE REST AND STRANGERS' WELL.

Concourse of Zulu Warriors.

ARRIVAL OF KING CETEWAYO.

War Council—Approach of the British Envoy—War Proclaimed—War Dance—Grand Review of the Zulu Warriors—Congress of the Chieftains—Dennis, Special War Correspondent to the *Tipperary Telegraph*—His Courage under Difficulties—Rescued from Death by the lovely Amazulu—The Flight of Dennis with Amazulu—The British Encampment at Isandula.

Camp by Moonlight. Bivouac by the Camp Fire.

PATRIOTIC WAR SONG BY THE SOLDIERS.

The Surprise—"The Zulus are coming down upon you in thousands."

THE BATTLE OF ISANDULA.

The Gallant 24th—Flight of Coghill and Melville with the Colours, pursued by the Zulus—Terrific Combat for our Country's Honour,

DYING TO SAVE THE COLOURS.

Night—Search for the Dead and Wounded—Recovery of the Colours—Solemn Procession—Dennis O'Donnybrook tries to escape from his would-be Bride, but finds he has caught a Tartar.

RORKE'S DRIFT—THE DEFENCE

Preparations for the Reception of the Zulus—"If we fall, let us die as men and soldiers"—Piling up the Mealie Bags—Advance of the Zulus—Concentration of the British Forces.

REPULSE OF THE ENEMY.

Plate 17 (above left): War tableaux were a popular feature of travelling exhibitions. Programme cover for Poole Brothers' Panorama and Cinematograph show, 1904 (NFA).

Plate 18 (above and left): Cover of circus programme and centre insert advertising the 'War in Zululand' demonstrates the interest in South Africa before the Anglo-Boer War, 1891 (NFA).

Plate 19: Programme for the Alhambra Palace, Morecambe, 1901. The music hall was a patriotic supporter of the Boer War and many performers produced songs and sketches in support of the gallant soldier boys (Barnes Collection).

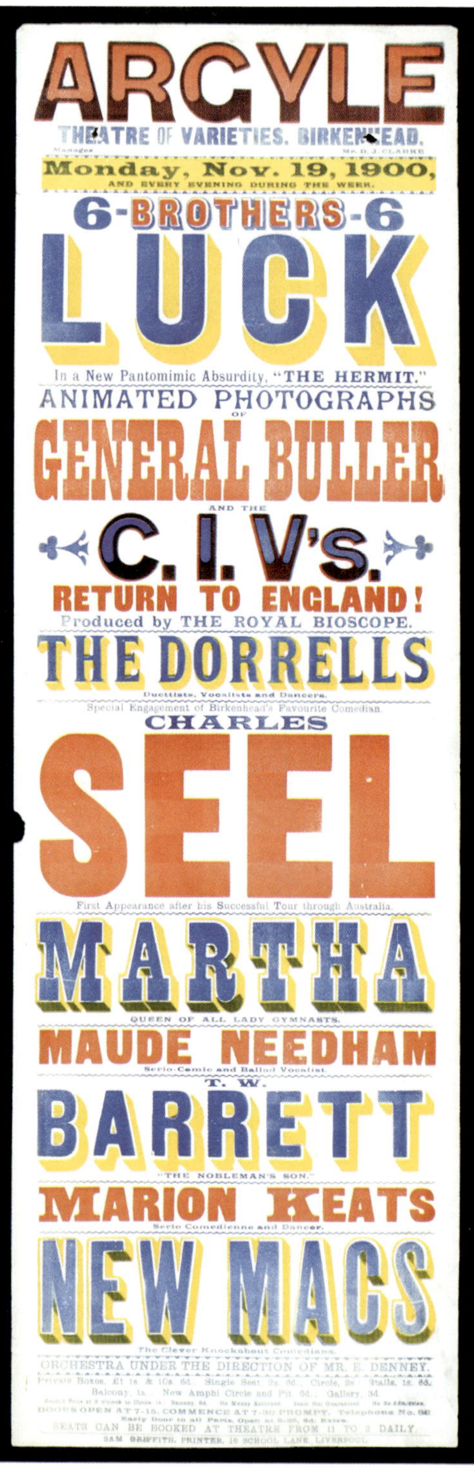

Plate 20: Films of the volunteer forces and General Buller were a popular feature at the Argyle Theatre, Birkenhead in 1900 (NFA).

in the case of the cinematograph, a particular company's titles. See Toulmin, 'The Cinematograph at the Goose Fair', for further information.

50 See the account of Arthur Cheetham filming football and local scenes in *Photography* p. 656.

51 Cecil Hepworth, *Came the Dawn: Memoirs of a Film Pioneer* (London: Phoenix House, 1951), pp. 58–9.

52 See M&K 420, 421, 422, 430, 777: *Lord Roberts's Visit to Manchester*, in particular 422, for a glimpse of Cecil Hepworth filming the unveiling of the statue of Queen Victoria by Lord Roberts.

53 See *The Showman*, 21 June 1901, for an example of Hepworth offering to provide in advance local pictures for each town the showmen visit. This advertisement continues throughout June and July.

54 Mellor, *Movie Makers and Picture Palaces*, pp. 76–7.

55 *The Showman*, 24 May 1901, p. 328.

56 *Optical Lantern and Cinematograph Journal*, September 1906, p. 201

57 For the Warwick Trading Company see *The Era*, 5 April 1901, p. 32; for Sheffield Photo Company see *The Era*, 20 June 1903, p. 28.

58 M&K 256–60, 364: *Visit of HRH Princess Louise to Blackburn.*

59 See Stephen Herbert and Luke McKernan, *Who's Who of Victorian Cinema* (London: BFI, 1997); for details on Jasper Redfern see Vanessa Toulmin, 'Moving Images: The Early Days of Cinema in Yorkshire', *Yorkshire Journal*, Winter 1995, pp. 32–41; and Clifford Shaw and Stuart Smith, *The Early Years of Cinema in Sheffield, 1896–1911* (Sheffield: Sheffield Cinema Society, 1995).

60 *Hull Daily Mail*, 7 April 1902, for a report of Clive Wilson's return from the war to Hull. 'During the proceedings, Mr Jasper Redfern and the NAAPCo secured some excellent cinematographic pictures, and they will be reproduced at the Assembly Rooms and the circus during the week.' The title in question is M&K 663–6: *Lieutenant Clive Wilson and Tranby Croft Party*, in particular M&K 665, which shows Jasper Redfern filming.

61 Memo from Mitchell & Kenyon to Sydney Carter of the St George's Hall, 17 February 1902, WYAS (Bradford).

62 Frank Sunderland, 'How the Picture Show Evolved', *The Bioscope*, 4 February 1917, p. 28.

63 For further information on New Century Pictures see Richard Brown, 'New Century Pictures: Regional Enterprise in Early British Film Exhibition', in Toulmin *et al.* (eds), *The Lost World of Mitchell & Kenyon*, pp. 69–83.

64 *The Music Hall and Theatre Review* (incorporating *The Showman*), 12 September 1902, p. 181. See also *The Era*, 6 September 1902, p. 22, for a more detailed account.

65 For further information see the Carter Papers in the WYAS in Bradford.

66 *The Era*, 21 June 1902, p. 29. For details of the film advertisements placed by Warwick, R. W. Paul and the Prestwich Manufacturing Company see *The Era*, 9 and 16 August 1902, p. 28, M&K 826: *Coronation of Edward VII* (1902).

67 *The Era*, 8 November 1902, p. 36, for details of M&K 214–2: *A Trip to North Wales on the St Elvies* (1902); for details of M&K 193: *The King's Ride in the Isle of Man*, see *The Era*, 18 October 1902, p. 32.

68 *The Talking Machine News*, January 1904, p. 189.

69 Cited in obituary, 'Cinematograph Pioneer: Death of Mr James Kenyon', *Blackburn Times*, 14 February 1925. For more information see Tim Neal, Vanessa Toulmin and Rebecca Vick, 'A Successful, Pioneering and "Travelled Partnership of Production"', in Toulmin *et al.* (eds), *The Lost World of Mitchell & Kenyon*, pp. 6–12.

70 For full details see Jon Burrows, 'When Britain Tried to Join Europe: The Significance of the 1909 Paris Congress for the British Film Industry', *Early Popular Visual Culture*, Vol. 4 No. 1 (2006), pp. 1–19.

71 *Walturdaw Catalogue*, 1907, pp. 38 and 109.

72 Burrows, 'When Britain Tried to Join Europe'.

73 M&K 338–9, 341–3: *Whitsuntide Processions at Clitheroe* and M&K: 347–50: *Mayor's Sunday at St Mary's Church, Clitheroe.*

74 *Blackburn Times*, 10 October 1952, p. 5 (obituary).

75 Brown, 'New Century Pictures' p. 69.

76 See Stephen Bottomore, 'From the Factory Gate to the "Home Talent" Drama: An International Overview of Local Films in the Silent Era', in Toulmin *et al.* (eds), *The Lost World of Mitchell & Kenyon*, pp. 33–48 (33).

77 Low and Manvell, *The History of British Film,* pp. 22–3.

2
The Films

> The firm of Mitchell and Kenyon, of Lancashire . . . is typical of the small but hardy companies which sprung up early in England . . . This company, however, has left little trace. On the whole it is probably safe to say that although it made a solid contribution to the considerable British output of the time, it does not seem to have exerted any influence on the development of cinema technique.[1]

Introduction

Before the discovery of the three collections in the 1990s, little trace of the films produced by Mitchell & Kenyon existed in national and regional archives.[2] Over a decade later, we now know that over 900 films have survived from various sources, resulting in the third largest corpus of work associated with one company from the early cinema period.[3] Mitchell & Kenyon's total output has always been difficult to estimate, as in some cases the local films were never distributed, and it is only their existence in the collection that allows us to relate them to the company. As we have seen in Chapter 1, the collection consists of film genres produced by Mitchell & Kenyon and their contemporaries, and includes non-fiction, fiction and reconstructions. While these are the classifications employed by today's archivists and historians, they were not necessarily utilised at the period of production. The classification of material from the early cinema period can be quite problematic and recent publications have emphasised that the categories applied at the time were often fluid: for example, actualities (a word derived from the French 'actualités' denoting a factual film), was sometimes applied to films that were re-enactments of events from real life but was also used as a synonym for reality.[4] This fluid terminology also occurred in fiction titles, with contemporary catalogues using groupings such as 'story films', 'chase films', 'comedy', 'melodrama', etc. For the sake of the modern non-specialist reader, the terms 'non-fiction', 'fiction' and 'reconstructions' will

The Police Annual Inspection at Birchfields Park, Manchester (1901) – an example of one of the many local films produced by the company

be applied to the overall genres with the individual categories used at the time divided into subsections within these fields.

The following sections outline the main types of films produced by the company, alongside similar titles advertised by their contemporaries. In addition to the genres identified above, there are a number of interesting variations, and, on one occasion, perhaps the creation of a new genre: the 'reconstructed actuality'. Within each specific group, there also exists a range of subjects that have their own distinct category. For example, non-fiction can include local films, actualities, news events or celebrity films, advertising subjects, sporting titles and factory gates. Re-enactment films also fall into subcategories: such as war titles and the 'reconstructed actuality', while the fiction genre includes comedies, tragedies and chase films, to name but a few. These differing and wide-ranging themes will be analysed in the context of similar titles or subject matter made by their contemporaries, and their importance or significance within the genre evaluated. Due to the fact that a large amount of the collection was commissioned, it is difficult to estimate which of the titles were actually produced by Mitchell & Kenyon for national distribution and which were supplied to individual showman either on a sole rights basis or filmed by the showmen themselves. Inevitably, this means that certain sections will be covered in more detail. The following chapters will also consider the role of the showmen in commissioning these titles and their efforts to create or promote specific types of films that were popular with the early film audiences. The films were also part of Edwardian visual culture and as such reflected or precipitated trends at the time, factors that will be considered when examining particular influences on individual films.

Non-Fiction

The non-fiction titles encompass many subjects, including factory gates, school exits, processions and calendar customs, sporting events, transport films and phantom rides, public entertainment and leisure, and celebrity films (depicting prominent personalities of the day). These in turn can also encompass many subgenres, including actualities, news events or topicals, and those of a local nature (the latter being the mainstay of Mitchell & Kenyon's output). The French term 'actualités' in early film history embodies a variety of meanings, but is generally used to denote the filming of a current event, such as state visits, sports films, parades and processions, or anything that can be construed as 'news'.[5] The subject matter of the non-fiction titles filmed by Mitchell & Kenyon in the Edwardian era was not unique and representatives of different types can be found in other film-makers' catalogues at the time. Active dialogue between European scholars is providing new insights into how we understand and differentiate local and topical films, and how they contributed to the development of the newsreel and other types of non-fiction material.[6] When particular titles produced by Mitchell & Kenyon are compared to those of one of their rivals there does appear to be a difference in how the event was filmed. Due to the vast amount of material in the collection, in contrast to other British and European material, particular types of non-fiction films will be compared with those produced by different film companies, selecting the titles that are closest in content and date.

Factory Gates

The first and earliest non-fiction films in the Mitchell & Kenyon Collection are the factory gate films. The concept of filming factory gate exits can be traced back to the Lumière Brothers, who filmed *Workers Leaving the Factory* in March 1895, and followed this with two remakes later the same year.[7] Although there are only three examples in the Lumière filmography, it soon became a subject covered by other pioneers of the cinema.[8] Cecil Hepworth mentions filming factory gate exits in his autobiography, *Came the Dawn*, and the Warwick Trading Company advertised *Workmen Leaving the Factory* in 1900.[9] They were also a popular choice for early fairground exhibitors such as Edwin Lawrence:

> Cameramen were not plentiful in those far off days, so to find a man with a cinematograph camera must have been a piece of inspiration on the part of Billy Clark. He found and engaged this man to take a short film of about fifty to sixty feet showing the employees leaving their work at the dinner hour at a local hat factory at Stockport, which he then exhibited at Stockport fair.[10]

The factory gate film as produced by Mitchell & Kenyon linked production to exhibition, with the workers who were filmed during the day becoming the audience who later viewed the show. The company produced factory gate films as both local subjects,

A typical factory gate exit filmed by the company, showing the *Workforce of Scott & Co., Shipyard, Greenock* (1901)

which they advertised in the showmen's press, and as commissioned films for the showmen exhibitors. Over 124 examples of factory gate films survive in the collection, all of which are very different in format and execution to the original title produced by the Lumière Brothers in 1895, and those by other film-makers such as the American Biograph Company. The most striking difference is that the Mitchell & Kenyon films make the workers the centre of attention, as opposed to the architecture of the factory in the French and American examples. The Lumière Brothers filmed their own factory in Lyon purely to show the size of the building and the workforce and to convey motion in pictures. The workers captured on film were not the intended audience and they were instructed to walk away from the camera or across the line of vision. As Tom Gunning writes, *Workers Leaving the Factory* 'was presented to elite audiences in order to demonstrate the success of the latest Lumière photographic experiment, for which the workers were guinea pigs, rather then the intended audience'.[11] Indeed, the camera was placed in such a position so as not to distract the workers, and some scholars believe that they must have been ordered not to look at the camera.[12] This is in complete contrast to any of the Mitchell & Kenyon films where, as the people captured on film are the intended audience, their faces fill the screen and become the most important aspect. These films glow with humanity and vitality as the workers respond with a variety of gestures to the appearance of the cinematograph at their place of work. Church exits provide another

Workforce Leaving Alfred Butterworth and Sons, Glebe Mills, Hollinwood (1901). The children are fascinated by the presence of the cinematograph

point of comparison between the Lumières and Mitchell & Kenyon; there are only three examples in the Lumière catalogue, while Mitchell & Kenyon shot over twenty-one films of this type. Again, Mitchell & Kenyon concentrated on filming the crowds, with close-ups and pans of the congregation, whereas the Lumières focused on the structure of the building. In one example from Stockholm, members of the Lumière company can be seen using sticks to prevent people from crossing the view of the camera![13]

Celebrity Subjects and News Events

Certain subjects, in particular the films marking specific civic events such as the visits of Boer War generals, were almost certainly promoted outside their locations and used to augment the travelling exhibitors' programmes. Sometimes classified as celebrity films within the collection, they consist of films of Boer War military heroes such as Kitchener, Buller and Roberts, or particular royal events, including the *Visit of HRH Princess Louise to Blackburn* (1905).[14] Mitchell & Kenyon's treatment of this material is very similar to those of their contemporaries, such as Robert Paul and Cecil Hepworth, for example, who advertised many examples of this kind of filming in contemporary catalogues. Perhaps the most famous of the celebrity subjects filmed by the company was the *Funeral of Queen Victoria* (1901), an occasion also covered by their contemporaries.[15] The film has survived and in form and style is similar to the Hepworth title already held at the NFTVA in London.[16]

Funeral of Queen Victoria (1901) was one of the first non-fiction titles that the company sold nationally

As this event was covered by a variety of companies, it is also interesting to compare Mitchell & Kenyon's film of King Edward VII's visit to Manchester in 1902 with the Sheffield Photo Company's record of his visit to Sheffield.[17] Edward VII visited Sheffield on 12 July 1905, to open the newly inaugurated University of Sheffield. The film starts with a shot of his arrival at the Vickers factory, where a message of welcome has been written over the gateway. This is followed by various shots of the royal train as it draws into the station and of the King and Queen alighting, the procession of carriages through the streets of Sheffield and their arrival at the university. The final sequence reveals the 'The King opening Sheffield University', as the ceremony is filmed over the heads of the spectators. We then see a parade of troops, blessing the colours and the presentation to the King in Western Park. The film is constructed in a very formal civic fashion, with little interaction between the camera and the spectators filmed along the route.

The Manchester title, although similar in subject matter (the visit of the monarch to the university), centres solely on the formal parade of the royal and civic dignitaries through the streets of the city. The camera focuses purely on the dignitaries in their carriages, and little if no attention is paid to the streets through which they pass, as the film concentrates on the VIPs who await the monarch the University College. The Sheffield Photo Company title was produced for both a local and national audience: by showing the landscape of the city environment, the close-ups of the Midland Station, the factories visited by the King and also the route taken by the parade, there is an inherent storyline within the structure of the event. In contrast, the Mitchell & Kenyon title is filmed as a series of close-ups of the dignitaries, and focuses on the splendour of the parade itself, with little attention paid to any city landmarks. It lacks the contextual setting of the Sheffield Photo Company film and appears to be produced for a local audience rather than as a news event feature that could be shown outside the area. Having said this, of course, there are many films within the collection, that display the characteristics of the Sheffield Photo Company title, including the royal visits to Rhyl, Bangor and the Isle of Man, and the latter title was certainly advertised in *The Era*.[18] It is interesting to see that even within the category of news events, Mitchell & Kenyon were also adapting their filming for local criteria.

Sporting Titles

Films depicting sporting events of national interest were often commissioned by the travelling exhibitors and formed part of their programmes as items of national or news interest. Within the collection, two titles were exhibited in this way: the *AAA Championships at Fartown Huddersfield* (1901) and *Arthur Mold Bowling to A. N. Hornby* (1902). Despite being of national interest, there is little evidence in the trade press that Mitchell & Kenyon offered these titles for sale, in contrast to the marketing of the films of Queen Victoria's funeral or the coronation of Edward VII mentioned earlier. This is despite the overwhelming popularity of such subjects with other film-makers at the time. Indeed, sporting events were among the first subjects to be filmed, the 1895 Paul-Acres Derby title and the Oxford and Cambridge University boat race being obvious examples.[19] Boxing was also a very popular subject for the kinetoscope, with both Birt Acres and Thomas Edison producing titles in 1894 and 1895.[20] Although football matches were filmed by Robert Paul in 1896, and by the Lumières in 1897, the earliest surviving film was made in 1898 by Arthur Cheetham of Blackburn Rovers v. West Bromwich Albion. The reporter in *Photography* states:

AAA Championships at Fartown Huddersfield (1901) showing William Coe, the winner of the shot put competition posing for the camera

> We thought that before long the kinematograph would come into the football field. At the beginning of the season and at the end of it, of course the light is good enough but the play may not be of the best.[21]

Some of the earliest football films were made by Jasper Redfern who travelled with Sheffield United in 1899 and filmed at least four matches.[22] The fact that Redfern was based in Sheffield probably explains why Sheffield United was chosen for such prominent coverage. But they were also a very successful football club at the time, going on to win the FA Cup in May, and would therefore have attracted national interest. Although association football matches dominate the sporting material produced by Mitchell & Kenyon, it is interesting to compare their film of *Hunslet v. Leeds* (1901) with the *Rugby Football Match* (1901) made by Bamforths of Holmfirth.[23] On first viewing, both titles are constructed in a similar fashion and involve three groups of shots: the arrival of the teams on the pitch, shots of the action and then a general pan of the crowd. This is certainly the case with the Bamforth title, as it displays all the characteristics of the Mitchell & Kenyon filming of sporting events at that time. As the Bamforth title appeared eight months after the Hunslet game, a case could be made that this three-shot composition of sporting titles was an innovation introduced by Mitchell &

Hunslet v Leeds (1901) showing the Hunslet team lining up for the cinematograph, including the legendary Albert Goldthorpe

Policeman and crowds watching the Northern Union match between *Hunslet v Leeds* (1901). Around 4,000 spectators attended the game, Parkside, which Hunslet won by 16 points

Kenyon. An examination of *Hunslet v. Leeds* reveals that it has a more complex construction. Although still divided into three sections – players entering the field of play, shots of the action and the spectators – the composition and grouping of shots are far more advanced. For example, the film includes individual shots of each team lined up in front of the camera, displaying wonderful moments of interaction between the cameraman and the players, who jostle and wave at the camera. In addition, within the three-shot composition, there are seven individual edits on the field of play, seven or eight close-ups of the crowd, along with a great deal of interaction and waving at the camera, as well as a final pan across the spectators. Mitchell & Kenyon's treatment of sporting events is complex, innovative and more progressive than those of their contemporaries, and the characteristics noted in *Hunslet v. Leeds*, are certainly prevalent within the Northern Union films produced by the company between 1901 and 1903.[24]

Phantom Rides

Phantom ride films were usually filmed from the front of a moving vehicle, invariably a train, and were an attempt to reproduce the effects of continuous movement into the landscape. They were a feature of the American Mutoscope and Biograph Company, whose famous films of *Brooklyn Bridge* and *Haverstraw Tunnel* (1898) are but two examples.[25] Although Mitchell & Kenyon did film journeys from the front or the side of a train in Dundee and Blarney, and also used steamboats to shoot a panoramic voyage down the Menai Straits, it was the electric tram that became their preferred choice of locomotion.[26] Crossing over two different subjects, these films became more than a re-creation of a journey through a particular landscape but were advertised as an animated excursion through one's locality, a living, moving panoramic view of the city or

An example of one of the company's phantom ride sequences taken from *Lytham Trams and Views along the Route* (1903) and promoted as an animated journey through one's locality

town inhabited by the audience. Very rarely is the non-urban landscape captured by the company, as they sought to use the phantom tram journey as a means to extend the range of the local subject and, of course, film the local spectators who participated in the production.

Local Films

> It is astonishing what a great attraction a local film is; crowds flock to see it, and there is generally some comical feature that causes much merriment. Considerable delight is expressed when popular characters come on the screen, and great laughter as some grinning face appears . . .[27]

Another type of local film were those featuring prominent personalities visiting the town – as seen in the *Inspection of the Ambulance Drill Hall in Accrington by Inspector-general Baden Powell* (1904)

Local films, as defined in early film studies, are those that were exhibited purely for a local audience where part of the rationale of the filming lay in the audience paying to view their friends, neighbours, locality or themselves on the cinematograph. As Tom Gunning writes, 'it is the cry of recognition that baptizes this cinema of locality', and nothing demonstrates this more than the Mitchell & Kenyon Collection, of which over 90 per cent falls into the category of the local film genre.[28] The local film encompassed sporting events, the arrival of civic dignitaries and the factory gate genre, where the original commissioning and production was in connection with a local show or exhibition. Although some of the subcategories previously mentioned can also be defined as local, the most important rationale for defining the local is that: 'a film is "local" only if there is considerable overlap between the people appearing in the film and those who watch it or are intended to watch it.'[29]

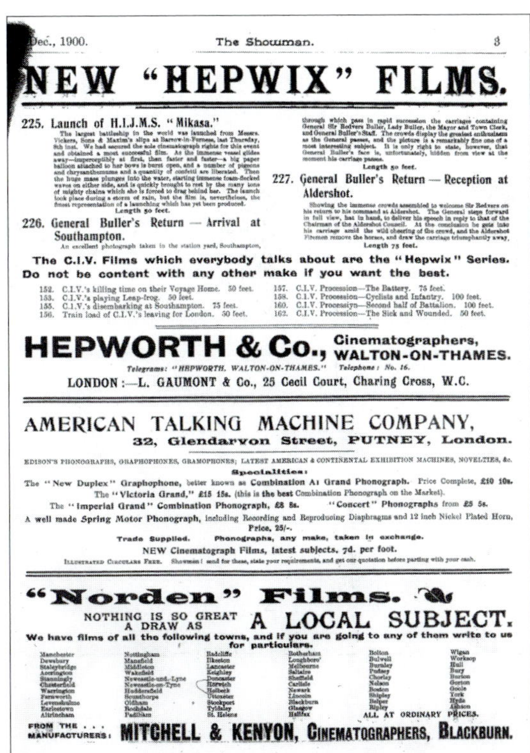

Dec., 1900. The Showman. 3

NEW "HEPWIX" FILMS.

225. Launch of H.I.J.M.S. "Mikasa."

The largest battleship in the world was launched from Messrs. Vickers, Sons & Maxim's slips at Barrow-in-Furness, last Thursday, 8th inst. We had secured the sole cinematograph rights for this event and obtained a most successful film. As the immense vessel glides away—imperceptibly at first, then faster and faster—a big paper balloon attached to her bows is burst open, and a number of pigeons and chrysanthemums and a quantity of confetti are liberated. Then the huge mass plunges into the water, starting immense foam-flecked waves on either side, and is quickly brought to rest by the many tons of mighty chains which she is forced to drag behind her. The launch took place during a storm of rain, but the film is, nevertheless, the finest representation of a launching which has yet been produced.

Length 50 feet.

226. General Buller's Return — Arrival at Southampton.

An excellent photograph taken in the station yard, Southampton, through which pass in rapid succession the carriages containing General Sir Redvers Buller, Lady Buller, the Mayor and Town Clerk, and General Buller's Staff. The crowds display the greatest enthusiasm as the General passes, and the picture is a remarkably fine one of a most interesting subject. It is only right to state, however, that General Buller's face is, unfortunately, hidden from view at the moment his carriage passes.

Length 50 feet.

227. General Buller's Return — Reception at Aldershot.

Showing the immense crowds assembled to welcome Sir Redvers on his return to his command at Aldershot. The General steps forward in full view, hat in hand, to deliver his speech in reply to that of the Chairman of the Aldershot Council. At the conclusion he gets into his carriage amid the wild cheering of the crowd, and the Aldershot Firemen remove the horses, and draw the carriage triumphantly away.

Length 75 feet.

The C.I.V. Films which everybody talks about are the "Hepwix" Series. Do not be content with any other make if you want the best.

152. C.I.V.'s killing time on their Voyage Home. 50 feet.
153. C.I.V.'s playing Leap-frog. 50 feet.
155. C.I.V.'s disembarking at Southampton. 75 feet.
156. Train load of C.I.V.'s leaving for London. 50 feet.
157. C.I.V. Procession—The Battery. 75 feet.
158. C.I.V. Procession—Cyclists and Infantry. 100 feet.
160. C.I.V. Processiyn—Second half of Battalion. 100 feet.
162. C.I.V. Procession—The Sick and Wounded. 50 feet.

HEPWORTH & Co., Cinematographers, WALTON-ON-THAMES.

Telegrams: "HEPWORTH, WALTON-ON-THAMES." Telephone: No. 16.

LONDON :—L. GAUMONT & Co., 25 Cecil Court, Charing Cross, W.C.

AMERICAN TALKING MACHINE COMPANY,
32, Glendarvon Street, PUTNEY, London.

EDISON'S PHONOGRAPHS, GRAPHOPHONES, GRAMOPHONES; LATEST AMERICAN & CONTINENTAL EXHIBITION MACHINES, NOVELTIES, &c.

Specialities:

The "New Duplex" Graphophone, better known as Combination A1 Grand Phonograph. Price Complete, £10 10s.
The "Victoria Grand," £15 15s. (this is the best Combination Phonograph on the Market).
The "Imperial Grand" Combination Phonograph, £8 8s. "Concert" Phonographs from £5 5s.
A well made Spring Motor Phonograph, including Recording and Reproducing Diaphragms and 12 inch Nickel Plated Horn, Price, 25/-.
Trade Supplied. Phonographs, any make, taken in exchange.
NEW Cinematograph Films, latest subjects, 7d. per foot.
Illustrated Circulars Free. Showmen! send for these, state your requirements, and get our quotation before parting with your cash.

"Norden" Films.

NOTHING IS SO GREAT A DRAW AS **A LOCAL SUBJECT.**

We have films of all the following towns, and if you are going to any of them write to us for particulars.

Manchester, Dewsbury, Staleybridge, Accrington, Stanningly, Chesterfield, Warrington, Farnworth, Levenshulme, Earlestown, Altrincham, Nottingham, Mansfield, Middleton, Wakefield, Newcastle-und.-Lyne, Newcastle-on-Tyne, Huddersfield, Scunthorpe, Oldham, Rochdale, Padiham, Radcliffe, Ilkeston, Lancaster, Keighley, Doncaster, Horwich, Holbeck, Uttoxeter, Stockport, Tyldsley, St. Helens, Rotherham, Loughboro', Melbourne, Saltaire, Sheffield, Carlisle, Newark, Lincoln, Blackburn, Glasgow, Halifax, Bolton, Bulwell, Burnley, Pudsey, Chorley, Nelson, Boston, Shipley, Belper, Ripley, Wigan, Worksop, Hull, Bury, Burton, Gorton, Goole, York, Hyde

ALL AT ORDINARY PRICES.

FROM THE . . . MANUFACTURERS: **MITCHELL & KENYON, CINEMATOGRAPHERS, BLACKBURN.**

Advert for Norden Pictures, the trade name for Mitchell & Kenyon, advertising the range of local films available for purchase in December 1900 (NFA)

These films exist in archival collections around the world, but have been ignored by academics and archivists alike for a number of reasons: they were not advertised in trade journals, and were available originally only in small numbers and for purely local exhibitions.[30] The motivation behind the local film was to entice those being filmed into the cinematograph screening, so the spectator also became part of the paying audience. This exploitation of the local film by showmen and film-makers alike was an important economic factor in the development of early film shows and explains the large amount of this material in the Mitchell & Kenyon Collection. Recent research has demonstrated that local films played a prominent role in the context of local cinema competition in the UK before the First World War, and this is also apparent in Germany.[31] This trend for local views continued within international cinema exhibition into the sound era. Local films were exclusive and unique programme 'numbers' that could attract large audiences interested in recognising themselves on the screen. They were produced in the UK from as early as 1897, with film companies offering this service in trade advertisements and catalogues. Other exhibitors were quick to spot a potential market, including Cecil Hepworth, who ran an extensive advertisement on the front page of a newspaper for eight consecutive weeks from June onwards offering local subjects.[32] Hepworth's association with local films is reaffirmed in *The Showman* in 1902:

> Hepworth and Co., as the majority of our readers well know, make a speciality of taking local films in any part of the country, for showmen and entertainers running a hall or booth in their town. They are not content with merely securing pictures of the streets and ordinary incidents, and their staff of photographers are in possession of several mighty secrets, by which they can generally stage manage a sensational turn out of the local fire brigade or something similarly attractive.[33]

The Crowd Entering St George's Hall Bradford (1901) was filmed by Thomas during a matinee performance, and shown on screem later the same day

This practice continued throughout the Edwardian era with both the Warwick Trading Company and the Sheffield Photo Company making local films in 1906.[34] It is difficult to compare the commissioning, exhibition and reception of the titles made by other film-makers, as their links with the showmen have not been investigated as fully as in the Mitchell & Kenyon Collection, and many of the examples made by other companies have not survived. The purest example of a local title is one in which the subject is solely the audience that will view the film when exhibited. An important example in the collection is *The Crowd Entering St George's Hall, Bradford* (1901).[35] The film was part of a two-hour programme presented at the St George's Hall in Bradford by the showman A. D. Thomas. As an added incentive to bring the audience back to the evening's show, the crowds were filmed entering the building, and the film exhibited four to six hours later during the evening's presentation. Examples of this kind of showmanship can also be found also in Germany, with Peter Marzen from 1907 onwards, and in America in the 1930s.[36] Although filming the audience is the main premise of Mitchell & Kenyon's activities, this title reveals a more intimate and detailed example of such a practice. *Crowd Entering St George's Hall, Bradford* was a ploy to entice customers from a previous show to return later that evening and its remit is perhaps the most narrow of this type.

Re-enactments

According to film historian André Gaudreault, 'a re-enactment is a category of moving pictures that can include both past and current events'. As either the time or location meant that the camera was unable to capture a fully realistic cinematographic record, so 'other means were brought into place to reconstruct from scratch aspects of an event that had taken place out of the camera's view'.[37] One of the most famous examples of this was Méliès's *Reproduction, Coronation Ceremonies King Edward VII* (1902), which was actually produced before the real coronation of Edward took place in September that year. Other types of re-enactments consisted of actual news events incorporating dramatisations within actuality footage, such as the Edison Company's *Execution of Czolgosz* (1901), as well as reconstructed actualities. In Britain, the most common forms of 'faked' or reconstructed events were the 'fake' war titles associated, in particular, with the Boer War (1899–1902).

Fake War Films

The area of production that brought notoriety to Mitchell & Kenyon (and the canon of work with which people might have been more familiar prior to the emergence of this collection) was their reconstructions of war films, described at the time as 'imaginative reconstructions'.[38] The outbreak of the Boer War in October 1899 prompted the pair to re-create or 'fake' (essentially fictionalise) scenes from the battlefields. Other companies who produced these types of fiction included James Williamson and R. W. Paul in the UK, and James White for Thomas Edison in the United States.[39] From 1900, Mitchell & Kenyon produced fake war films of events in the Transvaal and the Boxer Rebellion in China, shot in the countryside around Blackburn. The term 'fake' was not one used by Mitchell & Kenyon, as

Scene from Williamson's *Attack on a China Mission* (1901).

they explained in a 1907 interview: 'Messrs Mitchell and Kenyon gave me one other interesting illustration of how pictures are "faked", though they do not like the use of the word, as it implies dishonesty where none is practiced.'[40] This sentiment was also echoed by Charles Urban, who wrote to the trade press in December 1900 to express his concerns over the use of the terms 'fake' or 'trick' films.[41] As Simon Popple has written, the films fall into subcategories that range from re-enactments of combat, scenes of individual deeds of heroism and sacrifice, the comedic and satirical, to full-blown representations of enemy atrocities.[42] The titles were available direct from the manufacturers but were also distributed by Gaumont, Walturdaw and Charles Urban. Many of these reconstructions survive, including *The Dispatch Bearer* (1900), *Winning the VC* (1900), *Sneaky Boer* (1901), *The Clever Correspondent* (c. 1901) and *Attack on a China Mission*, the latter being one of the few films featuring Mitchell himself. These reconstructions were extremely popular and were extensively shown throughout 1901. Other companies also manufactured them, including James Williamson's *Attack on a China Mission* (1900), while John Wrench and Son advertised a number of titles for sale in May 1900.[43] An advert carried in *The Showman* in September 1901 listed a further series of Boer War films produced by Mitchell & Kenyon, including their new amusing trick

Advert from the *Showman's Year Book*, 1901, offering Boer War films and local titles for sale (NFA)

ADVERTISEMENTS.

Local Films Hundreds Now Ready.

6d. Per Foot.

New Comic Films always coming out.

THE

BOER WAR FILMS

In the BIG SHOWS are our make.

Look out for New Gags, we are doing them.

The well-known Kenyon's Penny-in-the-Slot-Business will from January 1st, 1902, be carried on by us, and Exhibition Proprietors may look out for some new money making ideas.

Mitchell & Kenyon,

Norden Film Works,

22, Clayton Street,

BLACKBURN.

Sept., 6, 1901. The Showman. xi.

TOM NORMAN,
SILVER KING (Registered).

THE RECOGNISED
SHOWMAN'S AUCTIONEER, VALUER, and VARIETY AGENT.

47 Camden Hill Road, Upper Norwood, Feb. 8th, 1901.

With very best wishes, Faithfully yours,
FRED GINNETT.

Our New Series of
Boer War Films
LAST WEEK IN SEPTEMBER.

Startling, Realistic, Pathetic.

Also a
New Laughable Trick Film
Entitled
'Chasing De Wet.'

The Fight for the Gun.
Hands off the Flag.
Poisoning the Well.
Tommy's Last Shot.
Surprise of a Boer Camp.
Saved by a Woman.
A Sneaky Boer.
A Tight Corner, in 4 Tableaux—
1. A Dash for Help.
2. Through the Enemy's Lines.
3. The Message Delivered.
4. Just in Time.

We are still making the ever popular subjects:
Despatch Rider,
Washing Boer Prisoner,
Winning the V.C., and
The Lost Scout on the Veldt.

50ft. Local Pictures 25/-
300 Sbjects Now Ready.

Customers own Subjects Developed and Printed.
BEST FILM STOCK SUPPLIED.

MITCHELL & KENYON
Norden Film Works,
22 Clayton St., BLACKBURN.
Telegraphic Address:
"Films," Blackburn.

SPECIALITIES.
G. ORNUM & CO.
4 Duke St., Charing Cross, LONDON, W.C.

Aerial Gold Fishing Trick.
Best, quickest, and latest method. The same as performed by leading professional conjurers. Can be worked in evening dress. Price 32/6 complete.
Call and inspect at
G. Ornum & Co.

The Wonderful Rising Wand.
Absolutely a perfect imitation of a genuine Wand. Can be given for examination. Wand rises in the hand at command. Inexplicable and indetectable. Best quality, price 6/-
G. Ornum & Co.

Ubiquitous & Multiplying Thimble.
Eight thimbles mysteriously produced on the finger tips. Call and see it worked at 4 Duke Street. The only way to learn the various sleight. Complete trick 3/6

Novel Vanisher for Ball, Egg or Coin
Price 2/-
At G. Ornum & Co.

Variegated Spring Flowers, 5/- per 100.
Silk Spring Flowers. All sizes, from 9/- per 100.
6-in. Hat Coils. Absolutely the best, 3/9 per doz., post free 4/3.
Spring Snakes, from 1/6 each.
Carrots and Fishes, from 1/- each.
Throw-out Ribbons, from 2/6 per doz.
Tri-coloured Mouth Coils, 9d. doz.
Leaf Garlands, for Hat production, &c., &c., from 1/6.
Conjurer's Wax, from 4d. per box.
Invisible Thread, 10 yards 1/-.
Send for Catalogue.
G. ORNUM & Co.,
4 Duke St., Charing Cross, W.C.

The Latest Trick.
"Horizontal Sailing Card."
Card leaves pack and sails in front of performer, when it is caught in the hand. Simple, but very effective.
Also new method for "Rising" Card. Both complete, 5/.
G. Ornum & Co.

Marvellous Flag Production.
Performer mysteriously produces a silk Union Jack (5 ft. long by 2 ft. 6 in. wide) on a silver-plated staff. A sure applause producer. Also supplied with Stars and Stripes flag. Price 27/6.

G. ORNUM & Co.,
4 Duke Street, Charing Cross, LONDON, W.C.

Advert in the *Showman* newspaper for Mitchell & Kenyon's Boer War titles and local pictures, 6 September 1901 (NFA)

film, *Chasing De Wet* (1901), and *Saved by a Woman* (1901), both of which survive in the Cinema Museum's collection.[44] They continued advertising these types of film until the end of the Boer War in 1902, when they listed fifteen titles under the heading 'the war is won and now the country is eager to know how Tommy won South Africa'.[45]

Reconstructed Actualities

> When a crime is represented in the cinematograph films it is extraordinary to what trouble a firm goes in order to obtain the best results. The firm's representatives will visit the house of the criminal, will obtain some of his very belongings, perhaps will persuade his relatives to come and play over again the scene when he was arrested. The very detective who took the main in charge may even be present. And descriptions of weight, stature and appearance of the central figure are compared with official records.[46]

In December 1901, Mitchell & Kenyon added a new type of filmic representation to their already impressive output, a reconstructed actuality of a crime event, the *Arrest of Goudie* (1901).[47] Although similar to the 'fakes' described above, the marked difference was that the film depicts the events of, and the lead-up to, the real-life arrest of an embezzler, Thomas Peterson Goudie, who had stolen £170,000 from the Bank of Liverpool.[48] The discovery of this theft, Goudie's disappearance and the worldwide hunt for both him and the money captured the imagination of the public. This was especially the case when he was discovered living in lodgings less than half a mile from a local police station in Bootle, while his pursuers were following leads in London, Paris and Brazil!

Although the Biograph Company in Europe and America, and Méliès in France,[49] had regularly reconstructed and re-enacted scenes of topical news back in their studios, the filming of the Goudie case was different in two distinct ways. First, it used the actual locations where the event occurred and advertised the film as a factual and authentic account of the arrest and, second, it was filmed less than two days after the arrest had taken place.[50] In order to understand the rationale behind the film's construction, it is important to compare the *Arrest of Goudie* with similar films from the period and slightly after. Crime reports were a popular feature of Victorian newspapers and serials, with dedicated newspapers such as *The Police Budget* and *The Illustrated Police News* providing a staple diet of sensational stories, murders and rapes, all elements that would go on to make up the essential components of the Sensation novel.[51] Madame Tussaud's Chamber of Horrors, which began life as the 'Separate Room' until *Punch* magazine renamed it in 1846, has been an essential component of the waxwork museum for two centuries and remains so to the present day.[52]

Considering the popularity in the Victorian era for all aspects of criminality, it is surprising that early cinema only adopted crime as a subject in the early 1900s, with the *Life of Jack Shepherd* (1900), a legendary criminal from the early nineteenth century. As Andrew Clay

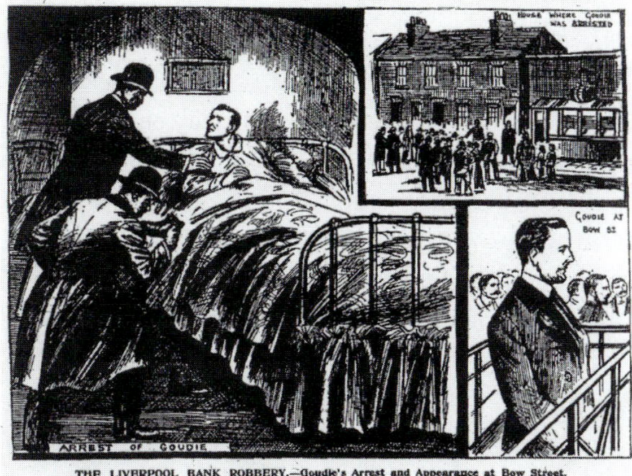

December 14, 1901. THE ILLUSTRATED POLICE NEWS. 3

THE LIVERPOOL BANK ROBBERY.

GOUDIE'S ARREST AND APPEARANCE AT BOW STREET.

THE ARREST.

GOUDIE AT BOW STREET.

A DOUBLE EXECUTION.

THE LIVERPOOL BANK ROBBERY.—Goudie's Arrest and Appearance at Bow Street.

A BOOK FOR LADIES.

writes, 'crime as a subject-matter for films was insignificant in 1900: by 1905 it had become a common source material in all genres'.[53] Although criminality was an element in some of the early films, it usually consisted of tramps stealing food or clothes, or in representations of crime in early chase films. A comparable example of the filming of a crime reconstruction soon after the event was the *Moat Farm Mystery*, shot by Gaumont, Robert Paul and Harrison in 1903.[54] The films were based on the arrest and subsequent trial of Samuel Herbert Dougal for the murder of his wife, Camille Cecile Holland, in 1899 at Moat Farm. After murdering his wife, Dougal remained at the farm and told people that his wife had disappeared.[55] The discovery and identification of the body on the farm and the subsequent arrest and trial of Dougal captured the public's imagination. Gaumont and Paul were only part of the large media activity surrounding the crime scene. Unfortunately, none of the Moat Farm films survives, but the description that appeared in *The Era* of the Gaumont title reveals that the film was 110 feet in length, comprised four parts and showed actual footage of the farm buildings where the murder took place.[56] Other crime reconstruction films were produced by the American Biograph Company, in particular the Thaw White murder case in 1906 and the trial and hanging of Mary Rogers for the murder of her husband in 1905.[57] Both these films were made after two British film companies each produced their own crime reconstruction fiction film in 1905, on the life and career of the legendary criminal from the 1870s, Charles Peace.

(Above left) Close-up of the steel engraving from the *Illustrated Police News* showing the arrest of Goudie, 14 December 1901 (NFA); (above left) Dramatic reconstruction from the *Illustrated Police News,* 14 December 1901, showing the sleeping Goudie arrested in his bed by police (NFA)

A contrast can be made between the *Arrest of Goudie* and later criminal reconstruction events such as the *Life of Charles Peace*, filmed by both the Sheffield Photo Company and William Haggar in 1905. Charles Peace was a notorious burglar whose exploits had gripped the imagination of the Victorian public since his capture and subsequent execution in 1879 for the murder of Arthur Dyson, his neighbour in Sheffield, in 1876. By the 1880s, his life had been transformed into a play, a penny dreadful and displayed as a waxworks in Madame Tussaud's. Clearly, double life as a respectable churchgoing citizen by day and a daring cat burglar by night had transfixed the public (see Plate 4).[58]

In 1905, the life of this villainous character, who over time had become transformed into a more sympathetic figure, was finally captured on film by William Haggar from Wales and Frank Mottershaw of the Sheffield Photo Company.[59] Although only the Haggar version has survived, the catalogue description of the Mottershaw title contains a full synopsis of the film that we can use to compare the different approaches. First, the later Charles Peace films were both filmed many years after the event and utilised the dramatic retelling of Peace's life in melodramatic style. Second, the development of the fiction film from 1903 had given rise to more dramatic plot developments, a stronger narrative structure and a move away from single-shot representations. In contrast, *Arrest of Goudie* is stripped down in terms of narrative structure and dramatic incident. Nevertheless, one similarity is that both Mitchell & Kenyon and Mottershaw filmed in the actual places where the crime took place. Indeed, Mottershaw advertised that the engine driver used in the film was 'the very same man who escorted Peace on his journey'.[60]

The realisation of cinema was as Michael Booth argues 'one of the many responses of an increasingly sophisticated entertainment technology to the demand for pictorial realism'.[61] As Jonathan Auerbach discusses in his article 'McKinley at Home: How Early American Cinema Made News', the Edison Company's film *Execution of Czolgosz, with Panorama of Auburn Prison* was 'an unusual hybrid of actuality footage and theatrical re-enactment' that closely followed eyewitness newspaper accounts.[62] The depiction of the execution of

Sequence from the first *Arrest of Goudie* film, showing the actual street where Goudie was in hiding, the bridge and crowd scenes, the top room in the boarding house where Goudie was lodging, views of the Bootle police station, and shots of the arresting officers

President McKinley's assassin in October 1901 was an attempt to capture on film the death by electrocution of Leon Czolgosz, who had shot President McKinley at the Pan-American Exposition in September 1901. Permission to film the event was refused and instead they combined actuality footage of the prison with restaged scenes.[63]

A comparison of *Arrest of Goudie* with *Execution of Czolgosz, with Panorama of Auburn Prison* throws up several dramatic differences. First, as Charles Musser argues, the Czolgosz film 'did not present the scenes along a simple, linear time line'. Rather, it is a mixture of reconstructed scenes of the execution made in the Edison studio with two shots of actuality footage of sweeping panoramas of Auburn State Prison taken on the morning of Czolgosz's execution, followed by two representational staged scenes of the execution itself. The reconstructed studio scenes commence with shots of the prisoner in his cell and being escorted to his execution, followed by the final sequence demonstrating the testing of the electric chair, the prisoner's entrance and then his actual execution. Compare this to the first nine-shot sequence of the first reel of *Arrest of Goudie* and the subsequent four-shot sequence of the second part. In the first film, we are given the background to the story: the photographic evidence of the event, including shots of Goudie's lodgings, the police station and the railway bridge, where eager crowds had gathered to see a view of the house where Goudie was arrested. News of his arrest had spread quickly throughout the locality and the scenes of onlookers watching the house are possibly footage of the crowds who continued to gather for days after his arrest. The second film, which is shorter and more tightly constructed, takes us straight to the central part of the story itself, as Mrs Harding, the landlady, becomes suspicious of her lodger and goes to the police station in Bootle to inform them of his whereabouts. The final scene depicts the arrest of Goudie by the CID, who are distinct from the uniformed police in their formal and smart attire.

Four-shot sequence from the second *Arrest of Goudie* film, showing the entrance to Berry Street; the arrival of the landlady, Mrs Harding, to inform the police of her suspicions; the CID officers taking Goudie to be questioned; and the final crowd shots

At the end of the film, groups of young men appear from behind the camera and act as if in a local film, where the audience play up to the camera eager to get their faces on film.

Although *Execution of Czolgosz* is more ambitious, with its use of dissolve, actuality and reconstruction, and portions of scenes that occur simultaneously, *Arrest of Goudie* is innovative in other ways: for example, the employment of exact locations to re-enact the event; the contrast between the two titles that make up the film; the means by which Mitchell & Kenyon introduce the key components of the story; and the four-shot sequence in the second film that concludes with Goudie's capture. The film was organised in this manner to create greater pictorial realism (rather in the way of a lantern show) for the narrative structure of the lecture that accompanied the film.

Ralph Pringle, the showman who exhibited *Arrest of Goudie*, emphasised in his advertisement that the film was authentic and realistic, and that it was not a re-enactment in the tradition of melodrama or the Boer War and Boxer Rebellion films. Moreover, the possibility of likeness between the real arresting officers and the persons employed by Mitchell & Kenyon could also add to its authenticity. In 'The Romance of the Cinematograph Film', published in 1907, the reporter states that the very detective who arrested the assailant may even be present on film, and that central characters were hired who resembled the real people.[64] This represents an antecedent to the modern-day *Crimewatch* re-enactments, where greater realism is achieved through the use of reconstructed actuality footage of a story that is already in the public domain. On first viewing, it is quite an unremarkable film, as it lacks the melodramatic components of fake war titles, the narrative structure of the Peace films or the dramatic content of the Edison Company's *Execution of Czolgosz*. However, by investigating beyond the text of the film to understand the rationale and context in which it was produced, it becomes apparent that *Arrest of Goudie* was an attempt to make the fake film more authentic and more like a visual newspaper. Through utilising the locality where the events occurred and the factual structure from the newspaper accounts of the arrest, Mitchell & Kenyon were anticipating a new development in film as a medium – the reconstructed actuality as opposed to the dramatic reconstruction. It could be argued that if the event had been filmed at a later stage, when the narrative structure of the episode had become enhanced and sensationalised through the print media, a stronger dramatic story may have been produced. Mitchell & Kenyon and Pringle would have been aware of the main components of the story – Goudie's secret life, his gambling debts – but chose instead to produce a factual reconstruction of the arrest as opposed to a dramatisation of the event as a whole. With the *Arrest of Goudie*, it appears that, for the first time in England, film predated theatrical and pictorial media in delivering the event to the public.

'Docudrama' or Drama Documentary?

Although the term 'docudrama' is not used in relation to films produced in the early cinema period, John Parris Springer, writing in *Docufictions*, believes that it can be applied to films that combined actualities with narrative or fictional reconstructions:

> While the fusing and blurring of documentary devices and fictional narrative elements might at first seem a contemporary, even postmodern cultural phenomenon, arguably such docufictional synthesis was at its height during the period of Early Cin-

> ema (1893–1905), precisely because film's critical identity as a vehicle for fictional narrative was not yet fixed and taken for granted by either filmmakers or audiences.[65]

Springer uses this term when referring to Edwin Porter's *Life of an American Fireman* (1902–3) and the same model could also be applied to Charles-Lucien Lépine's *A Policeman's Tour of the World* (1906), which uses an elaborate mixture of actuality footage and fictional narrative.[66]

In the early 1900s, British film-makers, in particular, were involved in what Rachael Low calls 'a film of exploration, film as a demonstration of processes of actual life'.[67] Film-makers who explored this particular type of 'embryonic documentary' included James Williamson, with his *Country Life Series* (1899), Robert Paul in *Army Life or How Soldiers are Made* (1900) and Cecil Hepworth in *The British Army* (1900).[68] By 1904, what had originally been examples of picture scenes from reality grouped together as a subject had become more sophisticated, as both Paul and Hepworth were producing titles with a narrative structure and storyline: for example, Hepworth's *A Day with the Hop Pickers* (1903), *A Day in the Hay Fields* (1904), *The Story of a Piece of Slate* (1904) and Charles Urban's *Newspaper Making* (1904). The combination of a fictional character intertwined in a pictorially realistic backdrop made from actuality footage is apparent in Mitchell & Kenyon's *Black Diamonds – The Collier's Daily Life* (1904).[69] Sold exclusively by the Charles Urban Trading Company, possibly their most ambitious title, it told the parallel stories of a miner's life and coal, or the 'Black Diamonds' of the title.[70] The company filmed at a disused mine and employed miners to re-create the appearance of a fully operational mine.[71] The film is a mixture of drama and non-fiction, combining actuality shots with dramatic events staged for the camera, such as an underground explosion.[72] Parts of the film have survived in the collection, although it is interesting to note that they are not easily distinguishable from other factory gate films, such is the 'realistic' nature of the mining scenes.[73]

> Everybody uses coal, and everybody will be interested to see this true and faithful pictorial representation of the way coal is got. No expense has been spared to make this

Scenes form *Black Diamonds – The Collier's Daily Life* (1904) showing the miners entering the pit head and the coal coming out of the mine. The scenes were shot at a real mine in the Black Country to add authenticity

> film most interesting and realistic. No. 3,300. – Length, about 650ft. Ready Next Week.
>
> NOTE – The above is the Latest 'Mitchell & Kenyon' Production of which we have acquired the Exclusive Sale.[74]

Parts of the film were tinted: for example, the explosion scene, which was 'tinted to import a subdued light', and in the final section, where a 'warm and cosy fire – showing the blazing coal in an open grate' was 'coloured to the natural glow and blaze of the fire'. Copies were priced at £17 10s. for a total length of 675 feet from Charles Urban on condition that 'they were not exhibited or re-sold in England or the United States', as the exclusive rights had been secured by Urbanora.[75] *Black Diamonds* was a very ambitious project for Mitchell & Kenyon and was made at the time when coal had apparently become a popular subject for early film-makers: in 1902, Gaumont had made *The Coal Miner – A Day from the Collier's Life*, ten scenes of mining life in Wigan. A later title from Pathé in France, *Au Pays Noir* (1905), also features a coal mine, and although predominantly dramatic, it concludes with actuality footage of the funeral of trapped coal miners.[76] Paul also produced a film about coal entitled *A Miner's Daily Life* (1904).[77] Examination of the synopsis reveals that it is not as ambitious as Mitchell & Kenyon's *The Collier's Daily Life*,which, as well as the reconstructed pit explosion and tinted sequences, consists of fifteen to eighteen scenes as opposed to Paul's five.[78] In the Mitchell & Kenyon title, the narrative of the 'Story of Coal' is constructed around a day in the life of one individual miner and begins as he leaves home for work.[79] The next six scenes are filmed as actuality sequences and two of these survive in the collection and appear very similar in form and structure to the company's factory gate films.[80] These scenes introduce the other 'leading man' – the 'black diamond' that is the title of the film – and we are shown how it is extracted from the pit, passed from tub to tub, travelling upwards on an endless belt, to be sorted by pit men and girls. In scene nine, the narrative returns back to our original miner, who, along with his workmates, is buried in debris after an explosion, and is heroically rescued by his colleagues. Scenes ten to twelve employ the actuality format once again, with the fictional narrative returning in scene thirteen, when the miner, or 'Daddy' as he is now described in the synopsis, comes home to his children. The final two scenes include a comic washing scene interlude that Urban describes as 'a wet reception', 'speeding the parting guest', followed by the real hero of the story, 'the blazing coal', in an open grate with the film tinted to reflect the natural glow and blaze of the fire!

While further research is needed on the development of these types of actuality, along with more in-depth comparisons of all surviving examples, this brief overview does place *Black Diamonds* firmly alongside films that incorporated elements of both fiction and actuality material, and demonstrates again how distinct genres were less defined in the early cinema period. The synopsis for *Black Diamonds* appears to place it outside the type of films described by Low as 'embryonic documentary' and not fully in the realms of what Springer considers as 'docudrama'; rather, it is either a dramatisation or reconstruction of an actual event, or a fictional account with actuality footage. In the early cinema period, neither drama nor documentary forms were mutually exclusive, a fact that *Black Diamonds* and other titles produced at the time clearly demonstrate. It may also have anticipated

Charles Urban's *A Day in the Life of a Coal Miner* (1910), which mixed drama with documentary footage. The film does demonstrate how Mitchell & Kenyon, at this time, were expanding their repertoire as film-makers and also extending the form and structure of their non-fiction titles. The film was successful and was sold exclusively by Charles Urban from 1904 onwards. It was shown by a number of exhibitors in 1905, including New Century Pictures in Blackburn and by Ralph Pringle in Rochdale.[81]

Fiction

> On this little stage grim tragedies have been enacted. There have been here the atrocities of the Congo, the imprisonment of criminals. Little homely stories have run their length to a finish of happiness, and there has been wild burlesques. A doctor has stooped over the dying husband, hospital nurses have busied about the beds of the sick. Romance in the daintily-decked person of one and twenty has loitered here as though it were a spring garden – all on the rough stage in the heart of a black and smoky town . . .[82]

This description of Mitchell & Kenyon's fiction output from the periodical *Ideas* published in 1907 gives a complete overview of the types of subjects tackled by the company. War films, tragic romances, burlesque comedies and crime stories were all subjects utilised in their fiction narratives. If we exclude the Boer War material and concentrate on the comedy, chase, melodrama and the burlesque, forty new fiction titles now exist in the collections at the Cinema Museum in London and Lobster Films in Paris. These were filmed between 1899 and 1907 in various locations in the east Lancashire countryside or on a specially constructed stage at their premises in Blackburn. Additionally, another six titles form part of the collection and include the first fiction titles produced by Mitchell & Kenyon in 1899. The majority of the fiction titles currently reside in private hands but

Scenes from Mitchell & Kenyon's fiction titles including (from top left) *Kidnapping by Indians* (1899); *Snowman*, shot at Green's Carnival (1901); Perci Hondri's *Mr Moon* act; *The Sporting Colliers and the Bobby* (c.1901); and an unidentified actor performing for the camera at Lizar's in Edinburgh in 1904

details of the films supplied by the Cinema Museum in London have enabled the following attempt at a chronology of their fictional output, along with a comparison of Mitchell & Kenyon's most successful film, *Diving Lucy* (1903), and a later remake, *Sold Again* (1907), produced by the Sheffield Photo Company.[83]

The earliest fiction films produced by the company were first advertised for sale in September 1899, two weeks after the date of filming on the negative for *Kidnapping by Indians*.[84] The two other titles, *The Tramp's Surprise* and *The Tramps and the Artist*, were also advertised in *The Optician and Photographic Trades Review*. The company's fiction production was not as prolific as their non-fiction output, but by 1903 their premises in Clayton Street included an outdoor studio and they also filmed on location. The types of subjects included chase films, comedies, melodramas such as *A Tragic Elopement* (1903) and what Tony Fletcher defines as 'snow comedies', where the main comedic element involves snowball fights or chases in the snow. Throughout the Edwardian era, as fiction subjects became more popular, additional scenes were included, along with innovative use of animated intertitles to maintain the narrative structure of the films.[85] *A Tragic Elopement*, distributed by Charles Urban and comprising a six-part tableau, marks their transition to more elaborated scenarios. *Driven from Home* (1904), and *Miser and His Daughter* (1904), both serious dramas verging on the maudlin, were also advertised at this time.[86] Like their contemporaries, in particular Bamforths of Holmfirth, they utilised the figure of the tramp to introduce comic elements. This was in the tradition of Tom Browne's Weary Willie and Tired Tim series, where the character of the itinerant is a figure of misrule whose presence results in mischief and chaos. Two of their first fiction titles, *The Tramp's Surprise* and *The Tramps and the Artist*, feature unruly tramps, as do later titles, such as *Cool Proceedings* (1902) and *The Interrupted Picnic* (1906). The storylines and comedic characters utilised by Mitchell & Kenyon can be found in many other films from the time.[87] Perhaps one of the most successful fiction titles produced by the company was *Diving Lucy*, a film described by the *Talking Machine News* in the following terms:

> Another film by Messrs. Mitchell and Kenyon, entitled 'Diving Lucy', is also very comic. The lady at first sight appears to have dived head first into the mud and stuck at the bottom of a pond. Two tramps, assisted by a policeman, push a plank out from the shore and attempt a rescue, only to find that they have been hoaxed and all their trouble was in vain. The ingenious way in which the descriptive title is arranged is a decided novelty, and we do not remember seeing anything similar before.[88]

The reviewer's reference to the animated picture titles points to Mitchell & Kenyon's innovative use of animation titles in their films. Animated titles were also used in other films produced by the company, including *A Trip to North Wales on the St Elvies*.[89] This title predates *Humorous Phases of Funny Faces* (1906), in which the letters of the title form themselves from moving bits of paper.[90] Little if any animation has emerged in the UK prior to these dates, but *Diving Lucy*, in the Cinema Museum's Collection, and *Trip to North Wales on the St Elvies* certainly demonstrate that Mitchell & Kenyon were using such techniques successfully before other companies in the UK and possibly America.

Diving Lucy was successfully sold in the United States, where it was billed on its release in February 1904 as 'The biggest English comedy hit of the year'.[91] The subject proved

Scenes from *A Trip to North Wales on the St Elvies* (1902) – one of the successful travelogues produced by the company

so popular that the Sheffield Photo Company produced a very similar film four years later, entitled *Sold Again*. Both films employ the same storyline in which a group of men and a policeman are walking in a park when they see two legs sticking out of the water in the middle of a pond. A rescue is attempted in both versions, as the policemen use either a bench or a ladder to crawl out towards the legs. The policeman then realises that the legs are in fact dummies and that he has been fooled. In the Mitchell & Kenyon version, he falls off the ladder held by his 'helpers', while in the Mottershaw title, the policeman is pelted with snowballs by a group of young boys in the park. Although the storylines are identical, there are interesting differences in the comic narratives. In *Diving Lucy*, the legs are first spotted by the two men, who attempt a Good Samaritan rescue before the arrival of the policeman. When the policeman appears, the scenario is transformed into a comic trick played on the unsuspecting official. The legs have been planted in the pond and the policeman is tricked into pulling them out. The gag is heightened further by the inscription 'Rats', picking up the joke from the initial animated intertitles at the start of the film, which read '£100 Reward. Lost!!! Diving Lucy!' and then reassemble to state: 'Her Husband Thinks She May Have Been Stuck at the Bottom. But Somebody Said Rats!!!'

Sold Again has a less complex narrative structure. The film starts with a group of onlookers and a policeman standing on the banks of a frozen pond on which there is a sign that

(Overleaf) Mitchell & Kenyon's skilful treatment of the local film is evident in the crowd sequences in *The Champion Athletes at Birmingham* (1902)

reads 'Dangerous', a clear indication for the audience that something perilous is going to happen or has already happened. In contrast to the Mitchell & Kenyon title, the policeman attempts the rescue alone and although the same discovery is made (i.e. the legs appear to be false), there is no direct inference that he was set up by the other individuals in the film. In the final scene, the policeman is pelted by snowballs, but his humiliation is not as great as in *Diving Lucy* which ends with the policeman falling into the water due to the actions of his 'co-helpers'. Although produced four years earlier, the Mitchell & Kenyon version has a more ambitious approach and is certainly more innovative in execution and presentation.

Conclusion

This summary of the films produced between 1899 and 1913 by Mitchell & Kenyon has attempted to place them within contemporary modes of production. With certain types of material, in particular the sporting films, Mitchell & Kenyon utilised groundbreaking editing techniques, while a strong case for innovation could be made for some of their fiction films. What is apparent from this overview is that the company practised and became expert in the film language of the time.[92] Indeed, further research is needed on their fiction output in order to assess fully their contribution to the development of narrative film

Darwen Street Scenes (1901) – filmed as a series of local views, but capturing as many faces on film as possible

in the UK. In terms of their greatest output, the non-fiction titles, the company operated during cinema's movement 'into the daily life of the modern age'. They not only focused on making films for and about the working classes but, in line with the middle-class programmes presented by their contemporaries, they also supplied films for showmen such as Sydney Carter and a more select clientele. Moreover, the way in which they incorporated innovative methods in the non-fiction genre can be seen in individual titles such as *Arrest of Goudie* and *Black Diamonds*. The Mitchell & Kenyon Collection also demonstrates the intense deployment of the non-fiction idiom from 1900 onwards. The phenomenon was active in other countries, where similar patterns of showmanship combined with non-fiction to provide exhibitors with an advantage over their competitors.[93]

In the context of the development of cinema as an institution and the language of film that evolved during this period, it is the emergence of the 'local' that is now readily associated with Mitchell & Kenyon. Nowhere in early film history is the enigmatic presence of the audience felt so acutely as in the local film and its skilful manipulation by the commissioners and Mitchell & Kenyon. The participatory fervour so evident in the films themselves is echoed in the comments of the reviewers: 'The public taste for animated pictures is as strong as ever, but it is the skilful treatment of local events that does much towards filling the building every night . . .'[94] The local films in the Mitchell & Kenyon Collection are also the ones most directly associated with the showmen commissioners and as such are a business record of the transaction between the company and the individual exhibitors. It is only when the collection is placed in the context of this world of commissioning and exhibition that the importance of the material can really be understood. The 'skilful treatment of the local event' was an important factor for both the growth of Mitchell & Kenyon as a film business and also the increasing popularity of the cinematograph exhibition as toured by the itinerant showmen. These films stand out within the collection for their use of close-ups, the interaction between the cameramen and the audience, and the intimacy of the shots. This is partly due to the presence and influence of the showmen on the making and commissioning of the material. Their contribution to film history has only previously been examined within the context of exhibition practices rather than the evolution of the language of film. The showmen are the silent partners in this business relationship and their movements have gone largely unrecorded and unrecognised by later historians. It is only through examining the world of Edwardian exhibition practices, the world in which the cinematograph evolved and developed, that their true contribution to the development of early film will be understood.

Notes

1 Rachael Low and Roger Manvell, *The History of British Film, 1896–1906* (London: George Allen, 1948), pp. 22–3.

2 Only twenty titles existed in the NFTVA, the North-West Film Archive and the Imperial War Museum.

3 The other collections being the Lumière Collection in France and the Edison Collection in America.

4 See Frank Kessler's entry 'actualités' in Richard Abel (ed.), *Encyclopedia of Early Cinema* (Oxford: Routledge, 2005), pp. 5–7.

5 For further definition see Luke McKernan, 'News Event Films', in Abel (ed.), *Enclyclopedia of Early Cinema*, pp. 474–6.

6 Frank Kessler (ed.), 'Visible Evidence – But of What? Reassessing Early Non-Fiction Cinema', *Historical Journal of Film, Radio and Television*, Vol. 22 No. 3. (2002).

7 The original French title was *Sortie d'usine.*

8 The three other eamples are No. 1275: *Sortie de la briqueterie Meffre et Bourgoin à Hanoi*, 1900 by Gabriel Veyre, showing workers leaving a factory in Hanoi, Indochina; No. 1279: *La Sortie de l'arsenal*, taken between 28 April 1899 and 2 March 1900 by Veyre in Hanoi; and No. 1279: *La Sortie de l'arsenal*, again taken between 28 April 1899 and 2 March 1900 by Veyre in Hanoi, showing workers passing a cranking cinematograph cameraman. See Michelle Aubert and Jean-Claude Seguin (eds), *La Production cinématographique des Frères Lumière* (Paris: Bibliothèque du film, 1996).

9 Cecil Hepworth, *Came the Dawn: Memoirs of a Film Pioneer* (Phoenix House: London, 1951); and for the Warwick Trading Company see film 01359 (July Catalogue), cited in Dennis Gifford, *The British Film Catalogue Volume 2: Non-Fiction Films 1888–1994* (London: Fitzroy Dearborn, 2000), p. 54.

10 Edwin Lawrence, 'The Infant Cinema, Part 2', *The World's Fair*, 10 June 1939, p. 35.

11 Tom Gunning, 'Pictures of Crowd Splendour: The Mitchell and Kenyon Factory Gate Films', in Vanessa Toulmin, Simon Popple and Patrick Russell (eds), *The Lost World of Mitchell & Kenyon: Edwardian Britain on Film* (London: BFI, 2004), pp. 49–59 (51).

12 Ibid., for a fuller discussion of this.

13 I am indebted to Professor Martin Loiperdinger for supplying this information. See also Martin Loiperdinger, *Film & Schokolade: Stollwercks Geschäfte nuit leben de Bilden* (Basel: KINtop Schriften, Stroemfeld/Roterstern, 1999), p. 209.

14 M&K 256–60, 364: *Visit of HRH Princess Louise to Blackburn.*

15 See Gifford, *The British Film Catalogue Volume 2*, for 1901 for details of the films produced by other companies.

16 M&K 807, 817: *Funeral of Queen Victoria.*

17 M&K 435-6: *Royal Visit to Manchester, Owen's College* (1902).

18 M&K 494: *Royal Visit to Rhyl* (1902); M&K 495: *Royal Visit to Bangor* (1902); M&K 192–4: *The King's Ride in the Isle of Man* (1902), which was advertised for sale in *The Era*, 18 October 1902.

19 John Barnes, *The Beginnings of the Cinema in England, 1894–1901, Volume 1, 1894–96*, revised and enlarged edn (Exeter: Exeter University Press, 1998), pp. 229–30.

20 For a discussion of sport and early cinema see Luke McKernan, 'Sport and the First Films', in Christopher Williams (ed.), *Cinema: The Beginnings and the Future* (London: University of Westminster Press, 1996), pp. 107–16.

21 *Photography*, Vol. 10 No. 517 (6 October 1898), p. 656.

22 Jasper Redfern filmed Sheffield United v. Derby, Sheffield United v. Liverpool and two cup ties at Nottingham and Bolton. For further information see Barnes, *The Beginnings of the Cinema in England*, p. 224.

23 The match was between Leicester and Plymouth, 26 October 1901, at Welford Road, Leicester, filmed by the Bamforth Company. A copy of this title is held by the NFTVA; M&K 151: *Hunslet v. Leeds*, filmed on 2 February 1901.

24 Although Leo Enticknap maintains that the overall production standards of the company are no more advanced than their contemporaries, he does believe, as I do, that this may not be the case with the football titles they produced and this is certainly the case when one examines the sporting material filmed. See Leo Enticknap, 'A Real Brake on Progress? Moving Image Technology in the Time of Mitchell and Kenyon', in Toulmin *et al.* (eds), *The Lost World of Mitchell & Kenyon*, pp. 21–33.

25 See Lauren Rabinovitz, 'Phantom Train Rides', in Abel (ed.), *Encyclopedia of Early Cinema*, pp. 514–15.

26 See M&K 241: *Over the Tay Bridge on an Express Train* (1901) and M&K: 723, 243: *Ride from Blarney to Cork on Cork & Muskerry Light Railway* (1902), for example.

27 *The Showman*, 9 August 1901, p. 3.

28 Gunning, 'Pictures of Crowd Splendour', in Toulmin *et al.* (eds), *The Lost World of Mitchell & Kenyon*, p. 55.

29 Stephen Bottomore, 'From the Factory Gate to the "Home Talent" Drama: An International Overview of Local Films in the Silent Era', in Toulmin *et al.* (eds), *The Lost World of Mitchell & Kenyon*, pp. 33–48 (33).

30 Uli Jung, 'Local Films: A Blind Spot in the Historiography of Early German Cinema', *Historical Journal of Film, Radio and Television*, Vol. 22 No. 3 (2002), p. 255.

31 See Bottomore, 'From the Factory Gate to the "Home Talent" Drama'; and also Janet McBain, 'Mitchell and Kenyon's Legacy in Scotland – The Inspiration for a Forgotten Film-Making Genre', in Toulmin, *et al.* (eds), *The Lost World of Mitchell & Kenyon*, pp. 113–25, for an introduction to the local material produced by and for cinema owners in Scotland from the 1910s to the 1950s. For Germany see Brigitte Braun and Uli Jung, 'Local Films from Trier, Luxembourg and Metz: A Successful Business Venture of the Marzen Family, Cinema Owners', *Film History*, Vol. 17 No. 1 (2005), pp 19–29.

32 *The Showman*, 21 June 1901, front page until the end of August.

33 Ibid., 7 March 1902, p. 45.

34 For Hepworth see *The Showman*, June and July 1901; and for Warwick Trading Company see *Cinematography and Bioscope Magazine*, December 1906.

35 This film has survived in the Mitchell & Kenyon Collection as M&K 637: *The Crowd Entering St George's Hall, Bradford.*

36 See Vanessa Toulmin and Martin Loiperdinger, 'Is it You? Representation and Response in Relation to the Local Film', *Film History*, Vol. 17 No. 1 (2005), pp. 7–19.

37 Abel (ed.), *Encyclopedia of Early Cinema*, p. 547.

38 Further information supplied by Richard Brown.

39 See Simon Popple, "But the Khaki-Covered Camera is the *Latest* Thing": The Boer War Cinema and Visual Culture in Britain', in Andrew Higson (ed.), *Young and Innocent? The Cinema in Britain 1896–1930* (Exeter: Exeter University Press, 2002), pp. 13–27.

40 'The Romance of a Cinematograph Film', *Ideas*, 31 January 1907, p. 15.

41 *The Optical Magic Lantern Journal and Photographic Enlarger*, Vol. 2 No. 139, December 1900, pp.153–4.

42 Simon Popple, '"Startling, Realistic, Pathetic": The Mitchell and Kenyon "Boer War" Films', in Toulmin *et al.* (eds), *The Lost World of Mitchell & Kenyon*, pp. 50–7.

43 *The Optician and Photographic Trade Review*, 18 May 1900, p. 347.

44 *The Showman,* 6 September 1901, p. xi.

45 *The Era,* 7 June 1902, p. 29.

46 '*The Romance of a Cinematograph Film*', pp. 14–15.

47 M&K 757–8: *Arrest of Goudie.*

48 For a full account of the background to Thomas Goudie and the events surrounding the case see Charlie Simpson, 'Tragic Story of a Lerwick Man', *The Shetland Times*, 28 December 2001, pp. 20–1; John Gannon, 'The Bank Clerk from Shetland Who Stole a Fortune', *Shetland Life*, November 1987, pp. 39–43; and Frederick Edwin Smith, Rt Honourable the Earl of Birkenhead, *Famous Trials of History* (London: Hutchinson, 1926), pp. 229–36.

49 For details of the Biograph Company's non-fiction production see Stephen Bottomore, 'Every Phase of Present-Day Life: Biograph's Non-Fiction Production', *Griffithian 69/70, The Wonders of the Biograph* (1999–2000) (Baltimore, MA: Johns Hopkins University Press, 2000), pp. 147–211; and for George Méliès see Paul Hammond, *Marvellous Méliès* (London: Gordon Fraser, 1974).

50 *Liverpool Daily Post*, 5 December 1901, p. 1.

51 For an in-depth study of the Victorian craze for crime reporting see Thomas Boyle, *Black Swine in the Sewers of Hampstead* (London: Viking, 1989); and for information pertaining to the *Illustrated Police News* see Leonard De Vries, *'Orrible Murders: An Anthology of Victorian Crime and Passion Compiled from The Illustrated Police News (*London: Macdonald, 1974).

52 For information about Madame Tussaud see Pauline Chapman, *Madame Tussaud in England: Career Woman Extraordinary* (London: Quiller Press, 1992), and Pauline Chapman, *Madame Tussaud's Chamber of Horrors: Two Hundred Years of Crime* (London: Constable, 1984).

53 Andrew Clay, '"True crime?": Charles Peace and the British Crime Film, 1895–1905', in Linda Fitzsimmons and Sarah Street (eds), *Moving Performance: British Stage and Screen 1890s–1920s* (Trowbridge: Flicks Books, 2000), pp. 123–37 (123).

54 I am indebted to Stephen Bottomore for information about this case. The event was filmed by three different companies – *The Moat Farm Mystery* (Gaumont), *The Moat Farm Tragedy* (Harrison) and the *Moat Farm Murder* (Robert Paul) – and can be found in Gifford, *The British Film Catalogue Volume 2.*

55 For further details of the Moat Farm Murder see *History Notebook*, Essex Police Museum, Issue No. 37 at /<www.essex.police.uk/pages/offbeat/o_his37.htm>

56 For details of the Moat Farm films see *The Era*, 23 May 1903, p. 3, and 27 June 1903, p. 29.

57 For details of the *Hanging of Mary Rogers* (Biograph, 1905) see Bottomore, 'Every Phase of Present-Day Life', pp. 147–211.

58 For further details of the life and career of Charles Peace see Gordon Honeycombe, *The Complete Murders of the Black Museum, 1835–1935* (London: Random House, 1995), pp. 1–17.

59 For further information on Frank Mottershaw and the Sheffield Photo Company see Geoff Mellor, *Movie Makers and Picture Pioneers: A Century of Cinema in Yorkshire, 1896–1996* (Bradford: Bradford Libraries, 1996).

60 For reference to the use of the engine driver see Dave Berry, *Cinema and Wales* (Cardiff: University of Wales Press, 1994), p. 50, in which he cites the Sheffield Photo Company catalogue for 1906 as the source for this claim.

61 Michael R. Booth, *Victorian Spectacular Theatre, 1850–1910* (London: Routledge, 1981), p. 14.

62 Jonathan Auerbach, 'McKinley at Home: How Early American Cinema Made News', *American Quarterly*, Vol. 51 No. 4 (1999), pp. 797–832 (822).

63 Ibid.

64 *'The Romance of a Cinemotograph Film'*, p. 15.

65 John Parris Springer, 'The Newspaper Meets the Dime Novel: Docudrama in Early Cinema', in Gary D. Rhodes and John Parris Springer (eds), *Docufictions: Essays on the Intersection of Documentary and Fictional Filmmaking* (Jefferson: McFarland 2005), p. 28.

66 Philip Rosen, 'Disjunction and Ideology in a Preclassical Film: *A Policeman's Tour of the World*', *Wide Angle*, Vol. 12 No. 3 (1990), pp. 20–36.

67 Low and Manvell, *The History of the British Film, 1896–1906*, p. 55.

68 See ibid., pp. 56–8 for more details.

69 Although listed by Gifford as made in 1905 see *The Era*, 10 December 1904, p. 35, in which the Urban Trading Company are advertising the film for sale.

70 Charles Urban Catalogue, June 1905, p. 240.

71 See Robin Whalley and Peter Worden, "Forgotten Firm": A Short Chronological Account of Mitchell and Kenyon, Cinematographers', *Film History*, Vol. 10 (1998), for more information relating to this film, and *Ideas*, 31 January 1907, pp. 14-15, for a description of the working practices of Mitchell & Kenyon's outdoor studio in Blackburn.

72 *The Era,* 10 December 1904, p. 35.

73 M&K 92, 765: *Black Diamonds – The Collier's Daily Life*, tableau seven: 'Men Sorting'; tableau six: 'Pit Brow Girls Sorting'.

74 *The Era*, 10 December 1904, p. 35.

75 Ibid., for the first advert, and also *Charles Urban Catalogue*, June 1905, p. 240, which has a slightly different scenario and foot length and includes a fuller synopsis and details of the tinting.

76 See Roland Cosandey, *Welcome Home, Joye! Film und 1910: aus der Sammlung Joseph Joye* (NFTVA, London) *KINtop Scriften 1* (Basel: Stroemfeld/Roter Stern, 1993), I am indebted to Luke McKernan for supplying this and additional information relating to Charles Urban.

77 Also advertised as *A Collier's Life* and cited by Low and Manvell, *The History of the British Film*, p. 56. See also Gifford, *The British Film Catalogue Volume 2*, for another coal-related title made by Robert Paul, *How Coal is Made – Down a Coal Mine*, advertised 20 August 1904, No. 02604.

78 The Urban advert in *The Era* lists eighteen scenes and cites the length as 650 feet; by June it is listed in their catalogue as sixteen scenes and 675 feet.

79 See 'The Romance of a Cinematograph Film' for further information on how Kenyon produced the film, which was filmed in an open-cast mine in the Black Country.

80 See M&K 92, 765: *Black Diamonds – The Collier's Daily Life*.

81 *Blackburn Times*, 7 October 1905; and *Rochdale Observer*, 11 February 1905. p. 1.c.3.

82 'The Romance of a Cinematograph Film', p. 15.

83 I am indebted to Martin Humphries and Tony Fletcher of the Cinema Museum in London for supplying unpublished details of this material. It is hoped that increased awareness of the Mitchell & Kenyon Company will lead to greater interest in their fiction output and the incredible collection owned by the Cinema Museum.

84 *The Optician and Photographic Trades Review*, 29 September 1899, p. 46.

85 *The Era*, 18 October 1902, p. 32.

86 Ibid., 13 August 1904, pp. 30–1.

87 For more information on film styles from 1903 onwards see Simon Popple and Joe Kember, *Early Cinema: From Factory Gate to Dream Factory* (London: Wallflower Press, 2004).

88 *The Talking Machine News*, January 1904, p. 89.

89 See Dave Berry, 'Mitchell and Kenyon in Wales', in Toulmin *et al.* (eds), *The Lost World of Mitchell & Kenyon*, pp. 102–13, for a more detailed discussion of the animated intertitles in M&K 212–22: *A Trip to North Wales on the St Elvies*.

90 Donald Crafton, *Before Mickey, 1898–1928* (Chicago: University of Chicago Press, 1993), p. 21.

91 Kemp R. Niver (ed.), *The Biograph Bulletins, 1896–1908* (Los Angeles: Los Angeles Local Research Group, 1971), 23 February 1904, p. 111. Many thanks to Richard Brown for providing this reference.

92 Ben Thompson and Rebecca Vick of the NFTVA are currently studying the original negative of *Arrest of Goudie* in order to determine how innovative the company was in post-production editing, as part of their continuing research into the original camera negatives.

93 Jung, 'Local Views: A Blind Spot in the Historiography of Early German Cinema'. This article provides a detailed discussion of Peter Marzen, a travelling exhibitor who later opened a stationary movie theatre in Trier.

94 *The Showman*, 30 May 1902.

-3-

Showmanship

> But you could indeed exhibit anything in those days. Yes anything from a needle to an anchor, a flea to an elephant, a bloater you could exhibit as a whale. It was not the show it was the tale that you told.[1]

Introduction

The role of the showman in shaping and organising trends in popular entertainment has been until recently largely ignored by writers on the subject. With the exception of the many studies on American showmen such as P. T. Barnum and Buffalo Bill Cody, the names of their British counterparts are limited to footnotes or regional histories (see Plate 5).[2] Although the world of the fairground, circus and music-hall showmen has produced many autobiographies and biographies, their overall contribution has been largely left to local historians or enthusiasts who chronicle each act and show

Showmen for A. D. Thomas in Halifax, displaying the posters that Thomas covered towns with to promote his cinematograph exhibitions (1901)

Showman advertising Tweedale's Bio-Motograph Show, playing at the Theatre Royal in unidentified Town Centre (c. 1902)

lovingly, and is rarely included in standard works on the period.[3] In line with this, the early cinema exhibition has been treated by historians as a romantic interlude, a kind of sideshow that deviates from the development of film genres and the emergence of the cinema theatre.[4] Recent scholarship in America by Charles Musser and Greg Waller, and Ivo Blom in the Netherlands, in particular, has sought to reassess the role of the exhibition and the showman in the history of cinema.[5] However, with the discovery of the collection, we now have a body of work in the UK that directly links the commissioning of particular films and genres to the show and the exhibitor. The films that have survived to form the Mitchell & Kenyon Collection were commissioned by travelling exhibition showmen who used this material to shape and build a film programme. The importance of the travelling exhibitor cannot be underestimated, as it is only through their patterns of exhibition, business practices and pure feats of showmanship that the collection can be understood. Their presence dominates the filmic record: we see showmen directing the people in front of the camera, using advertising bill boards and gag cards, and plastering the town with posters for their show. In order to understand the films, we must interpret them as records of entertainment history that reveal the dynamic relationship that existed between the exhibitor and his or her audience and the show they presented.[6]

Nineteenth-Century Shows

Shows, as the term 'showman' implies, were one of the main forms of popular entertainment in the Victorian era. Shows were found in the fairground arena, within a travelling or fixed circus, as part of a programme of optical and scientific wonder at permanent halls or on the high street.[7] Everything and anything was exhibited under the banner of education and entertainment, including displays of the body beautiful or grotesque, painted panoramic scenes, fasting men and fat women, and magic and illusion tricks. The nineteenth century was the age of the showman – from the great American figures like P.T. Barnum and Buffalo Bill Cody to the optical wizards such as Professor Pepper and the great magicians at the Egyptian Hall. Tom Norman provides an inside view of the world of the Victorian showman in his unpublished autobiography, *The Silver King*, when he writes:

> My friends there was a time in my career as a showman where I would exhibit any mortal thing for money and it must be understood there was always large crowds who were only too eager to pay to see.[8]

The secret of the show lay in the showman's ability to hoodwink and entertain the pubic into suspending their disbelief for the duration of the exhibition. Showmanship was the essential component unifying the different types of exhibitions in which the cinematograph first found its home (see Plate 6). In his autobiography, E. H. Bostock understood that the secret was to present a good frontage to attract the public; Tom Norman maintained that it was not the show but the tale that you told; while P.T. Barnum believed that it was merely 'the knack of knowing what people will pay money to see or support'.[9] The nineteenth century was the golden age of the showmen, who adapted and incorporated the latest novelties and attractions in an increasing array of venues to capture the attention of the show-going public.[10] Whatever the style of show, the public fascination always resulted in an ever-receptive audience.

By the end of the 1890s, new technology would find its way into the shows, with the cinematograph replacing Pepper's Ghost as the latest optical attraction. Competition to exhibit the latest innovation was very intense, and the travelling showman had to keep up to date with every new development:

> On asking our worthy friend what the showmen of twenty years ago would have said about the possibility of showing moving pictures in the twentieth century, he replied, 'that he had never given the matter a thought.' But a showman is always the first to seize on anything new, and is too much occupied in pleasing the public taste to have time for reflecting.[11]

The Cuckoo in the Nest

From its emergence in 1895 in Paris, the cinematograph became assimilated into all types of nineteenth-century shows. It appeared like a cuckoo laying its eggs in a variety of nests and, by 1900, most entertainment venues had incorporated moving pictures as part of the attractions on offer (see Plate 7).[12] Venues ranged from shopfronts to music halls to fairgrounds and circus shows, with travelling exhibitors adapting the programme to suit the public taste:

> The management of the Queens Theatre, Holbeck, are providing a light and miscellaneous kind of entertainment for next week, embracing a cinematograph show (the pictures including a representation of the return of Lord Kitchener), a performance by Shawlene the Tramp Whistler, and 'turns' by Miss Beatrice Vere and Mr Kenneth Jason, the actor vocalist. A show of this kind is certainly preferable to melodrama on a hot July evening, and Mr Longden's example might very well be copied.[13]

The film exhibitor drew on a vocabulary derived from earlier entertainments that shared a common language of spectacle and spectatorship:

> The cinématographe was seen, above all, as a new way of presenting already well-established entertainment 'genres': magic and fairy shows, farce, plays and other kinds of stage performances. It wasn't until cinema's practitioners arrived at a reflexive understanding of the medium and until the cinema achieved a certain degree of institutionalisation that the medium became autonomous.[14]

Research conducted by Jon Burrows and Tony Fletcher in London has revealed a whole variety of shows from 1900 onwards in which film formed a part, from penny arcades, shopfronts, music halls and venues previously unconnected with popular entertainment.[15] By the early 1900s, the cinematograph exhibitors had developed a structure and a language of exhibition that could be adapted to a variety of different venues. Living pictures could be a one- to three-minute turn in a music-hall programme; a fifteen-minute performance in a fairground bioscope show; a cine-variety performance interspersed with live acts and variety artists; or a two-hour stand-alone film show where the singular attraction was the variety of film titles on offer.[16] As John Bird wrote in *Cinema Parade*:

> Hundreds of those early picture shows excited crowds on fairground, in empty shop, in town hall, temperance room and music hall. And when the cinema came, the manager was often a blend of the fairground showman, the travelling theatre proprietor and the panorama lecturer.[17]

Work by Greg Waller and others on American film exhibition has shown the importance of both the venue and the locality for the development of the cinema in non-urban centres.[18] In the UK, the importance of regional diversity in the transition period from travelling exhibitions to the development of cinema was significant, as no one model of commissioning, exhibition and rental can be applied. The showmen led Mitchell & Kenyon in particular directions and provided them with the web of connections that guaranteed the company growing success throughout the early years of the 1900s. The dynamics of the showmen's circuits provided the geographical structure for the company's association with the exhibitors, encompassing Scotland, Ireland, Lancashire, Yorkshire, the north-east and the Midlands, with occasional shows in the south-west. Many of the exhibitors who first presented travelling film shows in Scotland, such as J. J.

Bennell, manager of New Century Pictures in Scotland, for example, subsequently opened the first permanent cinemas in their localities.[19]

The collection draws us into a world before cinema became an institution, where different strands of performance and exhibition history impose their own particular modes of apparatus on its exhibition. By examining the role of the showmen, we can start to understand how they shaped this new medium until it became a stand-alone attraction. This is not achieved by analysing exhibition patterns or describing in detail the individual exhibitors and their types of show. Instead, we must utilise the collection and contemporary newspaper accounts, to understand the manner in which the films were presented, the importance of the showmen in the development of film as an attraction and the relationship between the spectator and the spectacle.[20] As the reporter for *The Showman* writes, it is the ability to attract the public that underpins the showman's art:

> To attract the public is the object of every would-be successful showman or entertainer, and to do that, two methods of procedure are open to him. He can either plan a show or entertainment that will be entirely novel in idea, as well as in execution, and so give the public a new sensation, which method will generally be successful or he must arrange his show that will harmonise with some particular event that is exciting the public mind, and exhibit in realistic fashion, things that are attracting general attention . . .[21]

The Showmen

> The showman, and the man who gets his living on the fairground, is nothing if not enterprising. He can always be expected to make the most of his opportunities, and the public in this respect are not disappointed . . .'The Best Show for Local Pictures' is the legend that greets the visitor wherever his face is turned along this line of 'living picture' exhibitions . . .This is science served up to the public steaming hot, at a price which is, to borrow a phrase of the showman,' within the reach of all' . . .[22]

Musser and Nelson's study of Lyman H. Howe's travelling exhibition in America between 1880 and 1920 examines the importance of the showmen in incorporating innovations such as projected motion pictures. Howe, in line with other travelling exhibitors, varied his programme according to his audience and survived in the competitive world of early film exhibition through showmanship, his use of the educational programme, the knowledge he had built up of the exhibition circuit during his time with the phonograph and his concern for technical excellence.[23] No equally comprehensive study has been attempted on film showmen in the UK, and how their role in selecting and organising the films created an audience for the new medium.[24]

Over forty different showmen-commissioners are associated with the Mitchell & Kenyon Collection, and many of them feature in the films themselves, either directing the action, as in *Messrs Lumb and Co Leaving the Works, Huddersfield* (1900), or mimicking the live show by acknowledging the audience, as in *Preston Egg Rolling* (1901), in which a member of the Poole family gracefully bows to both the camera and the soon-to-be film audience.[25] In *Factory Workers in Clitheroe* (1901), the same showman tips his hat

A member of the Poole family gracefully bows to both the camera and the soon-to-be film audience in *Preston Egg Rolling* (c. 1901)

Tweedale's advertising cart promoting a film show at the Victoria Hall later that week, is prominently on view in *The Mayor Entering his Carriage Near the Town Hall, Halifax* (1902)

and bows to the camera, as does Tweedale in *Street Scenes in Halifax* (1902).[26] Waller Jeffs, the manager for New Century Pictures in Birmingham, can clearly be seen participating in the Boys' Brigade procession, as can A. D. Thomas in many of the Manchester films.[27] He is particularly prominent in the *Manchester and Salford Harriers' Cyclists Procession*, in which he holds up a large bag of money to the camera, and in *Manchester Street Scenes*

Unknown exhibitor mimicking the actions of the sporting crowd in *Dewsbury v Manningham* (1901)

(1901), where he jokes with the spectators and then hands a free ticket to a Boer War veteran and his son.[28] In *Parade on Morecambe Central Pier* (1902), the cameraman leads the promenade along the pier and in one shot holds up a copy of the showmen's newspaper *The Era* to be filmed; likewise in *A Tram Ride through Sunderland* (1902), the exhibitors dance in front of the Roker Hotel.[29] Perhaps the most spectacular example is the unknown exhibitor working for Ralph Pringle who mimics the actions of the sporting crowd in *Dewsbury v. Manningham* (1901) in order to elicit some response from the spectators, and then there is the silent interview that Ralph Pringle conducts with Private Ward of Leeds in 1901.[30] Speaking in 1933, Alfred Bromhead divided early film showmen into three main types of exhibitors: the Music Hall, the Fairground and the Town or Public Hall showmen.[31] The travelling exhibitors who commissioned films from Mitchell & Kenyon fall into Bromhead's original categories: fairground showmen who turned to moving pictures from already existing fairground shows; independent travelling showmen who presented temporary film shows in public venues and rented spaces; theatrical exhibitors who used agents to present a variety of music-hall bookings in fixed theatrical venues. There was also a fourth type: the early cinema owners in the east Lancashire region who commissioned the firm to produce local topicals. Despite the wide range of venues, it was showmanship and the ability to present an up-to-date show, a talent, as we have seen, common to all showmen, that guaranteed in large audiences. According to Frank Sunderland of New Century Pictures, one of the major exhibition companies associated with Mitchell & Kenyon, the secrets of a successful exhibition were that

> The films were good and well shown; there was always a good lecturer, frequently the local military band was engaged and the advertising was on a big scale, as much as 5,000 sheets of posting being put out before the opening night.[32]

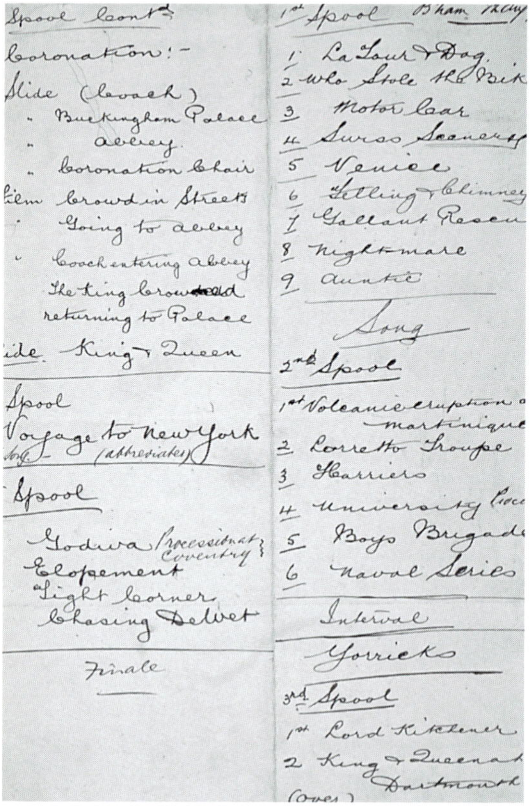
Spool (cont)
Coronation:-
Slide (Coach)
" Buckingham Palace
" Abbey
" Coronation Chair
Film Crowd in Streets
" Going to Abbey
" Coach entering Abbey
The King Crowned
returning to Palace
Slide King & Queen
Spool
Voyage to New York (abbreviated)
Song -
Spool
Godiva Procession Coventry
Elopement
Light Corner
Chasing [illegible]
Finale

1st Spool
1 La Tour & Dog
2 Who Stole the Bik
3 Motor Car
4 Swiss Scenery
5 Venice
6 [illegible] Chimney
7 Gallant Rescu
8 Nightmare
9 Auntie
Song
2nd Spool
1st Volcanic eruption Martinique
2 Loretto Troupe
3 Harriers
4 University Proce
5 Boys Brigade
6 Naval Series
Interval
Yoricks
3rd Spool
1st Lord Kitchener
2 King & Queen at Dartmouth
(over)

Handwritten notes outlining the programme that A. D. Thomas presented at the St George's Hall, Bradford in 1901

The showmanship of the exhibitors underpinned all aspects of the travelling cinematograph entertainment and incorporated three elements: the ability to create an audience through advertisements; the film programme or selection of films exhibited; and the execution of the show itself. This is clearly evident when one examines the development of the two-hour stand-alone film show pioneered by the town-hall or stand-alone showmen such as Ralph Pringle, A. D. Thomas and New Century Pictures.

Creating an Audience

> Cinematograph operations are, generally speaking, remarkably good advertisers, and know well how to boost their own shows and use the most attractive posters.[33]

The stand-alone film showmen associated with Mitchell & Kenyon created an audience for their exhibition by combining a policy of mass advertisement with a film programme that was tailored to each locality. As we have seen, in the case of Mitchell & Kenyon, it was primarily the programming of local films that satisfied the public craze for the cinematograph in the early 1900s. Printed advertisement was the main method of attracting an audience. Although the poster was perhaps the most visible form of advertising utilised by the showmen, it was only part of the huge plethora of printed ephemera available in the early 1900s, which included handbills, postcards and programmes (see Plate 8). The impact of advances in printing technology on advertising in the latter part of the nineteenth century, and the cheapness of new printing techniques, allowed a greater range and type of advertising material to be printed in large quantities. As Catherine Haill writes in *Fun without Vulgarity*:

> Entertainment has always needed advertisement . . . They served both as advance notice and programme and gave basic information about the entertainment on offer – the titles of the plays, the times of the performance, the availability of the tickets and names of the best known performers.[34]

By 1900, films had increasingly become the focus of the exhibition, and the handbill, banner or gag card were the means by which films were advertised or programmed. The film programme either became part of the actual physical scenery of the show, through banners or gag cards, or reflected the ephemeral nature of the attraction through the use of the handbill – the staple of entertainment advertising.[35] The showmen followed the advice of the trade press, who proclaimed 'a man with a well got up circular programme, or poster always secures the preference over his brother performers who do not invest a little money in their printing'.[36] The collection contains many instances of showmen advertising the films to the audience they are filming. *Llandudno May Queen* (1907) ends with a billboard advertising Parisian Animated Pictures to be held at the Prince's Theatre, along with the exhibitor Mr Ritson, who appears in the foreground of the scene.[37] In Manchester, the *Manchester Spiritualists' Procession* (1901) features an advertising cart with posters for Edison's Animated Photo Company, which is bettered by the hoarding for 'Tweedale's Bio-Motograph A Trip Round the World', including films of Halifax, a trick he repeats in West Bromwich.[38] *Salford v. Batley (*1901*)* starts with the showmen opens with a shot of the poster for a show of the soon to be filmed rugby match, while the film of *Blackburn Rovers v. Sheffield United* begins with the showmen advertising Green's cinematograph.[39] Another prominent poster board appears in *Miners Leaving Pendlebury Colliery* (1901) and again on the front of *Sedgwick's Bioscope Showfront at Pendlebury Wakes* (1901), where it is held by James Kenyon.[40] *Champion Athletes at Birmingham* (1902) includes a crowd shot in which a showman advertises films of Lord Kitchener to be shown at the Curzon Hall. One of the funniest uses of the gag cards occurs when Relph and Pedley repeatedly place their name card on the front of the new electric trams in the *Opening of Accrington Electric Tramways* in 1907.[41] Ralph Pringle is perhaps the most prolific self-advertiser: in *Living Wigan* (1902), posters for the North American Animated Photo Company are plastered around the town, and in *Tram Rides through Nottingham* (1902), the tram stops to film a large billboard poster advertising the company.[42] Whether this was a form of product placement or a subtle form of copyright protection, the importance of the poster as a means of advertisement was recognised by all showmen, with the most lavish example in the collection being the lengthy procession of eight portable hoarding boards wheeled down Royal Avenue in Belfast advertising Pringle's show at the Ulster Hall.[43] A. D. Thomas, the subject of our case study later in this chapter, was particularly fond of the poster as means of advertising his show, as Cecil Hepworth recalls:

> He plastered the whole town wherever he went, and he went nearly everywhere, with tremendous posters in brilliant colours describing his wonderful shows and his still more wonderful self . . . He would parade the town in person, mounted high on an open lorry, actively turning his camera on every little knot of people he passed. As the

(Above) Farrar and Tyler's cinematograph show at Hull Fair – the show held up to 1,000 people, 1908 (NFA); (left) Showmen from Biddell's cinematograph exhibition advertising the entertainments on show (NFA)

Mr Ritson, manager of the Prince's Theatre, Llandudno poses for the camera in front of an advertising cart showing the times of the cinematograph exhibition (1907)

Two of the exhibitors for Thomas-Edison's Animated Photo Company advertising the 'film of the game' during the filming of *Salford v Batley* (1901)

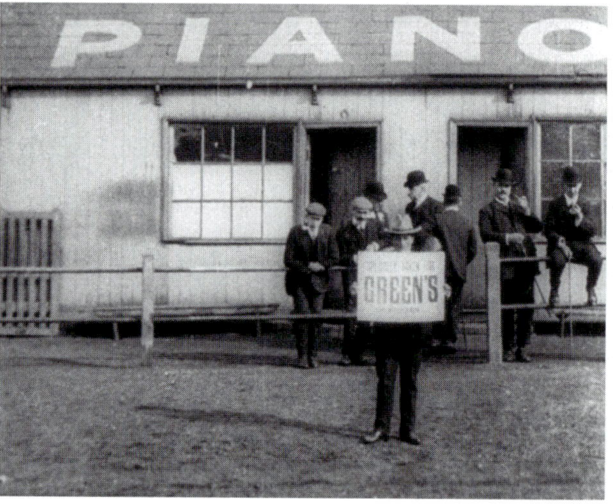

Gag card for Green's cinematograph prominently displayed during the filming of *Blackburn Rovers v Sheffield United* (1907)

Another prominent poster board appears in *Pendlebury Colliery* (1901) advertising Sedgwick's cinematograph and lantern show

A crowd shot during *Champion Athletes at Birmingham* (1902) reveals the showman advertising films of Lord Kitchener to be shown at the Curzon Hall

Ralph Pringle utilised all methods of showmanship to advertise his presence – for example, the use of walking billboards in *Ride on a Tramcar Through Belfast* (1901) for the show at the Ulster Hall.

> lorry was plastered with his colourful posters telling them to come and see themselves at such and such hall tonight, it left the people in no doubt as to what he was doing.[44]

Another means by which the exhibition was advertised was through local newspapers. The showmen would often promote a particular commissioned or local film by advertising it in the newspaper in the days leading up to the holidays. In addition, the reviews of the show that followed reveal that the audience were a major fact in the advertisement and execution of the show itself. If the poster was the drawing card for the audience, it was the programme as executed by the showmen that brought about the continued success of the show, for, according to John Prestwich, writing in 1901:

> The film subjects are a matter of choice for the exhibitor himself, and must depend upon the class of exhibition. They may include comic trick subjects, scenes of everyday life, of historical interest, or set pieces representing familiar stories, which we, and those before us, were acquainted with in our very early days . . .[45]

Entertainment ephemera ranged from lavish posters and programmes, to the daily inserts in the handbill from the Manchester Programme, such as this advertisment for Edison's Animated Pictures at St James's Hall, 1901 (NFA)

The Film Programme – Local Films for Local People

As John Prestwich reveals, the exhibitors who first presented the cinematograph used a variety of film subjects. The length of the programme depended largely on the venue and the audience. A fairground show, for example, lasted no more than fifteen minutes, whereas a town-hall exhibition could run for up to two hours.[46] Richard Brown has argued that New Century Pictures invariably excluded factory gate films from their programme as they were performing to a largely middle-class audience.[47] Fiction films, as produced by any number of companies as well as Mitchell & Kenyon, were shown alongside travel films, variety subjects and the ever-popular trick films produced by Pathé and Méliès.[48] However, it is the prevalence and dominance of the local film that concerns us in this section, as they were particularly dictated and commissioned by the stand-alone film showmen for the particular locality in which they were exhibiting. The use of the print media as a means of advertising and publicising the local shows, and the selection of material advertised, is also an important aspect in understanding the growing popularity of the cinematograph during the early 1900s:

> IS IT YOU?
>
> If you recognise your Photo on the Screen you are entitled to the sum of £1 on making immediate claim.
>
> CUT THIS OUT
>
> Half Price Family Voucher . . .[49]

Local scenes such as *Street Scenes in Halifax* (1902) solicited a popular response from the audience

The promotion of local material in the film programme and newspapers was an essential factor in soliciting an audience for the film show, and audience reaction and participation were equally part of the exhibitors' marketing strategy:

> To Showman. The most popular Cinematograph Film in a Travelling show is Always a Local Picture containing Portraits which can be recognised. A Film showing workers leaving a factory will gain far greater popularity in the town where it was taken than the most exciting picture ever produced.[50]

News reports from 1901 onwards reveal a common reaction as the audience recognises familiar faces and landscapes. The gait, appearance and even vanity of the audience being filmed are consistent features of the reports that appear in daily reviews. The sight of notable personages was greeted with 'amusement and gratification', as this review from Lytham St Annes reveals:

> The cinematograph reproduction of Lytham Club Day procession is a splendid success, and Mr Kingston is to be congratulated on his enterprise. The photographs come out with remarkable clearness, and a number of persons can be easily recognised on the screen, much to the amusement and gratification of the audience . . .[51]

The film show at the Palace of Varieties in Lancaster on 26 April 1902 was also greeted with 'much amusement when well known faces and characters were recognised'.[52] A later review comments on the vanity of the people concerned when they realise they are being filmed and their wish to create a good impression for the camera and their audience.[53] This theme of recognition and response continues throughout the run of the exhibition, as later reviews comment on how the show is still a great attraction, with 'the local pictures in particular calling forth the admiration of the audience'.[54] Reviews from Tweedale's show in Halifax in January 1902 elicit the same response: 'local street scenes, of which there are many . . . create roars of laughter as fellow townsmen are recognised hurrying to and from business'.[55] A later reviewer is moved to write that the local films 'reflect in a remarkable degree the traits of Halifax people'.[56] This pattern is also evident at Edison's show in Chesterfield, where the reviewer comments that 'much amusement has been caused, as many well known Chesterfield people have been recognised on the canvas'.[57] A reviewer of an unknown show at Southport in September 1902 continues the theme when he writes, 'members of the younger generation present may frequently be heard to raise up their voices with joy at discovering some friend or acquaintance'.[58] This concept of the reflected image or living portrait was an important tool of advertising for the early exhibitors:

> 'Lor', Bil', that's me!' – An enterprising cinematographist, who was giving a series of lantern entertainments in a town up North exposed a film at the gates of a large factory as the men were coming out for their dinner hour. This was in due course projected on the screen, when great amusement was caused to the audience by an enthusiastic member, who on recognizing himself in the picture, shouted out to a companion, 'Lor', Bil', that's me with the square basket!' We are informed that this small incident was the means of bringing a huge audience on the following evening of men engaged at the said works, and after this particular film had been projected, they insisted on an encore, which was of course honoured . . .[59]

This issue of recognition, either of oneself or the locality, played an important part in the development of the local in early cinema history and throughout the later silent period.[60] As Tom Gunning remarks, it 'is the cry of recognition which baptizes this cinema of locality, as the amazement of a direct connection marks the viewing process'.[61] The relationship between the subject and the audience was further heightened when the showmen filmed local personages and invited them to view the films. Perhaps one of the most interesting examples of the centrality of the audience in the film exhibition is the Thomas-Edison show in Bradford, when Thomas filmed the afternoon crowd entering the cinematograph show[62] and then exhibited it as part of the evening's entertainment:

> The crowded state of the St George's Hall last night shows that Bradford people know how to appreciate 'a good thing' . . . Tonight a further luxury is promised, namely, a film showing the crowd entering St George's Hall to witness a performance by the Edison Company, which will doubtless attract the interest of quite a host of people . . .[63]

The Exhibition as Performance

Although the length and numbers of films exhibited were dictated by the type of presentation, the show itself comprised standard features that were common to all types of performance: a lecturer to provide commentary, special effects to heighten their impact and

The showman employed every possble means to advertise exhibitions – as demonstrated by this advertising cart in *Mayor Entering his Carriage Near the Town Hall, Halifax* (1902)

musical accompaniment. Early films shows were often presented with a lecturer, as Ansje van Beusekom reveals in relation to the Netherlands: 'from the moment . . . that itinerant film exhibitors put together short strips of film, they began to explain moving pictures'.[64] The importance of the lecturer in constructing a narrative for the films was emphasised in the trade press at the time:

> The idea of having a lecturer to explain the pictures is a good one, for audiences often miss the good points of a film unless they have been previously pointed out to them, and this is not always possible to do by means of a lantern or announcement slide.[65]

Many of the showmen who exhibited films from the collection often played the role of lecturer, including Loder Lyons and Ralph Pringle in Huddersfield, and J. J. Bennell in Glasgow, while A. D. Thomas employed specialist lecturers such as Leon Gould for his exhibitions. Signor Pepi, the quick-change artist, exhibited the films as part of his act and Loder Lyons doubled as a ventriloquist during the variety component of the North American Animated Photo Company's show in Liverpool.[66] The lecturer not only provided a live commentary to the films but also acted as master of ceremonies for all stages of the theatrical and filmic performance: 'If you happen to be a good speaker, it is better to announce the titles in a small hall, as you can generally add considerable interest to the entire entertainment by introducing a jest or short anecdote.'[67]

Incorporating live or special effects into the proceedings was also an essential part of the performance; modern viewings of early film complete with a piano accompanist create a false impression of a hushed and rarified viewing environment.[68] J. J. Bennell reveals that early exhibitors 'invariably carried a lecturer to describe the pictures and an effects worker to imitate galloping horses, rushing water etc'.[69] According to *The Showman*, the effects were fundamental to the success of the cinematograph show:

> A cinematograph exhibition is greatly improved by sound effects, such, for instance, as the banging of a drum to represent the firing of a big gun, or stamping of feet to represent soldiers marching, and the blowing of a whistle as a railway scene is projected upon the screen. These effects are very easy to arrange, and are often the making of a show.[70]

An exhibitor in Bolton took the advice of the trade press and incorporated special effects when showing war-related titles and military films:

> Three of the sets, an attack by the Boxers . . . a street scene in Peking, and the bombardment of the Taku Forts by the Allied squadrons, which were rendered startlingly realistic by the aid of gunpowder and various mechanical effects, and to the accompaniment of military music, fairly took the audience by surprise, and a repetition was demanded.[71]

Sydney Race recalls seeing this effect at a cinematograph show in Nottingham in 1897, but unlike the spectator in Bolton, he remained unconvinced:

> In Williams I saw picture said to have been taken during the Greek and Turkish war – but I much doubt it . . . To heighten the reality of the picture a boy whose principal work was to attend to a barrel organ, fired several shots from a pistol – which startled the ladies into real fear . . .[72]

Cecil Hepworth believed that using live gunshot as a special effect in this way was 'carrying realism to an absurd pitch'.[73] Hepworth and other exhibitors utilised a different type of live effect for the popular title *Rescued by Rover* (1905), in which a collie dog is the hero of the film. During screening, early film exhibitors planted a dog behind the screen so that when 'Rover on the screen was seen to be barking, Rover behind the screen was barking also'.[74]

Unlike cinematographic presentations in music hall, the live action or variety acts in the stand-alone film shows were in the minority on the bill and were linked to the film presentations. On the fairground, music was provided by the fair organ, which was employed both to attract the audience to the show and as an accompaniment to the films. Similarly, in the town-hall shows, local military bands were often used by the showmen as both an advertising ploy to encourage local visitors and as a musical accom-

Procession in Accrington Park (1900) includes the local silver band – which were often incorporated into exhibitions

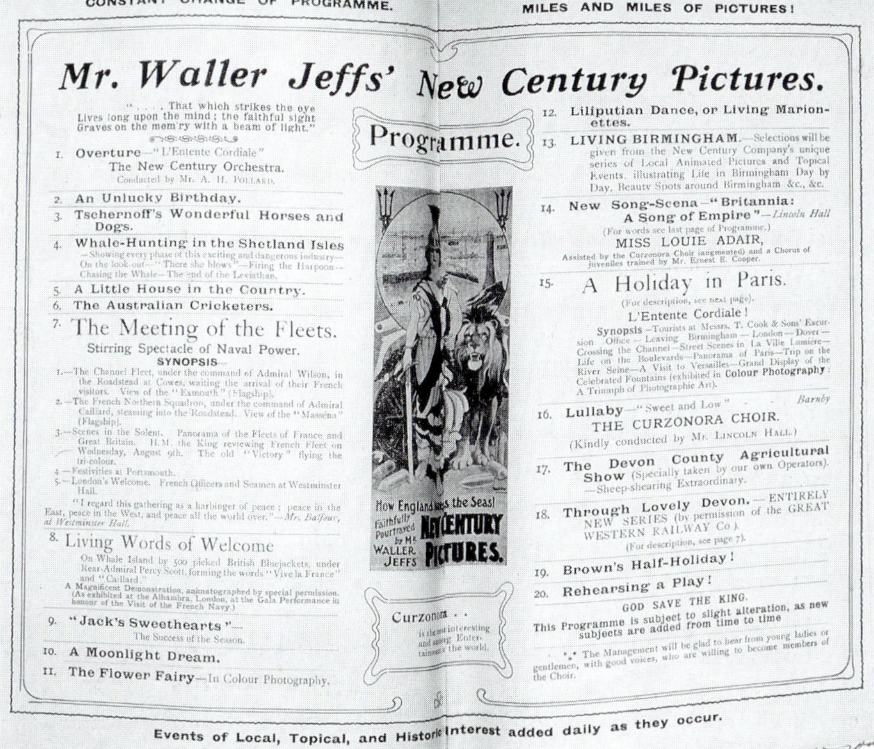

CONSTANT CHANGE OF PROGRAMME. MILES AND MILES OF PICTURES!

Mr. Waller Jeffs' New Century Pictures.

"…. That which strikes the eye
Lives long upon the mind; the faithful sight
Graves on the mem'ry with a beam of light."

Programme.

1. **Overture**—"L'Entente Cordiale"
The New Century Orchestra.
Conducted by Mr. A. H. Pollard.

2. **An Unlucky Birthday.**

3. **Tschernoff's Wonderful Horses and Dogs.**

4. **Whale-Hunting in the Shetland Isles**
—Showing every phase of this exciting and dangerous industry—On the look-out—"There she blows"—Firing the Harpoon—Chasing the Whale—The end of the Leviathan.

5. **A Little House in the Country.**

6. **The Australian Cricketers.**

7. The Meeting of the Fleets.
Stirring Spectacle of Naval Power.
SYNOPSIS—
1.—The Channel Fleet, under the command of Admiral Wilson, in the Roadstead at Cowes, waiting the arrival of their French visitors. View of the "Exmouth" (Flagship).
2.—The French Northern Squadron, under the command of Admiral Caillard, steaming into the Roadstead. View of the "Masséna" (Flagship).
3.—Scenes in the Solent. Panorama of the Fleets of France and Great Britain. H.M. the King reviewing French Fleet on Wednesday, August 9th. The old "Victory" flying the tri-colour.
4.—Festivities at Portsmouth.
5.—London's Welcome. French Officers and Seamen at Westminster Hall.
"I regard this gathering as a harbinger of peace; peace in the East, peace in the West, and peace all the world over."—*Mr. Balfour, at Westminster Hall.*

8. Living Words of Welcome
On Whale Island by 500 picked British Bluejackets, under Rear-Admiral Percy Scott, forming the words "Vive la France" and "Caillard."
A Magnificent Demonstration, animatographed by special permission. (As exhibited at the Alhambra, London, at the Gala Performance in honour of the Visit of the French Navy.)

9. **"Jack's Sweethearts"**—
The Success of the Season.

10. **A Moonlight Dream.**

11. **The Flower Fairy**—In Colour Photography.

12. **Liliputian Dance, or Living Marionettes.**

13. **LIVING BIRMINGHAM.**—Selections will be given from the New Century Company's unique series of Local Animated Pictures and Topical Events, illustrating Life in Birmingham Day by Day, Beauty Spots around Birmingham &c., &c.

14. **New Song-Scena—"Britannia: A Song of Empire"**—*Lincoln Hall*
(For words see last page of Programme.)
MISS LOUIE ADAIR,
Assisted by the Curzonora Choir (augmented) and a Chorus of juveniles trained by Mr. Ernest E. Cooper.

15. A Holiday in Paris.
(For description, see next page).
L'Entente Cordiale!
Synopsis—Tourists at Messrs. T. Cook & Sons' Excursion Office—Leaving Birmingham—London—Dover—Crossing the Channel—Street Scenes in La Ville Lumière—Life on the Boulevards—Panorama of Paris—Trip on the River Seine—A Visit to Versailles—Grand Display of the Celebrated Fountains (exhibited in **Colour Photography**: A Triumph of Photographic Art).

16. **Lullaby**—"Sweet and Low" - - - *Barnby*
THE CURZONORA CHOIR.
(Kindly conducted by Mr. Lincoln Hall.)

17. **The Devon County Agricultural Show** (Specially taken by our own Operators).—Sheep-shearing Extraordinary.

18. **Through Lovely Devon.**—ENTIRELY NEW SERIES (by permission of the GREAT WESTERN RAILWAY Co.).
(For description, see page 7).

19. **Brown's Half-Holiday!**

20. **Rehearsing a Play!**

GOD SAVE THE KING.

This Programme is subject to slight alteration, as new subjects are added from time to time

⁂ The Management will be glad to hear from young ladies or gentlemen, with good voices, who are willing to become members of the Choir.

Events of Local, Topical, and Historic Interest added daily as they occur.

Programme for Waller Jeffs' New Century Picture Show at the Curzon Hall Birmingham

paniment for the evening's entertainment. According to his surviving programmes, Edison's Military Band was used to accompany the war films or the 'Grand Allegorical Tableaux of Britannia's Welcome to her Valiant Sons', while in Durham, he hired the Durham Light Infantry to play selections during the film show.[75]

The lecturer, the use of special effects and the musical accompaniment created a new kind of performance in which the cinematograph was the heart of the exhibition, rather than a mere addition to the music-hall programme or just one of a variety of fairground attractions. The two-hour spectacular promised by the showmen, complete with military band, local films, an effective spieler for the commentary and a change of programme daily, marked the start of a new and distinct form of leisure activity. Through their business relationship with Mitchell & Kenyon and other companies, the showmen provided a model of how to create a cinemagoing habit. By constantly adapting the programme on a daily basis and scheduling the exhibitions for ten- to twelve-week runs in urban centres such as Manchester, Bradford, Liverpool and Birmingham, the stand-alone film exhibitors were anticipating the advent of permanent cinema theatres. Fifty per cent of the films in the collection are associated with this type of showman, many of whom subsequently became managers or owned their own picture house. Ralph Pringle became a proprietor of several cinemas in Bristol, Edinburgh, Huddersfield and Newcastle, while J. J. Bennell was the founder of B.B. Pictures in Glasgow, which he began after operating a successful stand-alone show at the Wellington Palace for New CenturyPictures in 1906:

> For years these tours were both pleasant and profitable, but ten years ago I became convinced that the future of the kinematographe was in the permanent shows . . . I looked around for a suitable hall which would present a reasonable prospect of success as a temporary or permanent home for the kinematographe . . . that same building has now run for nearly ten years as a high class picture show to a working class clientele, who for the most part, pay, 2d . . .[76]

Although fairground showmen such as George Kemp and George Green opened cinema circuits in Scotland, the majority of the fairground and music-hall exhibitors stayed within their original sphere of operation. In later reminiscences, these former travelling exhibitors often recalled the days of early exhibition as chaotic, disorganised and haphazard. Yet, the films in the collection, and the business records and advertising posters in local archives, reveal a world where the spirit of enterprise coupled with natural showmanship could yield great rewards:

> There is . . . as every showman knows, plenty of hard work and energy required in the business, but the man who keeps up with the times and knows how to push himself forward is certain to be rewarded with the success he deserves, and to reap the benefit thereof in hard cash.[77]

The importance of the showmen in early film exhibition cannot be underestimated, for they 'reared the infant cinema' and 'brought it up to health and strength', and none more so than a former farmer from Devon who exhibited under the name of the Thomas-Edison Animated Photo Company.[78]

Case Study: Arthur Duncan Thomas: The English Thomas-Edison

> A. D. Thomas and his brother Ike were great characters and no history of the exhibition side of the industry can ignore their energetic pioneer work in the moving picture business. He was a showman to his finger tips and many of the kinematograph men who have made good, took their first lessons in management and operating from him.[79]

Arthur Duncan Thomas was one of the most colourful and incorrigible characters in early British film. Cecil Hepworth, in *Came the Dawn*, describes him as an utter scamp, a very lovable fellow and one of the greatest showmen who ever lived (see Plate 9).[80] As with other showmen of the late 1890s, he graduated from exhibiting Edison phonographs to projected film shows, which he billed as being provided by Edison himself. Although the Edison-Bell Company obtained a permanent injunction against him for exhibiting the phonograph without a licence, apparently they did not object to the use of Edison's name.[81] His continued use of Thomas Edison's name was deliberate as Hepworth reveals in his autobiography:

> His name . . . soon changed to Edison-Thomas and then, later on Thomas-Edison, and if people got it into their heads that he was the Edison, the great 'inventor' or moving pictures and many other things, well that was their look-out. He didn't do anything to disillusion them.[82]

This misappropriation of the real Thomas Alva Edison's name was a common phenomenon in entertainment history. Within the world of popular entertainment, the impresario's name was often the drawing card for the show and the impersonation of a famous showman or music-hall act was a common occurrence.[83] During Thomas's long and colourful career, he masqueraded as both P.T. Barnum and to a greater degree, Thomas Edison, but displayed the advertising ability and showmanship of the former (see Plate 10):

> Edison's Animated Pictures must not be confounded with other exhibitions of Biographs and Cinematographs. The name of EDISON STANDS ALONE in the domain of Scientific Invention, and is a guarantee of the perfection attained by the genius of EDISON, the MASTER MIND OF THE WORLD.[84]

Between 1898 and early 1900, Thomas appears to have been based in the south of England, staging regular film shows in Brighton[85] and venues throughout London as part of a cine-variety bill.[86] By 1899, he claimed to have control of twenty-one film shows and ownership of 4,000 film titles. He also appears to be operating both the Edison-Thomas Royal Vitascope and the Edisonograph in music halls, under the management of F. G. Bradford (see Plate 11).[87] In late 1899, Thomas moved to the north of England and based his operations in Manchester. His business flourished, with multiple shows touring throughout the north and the parallel music hall-type show in the south-east region named the Edisonograph. By 1901, Thomas had camera crews filming actualities in Ireland and the north of England, many of which now survive in the Mitchell & Kenyon Collection. In 1901 alone, the company was presenting stand-alone film shows in twenty-seven different ven-

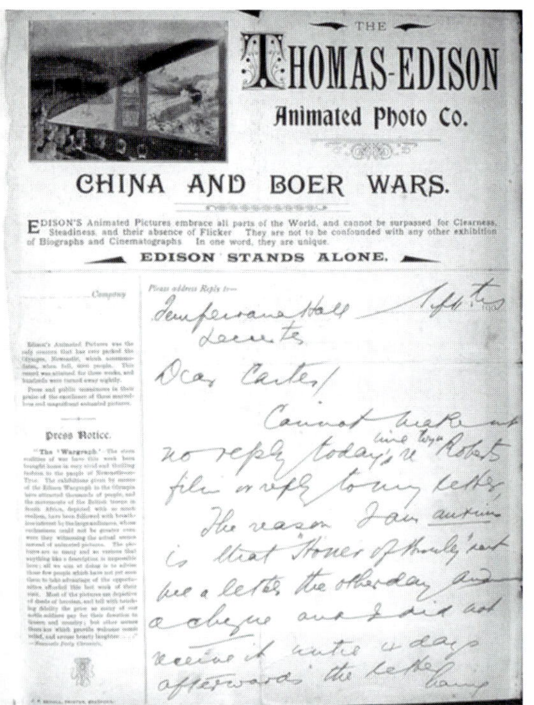

THE
THOMAS-EDISON
Animated Photo Co.

CHINA AND BOER WARS.

EDISON'S Animated Pictures embrace all parts of the World, and cannot be surpassed for Clearness, Steadiness, and their absence of Flicker. They are not to be confounded with any other exhibition of Biographs and Cinematographs. In one word, they are unique.

EDISON STANDS ALONE.

Press Notice.

Please address Reply to—

Temperance Hall

Dear Carter/

Letter from A. D. Thomas of Thomas-Edison Animated Photo Company, outlining the terms and conditions of his exhibition, 1901 (NFA)

ues throughout the north of England, the Midlands and Scotland (see Plate 12).[88] Many of these were simultaneous productions, so that while Thomas staged his show in Manchester from April onwards, his managers were also exhibiting in Glasgow, Dundee, Birmingham, Grimsby, Morecambe and Halifax.

After his bankruptcy hearing in November 1902, where it was revealed that the company had run up debts of £9,000, Thomas reputedly left for the West Indies.[89] According to Rachael Low, he left England and went to Canada, returning once again to tour Britain with his Royal Canadian Animated Photo Company in 1905.[90] This myth persisted following his appearance at the 1933 Cinematograph Veterans evening. It seems likely that Thomas actually never left the country. After his bankruptcy, he continued as an exhibitor, working for, among others, Walter Gibbons and the Warwick Trading Company in 1902, and many of the shows associated with the 'Thomas-Edison' name remained in operation. By 1903, he had changed the name of his touring show to Edison and Barnum's Electric Animated Pictures and continued presenting regional film shows in towns and cities throughout the north of England.[91] By 1904, he was general manager of a show in Liverpool under the name of The New Century Animated Pictures, which either ran in association with New Century Pictures of Bradford, or in competition. The relationship is unclear, as New Century Pictures existed as a network of affiliated exhibition companies with general managers in each region, while the company itself was still owned by Sydney Carter and Frank Sunderland. By May 1905, Thomas had left Liverpool and sold the stock, goodwill, together with all equipment, stationery, posters and local films to Sydney Carter for £112. Prior to his management of the Liverpool show and certainly from 1903, he was also operating as the Royal Canadian Animated Photo Company (see Plate 9) and presenting shows in Glasgow in 1903 and Manchester in 1904.[92] It is clear that filming links with Mitchell & Kenyon continued, as the collection contains films from this period of King Edward's visit to Manchester in 1905.[93]

The nature of the relationship between Mitchell & Kenyon and Thomas is complex and one that has still not been completely revealed. On one level it appears that the company developed and printed films for Thomas, as he had his own camera crew operating in Manchester as well as a company in Ireland. However, the presence of James Kenyon on some of the Manchester titles presented by Thomas shows that the relationship was not simply that of developing and printing or commissioning.[94] In addition, Clercq's notebooks from 1902 also indicate that Wilkinson, a Mitchell & Kenyon cameraman, was working with Edison's unit in Dublin.[95]

Thomas the Showman

As Hepworth reveals, Thomas was one of the most consummate showmen to present the cinematograph in the early 1900s. His style of show evolved from exhibiting films as part of a music-hall performance in the south-east to operating stand-alone film shows by 1899

A rare glimpse of A. D. Thomas, seen at the end of the *Manchester and Salford Harriers' Cyclists Procession* (1901)

in Manchester. Thomas marketed his shows through prolific newspaper advertisements and posters. His use of Thomas Edison's name in a variety of forms continued from 1899 to 1903 and he added to the legend by proclaiming that 'Edison Governs the World in Animated Photography', 'Edison the Picture King', 'Edison is Supreme' and 'Edison the Wonder Worker' in newspaper adverts and in his own four-page programmes.[97] He first tasted success with his Boer War films, which incorporated local army or military bands, the presence of local dignitaries and patriotic advertising. These films were advertised as 'a true record of the Boer and China Wars as depicted by the Telephoto Lens with 1,000 Animated Pictures, accompanied by a military band with forty performers'.[97] When interest in the Boer War material faded, the local film became a prominent feature of his advertisements. Using the local film as a main feature of the programme, he was able to create a two-hour show that could be adapted for any town or city in which he was exhibiting.[98] He would also parade through the streets with a handcart or horse and carriage during filming to advertise the fact that these films would be on show that evening.[99]

Thomas's business operations are complex and difficult to interpret, as no records or accounts have survived. Indeed, all we have is the information contained in the bankruptcy records, which reveal that, at their peak, one of his shows in Newcastle was taking £100 per week. While most of his claims over the years have been dismissed, it was not until the discovery of the Mitchell & Kenyon Collection that his real importance in early cinema exhibition was fully appreciated. Contemporary biographical accounts echo Hepworth's description of him as a scoundrel, and his subsequent bankruptcy only adds to the mystery. Charles Urban recalls how his dealings with Thomas ended unfavourably in 1902 following his involvement, along with Walter Gibbons, in the illegal duping of Warwick Trading Company films.[100]

The variety of names under which Thomas advertised over the years has added to the mystique, as do his own claims to have travelled in Canada and the West Indies and Europe. After 1907–8, A. D. Thomas the exhibitor disappears from contemporary records as his kind of show is superseded by the arrival of the purpose-built cinema houses. Later investigations have revealed that his real name was Arthur Dewdney, and he was originally a farmer from Devon. No trace of his subsequent activities as a film exhibitor after 1908 has so far come to light. Reference to a meeting with a fellow cinema veteran in New York in 1924, his appearance at the 1933 address by Colonel Bromhead and a letter from Waller Jeffs in 1938, in which he reveals that Thomas is living in Devon, all prove his existence.[101] Despite the false leads, changes of name and air of general ill-repute that follows A. D. Thomas, his contribution to early film exhibition is clearly evident in the Mitchell & Kenyon Collection. Over 140 titles are associated with his various companies and many of his fellow exhibitors owed their training and entry into the business to his shows. New Century Pictures continued to trade with him despite the many inconveniences he had caused them; Waller Jeffs and Ralph Pringle served as managers for his show; and Leon Gould, who worked as a lecturer for his company, went on to operate the North of England Film Bureau and opened cinemas in Carlisle.[102] Finally,

The close-ups and intimate shots were a feature of A. D. Thomas's films – as seen in the crowd shot from *Life in Wexford* (1902)

the films associated with A. D. Thomas in the collection are by far the most interesting and intimate of the ones that survive. The use of close-ups, audience participation and the presence of the showmen in the films allow us an insight into the world of the Edwardian showman and the man who, in the words of Cecil Hepworth, 'was one of the most remarkable personalities of the entertainment world of that or any other time'.[103]

Conclusion

The skill of the Edwardian showmen as illustrated by A. D. Thomas and others associated with the collection was to create an audience for the new and emerging medium of film exhibition. Using already existing titles, subject matter and specially commissioned titles, their role in the selection and exhibition of the material is central to understanding the institutionalisation of cinema prior to the Great War. However, their importance in choosing and commissioning certain subjects and developing non-fiction as a medium must also be reconsidered. The wide range of non-fiction material filmed by the company and utilised by the showmen may be the roots from which later forms of actuality productions such as newsreels, local topicals and, according to John Parris Springer, 'docudrama' developed.[104] It is possible that the growth of narrative film after 1903, and the increasing dominance of fiction titles within the film programme internationally, has obscured the importance of non-fiction in early film production and its subsequent influence; these links should now be re-examined. Mitchell & Kenyon operated within the intensively competitive worlds of both film production and exhibition. The importance of the collection for film history is that it enables us to understand the links between what has previously been regarded as two disparate groups, with the film-makers acting as suppliers to a passive but receptive medium that provided the channel through which cinema developed. The collection demonstrates the dynamic and often overlapping relationship and the role it played in popularising particular genres. Early cinema exhibition and the showmen who presented it functioned within the entertainment and leisure industry of the late-Victorian era, in which there were competing attractions. The collection not only captures this era but also allows us to evaluate the importance of the films as historical documents of the industry and society in which it evolved. The following chapter will now concentrate on the films that capture the Edwardians at play, demonstrating how the Mitchell & Kenyon Collection can be utilised as documents of social history from the first decade of the twentieth century.

NOTES

1 Tom Norman, *The Penny Showman: Memoirs of Tom Norman 'Silver King' with Additional Writings by His Son, George Norman* (London: privately published, 1985), references are taken from Memoirs of Tom Norman the Silver King, late Vice President Showmen's Guild, auctioneer, shownman, manuscript copy, NFA Q/NORM/57S, p. 13.

2 The most famous being Lord George Sanger, *Seventy Years a Showman* (London: Arthur Pearson, 1908; new edn. London: J. M. Dent and Sons, 1952); W. F. Wallett, *The Public Life of W. F. Wallett* (London: Bemrose and Sons, 1870); Thomas Horne, *Humorous and Tragic Stories of Showman Life* (London: *The Era*, 1909); E. H. Bostock, *Menageries, Circuses and Theatres* (London: Chapman and Hall, 1927).

3 For example, see Freda Allen and Ned Williams, *Pat Collins, King of Showmen* (Wolverhampton: Uralia Press, 1991); John Turner, *Dictionary of Victorian Circus Performers* Vol. 1 (Formby: Lingdale Press, 1995); Kevin Scrivens and Stephen Smith, *The Harry Lee Story* (Fairground Society, 1996).

4 Deac Rossell, 'A Slippery Job: Travelling Exhibitors in Early Cinema', in Simon Popple and Vanessa Toulmin (eds), *Visual Delights: Essays on the Popular and Projected Image in the 19th Century* (Trowbridge: Flicks Books, 2000), pp. 50–60 (51).

5 Ivo Blom, *Jean Desmet and the Early Dutch Film* (Amsterdam: Amsterdam University Press, 2003); Charles Musser and Carol Nelson, *High-Class Moving Pictures: Lyman H. Howe and the Forgotten Era of Traveling Exhibition, 1880–1920* (Princeton: University of Princeton Press, 1991); Greg Waller, *Main Street Amusements: Movies and Commercial Entertainment in a Southern City, 1896–1930* (Washington, DC: Smithsonian Institution Press, 1995).

6 Although the exhibitors associated with Mitchell & Kenyon were invariably men, women proprietors constituted 12 per cent of the fairground cinematograph shows. For further details see Vanessa Toulmin, 'Women Bioscope Proprietors – Before the First World War', in John Fullerton (ed.), *Celebrating 1895: The Centenary of Cinema* (Sydney: John Libbey, 1998), pp. 55–66.

7 See Richard D Altick, *The Shows of London* (London/Cambridge, MA: Belknap Press of Harvard University Press, 1978).

8 Tom Norman, The Penny Showman, p. 32. References are taken from Memoirs of Tom Norman, the Silver King, late Vice President Showmen's Guild, auctioneer, showman, manuscript copy, NFA Q/NORM/57S, p. 13. For more information on Tom Norman, see Vanessa Toulmin, 'Curios Things in Curios Places: Temporary Exhibition Venues in the Victorian and Edwardian Entertainment Environment', *Early Popular Visual Culture*, Vol. 4 No. 2 (July 2006), pp. 113–38.

9 Cited in Albert Smith, 'A Go-Ahead Day with Barnum', *Bentley's Miscellany*, Vol. 21, 1847, p. 524.

10 For the range and types of shows available see the illustrated articles that appeared in six parts by William G. Fitzgerald, 'Side-Shows', *The Strand Magazine*, Vols 13 and 14 (1897).

11 *The Showman*, 24 January 1902.

12 See Charles Musser, 'The May Irwin Kiss: Performance and the Beginnings of Cinema', in Vanessa Toulmin and Simon Popple (eds), *Visual Delights Two: Exhibition and Reception* (Eastleigh: John Libbey, 2005), pp. 96–115, for an example of how early films drew on and inspired theatrical performances.

13 *Yorkshire Evening Post*, 12 July 1902, p. 3.

14 André Gaudreault and Philippe Marion, 'A Medium is Always Born Twice', *Early Popular Visual Culture*, Vol. 3 No. 1 (2005), pp. 3–15 (3).

15 Tony Fletcher, 'The London County Council and the Cinematograph, 1896–1900', *Living Pictures: The Journal of the Popular and Projected Image before 1914*, Vol. 1 No. 2 (2001), pp. 69–83. See Jon Burrows's two-part article on film exhibition from 1906, 'Penny Pleasures: Film Exhibition in London during the Nickelodeon era', *Film History*, Vol. 16 No. 1 (2004), pp. 60–91, and 'Penny Pleasures II: Indecency, Anarchy and Junk Film in London's "Nickelodeons", 1906–1914', *Film History*, Vol. 16 No. 2 (2004), pp. 172–97.

16 For fairground cinema shows see Vanessa Toulmin, 'Telling the Tale: The History of the Fairground Bioscope Show and the Showmen Who Operated Them', *Film History*, Vol. 6 No. 2 (Summer 1994), pp. 219–37 and Mervyn Heard, '"Come In Please, Come Out Pleased": The Development of British Fairground Bioscope Presentation and Performance', in Linda Fitzsimmons and Sarah Street (eds), *Moving Performance: British Stage and Screen, 1890s–1920s* (Trowbridge: Flicks Books, 2000), pp. 101–11.

17 John H Bird, *Cinema Parade: Fifty Years of Film Shows* (Birmingham: Cornish Brothers Limited, 1947), pp. 21–2.

18 Greg Waller, 'Motion Pictures and Other Entertainment at Chautauqua', in Claire Dupre la Tour, André Gaudreault and Robert Pearson (eds), *Cinema at the Turn of the Century* (Quebec: Editions Nota bene, 1999), pp. 81–9.

19 Janet McBain, 'Mitchell & Kenyon's Legacy in Scotland – The Inspiration for a Forgotten Film-Making Genre', in Vanessa Toulmin, Simon Popple and Patrick Russell (eds), *The Lost World of Mitchell & Kenyon: Edwardian Britain on Film* (London: BFI, 2004), pp. 113–24.

20 See Vanessa Toulmin, '"We Take Them and Make Them" ': Mitchell & Kenyon and the Travelling Exhibition Showmen', in Toulmin *et al.* (eds), *The Lost World of Mitchell & Kenyon*, pp. 59–68.

21 *The Showman*, September 1900, pp. 16–17.

22 *Hull News,* 13 October 1900, p. 9.

23 Musser and Nelson, *High-Class Moving Pictures*: p. 53.

24 There are exceptions: see Christopher Dingley, *Waller Jeffs at the Curzon Hall: A Study in Early Film Showmanship* (unpublished MA thesis, University of Derby, 2000) and Jon Burrows, 'Waller Jeffs Scrapbooks', *Picture House: Journal of the Cinema Theatre Association*, No. 29 (2004), pp. 44–55. Also Richard Brown, 'New Century Pictures: Regional Enterprise in Early British Film Exhibition', in Toulmin *et al.* (eds), *The Lost World of Mitchell & Kenyon*, pp. 69–82; Frank Gray, 'The Sensation of the Century: Robert Paul and Film Exhibition in Brighton in 1896/7', in Toulmin and Popple (eds), *Visual Delights Two*, pp. 219–35; and Vanessa Toulmin, 'Local Film for Local People: Travelling Showmen and the Commissioning of Local Films in Great Britain, 1900–1902', *Film History*, Vol. 12 No. 2 (2001), pp. 118–37.

25 See M&K 28: *Messrs Lumb and Co. Leaving the Works, Huddersfield*, for both Loder Lyons and Ralph Pringle directing the crowd, and M&K 286: *Preston Egg Rolling*.

26 See M&K 336: *Factory Workers in Clitheroe* and M&K 606–13: *Street Scenes in Halifax*, in particular M&K 611. For further information on the films associated with the individual showmen see Vanessa Toulmin, Patrick Russell and Tim Neal, 'The Mitchell and Kenyon Collection: Rewriting Film History', *The Moving Image: The Journal of the Association of Moving Image Archivists*, Vol. 3 No. 2 (Autumn 2003), pp. 1–18.

27 M&K 514: *Church Parade of the Boys' Brigade in Birmingham* (1902).

28 See M&K 424, 428, 429: *Manchester and Salford Harriers' Cyclists' Procession* for A. D. Thomas (the scene in which Thomas holds up the money bag is actually in a section of the film housed in the North-West Film Archive), and M&K 172 and 443: *Manchester Street Scenes* for A. D. Thomas again.

29 See M&K 170–1: *A Tram Ride through Sunderland*, in particular M&K 170 for the scene in front of the Roker Hotel, and M&K 250: *Parade on Morecambe Central Pier*.

30 See M&K 155: *Dewsbury v. Manningham* and M&K 585: *Ralph Pringle Interviewing Private Ward VC Hero* (1901).

31 Colonel Bromhead, *Proceedings of the British Cinematography Society*, No. 21 (1933), p. 4.

32 Frank Sunderland, 'How the Picture Show Evolved: Ten Minute Programmes and 300 Feet "Features". Stories of Early Touring Days', *The Bioscope*, 4 January 1917, p. 28.

33 *The Showman*, 1 February 1901, p. 72.

34 Catherine Haill, *Fun without Vulgarity: Victorian and Edwardian Popular Entertainment Posters* (London: The Stationery Office, 1996), pp. 3–4.

35 For examples of showmen programming films on fairgrounds see Vanessa Toulmin, 'The Cinematograph at the Goose Fair, 1896–1911', in Alain Burton and Laraine Porter (eds), *The Showman, the Spectacle & the Two-Minute Silence* (Trowbridge: Flicks Books, 2001), pp. 76–86.

36 *The Showman*, 1 February 1901, p. 72.

37 M&K 223: *Llandudno May Day*.

38 See M&K 449–51: *Manchester Spiritualists' Procession*, in particular M&K 450, which features the sign 'Edison will reproduce this procession in Animated Photography twice daily St. James' Hall Manchester', and also M&K 612: *Street Scenes in Halifax*, and M&K 527: *Comic Pictures in the High Street West Bromwich* (1902).

39 M&K 151: *Salford v. Batley* and M&K 95: *Blackburn Rovers v. Sheffield United*.

40 See M&K 58: *Pendlebury Colliery* and M&K 772: *Sedgwick's Bioscope Showfront at Pendlesbury Wales*.

41 M&K 513: *Champion Athletes at Birmingham* and M&K 181–2, 543–5: *Opening of Accrington Electric Tramways*, and see M&K 181, in particular, for four sightings of Relph and Pedley and the gag card.

42 See M&K 175: *Living Wigan* and M&K 165: *Tram Rides through Nottingham*.

43 See M&K 183: *Ride on a Tramcar through Belfast* (1901).

44 Cecil Hepworth, *Came the Dawn: Memoirs of a Film Pioneer* (London: Phoenix House, 1951) pp. 58–9.

45 John Prestwich, 'How to Give a Cinematograph Show', *The Showman*, 6 September 1901, p. 571.

46 For examples of fairground showmen see Kevin Scrivens and Stephen Smith, *The Travelling Cinematograph Show* (Tweedale: New Era Publications, 1999).

47 See Richard Brown, 'New Century Pictures', in Toulmin *et al.* (eds), *The Lost World of Mitchell & Kenyon*, pp. 69–82.

48 For further background to the history of early film production in the UK see John Barnes, *The Beginnings of the Cinema in England, 1894–1901* (Exeter: University of Exeter Press, 1996–8): and also Richard Brown and Barry Anthony, *A Victorian Film Enterprise: The History of the British Mutoscope and Biograph Company, 1897–1915* (Trowbridge: Flicks Books, 1999). For Pathé see Richard Abel, *The Ciné Goes to Town: French Cinema, 1896–1914* (London/Berkeley: University of California Press, 1994). See also Colin Harding and Simon Popple, *In the Kingdom of Shadows: A Companion to Early Cinema* (London: Cygnus Arts, 1996); Thomas Elsaesser (ed.), *Early Cinema, Space Frame Narrative* (London: BFI, 1990) and John Fullerton (ed.), *Celebrating 1895: The Centenary of Cinema* (Sydney: John Libbey, 1998).

49 *Yorkshire Evening Post*, 28 August 1904, p. 1.

50 *The Showman*, 21 June 1901, front page onwards.

51 *Lytham Times*, 4 July 1902, p. 4.

52 *Lancaster Guardian*, 26 April 1902, p. 5.

53 Ibid., 3 May 1902, p. 5

54 Ibid., 10 May 1902, p. 5.

55 *The Showman*, 31 January 1902, p. 311.

56 *Halifax Evening Courier*, 4 February 1902, p. 3.

57 *Derbyshire Times*, 18 January 1902, p. 2.

58 *Southport Guardian*, 3 September 1902, p. 4.

59 *Optical Magic Lantern Journal and Photographic Enlarger*, Vol. 12 No. 140 (January 190)1, p. 2.

60 For a full overview of this see Steven Bottomore, 'From the Factory Gate to the Local Talent', in Toulmin *et al.* (eds), *The Lost World of Mitchell & Kenyon*, pp. 33–49.

61 Tom Gunning, 'Pictures of Crowd Splendor: The Mitchell and Kenyon Factory Gate Films', in Toulmin *et al.* (eds), *The Lost World of Mitchell & Kenyon*, pp. 49–58.

62 This film has survived in the Mitchell & Kenyon Collection as M&K 637: *The Crowd Entering St George's Hall, Bradford.*

63 *Bradford Daily Argus*, 26 Febuary 1901, p. 4.

64 Ansje van Beusekom, 'The Rise and Fall of the Lecturer as Entertainer in the Netherlands. Cinema Exhibition Practices in Transition Related to Local Circumstances', *Iris: A Journal of Theory on Image and Sound*, No. 22 (1996), pp. 131–44 (131). See 'The Moving Picture Lecturer', *Iris: A Journal of Theory on Image and Sound*, No. 22 (1996), for a range of articles on the role of the lecturer in France, Spain, America, Germany and Japan.

65 *The Showman*, 18 January 1901, p. 41.

66 See *The Huddersfield Examiner*, 3 November 1900, when 'Mr Lyons and Mr Pringle shared the duty of making reference to the pictures'.

67 John Prestwich, 'How to Give a Good Cinematograph Show', *The Showman*, 6 September 1901, p. 572.

68 For further information see Richard Abel and Rick Altman (eds), *The Sounds of Early Cinema* (Bloomington: Indiana University Press, 2001).

69 J. J. Bennell, 'In the Days of the Pioneer Showman', *The Kinematograph and Lantern Weekly*, 8 March 1917, pp. 19–21 (21).

70 *The Showman*, 5 January 1901, p. 14.

71 *Bolton Chronicle*, 2 February 1901, p. 8.

72 Nottingham Archives, M24, 420/A/16, transcribed by Dr Ann Featherstone. See also Ann Featherstone, *The Diaries of Sydney Race a Nottinghamshire Lad* (London: Society for Theatre Research, forthcoming). For information about these diaries see Ann Featherstone, 'There is a Peep Show in the Market: Gazing at/in the Journals of Sydney Race', *Early Popular Visual Culture*, Vol. 3 No. 1 (May 2005), pp. 43–59.
73 T. C. Hepworth, 'Music and "Effects" in Cinematography', *The Showman*, 6 September 1901, p. 574.
74 Bennell, 'In the Days of the Pioneer Showman', p. 20.
75 *The Showman*, 15 March 1901, p. 178.
76 Bennell, 'In the Days of the Pioneer Showman', p. 21.
77 *The Showman*, December 1900, p. 68.
78 Edwin Lawrence, 'The Infant Cinema: A Short History of the Moving Pictures', *The World's Fair*, 17 June 1939, p. 44.
79 Bennell, 'In the Days of the Pioneer Showman', p. 20.
80 Hepworth, *Came the Dawn* p. 58.
81 For further information on A. D. Thomas see Stephen Herbert and Luke McKernan, *Who's Who of Victorian Cinema* (London: BFI, 1996), pp. 140–1. See also Vanessa Toulmin, 'The Importance of the Programme in Early Film Presentation', *KINtop 11: Kinematographen-Programme*, edited by Frank Kessler, Sabine Lenk and Martin Loiperdinger (2002), pp. 19–33.
82 Hepworth, *Came the Dawn*, p. 58.
83 See Vanessa Toulmin, 'The Impact of American Showmen on British Popular Culture, 1840–1940', John Curtis Memorial Lecture, University of Central Lancashire, 23 November 2005.
84 There are many examples of A. D. Thomas's programmes in local archives around the UK, often listed under the real Thomas Edison! The majority of the programmes referred to are from private collectors, the Barnes Collection or the NFA. A. D. Thomas programme, c. 1900, printed by Wilson's of Leicester, Bannister Collection, Manchester Central Library, Vol. 41.
85 Programme for the Brighton Alhambra, Monday 5 March 1900, Brighton Public Libraries, BB 792/BRI, for details of Edison-Thomas Royal Vitascope. However, Thomas's run at the Alhambra commenced in September 1899 according to reports in *The Encore*, 11 January 1900.
86 See John Barnes, *The Beginnings of the Cinema in England, 1894–1901, Volume 3 1898: The Rise of the Photoplay* (London: Bishopsgate Press, 1983), pp. 77–9 for details of A. D. Thomas during this period, and also Tony Fletcher, 'The L.C.C. and the Cinematograph (1896–1900)', *Living Pictures: The Journal of the Popular and Projected Image before 1914*, Vol. 1 No. 2 (December 2001), pp. 69–83.
87 Information based on advertising letters belonging to both companies in the London Record Office, sent between 10 February, 19 August 1899 and 12 July 1900. See ibid. for further details. See also Colonel Bromhead, *Proceedings of the British Kinematograph Society*, p. 6, in which he details Thomas's involvement with the Edisonograph.
88 Figures based on a survey of reviews in *The Showmen* for 1901 and local newspapers associated with the film exhibitions for example.
89 *The Times*, 26 November 1902, for details of his bankruptcy hearings, and *The British Journal of Photography*, 1 August 1902, p. 616, for details of the sale of material to Walter Gibbons.

Fashionably dressed Edwardian ladies enjoying the leisure facilities at the *Great Yorkshire Show at Leeds* (1902)

toms continued alongside more industrialised forms of entertainment (see Plate 14).[6] Long-standing local traditions such as the visit of the fair were an integral part of people's lives, and the technological innovations introduced to travelling fairs in some cases ensured the survival of local customs.[7] Free time could be spent on holidays and excursions to seaside and countryside, in 'rational recreation', where pursuits were allied to educational activities and to the culture of 'self-improvement', as well as a range of popular entertainments, including music hall, circus and the fairground.[8] Popular urban recreational pursuits underwent a major transformation in the nineteenth century, with the judicial system and a range of legislations 'performing a critical function in moulding the major institutions and practices of urban leisure'.[9] The Edwardians were a people at play who enjoyed the benefits of reduced working hours, increased holiday time and improvements in transportation to participate in the full variety of popular amusements that were on offer. 'Victorians and Edwardians were constantly looking for an opportunity to celebrate their own achievements', writes James Walvin, and the showmen were not only eager to film the spectators but also to charge for the privilege of seeing themselves on screen.[10]

Recreation on Film

Temperance parades, such as *Manchester Band of Hope Procession* (1901), were also an opportunity for the Edwardians to enjoy themselves

Mitchell & Kenyon were not the first film company to capture the Edwardians at play: catalogues from other contemporary film-makers reveal that leisure was a popular subject for the cinematograph.[11] The uniqueness of the collection lies in the range of activities and localities that are covered, including performers, the audience and the entertainment venues popular with the holiday crowd. The new leisure industries highlighted by the collection are concentrated in the industrial north of England, in particular Lancashire and Yorkshire, and consist of sporting events, seaside resorts and travelling fairs, which, although featured infrequently on film, were initially the main vehicle by which the titles were exhibited. Conversely, the films also show evidence of earlier, well-established forms of holiday activities, including local parades and processions, calendar customs such as May Day celebrations and church feast days. A more esoteric example of a leisure activity includes *Preston Egg Rolling* (1901), taken at Avenham Park in Preston, Lancashire, and shown by the Poole family of showmen in their cinematograph show.[12] Egg-rolling on Easter Monday afternoon was at this time an established tradition in many parts of Britain, and is still widely practised in northern England. Other traditions

(Above) Children enjoying the festivities at *Preston Egg Rolling* (c.1901); (above right) President Kemp features in *Buxton Well Dressing* – an event that he not only filmed, but paid for (1904)

were not so long-standing and the Victorian era also marked the reinvention of earlier folk customs. One such example is the well dressing in Derbyshire, in particular Buxton, which, despite claiming an earlier origin, was first introduced by the 6th Duke of Devonshire in 1840. By the early 1900s, it had grown into an elaborate event complete with maypole dancing, morris dancers and a travelling funfair, all of which appear in *Buxton Well Dressing* (1904). The disruption caused by both the fair and the festivities associated with the event proved a veritable nightmare to the middle classes. In 1904, the festivities were cancelled, only to be reinstated a week later by the showmen President George Kemp and a local publican, when the cinematograph was used as both the venue for the maypole dancing and the finished film.[13]

Other recreational activities are featured in the collection, including local celebrations of national festivities and promenading on the pier or in the park after church. Edward's coronation in 1902 was commemorated with parades, galas and parties in towns and villages across the UK: for example, specially arranged coronation marches were filmed by Mitchell & Kenyon in Durham and Coventry.[14] Commercial centres of leisure were also filmed, including the Lancashire seaside resorts of Blackpool, Morecambe and Southport, alongside local spectacles such as the Tynemouth Amateur Swimming Club Annual Gala in North Shields, featuring the 60-yard comic obstacle race.[15] This event demonstrates the crossover that existed between sport and entertainment culture at the time, as the competitors swam the first thirty yards in 'ordinary costume, tall hat and gloves' and then completed the final thirty yards wearing a coat, vest, trousers and carrying an umbrella![16]

The holiday crowd, the spectating audience and local festivities of the 1900s were all captured by the cameras of Mitchell & Kenyon, creating a body of material that allows us to examine the age, class and gender differentiations of the audience. It has been argued that during the first half of the nineteenth century, certain types of leisure were largely enjoyed by working class men, with various activities restricted to women.[17] This could well be the case when examining the sporting audience filmed in the collection. However, the other leisure activities captured by the company demonstrate that by the early 1900s the reality was more complex and varied.[18] A large percentage of the children tripping haphazardly down the stairs of Sedgwick's cinematograph are

Eager crowds leaving *Sedgwick's Bioscope Showfront at Pendlebury Wakes* (1901)

young girls wearing the distinctive shawls of the Lancashire textile workers. A reporter who remarked on the popularity of the steam-powered roundabouts with the young women at Kirkcaldy could have been describing the passengers on *Green's Racing Bantams at Preston Whit Fair* (1906):

> All around the entrance was a crowd of boys and girls with eager upturned faces waiting for the signal. Girls first – and it was with difficulty the boys were kept back. When every girl was settled it started, every place filled and some horses seating two. What a sight it was! The happy faces whirling around laughing and beckoning to their friends in the crowds of onlookers . . .[19]

(Below left) The high-tech Edwardian fair as captured in *Whitsuntide Fair at Preston* (1906); (below) scenes from *Blackpool Victoria Pier* (1904) showing the huge holiday crowds that flooded the seaside resorts

By the start of the Edwardian era, both middle- and upper-class women were enjoying as wide a range of entertainments as their working-class counterparts.[20] The audience watching H. Flockton Foster's Entertainers at *Blackpool Victoria Pier* (1904) includes groups of women enjoying not only the entertainment, but being 'part of an all-embracing mixture of age, gender and (apparently) class, with no suggestion that some parts of the audience are more "respectable" than others in any systematic way'.[21] Leisure time was seen as a right for the large majority of the working population, and although divisions occurred on the basis of class and gender, these did not restrict members of the community from participating in their preferred activity. Mitchell & Kenyon did not capture the full range of recreational activities and facilities enjoyed by the Edwardians, and the filmic record is selective due in part to the technical problems of the apparatus itself. Notwithstanding this, the rest of this chapter will examine the leisure activities that feature heavily in the collection within the context of this wider leisure market: namely, those associated with northern seaside resorts, commercial entertainments and processions linked to festivals and fund-raising events.

Seaside

> Seaside resorts were not just an English invention, they also grew faster and further in the England of the nineteenth century and produced a uniquely extravagant variety of sub-species to cater for different classes and tastes . . . An impressive proportion of the population could expect to spend part of their lives as seaside residents.[22]

Mitchell & Kenyon were filming during a time of transition for the British seaside resorts, especially in Lancashire, where 75–80 per cent of working-class families could afford

The holiday crowd parading on *Blackpool Victoria Pier* (1904)

occasional seaside excursions.[23] As we have seen, increased wages, greater availability of cheap and regular transport, and a reduction in working hours resulted in the growth of seaside resorts in the north-west of England in particular.[24] By 1881, there were over one hundred resorts in England and Wales with a population of around one million.[25] At the same time, the entertainment industry in these resorts expanded, with the building of new variety theatres and piers, and the development of fairground entertainments by local entrepreneurs, catering for working-class pleasures and pockets. Five north-west seaside resorts are featured in the Mitchell & Kenyon Collection: Blackpool, Southport, Lytham, Morecambe and New Brighton. The variety of scenes captured reflects the diverse nature of the seaside holiday during the Edwardian era. Each resort attracted its own unique visitor, and there are obvious overlaps evident in the landscape of the promenade and the architecture of seaside piers. Southport and Lytham catered for respectable middle-class holidaymakers, while New Brighton attracted Liverpool day-trippers as well as longer-stay visitors, and Morecambe became the destination of choice for white-collar workers and their families from Yorkshire. Indeed, so popular was Morecambe with residents of the West Yorkshire towns that it became known as Bradford-by-the-Sea! However, with its traditional rowdy wakes holiday crowd and its visitor outreach extending to Scotland, Lancashire and the Midlands, the undisputed centre for the working class was Blackpool.[26]

Seaside on Film

The Mitchell & Kenyon films reveal the class differences that marked the development of these various seaside resorts, of which their views of the holiday crowds on the piers at Morecambe and Blackpool appear most similar in format and context. From the mid-nineteenth century onwards, Blackpool was undeniably 'the world's first working class sea-

The Blackpool skyline, as filmed from Blackpool North Pier, including the Giant Wheel – illustrates the rapid development of seaside resorts from the late-Victorian period onwards

Morecambe's Tower was never complete – as glimpsed in a *Panoramic View of the Morecambe Sea Front* (1901)

side resort', and by the 1890s, it was attracting two million visitors a year.[27] Visitor numbers from the textile towns of the north of England increased throughout the Edwardian era, and before the outbreak of the Great War, this figure had doubled to four million. John Walton's work on the rise of Blackpool reveals that the forces of class and social stratification prevalent in the Lancashire towns were transposed and acted out in their holiday homes at the seaside. By the 1890s, the level of investment in the entertainment industries resulted in an array of attractions to equal or surpass any leisure resort in the world.[28] Blackpool's ability to constantly increase and maintain the interest of its audience is reflected in the reviews of its newest visitor attraction, 'Les Montagnes Russes', an early scenic railway, in 1902:

> 'A Great Novelty at the Winter Gardens – Les Montagnes Russes. Blackpool's Latest Attraction' . . . If there is anything in the world worth seeing and having you can rest assured that Blackpool will be amongst the first, if not the first, to have it. Paris, the centre of gaiety, had its Tower: Blackpool must have one too. Chicago built a Great Wheel, Blackpool followed suit. And now we are to have another world's novelty, one of the latest of Parisian playthings.[29]

The inauguration of the electric tramway from Blackpool to Lytham, seen in *Lytham Trams and Views Along the Route* (1903), developed Lytham as a resort in the early 1900s

The full glory of the developments that took place in Blackpool in the 1890s is apparent in the panoramic shot taken from the North Pier, with its revealing views of the Bassett Big Wheel and Blackpool Tower.[30] The construction and financing of Blackpool Tower was the greatest achievement of Victorian seaside architecture, 'the architecture of pleasure, novelty, excitement and stimulation', and one that dramatically increased the numbers of visitors to the town in the 1890s.[31] Other resorts sought to copy this idea, but Morecambe's tower, seen in *Morecambe Church Lads' Brigades at Drill* (1901) and *Panoramic View of the Morecambe Seafront* (1901), was only partly built in 1901 and eventually had to be abandoned due to lack of finance.[32] New Brighton's tower was more successful, a glimpse of which appears in *New Brighton, Egremont and Seacombe Promenade* (1904), and a flourishing amusement park added to its popularity. Although it was higher than Blackpool's structure it never had the same impact on visitors from Lancashire and neighbouring regions.[33] Scenes of the newly electrified Lytham-to-Blackpool tram route, opened in May 1903, demonstrate the impact Blackpool had on neighbouring resorts in the Fylde.[34] Although Lytham was a more middle-class resort than its neighbour, the inauguration of the electric tramway between the resorts, which has survived

Southport Carnival and Trades Procession (1902) concentrates on local views and the annual carnival, as opposed to the holiday crowd

in the collection as *Lytham Trams and Views along the Route* (1903), could be viewed in two ways. First, it could be seen as a means of developing Lytham as a resort and attracting some of the overspill of the visitors to Blackpool; or it could be argued that Blackpool regarded its neighbouring seaside resorts as merely satellite towns feeding its own expansion. 'The inauguration of the scheme will very possibly have the effect of considerably swelling the number of visitors to St Annes and Lytham', writes the reporter for the *Blackpool Times and Fylde Observer*.[35] The phantom ride consists of sections of the six-mile journey between the two towns, featuring views of Lytham beach, St Annes beach, the children's camp, Fairhaven golf links and the sand-hills. The ride finishes on the South Shore, still an overwhelmingly respectable and middle-class district before the development of the Pleasure Beach complicated matters. By the 1904 holiday season, the route was featured as a visitor attraction in the local press:

> Equally attractive is the tram ride in the other direction, from South Shore Station to St Annes, Ansdell, and Lytham. The ride through the sandhills is very charming and now that the lumbersome old cars and the gas motor system have been replaced by overhead electric traction and smart and commodious cars, the journey has grown exceedingly popular.[36]

The holiday crowds that swelled the populations of these northern seaside resorts represented differing aspects of Edwardian society. Southport was without doubt the premier choice for the northern middle-class holiday-maker in the nineteenth and early twentieth centuries. Interestingly, the films reveal little of the holiday-makers but instead concentrate on local views and the annual carnival procession. *Southport Carnival and*

Lytham Club Day Carnival (1902) reveals more local views of this seaside resort

Trades Procession (1902) is similar to *Lytham Club Day Carnival* (1902), and features the annual crowning of the Rose Queen, held as part of the coronation celebrations for Edward VII.[37] Both resorts attracted a more select clientele than Blackpool, and although they developed piers and theatres to cater for the holiday audience, these never emulated the abundance and grandeur of the entertainments on offer in Blackpool. Neither film shows the seaside of the promenade, piers and amusements: instead, they focus on the varying array of carnival floats. In contrast to the holiday scenes of Blackpool and Morecambe, the views of Lytham and Southport shown at the resorts' theatres are 'local' in nature. The participants on the floats are tradesmen and businessmen, signalling to the local audience their importance to the community, and highlighting their particular industries or businesses. Of course, the audience for both the parades and the films may well have included holiday-makers, but they are similar in feel to civic celebrations held in other towns in the north of England at the time. The views of New Brighton captured in 1904 also reveal a different representation of the seaside resort. *New Brighton, Egremont and Seacombe Promenade* is a series of films of different locations in New Brighton, including the bowling green, the local tramway system and the landscape of the town centre.[38]

Piers and Promenades

The typical pictorial view of the Edwardian seaside featured the promenades and the piers, and this is reflected in the scenes that survive in the Collection of Blackpool and Morecambe. Both resorts reached out for a wider audience in the 1900s, and the views represented on film are similar in composition and subject to the scenes widely available as photographic postcards.[39] The piers and promenades dominate the landscapes of Blackpool and Morecambe and Mitchell & Kenyon filmed the holiday-makers enjoying the sea-

Blackpool Victoria Pier (1904) illustrates the pier's importance as an essential architectural feature of the seaside resort

side air and the array of entertainments on offer. Piers were an essential architectural feature of the seaside resort and, befitting its position as the premier resort, Blackpool constructed three piers – the North, the Central and Victoria (or South Pier) – each attracting a different clientele. Both the North Pier and the South or Victoria Pier are featured on film. The North Pier, built in 1863, offered an orchestra, tearooms and an air of social pretension and, 'at the turn of the century it was probably the most socially elevated public space in Blackpool'.[40] The Victoria Pier, built in 1893, also shared these aspirations and attracted a respectable middle-class visitor. It became renowned for its high-class vocal and instrumental concerts, variety entertainments and military and other band contests, with a Grand Pavilion that could seat 2,000 people. Although the respectable clientele would soon be compromised by the development of the Pleasure Beach fairground, in the early 1900s it 'still had nearly as many social pretensions as the North Pier'.[41]

Morecambe's promenade is perhaps the star of all the seaside views taken by Mitchell & Kenyon. Filmed from the front of a horse-drawn tram, the panoramic view reveals Morecambe's greatest treasure, the view across the sands framed against the backdrop of the South Lakes.[42] The holiday-makers at Morecambe are filmed promenading on both the West End Pier, built in 1896, and the Central Pier, which opened in 1893. The camera follows them as they parade in front of the lens, enjoying the kinetoscopes, fortune-

Scenes from *Panoramic View of the Morecambe Sea Front* (1901), filmed from a horse tram, reveals Morecambe's greatest treasure, the view across the sands framed against the backdrop of the South Lakes

tellers and phrenologists by the Stone Jetty and standing outside the Winter Gardens theatre on the promenade.[43] The views are also local in nature, with scenes of the Church Boys Brigade performing a drill for the camera or the holiday-makers programmed alongside a film of a church exit from Morecambe parish church.[44] The Morecambe titles were taken at the middle of the holiday season, in late June and early July, and shown at

Final sequence of *Panoramic View of the Morecambe Sea Front* (1901) reveals the cinematograph crowd outside the Winter Gardens Theatre – in front of the advertising posters for Thomas-Edison's cinematograph show

(Above) The splendour of the entrance to *Blackpool Victoria Pier* (1904); (above right) the electric tramway was an important means of taking visitors to *Blackpool Victoria Pier* (1904)

the Winter Gardens theatre by the showman A. D. Thomas. Although originally promoted as 'magnificent local animated view', they were then repackaged, along with the Blackpool films, into the Thomas-Edison Animated Photo Company's touring programme.[45]

Blackpool and Morecambe drew visitors from outside the Lancashire boundary. Although Blackpool was arguably the resort for Lancashire at play, in terms of its visitor radius, they both attracted holiday-makers from Yorkshire and the Midlands. Due to this wider appeal, unlike the other seaside resorts in the collection, films of both Morecambe and Blackpool found a prominent place in A. D. Thomas's touring programme. With their numerous and socially diverse visitors, their range of attractions and stratified tiers of respectability located around the promenade's piers, they encapsulated the popular image of the seaside. The views were packaged by the showmen as the ideal representation of 'holiday scenes at Morecambe and Blackpool' and shown to audiences from Malvern to Bradford from mid-1901 to 1902. It was the seaside of promenades, piers and amusements that was presented as the Edwardian ideal and reveals the importance of both the resorts outside the Lancashire region.

Public Entertainment

> There always are, always have been, always will be, people who are willing to be 'entertained' i.e., amused, by a 'show' of some kind. Not only willing are they, but eager for such amusement. And they will travel miles and part from their money with no other object than to view.[46]

The Edwardian era was the golden age for all types of entertainment, with the commercial industries incorporating fairgrounds, circuses and theatres. A variety of venues were built or adapted to incorporate the latest novelties and attractions, with the aim of capturing the attention of an ever-receptive audience.[47] Brookes McNamara divides popular entertainment into three categories: variety entertainment, popular theatre and the entertainment environment, usually a temporary or open-air arena in which a range of other activities took place.[48] Variety entertainment was one of the most important subjects of the cinematograph, with Thomas Edison capturing the stars of the American

The travelling fairground captured in *Hull Fair* (1902) enjoyed its golden age during the Edwardian period

variety stage and Wild West shows.[49] Within the collection, however, it is the entertainment environment that is captured on film, consisting of short-term events such as fairs and circuses or those held within a temporary or permanent self-contained environment, such as the pleasure gardens or expositions.

Music Hall and Variety

> Music hall was the most successful popular theatre form of the nineteenth century . . . Its humour and styles penetrated the Victorian and Edwardian mind, shaping ways of thinking about pleasure and entertainment.[50]

Films of circus, fairground, music-hall and vaudeville performers were all popular subjects for the cinematograph. Unlike other film companies, Mitchell & Kenyon rarely filmed such variety entertainers and, indeed, when they were captured it was within the context of a wider performance arena. One example of this are the Mazonda Tub Jumpers, who appeared nightly at the Tivoli Theatre in Leeds, and were filmed in Headingley as part of the local carnival parade.[51] The Mazondas at Leeds carnival, Flockton Foster's Entertainers at Blackpool, and the clowns and acrobats at Algie's and Bailey's circuses reveal the

The Mazonda Tub Jumpers, appearing nightly at the Tivoli Theatre in Leeds, filmed taking part in the *Leeds Athletic and Cycling Club Carnival at Headingley* (1902)

diversity of performance skills and acts that were available to the Edwardians.[52] The Mazondas, for example, appeared primarily in fixed venues such as music halls and circus buildings, but their popularity was based on the novelty of their act.[53] All these acts were part of a professional entertainment industry that had evolved from the 1840s onwards.

The music and variety theatre originally embraced the cinematograph by scheduling it within its programme, and from 1896 onwards, music halls were central for the development of the cinematograph within large urban populations. The Argyle Theatre in Birkenhead, St George's Hall, Bradford, and the Winter Gardens in Morecambe, for example, are just three of the venues captured by Mitchell & Kenyon.[54] The differing histories of each of these three venues present snapshots of the changing nature of the professional entertainment industry leading up to the 1900s. The Argyle Theatre began life in 1867 as the Prince of Wales Theatre, but by the 1890s, it had been renamed and became one of the premier variety theatres outside London, attracting headline stars. The St George's Hall in Bradford was built in 1853 with a capacity of 3,300 for high-class musical concerts, and attracted a largely middle-class audience, who attended educational and political lectures, pantomimes and respectable theatrical shows.[55] The Winter Gardens in Morecambe, originally named the Palace of Varieties when constructed in 1878, was renovated and expanded in 1897 to form the Victoria Palace and Oriental Ballroom.[56] The collection presents us with not only a view of the types of venues patronised by Edwardian leisure-seekers but also the audience who attended the shows. Each venue attracted a different clientele, with ticket prices ranging from 2d. at the Winter Gardens (see Plate 15) to one shilling at the St George's Hall. The Argyle catered for the Merseyside basin in Birkenhead and attracted audiences from a large local radius, while Bradford served the needs of the respectable and aspiring mercantile class, with the Winter Gardens audience comprising both locals and holiday-makers.

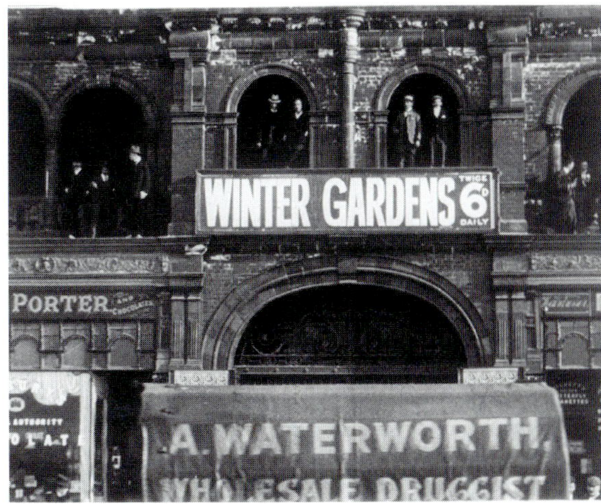

THE ENTERTAINMENT ENVIRONMENT

The environment filmed by Mitchell & Kenyon grew out of pre-industrial entertainment practices dating back to the eighteenth century. Fairs, circuses and pleasure gardens all have separate but intertwined histories, with the performing tradition and the spectator common to each cultural form. All of these environments feature in the collection and often provided the arena in which many of the films were first exhibited to the public. From the mid-nineteenth century onwards, they began to adapt to new conditions and embraced the modern and the different. Although the audience had changed and certain fairs had become increasingly unpopular with the urban bourgeoisie, the appeal of itinerant entertainment was on the increase among the working class.[57]

(Above left) The Argyle Theatre captured in *Carnival Processions in Birkenhead* (1902) was one of the premier music halls in the United Kingdom; (above right) Cinematograph crew standing at the top of the Winter Gardens captured of *Panoramic View of the Morecambe Sea Front* (1901)

Travelling Fairs

The local wakes fairs and feasts held in the north of England, although primarily centred on trading and economic activities in mid-Victorian times, had less than forty years later transformed into high-tech carnivals of fun featuring the latest modern attractions. Lancashire wakes and the Yorkshire feasts were an essential part of the factory workers' hol-

A view of *Hull Fair* (1902), the largest of all the travelling fairs in the United Kingdom

Green's Racing Bantams at Preston Whit Fair (1906) reveals the latest up-to-date attraction on the Edwardian fair

Advertisement for the *Whitsuntide Fair at Preston* (1906)

idays and became affirmations of community identity, both past and present, in which people expressed themselves through uninhibited pleasure-seeking.[58] Large urban events had largely died out in the south of England, but medieval Charter fairs in the north continued, as new fairs were held in association with agricultural shows and church festivities such as Whit Sunday. A fair could be the continuation of the original charter, as in *Hull Fair* (1902), a private business event located within the urban environment, a celebration held in association with the annual wakes, as seen in *Sedgwick's Bioscope Show at Pendlebury Wakes*, or held as part of an invented tradition such as *Buxton Well Dressing*.[59]

'By the late nineteenth century, fairs had been reconstituted. The chief attraction was mechanised swings and roundabouts, in place of the theatrical shows and dancing booths of the first half of the century.'[60] The Edwardian period heralded a golden age on the fairground, expressed in the lavish decorations and cacophony of sound emanating from the organ-fronted shows. The showmen opened up new experiences, by bringing in the latest attractions and manipulating them for their own audience.[61] *Whitsuntide Fair at Preston* (1906), complete with steam-powered roundabouts and the marvels of the travelling cinematograph show, was one of 150 events that took place weekly in the UK and demonstrates the full glory of the Edwardian fair.[62] An additional sequence highlighting *Green's Racing Bantams at Preston Whit Fair*, reveals the roundabout as the latest up-to-date attraction on the Edwardian fair.[63] Built by Savages of King's Lynn, the pagoda-top-platform cockerels was a rougher, faster ride than the galloping horses that were particularly popular in the mill towns of Lancashire.[64] These mechanical wonders had transformed the late-Victorian fair into a realm of speed and modernity, and what today is perceived as a relic from the apparently genteel age of steam power was in fact the latest high-tech attraction. The other roundabouts featured in the film also belonged

Scenes at *Hull Fair* (1902)

to George and John Green, two of the most successful travelling showmen of the nineteenth century. George went on to found the Green's circuit of cinemas in Scotland, while his brother John continued travelling in the Lancashire area.[65] The fair is located in the market square in Preston, and additional footage reveals the Victorian outdoor market, built in 1875, which is still the traditional site for the annual fair. The Edwardian fair was a kaleidoscope of motion, colour, light and noise, a marriage of modernity and medievalism allied to so-called ancient traditions.

Before the introduction of steam-powered roundabouts in the 1860s, shows were the principal ingredients of travelling fairs. *Hull Fair* reveals the range of shows that was on offer at travelling fairs in the Edwardian era, including Harry Hughes's boxing booth, Bailey's circus tent, Bostock and Wombwell's menagerie, photographic saloons and Randall Williams's cinematograph show. The cinematograph shows of the early twentieth century were the final expression of a once great spectacle that had dominated the fairground for over two hundred years. By 1900, these shows were a prominent feature on the fairground landscape. Built as ornate pavilions, with a frontage of eighty feet and capable of holding 1,000 people, all types of fairs would have featured such an attraction. The shows as illustrated in the collection became bigger and better, and the

President Kemp's bioscope – the setting for the maypole dancers at *Buxton Well Dressing* (1904)

showmen used the parades that formed part of a vaudeville act as the means of attracting an audience. Theatre or music-hall designs provided the main model for such portable shows, and the interiors of the exhibitions matched the lavish theatrical theme of the exterior. The showmen 'vied with each other in the lavishness of their adornments, their show fronts being one mass of gilt'.[66] Green's cinematograph show is featured in *Whitsuntide Fair at Preston*, while Randall Williams's exhibition is shown advertising local films in *Hull Fair*. President Kemp's bioscope is the setting for the maypole dancers in *Buxton Well Dressing*, and *Sedgwick's Bioscope Showfront at Pendlebury Wakes* reveals the exterior of the cinematograph show, with its variety show and parade continuing the performance aspect of the booth. This later title also features both Albert Sedgwick and James Kenyon on the front of the show holding the gag card that advertised the various attractions, and is a wonderful example of the dynamics at play between the film-makers and the showmen-exhibitors as they work together to create the spectacle. The environment of the fair, and its simultaneous attractions, was shaped by both the professional exhibitors and the audience. The showmen created the landscape of attractions on offer, while the spectator selected the order in which the entertainments were viewed, experienced and sampled.

Sedgwick's Bioscope Showfront at Pendlebury Wakes (1901) reveals the exterior of the cinematograph show with its variety show and parade – continuing the performance aspect of the booth. Also features James Kenyon and Sedgwick on the front of the show

The opportunity to sample the range of entertainments within one venue was also part of the success of the pleasure gardens, an example of which is illustrated in *Trip to Sunny Vale Gardens at Hipperholme* (1901). Pleasure gardens offered the spectator or leisure-seeker a mixture of attractions within one environment.[67]

Pleasure Gardens

Another feature of the increase in leisure time was the rise of the pleasure gardens on the edge of industrial and urban centres in the north of England. Pleasure gardens flourished in Europe in the eighteenth century, the most famous of these being Vauxhall Gardens (founded in 1661), whose popularity was at its height in the early nineteenth century. Although Vauxhall and Surrey Gardens in London had been popular for over a century, it was not until the mid-nineteenth century that Tivoli Gardens opened in Copenhagen in 1843.

Argued by some historians to be a forerunner of modern amusement parks, the pleasure gardens' entertainments included theatre shows, firework displays, dancing and drinking booths, and theatrical entertainment. Such was the success of both Vauxhall and the later Tivoli Gardens that both names became generic terms for other pleasure gardens in Europe and America. Vauxhall, unlike its European counterparts, fell into decay and by 1859 had closed, with historians citing the growth of the railway and holiday excursions as a reason for its falling visitor numbers. However, new-style gardens at the edges of large industrial centres had already opened, including Manchester's Belle Vue in 1836 and Crystal Palace in 1854. Combining the old-style pleasure gardens with the latest modern attractions, Belle Vue became the most famous example in the north of England. Pleasure gardens continued to develop throughout the UK, and Harrogate Spa and Gardens and White City in Manchester also served the needs of their locality. Considering their popularity in England at the time, it is surprising that the only film that survives in the collection is of Sunny Vale Pleasure Gardens, located between Halifax and Leeds.

Sunny Vale was the brainchild of Joseph Bunce, a native of London who moved to Yorkshire after his marriage. The pleasure gardens opened in 1883 at Hipperholme and attracted over 100,000 visitors each year in the early 1900s. The gardens had numerous attractions, many of which are featured in the films, including boating on the two lakes, a maze, a helter-skelter and swingboats. *Trip to Sunny Vale Gardens at Hipperholme*, the first title in the series, captures the customers entering through the turnstile, with the showmen leading the children towards the camera.[68] The second film reveals holiday-makers on the swingboats, dancing and in scenes that appear to have been specifically staged for the camera: in particular, a mock fight and a man who appears dressed as a woman.[69] Concerts were held regularly and rides could be enjoyed on the primitive switchback railway or mountain glide ride. Amusement tickets were priced at 1d. each or twenty-four tickets for 1/6d. The famous tearoom seated 1,000 people and would regularly serve meals to over 4,000 customers per day. Pathways were illuminated and a huge firework display marked the end of each season. Joseph Bunce died in 1918, but the gardens remained popular until the end of the Second World War; sadly, nothing remains today of its former glory.

Children and parties of young women enjoying the entertainments during their *Trip to Sunny Vale Gardens at Hipperholme* (1901)

Trip to Sunny Vale Gardens at Hipperholme, also reveals the high percentage of women who partook of leisure activities. Scene after scene reveals groups of women or children riding in the miniature railway, walking alongside the river, taking a boat out on the lake or enjoying the array of other entertainments on offer. The film reveals that leisure was enjoyed by all classes of people, and demonstrates how 'it had become generally accepted that everyone had a right to the enjoyment of leisure'.[70] Pleasure gardens, in particular, attracted a wide range of visitors and provided a social space for pleasure-seekers in search of entertainment and visitors wanting fresh air, exercise and more relaxing forms of amusement such as punting on the lake. Like the fairground, it presented a range of leisure activities that the public could pick and enjoy at their own pace. This was in contrast to the organised 'professional' spectating events such as the circus or music hall, where the entertainments were programmed by the showmen for a fee-paying audience.

Circus

George Speight defines the history of circus 'as the story of that entertainment of human bodily skills and trained animals that is presented in a ring of approximately 13 metres in diameter with an audience grouped all around it'.[71] Travelling menageries, acrobats and trick animal acts were all features of entertainment in the eighteenth century and earlier, but it was the combination of these features within a circular structure that became known as circus. The founder of modern circus, Philip Astley (1742–1814), staged a show in London in 1768 featuring trick horseback riding and live music. It was presented in a circular structure, and named Astley's Amphitheatre. He later added other acts, such as acrobats, a clown and a band to his performances. By the middle of the Victorian era, travelling circuses had become large commercial concerns, ranging from small tented affairs to gigantic enterprises housed in permanent buildings or amphitheatres. Circus historian John Turner has estimated that over 10,000 circus performers of all types appeared in the UK during the Victorian period.[72]

In the early 1900s, cinematograph filming was restricted to outdoor activities or those staged in an outdoor studio. As circus performances took place in an indoor venue such as a tent or specially constructed building, films capturing the full spectacle of the late-

The importance of the circus parade as an advertisement, is demonstrated in *Algie's Circus in Carlisle* (1901)

Victorian and early Edwardian circus were rarely attempted.[73] The outdoor spectacle of the circus parade is illustrated in *Algie's Circus in Carlisle* (1904), filmed earlier that day and exhibited within the corrugated iron circus building.[74] Vignettes of the acts parade in front of the camera, including performing dogs, white-face clowns, young girl acrobats and, of course, the would-be cinematograph and circus audience, who are now 'in the show'. According to Brenda Assael, circus inverted the order of things and created a world of richness and vulgarity, 'a fantastic, colourful gaudy dream' that, unlike other forms of the carnivalesque, was performed on a daily basis. Although originally presented as an itinerant exhibition, permanent circus buildings flourished throughout the nineteenth century in urban centres throughout the UK.[75] Although this is not apparent in the actual film, it does demonstrate the overwhelming popularity of this form of entertainment in the 1900s, capturing as it does a small local circus performing nightly for a population of approximately 40,000 in a regional town in England.

Parades as Performance

'To focus on the changing face of recreations in late Victorian and Edwardian Britain is to miss the many continuities linking past to present,' writes G. R. Searle. This is certainly the case when examining the popularity of the parade or procession in the 1900s.[76] The collection records a period when the parades were a particularly dynamic form of street activity. The processions can be examined as part of a parading tradition that had its origins in pre-existing industrial forms of leisure activities. Parades were organised by friendly societies, churches, schools, temperance groups and trade unions and were important expressions of political or religious identity. Over fifty different events dating

Parades were an important part of local pride and were often a means of commemorating national days of celebration, as in *Chorley Coronation Processions* (1911)

from 1901 to 1911 have survived in the collection, ranging from religious celebrations to political marches and national days of celebration.[77] Although their increase in popularity was due to the parade's resurgence in the Victorian era, the roots of this processional activity lay deeper. It was inevitable that there should be tension between older forms of street festivity and the middle-class adoption of processions as a vehicle for promoting respectability.[78] As Andrew Prescott writes, 'the Collection provides remarkable evidence of this exotic, largely forgotten, aspect of English urban history', reflecting social tensions, class distinctions and celebrations of both family and community identity.[79]

Their use of the social space of the time and their importance within nineteenth-century urban culture will be discovered in later chapters. However, it is the processions associated with local carnivals and calendar customs that reveal the parades as a form of street theatre. Unlike the industrialised professional entertainments discussed previously, these amusements were created by amateurs and performed largely within the context of the local parades. These 'amateur' performers, including morris dancers and participants in fancy-dress carnival processions, drew on both the traditions of folk amusements and trends in popular entertainment.

Parades as Street Theatre

> Carnival is not a spectacle seen by the people; they live in it, and everybody participates because its very idea embraces all the people.[80]

Carnival festivities held an important place in the life of medieval man and were an essential part of pre-industrial leisure activities. The manifestation of the carnivalesque tradition evident in the parades and processions in the collection was part of a flowering of such events that occurred in England from the nineteenth century onwards.[81] The nineteenth-century calendar parades and fancy-dress cycle parades filmed by Mitchell & Kenyon could be interpreted as containing elements of the carnival atmosphere, in which the participants cross the boundaries of rank, gender and race within the constraints of the formal procession through the streets of their own locality.[82] However, it is as an expression of street theatre – ritual spectacles performed by amateur players for a local audience – that carnivals are situated within the performance culture of the nineteenth century. The amateur players were a common feature of the processions and formed an essential part of the entertainments on view. Processions were held as part of a local feast day, a calendar custom such as May Day or formed the nucleus of new industrial events such as charitable fund-raising parades. They are different in concept and content to military parades, commemorations of important battles and civic pomp. The processions featured in the collection include participants wearing costumes and masks, entertainers appearing in blackface and men dressed in women's clothes. The costumes are both traditional and modern, with the influence of what Theresa Buckland calls the 'Merrie England' effect apparent, reflecting a yearning for a more idyllic pre-industrial age of cavaliers and English yeomanry.[83] This is apparent in *Llandudno May Day*, where the theme of the festivities was indeed 'Merrie England', which, according to the *Llandudno Advertiser,* also includes Wales![84] The costumed participants include a banjo-playing, blackface minstrel, clowns and chimney sweeps. Films of four May Day festivities from

Calendar customs such as May Day were an important aspect of Edwardian leisure. Elements of *Leyland May Festival* (1903) captured on film include the May Queen in her carriage and the local Morris men troupe performing the Leyland Processional Dance

a wonderfully diverse set of locations survive in the collection and cover Leyland, Knutsford, Llandudno and Bootle.[85] The parades are similar in format and generally include a formal procession of morris-dancing teams, as well as local May Queens and their attendants.[86] *Leyland May Festival* (1905) features morris-dancing teams from Cheshire performing in what folklorists have described as 'Carnival Morris', where the dress and costumes are similar to those of sporting leisure-based activities and the dancers perform in a competitive environment.[87] Morris-dancing teams are also present in other May Day parades in Bootle and charitable processions such as the *Leeds Lifeboat Procession* (1902).[88] Various sections of the Leeds parade were filmed, including a troupe of performing bears, the Horwich morris dancers and a number of cyclists in fancy dress, the theme of the parade being 'Past and Present'.[89]

Local fund-raising events such as *Royal Halifax Infirmary Annual Street Procession* (1908), *Leeds Lifeboat Procession* and *Crewe Hospital Procession and Pageant* (1907) all feature an array of costumes and decorated floats as complex and ornate as a professional theatre company.[90] The fancy-dress cyclists who accompany the processions appear to take their inspiration from popular culture and British history. *Carnival Procession in Birkenhead* (1902) and the *Manchester and Salford Harriers' Cyclists' Procession* (1901) reveal the popularity of the fancy-dress cycle parade. Established in the latter part of the nineteenth century as a Christian charitable fund-raiser, by the Edwardian era the cyclists' parade had

Leeds Lifeboat Procession (1902) with its array of decorated floats, attracted thousands of spectators

become an established part of the leisure calendar. Bicycles are decorated to match the attire of the participant with influences ranging from the Boer War to biblical characters. The impact of commercial entertainment is also prevalent, with one parader in the *Manchester and Salford Harriers' Cyclists' Procession* dressing as a Native American from Buffalo Bill's Wild West Show, which had exhibited in Manchester in 1892.[91] The importance of the mask as an essential component of the parade is manifest in the *Llandudno May Day* parade, which ends with a shot of two individuals in large masks that engulf their heads and torsos. The phenomenon of reversed class, gender and race is also revealed in the collection, with cross-dressing featuring regularly in the parades. During the *Manchester and Salford Harriers' Cyclists' Procession*, for example, one male cyclist is dressed as the Scales of Justice, complete with flowing locks and gown, while later in the same film, another gentlemen appears attired as a prairie flower.[92] Children dress as adults, men dress as women and Lancastrians disguise themselves as Native Americans. Fund-raising parades created an opportunity for divisions of class, race and gender to be displaced within the order and function of an organised event.

(Below left) *Hunslet Carnival and Gala* (1904); (below right) the diversity of costumes worn by the paraders in *Manchester and Salford's Harriers Procession* (1901) demonstrates the range of influences on the event

Ironically, the filming of these events changed the status of the amateurs, as they were repackaged and presented within the professionalism of a formal cinematograph exhibition. The carnival processions were shown in other locations, and one reviewer in Northampton

enviously compared the extravagance and professionalism of the Manchester parades to the Northampton cyclists' processions.[93] The seaside and parade films became part of the professional entertainment environment. Recreational events of this kind were popular subjects for the showman, as their appeal extended outside their locality, and they became a central part of the early cinematograph programme. When viewed from a modern perspective, the extravagant spectacle of parades linked to a fund-raising event or local carnival is startling. However, it is the recreational arena in which it operates that allows it the space and the opportunity to deconstruct and repackage these themes within the social and cultural context of the age in which it is presented. The films reveal a side of Edwardian leisure that has few modern comparisons: none more so than *Crewe Hospital Procession and Pageant*, one of the longest and most heavily edited parades surviving in the collection.[94]

Case study: Crewe Hospital Procession and Pageant

Crewe Hospital Procession and Pageant was filmed on Saturday 10 August 1907 and is an eight-minute film featuring sections of the local carnival and pageant parade. The parade was founded in 1906 by the workers of the London North Western Railway Company (LNWR) and other local institutions as a charitable fund-raising event for the Crewe Memorial Cottage Hospital. The hospital, which served both the local community and the LNWR workforce, opened in the mid-1890s and relied on charitable donations for its upkeep and maintenance. The importance of the railway works for Crewe as a town cannot be underestimated. The company had a major influence both politically and socially in the development of the town, promoting and running leisure activities through its various associated clubs, organisations and unions. This is a pattern

One of the most amazing of all the carnival films in the Collection – *Crewe Hospital Procession and Pageant* (1907) – attracted dancing troops supplied by the local LNWR company who paraded to raise money for their local hospital

'Original Stilters' from the Smithy Oldworks chose dances from all nations as their particular speciality for 1907

Performing Bears and Trainers representing scenes from British history

Troupe of Dutch Clog Dancers from the Crewe South Shed works

The formally attired dancers of the Colombo troupe were one of eight black-faced groups who contributed to the procession

Another stereotype representation of the minstrel show as demonstrated by original golliwogs' dance performed by the Fitting Shop from Crewe Old Works

Black-faced troupes were a popular theme in the 1907 procession and the new cakewalk craze executed by the North Steam Shed complete with formal evening dress, top hats and canes is a perfect representation of a minstrel show performance

in Britain in 1836 and soon became a prominent and popular part of both the music-hall show and more professional theatrical venues.[104]

The original American minstrel shows had evolved from professional acts or troupes within the context of a music-hall act or a whole show held at a variety theatre. In mid-Victorian Britain, it was a form of entertainment that attracted a more respectable audience than the music hall and fairground crowds, and it appealed to the largely lower-middle class family audience.[105] Its influence within popular culture was pervasive, and from the 1870s onwards it spread to street entertainments, seaside resorts, travelling fairs and pantomimes, where it became part of the 'burnt-cork' (or blacking-up) types of entertainments that were linked to earlier forms of folk entertainments.[106] By the 1880s, it had become a common part of amateur theatrical presentations and was adapted for street processions and parades of the time. In the context of the Crewe carnival, the minstrel show became assimilated into customary forms of popular traditional theatre, song and the mumming tradition. Many aspects of English traditional drama and dance had 'burnt-cork' elements in their repertoire, the most famous being the Britannia Coconut Dancers from Bacup.[107]

LNWR workers from the Locomotives store in drag appeared as Suffragist impersonators hints at the influence of contemporary political issues on the event

The parade itself was over a mile and a half in length and started in the late morning, making its way through the streets of Crewe to its final assembly point in Queen's Park. The troupes and paraders from the LNWR won the major prizes for the best float or display, and Mitchell & Kenyon appear to have edited the film to show the successful troupes in their best light. Although the parade would have taken over an hour to wend its way through Crewe, only eight minutes are captured on film and in no particular chronological order. The operators edited the final film to highlight the most spectacular displays, and featured eight of the minstrel troupes, the performing bears' sequence, the stilt walkers and fencing groups, Lady Godiva and the Court of George II. The stationary position of the camera and the use of close-ups reveal the level of professionalism shown by the amateur performers, all of whom dance with a high degree of skill. This is due to the amount of preparation that the workers from the LNWR put into their carnival parade. Weeks in advance, coaches were employed to put the workers through the routines, and the names of the trainers are listed in the newspaper report of the event. The minstrel dances performed by the LNWR workers range in style and convention, reflecting the various types of minstrel performers popular in the UK at that time. The modes of production range from the 'golliwog' dance performed by the Fitting Shop from Crewe Old Works, the new cakewalk craze executed by the North Steam Shed, complete with formal evening dress, top hats and canes, and the intricate steps of the Stone Yard and Forge and Mill troupes, who also perform in blackface. Both American-style shows and British influences are evident in the costumes, as English minstrelsy, in particular, shifted towards spectacular attire, a popular motif being elaborate costumes based on the English regency court dandy.[108]

Further work is needed to understand the variety of dances performed by the paraders in the film, and all of them were using the walkabout finale of the minstrel shows. The walkabout finale was a later development of the show and usually consisted of a solo or choral song accompanying a dance piece to an instrumental melody.

Although the minstrel troupes are the most spectacular feature of the parade, and most strongly aligned to the popular culture of the time, other influences are evident in the selected pageants. The fleeting glimpse of the Suffragist impersonators presented by the Locomotives Store hints at the influence of contemporary political issues on the event, while the array of colonial-type costumes reflects British imperial power at the time. The film itself is important for understanding the complexities and power of the pageant, the spectacle of the parade and its physical presence. The parade's significance as a historical record only becomes really apparent when viewed alongside contemporary newspaper reports of the entire procession and the leisure industry of which it forms a part. The film is heavily edited, with over forty-six stock joins, camera edits and post-production edits revealed on the negative.[109] As such, rather than a true historical record of an event that lasted over an hour, it is instead a heavily constructed synthesis of the main performance components selected by the showman. The film reveals the ritual spectacle of the parade, manifest as street theatre within a particular type of procession. The majority of the acts on film are the prize winners chosen by the judges. The additional material, such as the street performers who collect the money from the audience and the elaborately dressed pageants, displays a more filmic performance style and is suited to the arena in which the film was later exhibited, namely the travelling cinematograph show.

34 M&K 189, 195–9: *Lytham Trams and the Views along the Route.*

35 *The Blackpool Times and Fylde Observer*, 29 May 1903.

36 Ibid., 31 May 1904, 'Where to Go by Land and Sea'.

37 M&K 383, 385, 387: *Southport Carnival and Trades Procession* and M&K 356–9: *Lytham Club Day Carnival.*

38 M&K 769–70, 776: *New Brighton, Egremont and Seacombe Promenade.*

39 See John Hannavy, *The English Seaside in Victorian and Edwardian Times* (Princes Risborough: Shire Publications, 2003), for a range of photographic postcards of Morecambe and Blackpool that feature the promenades, piers and amusements on offer.

40 Walton, 'The Seaside and Holiday Crowd', in Toulmin *et al.* (eds), *The Lost World of Mitchell & Kenyon*, p. 162.

41 Ibid.

42 M&K 246, 251, 254: *Panoramic View of the Morecambe Seafront.*

43 M&K 754: *Scenes by the Stone Jetty, Morecambe* (1902).

44 M&K 248–9: *Morecambe Church Lads' Brigade at Drill* and M&K 252: *Old Poulton Parish Church, Morecambe* (1901–2).

45 *Morecambe Visitor*, 3 July 1901, p. 7, for a description of the local films shown; see also Programme for Edison's Grand Coronation Pictures, Monday 22 September 1902, Great Malvern Assembly Rooms, and Programme for Edison's Animated Pictures at the Temperance Hall, Grimsby, c. 1902, for 'Holiday scenes from Blackpool, Morecambe and other popular seaside resorts'.

46 G. J. Goodrick, *Tableaux Vivants and Living Waxworks with Directions for Stage Management* (London: Dean and Son, 1895), p. 5.

47 For information on Edwardian entertainments see Simon Popple and Vanessa Toulmin, (eds), *Visual Delights: The Popular and Projected Image in the 19th Century* (Trowbridge: Flicks Books, 2000), and Vanessa Toulmin and Simon Popple (eds), *Visual Delights Two: Exhibition and Reception* (Eastleigh: John Libbey, 2005).

48 Brookes McNamara, 'The Scenography of Popular Entertainment', *The Drama Review*, Vol. 18 No. 1 (1974), pp. 16–25.

49 See Charles Musser, *Edison Motion Pictures, 1890–1900: An Annotated Filmography* (Washington, DC: Smithsonian Institution Press, 1997), for details of the variety acts filmed by the Thomas Edison Company, including Annie Oakley and Eugene Sandhow. See also Charles Musser, 'The May-Irwin Kiss: Performance and the Beginnings of Cinema', in Toulmin and Popple (eds), *Visual Delights Two*, pp. 96–116.

50 Paul Maloney, *Scotland and the Music Hall, 1850–1914* (Manchester: Manchester University Press, 2003), p. 1.

51 M&K 553: *Leeds Athletic and Cycling Club Carnival at Headingley* (1902), for the Mazondas Tub Jumping champions.

52 M&K 674–5, 677: *Algie's Circus in Carlisle* (1901), for the circus parade with the white face clowns and performing animals; M&K 201: *Blackpool Victoria Pier*, for the H. Flockton Foster's Entertainers; and M&K 651–2: *Hull Fair* (1902), for the front of Bailey's circus booth at Hull Fair.

53 *Wigan Examiner*, 29 October 1902: 'The Mazondas are stated to be champions in their particular line, and exhibit some really marvellous tub jumping, which has the additional merit of being novel.'

54 M&K 401: *Carnival Processions in Birkenhead* (1902); M&K 637: *The Crowd Entering St George's Hall Bradford*; and see M&K 251: *Panoramic View of the Morecambe Sea Front*, for the final scene of the camera crew outside the Winter Gardens in front of a poster advertising the film show.

55 Dave Russell, 'Provincial Concerts in England, 1865–1914: A Case Study of Bradford', *Journal of the Royal Musical Association*, Vol. 114 No. 1 (1989), pp. 43–55.

56 Information supplied by the Friends of the Winter Gardens Trust in Morecambe.

57 See John K. Walton and James Walvin (eds), *Leisure in Britain 1780–1939* (Manchester: Manchester University Press, 1983); Hugh Cunningham, 'The Metropolitan Fairs: A Case Study in the Social Control of Leisure', in A. P. Donajgrodzki (ed.), *Social Control in Nineteenth Century Britain* (London: Croom Helm, 1977), pp. 163–84; and Alun Howkins, 'The Taming of Whitsun: The Changing Face of a Nineteenth-Century Rural Holiday', in Yeo and Yeo (eds), *Popular Culture and Class Conflict 1590–1914: Explorations in the History of Labour and Leisure* (Brighton: The Harvester Press, 1981), pp. 187–209.

58 Walton and Poole, 'The Lancashire Wakes in the Nineteenth Century', pp. 100–24.

59 See M&K 651–2: *Hull Fair*, M&K 772: *Sedgwick's Bioscope Showfront at Pendlebury Wakes* and M&K 540–2: *Buxton Well Dressing*.

60 Cunningham, 'The Metropolitan Fairs', p. 170.

61 Vanessa Toulmin, *Pleasurelands: 200 Years of Fun at the Fair* (Hastings: The Projection Box, 2002).

62 M&K 291: *Whitsuntide Fair at Preston*.

63 M&K: *Green's Racing Bantams at Preston Whit Fair*.

64 David Braithwaite, *Savages of Kings Lynn* (Norwich: Patrick Stevens, 1975).

65 Charles A. Harkins, *We Want 'U' In: The Story of a Glasgow Institution* (Erdington: Amber Valley Print Centre, 1995); for information on the history of fairground rides see David Braithwaite, *Fairground Architecture* (London: Hugh Evelyn, 1968).

66 *Eastern Morning News*, quoted in *The World's Fair*, 19 October 1907, p. 10.

67 M&K 588–90: *Trip to Sunny Vale Gardens at Hipperholme*.

68 M&K 588: *Trip to Sunny Vale Gardens at Hipperholme*.

69 M&K 589: *Trip to Sunny Vale Gardens at Hipperholme*.

70 Walvin, *Leisure and Society, 1830–1950*, p. 125.

71 George Speight, *A History of the Circus* (London: The Tanvity Press, 1980), p. 8.

72 John Turner, *Victorian Arena: The Performers* (Formby: The Lingdales Press, 1995).

73 There are exceptions and Walter Gibbons' 1901 title *Tally Ho* is an interior shot of Hengler's horses filmed in the Hippodrome in London.

74 M&K 674–5, 677: *Algie's Circus in Carlisle*.

75 Assael, *Circus and Victorian Society*, p. 155.

76 Searle, *A New England*, p. 556.

77 These consist of 163 individual reels of film. When one includes the parades associated with May Day, an additional four titles and twelve reels can be added to this total.

78 Andrew Prescott, '"We had fine banners": Street Processions in the Mitchell & Kenyon Films', in Toulmin *et al.* (eds), *The Lost World of Mitchell & Kenyon*, pp. 125–37.

79 Ibid., p. 125.

80 Mikhail Bakhtin, *Rabelais and His World* (Bloomington: Indiana University Press, 1984, translated by Helene Iswolsky), p. 7.

5
Sport in the Edwardian Era

> We are a nation at play. Work is a nuisance, an evil necessity to be shirked and hurried over as quickly and easily as possible, in order that we may get away to the real business of life – the golf course, the bridge table, the cricket and football field or some other of the thousand amusements which occupy our minds.[1]

INTRODUCTION

Denis Brailsford, writing in *British Sport – A Social History*, believes that the actuality of the Edwardian sporting world, so shattered by the events of the First World War, is hard to rediscover. Until recently, the history of the era has been mostly constructed by nostalgic biographers and early sports commentators remembering their schooldays:

> It tends to exist in a dream-like vision perpetuated by modern film makers of constant summer sunshine, of endless blue skies, with lithe flannelled youths playing graceful cricket on immaculate turf . . . It is a picture that never had more than the most partial and superficial relationship with the Edwardian realities . . .[2]

Recent sports scholarship by Tony Mason, Richard Holt, Tony Collins and David Russell has done much to change this view of the first decade of the twentieth century, positioning sport in the social context of working-class history and political and social divide. The tradition of Saturday play developed alongside the regulation of working hours, and, coupled with the decline in the Saint Monday tradition, when workers would enjoy the pleasures which had been denied to them on the Sunday and the rise of the Saturday afternoon off, created the 'match-day'.[3] According to Tony Mason, football's development relied on this increase in leisure time: by the late 1890s, most workers could count on having Saturday afternoon off by right. Without this, professional football as a

Football was perhaps the most professional and lucrative of Edwardian sporting activities, with 20,000 spectators attending *Everton v Liverpool* (1902) at Goodison Park

spectator sport could hardly have prospered.[4] By the mid-1890s, a variety of venues for spectator sport had been built in the UK, with an emphasis on the fee-paying public, as opposed to mere participation in the sport or rational recreation. This extended to football, athletics and motorcycle events, with sports grounds such as the Springfield Park in Wigan used for horse trotting, athletics, cycling and both association and rugby football. Sport was becomingly increasingly professional, as teams and spectators were able to travel up and down the country to attend events, with a fixed number of players per side in most team sports. The rise of professionals in rugby, cricket and football and the proliferation of the sports press resulted in specialist sports magazines and regular local and national newspaper columns. 'Spectating' gave way to 'consumption', writes G. R. Searle, as the policy of charged admission to football, cricket and rugby matches crossed over into other sporting events, including horse racing, athletics and trotting.[5] The issues of amateurism versus this new professionalism dominated the late-Victorian and early Edwardian period, with drastic results for some sporting bodies such as rugby union, where the split into two codes in 1895 led to the creation of the Northern Union (NU).

Football spectatorship rose dramatically throughout the Edwardian decade and the sporting crowd was as great an attraction for the showmen as the action on the pitch. Their importance is illustrated by shots of the Goodison crowd attending *Everton v Newcastle*, filmed 13 September 1902

Sport and the Cinematograph

The Mitchell & Kenyon Collection provides an additional and previously unexamined body of material that covers a whole range of sporting activities from this period, with new and important information on the spectator or audience, the participants or sportsmen and the venues. Over 12 per cent of the films that have survived feature some type of sporting activity, including road races, cycling contests, in which participants dressed up in costumes for the parade, athletics, rowing and, of course, football. The predominance of such sporting-related titles in the collection is not just a coincidence, as sporting fixtures were a popular feature in the early film programme. Cinematograph companies often covered national sporting occasions: for example, Robert Paul filmed the Derby in 1895, while Arthur Cheetham shot footage of Blackburn Rovers, one of the earliest football clubs to be filmed by him. Films of the FA Cup finals were always shown nationally: for example, the NFA holds two Argyle Theatre posters advertising the 1901 final between Sheffield United and Tottenham at Crystal Palace, and the subsequent replay at Burnden Park in Bolton. Mitchell & Kenyon usually filmed local rather than national events. There are exceptions to this within the collection, and these will be covered in more detail later. The decision to film a local sporting event was usually determined by when the cinematograph show was actually in town, and was therefore dictated by the leisure calendar rather than the sporting calendar. Moreover, as we have seen, the cinematograph itself was, throughout the Edwardian period, beginning to develop its own place in the cycle of leisure activities. The nature of the equipment and the show meant that it could be shown throughout the year, finding a home in the existing leisure seasons, be it the fairground, the music hall, the seaside piers or Winter Gardens. Thus, audiences could see living pictures from January through to December, unlike other entertainments that were restricted by custom or type of venue. Therefore, the filming of a particular game was dictated by the presence of the showmen in the town. The sporting titles that easily fall into the category of local films are the football titles, and include both association and rugby matches.

Filming the Local Game

The predominance of both association and rugby football titles in the collection is due in part to their close links with the local community, and as such they fitted the local rationale of the Mitchell & Kenyon showmen and operators.[6] The one surviving Lancashire League cricket match between Accrington and Church in the collection displays all the characteristics of a 'local' game.[7] Lancashire League cricket games, like football, had evolved to suit the interests of the factory workers, and were hugely popular in the county.[8] As well as the weekend matches, which began at 2p.m. on Saturdays and were completed in one day, there were also mid-week fixtures. Despite the popularity of the Lancashire League, however, association football matches dominate the filmic record. With the exception of two international games, the operators filmed teams in the Mitchell & Kenyon heartland of the north and the Midlands.[9] The collection contains fifty-six association football films made between 1901 and 1907, covering thirty-two separate games, of which nearly 70 per cent can be clearly identified by the date played and the teams involved. In addition, one title of a local schools' football competition has survived from Blackburn, featuring St Stephen's Football Club and Moss Street School. Although the majority are league fixtures (often First Division), non-league teams appear,

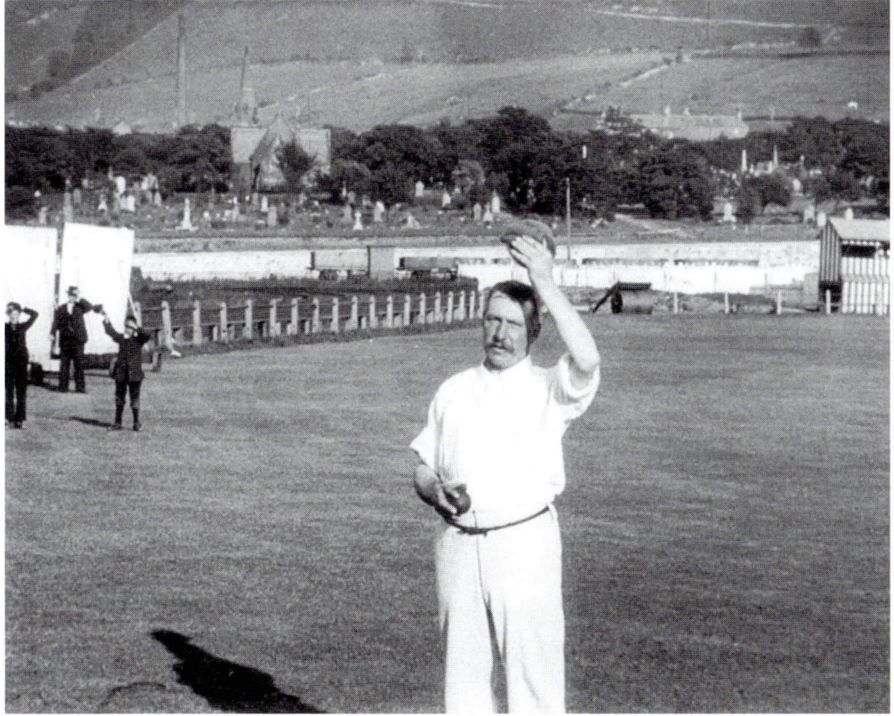

The one surviving Lancashire League cricket match in the Collection, *The Great Local Derby – Accrington v Church Cricket Match* (1902) displays all the characteristics of a 'local' game. Walter Hall is the bowler for Accrington captured on film

(Above) *Everton v Liverpool* filmed 27 September 1902 opens with Liverpool team (captained by Alex Raisbeck) filing past the cinematograph camera at Goodison Park; (above right) *Burnley v Manchester United* (1902). The inauspicious beginnings of the world's most famous football club, Manchester United, captured on film playing in the Second Division against Burnley in front of a crowd of less than 2000 spectators

such as Rotherham v. Thornhill, and at least one FA Cup tie, between Sunderland and Leicester in 1907 was filmed.[10] On one level, the dominance of football in the Mitchell & Kenyon Collection is understandable, as football was then the most commercial and thriving spectator sport in the country. Following the legislation of professionalism in 1885, the Football League was founded in 1888. By the time the Mitchell & Kenyon operators were filming across the north of England and the Midlands, First Division matches were attracting five million fans by 1905–6, with an average gate of 13,000 per game, which by 1913 had increased to 23,000 – figures that rival sporting codes such as the newly formed NU could not hope to emulate.[11]

Rugby football had long been established as a major working-class spectator sport in the north of England when filming first began. From its origins as a game for the privately educated sons of the northern industrial middle classes, by the 1880s it had become the dominant winter sport in Yorkshire and large sections of Lancashire, concentrated especially in the textile and mining towns that dominated the region.[12] When the first rugby films were made, there were no professional association sides in West Yorkshire.[13] Therefore, when the Mitchell & Kenyon showmen exhibited in these areas, rugby rather than association football featured as the preferred 'local' game in the film programme. A review of the local derby match in Hull shot by Mitchell & Kenyon reveals that it competed in the billing against other local scenes filmed in West Park:

> One of the new pictures that created great interest was the description of the match Hull v. Kingston Rovers, in which many exciting and amusing scenes are reproduced, to-night two new pictures of considerable interest will be submitted for the first time – the half-past twelve 'church parade' in West Park on Sunday last and the congregation leaving St James' Church . . .[14]

This particular game is among the earliest of the rugby titles to have survived in the national holdings, which consist of twenty films from the period 1901–3 (featuring eleven matches and thirteen different clubs) played under the auspices of the NU (from 1922, the Rugby League). If anything can be said to epitomise class division in British sport

(Above left) *Blackburn Rovers v Sheffield United* (29 March 1907) showing the Blackburn Rovers team coming out at Eywood Park; (above right) Pat McBride, the Prince amongst goalkeepers, leading Preston North End out to face Wolverhampton Wanderers in *Preston North End v Wolverhampton Wanderers* (19 November 1904)

it is rugby league. With the formation of the NU in 1895, the two codes were split according to locality and class, in which NU was identified with the working class, while rugby union attracted a middle-class base in the Midlands and the south of England. Of course, this simplistic division does not reflect the history and development of rugby in Wales, for example, but it can be applied to the material that exists in the collection, as all the films represent games from the newly formed NU. The rapid rise of working-class interest in rugby across the north of England in the early 1880s had caused deep consternation among the leadership of the Rugby Football Union (RFU), which, in 1886, introduced strict amateur regulations to head off the perceived threat of working-class

Action from the Northern Union local derby match *Hull F.C. v Hull Kingston Rovers* filmed on 26 April 1902

The preferred local game for filming in Yorkshire was Northern Union as typified in *Dewsbury v Manningham* (1901) at the Crown Flatt ground on 19 October

domination of the game. This did little to stem the tide. Over the following decade, the sport became polarised between the southern leadership of the RFU and the leading northern clubs, which drew their playing personnel and supporters from the industrial working classes and advocated allowing 'broken-time' payments to be made to players to compensate them for time taken off work to play rugby. The dispute came to a head in 1895 when, faced by an RFU determined to crush all opposition to amateurism, twenty-one of the top northern sides met at the George Hotel in Huddersfield on 29 August to form the Northern Rugby Football Union, better known as the Northern Union.

The material in the collection was filmed less than six years after the 1895 split.[15] Rugby historian Tony Collins believes that the rugby films are more important to the evolution of that particular sport than perhaps the cricket and other sporting titles in the collection, as they highlight the transition between the two codes. The early 1900s was a period in which the NU was grappling with ways to make rugby more attractive and to eliminate the endless stoppages of the union game. Initially, the NU played under RFU rules, but by 1897 it had begun to move away from its origins and institute a series of rule changes that would eventually lead to the new sport of rugby league. Unlike Mitchell & Kenyon's football and cricket films, captured at a point where, apart from minor changes, the playing rules would be recognisable today, the NU matches were filmed at the mid-point in its evolution from rugby union rules to what we now know as rugby league rules.

In 1897, the NU abolished the line-out, replacing it with a punt-out from touch, and, in order to make the scoring of tries more important than goals, the value of a goal was reduced to two points, one point less than a try. Even so, the game was still played by fifteen players per side and, as the films clearly show, a scrum was formed after every tackle, a rule that had been introduced in 1899 to move the game away from the endless ruck-

Salford v Batley (2 November 1901), Northern Union game taken at the New Barnes ground before Salford moved to the Willow in December 1901. Although the codes had split in 1895, the new Northern Union rules were still in transition at this point and the code played with fifteen players still until 1906

ing and mauling of the union game. It was not until 1906 that modern rugby league could be said to have arrived, when teams were reduced to thirteen a side and the 'play-the-ball' after a tackle was introduced.[16]

The collection, therefore, opens a window on the evolution of rugby league that was previously closed to historians. Although there was a great deal of contemporary newspaper discussion about the rule changes, we have never been able to see how they affected the way the game was played. The films show us how quickly scrums were formed after a tackle and also the speed at which the game was played, altering the common perception that the sport was essentially slow and static at that time. As such, they are a vital and unique source of information for historians of sport.

Although their importance today lies in their historical documentation, at the time, they were just one of many local events filmed as part of the exhibitors' daily shows. The events themselves were not a particular reason to watch the film programme. As with the football films, it was recognition of locality or even personality that characterised the spectators' experience in the exhibition:

> The Tweedale Edison Phono-bio-Motograph Co., are at the Victoria Hall, Halifax, this week, with their animated pictures . . . The local street scenes, of which there are many (including Saturday's football match, Halifax *v* Swinton) create roars of laughter as fellow townsmen are recognised hurrying to and from business . . .[17]

The Halifax v. Swinton title has not survived in the collection, so it is not possible to compare the action captured on film with the report on the match in the local press. However, an examination of the reviews of *Salford v. Batley* (1901), one of the more extrav-

Salford and Batley teams leaving the dressing rooms (a toilet in a local public house) – Salford played in the darker strip and were possibly playing one of their last matches on the New Barnes ground with the players arriving at the ground in a charabanc. The Batley team are guided by the showmen to work in front of the cinematograph in *Salford v Batley* (1901)

agant of all the rugby films, reveals that it was received like any other local title.[18] Edited in four sections, the action starts with the players leaving the local pub (which doubled as a dressing room), arriving at the venue on a horse-drawn tram, walking onto the field of play, interspersed with close-ups of the crowd, and footage of the match itself. When it was reviewed, the local Salford reporter was equally impressed by films of the local fire brigade:

> The Thomas Edison Company are paying a return visit . . . No event of local importance seems to escape the cinematographer operator's attention. One of the series of animated pictures shows a turnout of the Salford Fire Brigade, a performance of Little Tich and some of the exciting incidents in the match between Salford and Batley . . .[19]

The culture of spectating in late-Victorian and early Edwardian society and sporting events became entwined with viewing the game or oneself at the game at the cinematograph. The local sporting activity, in most cases football, and the local crowd are given equal prominence in the titles filmed by Mitchell & Kenyon, as these spectators would later become the paying audience. Match reports from the time echo the reviews of the cinematograph: in particular the *Bradford City v. Gainsborough Trinity* game filmed on 7 September 1903, which was Bradford's first game as an association football team:

> Each week novelties are introduced into the programme of the animated pictures at St George's Hall, and there is new interest this week in the shape of elaborate representations of the game between Bradford City and Gainsborough Trinity at Valley Parade on Saturday. So vivid and impressive are these illustrations that small boys in the audience are roused to enthusiasm and cry out 'Now City' as though they were again on the scene of play …[20]

Crowd scenes from *Blackburn Rovers v Sheffield United* (1907) where the spectators would later became the cinematograph audience

It is apparent that the true importance of the local sporting films lies in the links they reveal to the community at the time and the development of sports within this context. Very few sporting titles in the football material appear without a shot of the crowd, and on occasion this is the only surviving section of the film.[21] The real stars are not the players but the spectators who would ultimately become the paying audience. The cinematograph exhibition, with its views of local towns, friends and incidents, became an extension of both

Selection of shots from *Bradford City v Gainsborough Trinity* (5 September 1903) showing the celebrations to mark the first game played by the former Northern Union club Manningham who switched codes and reformed as Bradford City Football Club

One of the most amazing crowd sequences in the Collection, the Sheffield United fans captured at Bramall Lane watching Sheffield United win 1-0 in *Sheffield United v Bury* (1901)

the sporting and local community. As Richard Holt writes: 'By supporting a club and assembling with thousands of others like himself, a man could assert a kind of membership of the city, the heart of which was physically and emotionally his for the afternoon'.[22]

This theme of community identity is illustrated by J. B. Priestley when he wrote that

> football turned you into a member of a new community, all brothers together for an hour and a half . . . you had escaped with most of your mates and your neighbours, with half the town, and there you were, cheering together, thumping one another on the shoulders.[23]

By turning the camera on the crowd, the Edwardian football community then became the cinematograph community, as both the showmen and the sporting bodies relied on the economic participation of the crowd as both paying customers or viewers and spectators. It was this symbiotic relationship between the films and the fans that gave the 'spectators a further sense of their emotional ownership of professional football', an aspect highlighted by David Russell when he writes, 'if this is what is meant by football being the "people's game", then the local film has a part in making it such'.[24]

National Sporting Subjects

During the summer months when the football season had finished, sporting events such as road races, water polo, trotting and fancy-dress cycle contests filled the showmen's advertising boards.[25] Unlike the local football matches, many of the sports filmed formed part of the showmen's main touring programme and could be classed as events of national interest, or at least events that could attract an audience outside their locality. Three particular sporting events in the collection reflect this development: horse racing, athletics meetings and cycle racing.

Horse racing was one of the first sporting events filmed by the cinematograph, and the film of King Edward VII's horse Ambush was continuing in the tradition of Robert Paul's 1895 title, *The Derby*. The film itself consists of two titles shot in January 1902 by Louis De Clercq, a cameraman working for A. D. Thomas's show in Ireland. Ambush was one of several horses owned by Edward VII, which achieved glory when he was the Prince of Wales.[26] Ambush won the Grand National steeplechase on 30 March 1900, followed by Diamond Jubilee's triumph at the Derby in June that year. The film appears to be an attempt to produce a behind-the-scenes look at the King's racehorse in time for its appearance at the 1902 Grand National, where he was a strong favourite.[27] The first

King Edward's horse Ambush seen in *Ambush II at Eyrefield Lodge, Curragh* (15 January 1902), was a national favourite to win the Grand National but due to injury was withdrawn from the race

attempt at filming on 15 January 1902 failed when Ambush decided to take an afternoon nap in his stables. Instead, De Clerq and his fellow operators filmed other horses and apparently took part in and shot a mock reconstruction of Ambush's famous Grand National win, by jumping over some of the hedge fences in the stable grounds! Returning on 21 January, they took a number of shots of Ambush with his jockey and trainer cantering around the stable grounds.[28] Ironically, it appears that this title was never exhibited and no record of any screenings in Britain have been found. This could be due to two factors: first, Ambush was withdrawn from the Grand National a week before the race after suffering a fracture (splitting a pastern); second, A. D. Thomas, the owner of the Thomas-Edison company filming in Ireland, sold his Irish holdings and returned to England, soon to face bankruptcy hearings. Another aspect to consider is that the notes in De Clercq's diary reveal that Thomas operated his own film crew and used Mitchell & Kenyon to develop and print the films, thereby leaving the negatives in their possession. Mitchell & Kenyon may have chosen not to make further prints of a title that was not in the public eye and one whose ownership was in dispute. Nethertheless, the title itself is very important, as it is now the earliest surviving example of a Grand National film. More significantly, it shows how the company and its associated showmen made the transition from filming purely local sporting events to documenting those of national significance, which then became a staple of the touring exhibition programme.

Amateur v. Professional

As previously stated, one of the underlying issues that dominated late-Victorian and early Edwardian sport was the conflict between the gentleman amateur and the working professional. The ideal of fair play was part of the ideology of amateurism that the Victorian sporting elite held dear and which they upheld against rank professionalism and commercialisation. Neil Wigglesworth has argued that 'The north–south sporting split reflected a social, cultural and economic apartheid apparent elsewhere in society, which became even more pronounced over the turn of the century.'[29] While this reached a head with the splitting of the rugby codes, it also existed in cricket and, increasingly, in athletics. Although by the early Edwardian period, the majority of cricket clubs had professional players on their books, it was not until 1902, for example, that Lancashire Cricket Club abolished the practice of amateurs and professionals entering the field of play from separate entrances.[30]

The contrast between the semi-professional road races or pedestrian events and the genteel atmosphere of the athletics meetings also provides a sharp contrast in the collection.[31] Although this split as perceived by Wigglesworth existed in all types of sporting activities, the non-football events shot by Mitchell & Kenyon in the north of England were primarily amateur occasions. Such events were originally rooted in professionalism, but by the start of the Edwardian era had become increasingly defined by rigid amateur codes of practice.

Athletics

Unlike the majority of sporting events that moved into an increasingly professional arena, athletics actually went in the opposite direction. The founding of the Amateur Athletics Association (AAA) in 1880, with the ban on competing for money or against professionals a part of its original constitution, typified the attitude of late-Victorian sporting bodies to professionalism in sport.[32] Athletics was dominated by the Oxbridge

National sporting events were a popular theme for the cinematograph and *AAA Championships at Fartown, Huddersfield* (6 July 1901), features amongst others William Coe, the winner of the shot put competition in mid-throw

and public school culture, where one had to be an officer and a gentleman to belong to many of the London-based clubs, such as the South London Harriers and Blackheath Harriers.[33] Although the ban on working-class or artisan members was lifted by the AAA, by the end of the nineteenth century, participation in this particular sporting arena was for amateurs only.[34] Athletics as an event for spectators reached its pinnacle in the Edwardian era, when the 1908 Olympic Games were held in London. Before then, athletics meetings were a popular subject in the film canon and three meetings have survived in the collection, as well as children's sports days at Blackburn and a road race from Manchester to Blackpool.[35] The film of one of these meetings, a match between Cambridge University and the London Athletic Club (LAC) held on Saturday 14 March 1903, requires further study. The meeting at Birmingham in 1902 and the AAA Championship at Huddersfield in 1901 feature prominent world champion athletes posing for the camera, with the later title being of national significance.[36] The AAA championship meeting was the premier athletics event of the year in England, and from its inception in 1880 was held at various venues around the country until Stamford Bridge, London, became its permanent home from 1909, before another move to White City, London, in 1932. The AAA Championships at Huddersfield Cricket & Athletic Club grounds on Saturday 6 July 1901 was filmed by Mitchell & Kenyon in association with A. D. Thomas to form part of his touring programme. This film was subsequently shown the following week in Manchester, where it featured along with scenes from the local grammar school sports day.[37]

The international aspect of the meeting is reflected in the vignettes of the champions posing for the camera. The two short titles comprise mostly shots of some of the winners

(Above) Arthur Duffey (USA), winner of the 100-yards posing for the cinematograph. Duffey won this title for four consecutive years, 1900–3, and was the world's premier sprinter; (above right) the 120-yards Hurdles winner Alvin Kraenzlein (USA) posing after winning the event in a Pennsylvania University sweatshirt. He had previously won four gold medals at the 1900 Paris Olympic Games – in the 60-metres, 110-metres Hurdles, 200-metres Hurdles & Long Jump

of the individual events, including Arthur Duffey (USA), the world's premier sprinter and winner of the 100 yards. Duffey retained this title for four consecutive years 1900–3 and in 1902 ran 100 yards in 9.6 seconds, which remained the world record for twenty-four years. The dominance of the American athletes at the event is reflected in the filmic record and, although appearing as amateurs, the level of support and training regimes that underpinned their success was in stark contrast to the British athletes they competed against. Their move towards international dominance in track and field was personified by another athlete caught on film, the Olympic champion Alvin Kraenzlein. The holder of four gold medals at the 1900 Paris Olympic Games in the 60 metres, 110 metres hurdles, 200 metres hurdles and long jump, Kraenzlein was the winner of the 120 yards at this event. Another American Olympic champion captured by the cinematograph was Irving Baxter. Baxter was placed equal first in the pole vault at the AAA Championships but won the gold medal for the pole vault and high jump at the Paris Olympic Games. He also won the high jump and finished third in the 120 yards hurdles at the same meeting.[38] Out of the ten athletes featured in the Huddersfield film, four are American, two are Irish and four are English. Of the English athletes, only John Cleave was an overall winner of his event as W. Hodgson finished joint first with Irving Baxter.[39] For the showmen to have filmed these athletes for a national audience reveals that, regardless of their nationality, these sporting figures were prominent enough to be recognised by a cinematograph audience in 1901.

The Birmingham meeting that survives in the collection dates from July 1902. This was filmed by Mitchell & Kenyon for a local exhibition at the Curzon Hall in Birmingham. The Birmingham meeting took place a week after the AAA event at Stamford Bridge and again features Arthur Duffey and his fellow American Sam Jones, the 1902 AAA high jump champion. This six-section film covers all aspects of the meeting, including the 880 yards handicap race, with shots of the start, first lap and finish, and also the start and finish of the 100 yards won by Duffey. Unlike the Huddersfield title, where the attention of the cinematograph is focused on the athletes, this series of films is more local in nature, incorporating both crowd scenes and on-screen adverts for other film shows. Interestingly, the dominance of the American athletes is again reflected by the camera, as only Duffey

(Above left) Irving Baxter (USA) Pole vaulting, he placed equal 1st. He had won the Pole Vault & High Jump at the 1900 Paris Olympic Games. He also won the High Jump and finished 3rd in the 120-yards Hurdles at this meeting; (above right) First three in Hammer posing for camera: Ernest May (Oxford University), on left, 2nd place, a very sheepish looking Henry Leeke (Cambridge University) in centre, 3rd place, and Tom Kiely (Ireland), right, the winner

and fellow American Samuel Symington Jones are filmed as carefully posed vignettes. The film is also advertised as *Champion Athletes at Birmingham* (1902), with the emphasis placed on the American stars rather than the actual meeting.[40]

Cycling

Cycling films, both as a recreational pastime and a sporting occasion, are prevalent in the collection, either as fancy-dress cycle parades in Manchester, race meetings or scenes of particular club meetings. The films are divided between sport and recreation and include, for example, *Manchester and Salford Harriers' Cyclists' Procession* (1901), which took place at Broughton Rangers football ground.[41] Fancy-dress cycling was popular throughout the north of England at this time and events took place in Southport, Bradford and Sheffield. Reputedly founded in Manchester by Arthur R. Albert in 1894, the Fancy-Dress Cyclists' Parade was a charitable procession, in which 'the object is to get at the great public by means of humorous and picturesque outdoor display and then gather from the amused crowds contributions for the benefit of some noble charity'.[42] Although the films show the importance of the local cycling clubs and their rise to prominence in early Edwardian Manchester, the event is more carnivalesque than sporting or competitive, revealing a charity procession of members of the local club dressed in a range of fancy-dress costumes.[43] This link between cycling clubs and sporting events as a recreational and commercial activity was present at the sport's inception. The history of cycling as a sporting activity is linked to that of entertainment, pedestrianism and organised athletic activities, as Andrew Ritchie reveals:

> Some of the early bicycle racing grew in a social and class context similar to that of the older sport of pedestrianism, in which races were either held on an enclosed track or place to place on the open road . . . but in other respects, indoor bicycle competition was closer to circus or music-hall entertainment . . .[44]

Perhaps the most important cycling titles in sporting terms are those of the Manchester Wheelers' annual race meet, filmed at the Manchester Athletic Ground, Fallow-

Fancy Dress Cycling events were popular throughout the North of England at this time and include *Manchester and Salford Harriers' Cyclists Procession* (1901), which took place at Broughton Rangers Football Ground

field, on Saturday 13 July 1901. The nature of the event reveals the importance of the spectator and the development of cycling as a sporting and recreational activity in the late-Victorian era. The Manchester Wheelers started life as the Manchester Athletic Bicycle Club on 7 July 1883, changing their name to the Manchester Wheelers in 1890. Although one of the later various bicycle clubs in the Manchester region, by the early 1900s they were one of the most distinguished and prominent in the region, with their own club house and annual race meet. Eight films remain of the 1901 meeting and feature three

Race for the Muratti Cup at Manchester Wheelers Annual Race Meet filmed at the Manchester Athletic Ground, Fallowfield on Saturday 13 July 1901

The Manchester Wheelers Annual Race Meet (1901) also included a series of novelty events including this sequence where the winner of the '2 Miles Motor Match' is captured

distinct events in the race programme: the '2 Miles Motor Match', the Volunteers' Cyclists' Race and the Muratti Cup. The first sections of *Manchester Wheelers' Annual Race Meet* (1901) captures two laps of the Two Miles Motor Race and features the display of trophies, including the Muratti Cup, while *Race for the Muratti Cup at Manchester Wheelers' Annual Race Meet* (1901) includes highlights of the race.[45]

By the early 1900s, the Manchester Wheelers' Club was a purely amateur organisation and part of the National Cyclists' Union. The elements of promotion and spectatorship allied to a competitive amateur contest produced an event that was sporting in nature yet linked to earlier forms of leisure activities, with the spectator an economic contributor to the event. The match programme for the day reveals a series of events, in which competitive cycling was programmed alongside more recreational scenes, such as the Volunteer Cyclists' Race, which, as we have seen, is also featured in *Manchester Wheelers' Annual Race Meet*. The entertainment aspect was described in the cycling column of the *Manchester Evening News*: 'This year the novelty will consist of riding and firing competitions between teams from the various cyclists' sections of the six Volunteer Battalions of the Manchester Regiment . . .'.[46]

The culmination of the meeting was the Muratti Cup, which was established in 1899 when Messrs D. B. Muratti and Sons offered the first Muratti Cup for an amateur invitation race. This was contested on 8 July at the Fallowfield track, where a field of twenty-three riders competed in the ten-mile event, organised by the Manchester Wheelers.[47] In 1901, over 18,000 spectators witnessed the contest, which was won by Roland Janson of the London Polytechnic Cycling Club. The event was subsequently shown by A. D. Thomas at the St James' Hall, with prolific advertisements in both the Manchester and Lancashire newspapers. Additionally, Thomas advertised in the match programme that

The various cyclists pose with Thomas-Edison's exhibitors during *The Manchester Wheelers Annual Race Meet* (1901)

> Edison's operators will take animated photographs of these Sports and the Spectators and reproduce same at St James Hall . . . Do not miss seeing your own portraits in Animated Photography on the Screen – the Sight of a Lifetime . . .[48]

The decision of the showmen both to sponsor this event through advertisement in the match programme, and subsequently to exhibit the films at the St James' Hall is twofold. First, a crowd of 18,000 spectators attended the race meeting, which was larger than the average sporting crowds in Manchester, greater even than football and on a par with a near-capacity attendance for cricket at Old Trafford.[49] Second, cycling as a leisure and sporting pursuit was growing in popularity as the cost of equipment dropped considerably and was becoming

18,000 spectators witnessed the Muriatti Cup race during *The Manchester Wheelers Annual Race Meet*, won by Roland Janson of the London Polytechnic Cycling Club

within the means of the average working man as a form of transport. The film, therefore, had a cross-over appeal, in that it worked as both a 'local', because of the footage of the spectators, and had a subject matter that would attract keen interest outside its locality. As with the athletics meeting in Birmingham, the cycling events had both a local and national appeal. Both the sports event and the filming of the spectators were given equal prominence in the local advertisement. The showman produced two products from one event: a crowd shot for the locals and sporting title that could be exhibited to a wider audience.

This brief overview of some of the sporting titles in the collection has attempted to demonstrate how this new filmic record reveals the link between early sporting activities and leisure, and provides new evidence for the importance of sport in the local community. The final set of films does not fall into any of these categories and appears very modern in form and function. It is neither the day's action nor the spectators who make up the content of the films; instead they must be one of the earliest instances of the cinematograph or moving image functioning as an unofficial 'third umpire'.

Case Study: The Mold Bowling Controversy

Arthur Mold Bowling to A. N. Hornby – or *The Mold Cricket Controversy* (1901) are perhaps the most significant films in the sporting collection.[50] Filmed during a county championship match between Lancashire and Somerset on 11 July 1901 at Old Trafford, they feature two of the greatest cricket personalities of their day – Arthur Mold (1863–1921), of Lancashire and England (formerly of Northampton), and Albert Neilson Hornby (1847–1925), President of Lancashire Cricket Club.

The match lasted two days, and Lancashire eventually won by ten wickets. The controversy of the title referred to the actions taken by the Australian umpire, James Phillips,

Arthur Mold Bowling to A. N. Hornby (1901) at Old Trafford cricket ground. Thomas-Edison filmed Mold during the lunch break to ensure maximum publicity for his exhibition at the St James' Hall in Manchester

The Australian umpire, James Phillips, the villain of the piece, who accused Mold of 'throwing' rather than bowling the ball, captured in *Arthur Mold Bowling to A. N. Hornby* (1901)

on the first day of the proceedings, when he no-balled Arthur Mold, the Lancashire fast bowler, fifteen times in ten overs (including five times in one over) for his unorthodox bowling action.[51] This was in contravention of Rule 48 or, in laymen's terms, Mold was being accused of 'throwing' rather than bowling the ball.[52] This accusation caused much comment in the local press. Mold, a native of Northampton, had played for Lancashire since 1889 and was one of the most destructive fast bowlers of his time.[53] *The Manchester Evening News* issue on the evening of the game reflects that the gate increase in the afternoon was due in no small part to the spectators wishing to view the controversy unfolding rather than the resulting cricket match.[54]

All the elements of today's modern fan-based participations and phone-ins are captured in the public outrage that followed the controversy at Old Trafford. *The Manchester Evening News* invited its readers to make their own judgment on Phillips's conduct and wrote to leading umpires active in the game for their comments on Mold's bowling.[55] A. D. Thomas, the showman exhibiting at the St James Hall in Manchester, immediately sent down his camera crew to Old Trafford for the second day of play in order to involve the audience directly in the argument:

> MOLD CINEMATOGRAPHED – During the luncheon interval Edison's representative took a number of moving pictures of Mold in the act of bowling to A. N. Hornby on the practice ground. The pictures, which will be presented at the St James's Hall tomorrow evening, were taken from three of four points of view at short range and an opportunity will thus be afforded to those who have not seen him play of judging for themselves the fairness or unfairness of his delivery.[56]

An interested spectator smiles at the camera during the filming of *Arthur Mold Bowling to A. N. Hornby (1901)*, with Mold and Hornby caught on camera

The review that subsequently appeared in *The Manchester Evening News* credits the showman with confirming the opinion 'that his delivery is absolutely fair. The arm comes round with a perfect swing and there is absolutely no suspicion of throwing.' The reporter also informs us that the famous bowler himself, along with other equally well-known cricketers, attended the exhibition.[57] In later advertisements, A. D. Thomas claims to have resolved the issue when he encourages the public 'to see the controversy settled by Edison'.[58]

The decision to penalise Mold for the breaking of Rule 48 and the national interest it created is due in part to the standing of cricket within the public rationale. If football was the people's game, cricket belonged to the Empire, and, as Richard Holt reveals:

> Cricket was the English national sport in the sense that it was followed by the middle and working classes, both in the north and the south . . . although was often more difficult for working class boys . . . it was still keenly followed as a spectator sport . . .[59]

Gideon Haigh, writing in 'The Great Taboo', states that by the early 1890s, throwing was disturbingly pervasive in English cricket.[60] Mold was one of the perpetual serial offenders in this respect, and Phillips's actions were welcomed in some quarters. Mold had been previously no-balled by James Phillips in 1900 at Trent Bridge, and at a meeting of county captains held later that year, his delivery was condemned by eleven votes to one. Mold was not only breaking the rules of the game but was being accused of ungentlemanly conduct unbecoming of a true Englishman. As Keith Sandiford writes: 'In a fiercely nationalistic era Englishmen regarded cricket, an exclusively English creation unsullied by outside influences, as proof of their cultural supremacy.'[61]

The spectators watch Lancashire play Somerset, and the filming of *Arthur Mold Bowling to A. N. Hornby (*1901). The crowd grew in the afternoon, in no small part to spectators wishing to view the controversy unfolding – rather than the on-going cricket match

Interestingly, in the survey conducted by the local newspaper, some umpires agreed with Phillips. Perhaps the decision by Arthur 'Monkey' Hornby to take part in the filming of Mold's controversial bowling action was designed to ensure that the good name of Lancashire cricket remained untainted. Hornby's standing in the game both at the county and national level was impeccable. He was an all-round sportsman in the true Corinthian tradition and excelled at rugby and cricket, captaining England in both sports. Hornby also played for Blackburn Rovers and in his later years was President of the Lancashire Football Association. He captained England in the disastrous one-off cricket match against Australia in 1882 that led to the start of the Ashes, but despite this result was known for the brilliancy of his captaincy. After playing for Lancashire Cricket Club for thirty-three years (twenty years as captain), where he was their leading scorer for many seasons, he became President of the club, a position he held at the time of the Mold controversy.[62] The films themselves consist of reconstructions of Mold's bowling action and show him delivering to Hornby in the nets. The umpires and other officials associated with the match also feature, as shots are taken from various angles of Mold's bowling action.

This match was one of the last that Mold played for Lancashire, and he left the club at the end of the 1901 season. *Arthur Mold Bowling to A.N. Hornby* became part of A. D. Thomas's touring programme and was shown at venues throughout the country, including Burnley, Blackburn, Halifax and Bristol, among others.[63] In Northampton, the partisan nature of the audience was increased due to the 'local' nature of the film:

> Mold bowling to A. N. Hornby was a very popular picture, for Mold, as everyone knows, is a Northamptonshire man, and played for his native county before he qualified for Lancashire, while Mr Hornby has Northamptonshire connections . . .[64]

The controversy remained topical for many months after the event and was still part of Thomas's show in Birmingham on 22 October, where the reviewer noted, 'in view of the recent controversy, an exhibition of Mold's bowling is viewed with keen interest'.[65] Of the sporting events that have survived in the collection, the Mold titles appear to have been shown on numerous occasions, remaining a feature of the film programme for

Snapshots of *Arthur Mold Bowling to A. N. Hornby* (1901) including, Arthur Mold, the Lancashire bowler at the centre of the controversy – the Lancashire President and former England caption, Albert Neilson Hornby, comes out of retirement to prove that Mold's bowling action was within the rules of the game

a year after the event. The role of the media and the cinematograph in maintaining this controversy needs further exploration. It is apparent, however, that the filmic representation of this controversy is perhaps the earliest example of the cinematograph actively contributing and perhaps prolonging a sporting debate through its capacity to produce an instant replay of the incident. In terms of its historical importance, *Arthur Mold Bowling to A. N. Hornby*, provides us with clear evidence that, in this instance, the umpire was decidedly correct in his decision.

Conclusion

Both sporting and other leisure activities relied on the increased leisure time available to spectators and participants from the late-Victorian period onwards. Other factors enabled the professional and amateur arenas to flourish. These include increased mobility in transportation made available through cheap urban electrified tramway systems, the rise of public parks in urban centres for recreational activities, and ultimately a growth in urban populations, which created an audience for the leisure industry. The cinematograph developed and expanded within large urban centres, where the entertainment industry flourished and a range of subjects could be filmed. Street scenes, urban landscapes, city parks and city centres were all captured by the cameras of Mitchell & Kenyon, illustrating the great industrial urban centres that flourished during the Edwardian era.

Notes

1 Arthur Shadwell, 1907, cited in G. R. Searle, *A New England: Peace and War 1886–1918* (Oxford: Oxford University Press, 2004), p. 529.

2 Denis Brailsford, *British Sport – A Social History* (Cambridge: The Lutterworth Press), p. 103. For an overview of the role of sport in British Victorian and Edwardian society see

Derek Birley, *Sport and the Making of Britain* (Manchester: Manchester University Press, 1993), and Derek Birley, *Land of Hope and Glory: Sport and British Society, 1887–1910* (Manchester: Manchester University Press, 1995).

3 Douglas Reid, 'The Decline of St Monday, 1766–1776', *Past & Present*, No. 71 (1976), pp. 76–101.

4 Tony Mason, *Association Football and English Society, 1863–1915* (Brighton: The Harvester Press, 1983).

5 Searle, *A New England*.

6 Vanessa Toulmin, '"Local Films for Local People": Travelling Showmen and the Commissioning of Local Film in Great Britain, 1900–1902', *Film History*, Vol. 11 (2002), pp. 19–33.

7 For further details see M&K 319–21: *The Great Local Derby, Accrington v. Church Cricket Match* (1902), featuring a Lancashire League match filmed on 5 July 1902, with Walter Hall, Accrington's professional bowler, bowling Church out for forty-six runs.

8 Richard Holt, *Sport and the British: A Modern History* (Oxford: Oxford University Press, 1989).

9 These being M&K 136–8: *England v. Ireland at Manchester* (1905) and M&K 153–4: *Wales v. Ireland at Wrexham* (1906). For information on the latter see Dave Berry, 'Mitchell & Kenyon in Wales', in Vanessa Toulmin, Simon Popple and Patrick Russell (eds), *The Lost World of Mitchell & Kenyon: Edwardian Britain on Film* (London: BFI, 2004): pp. 103–12.

10 For further detail on the football films see David Russell, 'The Football Films', in Toulmin *et al.* (eds), *The Lost World of Mitchell & Kenyon*, pp. 169–80.

11 Wray Vamplew, *Pay up and Play the Game: Professional Sport in Britain* (Cambridge: Cambridge University Press, 1988), p. 63.

12 Tony Collins, *Rugby's Great Split: Class, Culture and the Origins of Rugby League Football* (London: Frank Cass, 1998).

13 David Russell, '"Sporadic and Curious": The Emergence of Rugby and Soccer Zones in Yorkshire and Lancashire, c. 1860–1914', *The International Journal of the History of Sport*, Vol. 5 No. 2 (1988), pp. 185–205.

14 *Hull Daily Mail*, 29 April 1902. The film mentioned is M&K 660: *Hull FC v. Hull Kingston Rovers* (1902). This was actually an 'ordinary' or friendly game played at the end of the season, which Hull won by fourteen points to six. See *Hull Daily Mail*, 28 April 1902, p. 3, for a report of the match.

15 The teams featured in the rugby titles are Batley, Dewsbury, Hull, Hull Kingston Rovers, Leeds, Oldham, Salford, St Helens, Swinton, Warrington, Wigan, as well as teams that no longer exist, such as Manningham and Runcorn.

16 Programme notes from 13 September 2005, 'The Rugby League Films in the Mitchell & Kenyon Collection', National Museum of Photography, Film and Television, Bradford.

17 *The Showman*, 31 January 1901, p. 311.

18 M&K 159, 158 141, 162: *Salford v. Batley*.

19 *Salford City Reporter*, December 1901, quoted in Tony Flynn, *The History of Salford Cinemas* (Manchester: Neil Richardson, 1987), pp. 28–9.

20 *Bradford Daily Argus*, 8 September 1903, p. 4.

21 For instance M&K 790: *Crowds Leaving Sports Event* (c. 1902) is just a shot of the crowd, while M&K 120, 122–3, *Notts County v. Middlesbrough* (1902), devotes two complete sections of the film to panning shots of the spectators.

22 Richard Holt, 'Football and the Urban Way of Life', in J. A. Mangan (ed.), *Pleasure, Profit, Proselytism: British Culture and Sport at Home and Abroad, 1700–1914* (London: Frank Cass, 1988), pp. 67–85 (79).

23 J. B. Priestley, *The Good Companions* (London: Heinemann, 1929), p. 4.

24 Russell, 'The Football Films', in Toulmin *et al.* (eds), *The Lost World of Mitchell & Kenyon*, p. 178.

25 Trotting was a particularly popular sport in Wigan, but the only trotting title in the collection is M&K 369–71: *Trotting Match at Springfield Park Wigan* (1904).

26 For further information on the Irish films in the collection see Robert Monks, 'The Irish Films in the Mitchell & Kenyon Collection', in Toulmin *et al.* (eds), *The Lost World of Mitchell & Kenyon*, pp. 93–102. For details of the film see M&K 5, 795: *Ambush II at Eyrefield Lodge, Curragh* (1902).

27 Edward Spencer, *The King's Racehorses: A History of the Connection of His Majesty King Edward VII with the National Sport* (London: John Long, 1902), pp. 162–70, for details of Ambush up to 1902. Ambush competed in both the 1903 and 1904 Grand National steeplechase but on both occasions failed to complete the course.

28 These films survive as M&K 5, 795: *Ambush II at Eyrefield Lodge, Curragh.*

29 Neil Wigglesworth, *The Evolution of English Sport* (London: Frank Cass, 1996), p. 98.

30 Information supplied by Lancashire County Cricket Club and see <www.lccc.co.uk> for a brief history of the club.

31 For more information on pedestrianism see Birley, *Sport and the Making of Britain*, pp. 278–82.

32 See Jeremy Crump, 'Athletics', in Tony Mason (ed.), *Sport in Britain: A Social History* (Cambridge: Cambridge University Press, 1989), pp. 44–77.

33 For the role of the public school movement in shaping the history of athletics see J. A. Mangan, *Athleticism in the Victorian and Edwardian Public School: The Emergence and Consolidation of an Education Ideology*, new revised edn. London: Frank Cass, 2000).

34 Peter Lovesey, *The Official Centenary History of the Amateur Athletic Association* (London: Guinness Superlatives, 1979).

35 M&K 388, 752: *Manchester to Blackpool Road Race* (1903).

36 M&K 510–11, 513, 515–16: *The Champion Athletes at Birmingham* (1902); M&K 506: *Cambridge University Sports Day* (1903); and M&K 591–2: *AAA Championships at Fartown, Huddersfield* (1901).

37 *Manchester Evening News*, 9 July 1901, p. 1, advert, including 'Scenes from the Grammar School Sports, and the International Sports, at Huddersfield, Saturday Last'.

38 Other prominent athletes who appear in these films include William Coe, Peter O'Connor and Tom Kiely. Kiely won the All-Round title at the 1904 St Louis Olympic Games, an event that predated the decathlon.

39 I am indebted to Kevin Kelly, athletics historian and member of Herne Hill Harriers, for identifying all the athletes in these titles and for supplying additional information on the events.

40 The films were shown locally at the Curzon Hall. See *Birmingham Daily Mail*, 15 July 1902, for a review of the films exhibited. Although listed alongside other local attractions, they are advertised as *Champion Athletes at Birmingham*; however, a review that occurs later in the

same paper only refers to them as animated pictures of the Birmingham Athletic Sports Club on Sunday.

41 M&K 424, 428–9: *Manchester and Salford Harriers' Cyclists' Procession* (1901).

42 See the *Manchester Programme*, 17 September 1904, for details of the history of the Fancy-Dress Cyclists' Parade.

43 Fancy-dress cycling events were popular throughout the north of England at this time, and events took place in Southport, Bradford and Sheffield. Reputedly founded in Manchester by Arthur R. Albert in 1894, the Fancy-Dress Cyclists' Parade was a charitable procession.

44 Andrew Ritchie, 'The Origins of Bicycle Racing in England: Technology, Entertainment, Sponsorship and Advertising in the Early History of Sport', *Journal of Sport History*, Vol. 26 No. 3 (Autumn 1999), pp. 489–520 (490).

45 For the full series of the films of the Manchester Wheelers' race meet see M&K 425–7: *Race for the Muratti Cup at Manchester Wheelers' Annual Race Meet* and M&K 744–746, 786, 801: *Manchester Wheelers' Annual Race Meet.*

46 *Manchester Evening News*, 4 July 1901, p. 2.

47 T. M. Barlow and Jack Fletcher, *A History of the Manchester Wheelers' Club, 1883–1983* (privately published in Manchester, 1983).

48 Programme for the 1901 Manchester Wheelers' race meet, Saturday 13 July 1901, p. 27. I am indebted to Ian Wilkinson, Secretary of the Manchester Wheelers' Club, for supplying a copy of this programme and all additional information on the Wheelers.

49 For details of cricket crowds in the late-Victorian era see Keith Sandiford, 'English Crowds during the Victorian Era', *Journal of Sports History*, Vol. 9 No. 5 (1982), pp. 5–22, in which he claims that first-class counties were playing cricket before crowds of between 8,000 and 24,000 per day. Richard Holt, in *Sport and the British*, p. 287, believes that crowds had fallen from an average of 15,000 in the 1890s to less than 10,000 between 1906 and 1910.

50 M&K 489–93: *Arthur Mold bowling to A.N. Hornby* – or *The Mold Cricket Controversy.*

51 See *Manchester Evening News*, 11 July 1901, for a full report of the match.

52 Rule 48: 'If either umpire be not satisfied of the absolute fairness of the delivery of any ball he shall call "no ball".'

53 For an overview of Arthur Mold's career at the time see *The Wisden Almanack*, Bowler of the Year, 1892 – Arthur Mold. Information taken from <content.cricinfo.com/ci/content/player/17059.html>, accessed 26 September 2005.

54 *The Manchester Evening News*, 11 July 1901, p. 5.

55 Ibid., 17 July 1901, p. 1.

56 Ibid., 12 July 1901, p. 1.

57 Ibid., 16 July 1901.

58 *Blackburn Times*, 17 August 1901, p. 1.

59 Holt, *Sport and the British*, p. 175.

60 See Gideon Haigh, 'The Great Taboo', first published in the July 2004 issue of *The Wisden Cricketer* and accessed on <content-usa.cricinfo.com/wcm/content/story/138634.html> on 23 February 2005.

61 Keith A. P. Sandiford, 'England', in Brian Stoddart and Keith A. P. Sandiford (eds), *The Imperial Game: Cricket, Culture and Society* (Manchester: Manchester University Press, 1998), pp. 9–33 (9). See also Keith A. P. Sandiford, *Cricket and the Victorians* (Aldershot: Scolar Press, 1994).

62 For further details on A. N. Hornby see Eric Midwinter, 'Hornby, Albert Neilson (1847–1925)', *Oxford Dictionary of National Biography* (Oxford: Oxford University Press, 2004) (<oxforddnb.com/view/article/50295>, accessed 19 September 2005).

63 For details of these showings see *Burnley Express*, 27 July 1901, p. 1, and *Blackburn Times*, 17 August 1901. For the Halifax showing see *The Showman*, 13 September 1901, p. 10, and *Bristol Times and Mirror*, 1 October 1901, p. 1. Examples of A. D. Thomas's programmes in the NFA also reveal that the films were shown in Grimsby and were part of the film programme until 1902.

64 *Northampton Mercury*, 17 September 1901, p. 1.

65 *Birmingham Daily Mail*, 22 October 1901.

6
The Edwardian City

> A moment of transformation had arrived. It hushed and gilded the moors above and then, just when Mr Oakroyd's tram reached the centre of the town, passing onto one side the Central Free Library and on the other hand the Universal Sixpenny Bazaar, it touched Bruddersford. All the spaces of the town were filled with smoky gold. Holmes and Hadley's emporium, the Midland Railway Station, the Wool Exchange, Barclay's Bank, the Imperial Music Hall, all shone like palaces. Smithson Square was like some quivering Western sea, and the Right Honourable Ebenezer Smithson himself, his marble scroll now a map of the Indies, was conjured into an Elizabethan admiral.[1]

Introduction

J. B. Priestley's depiction of the fictional town of Bruddersford published in 1929 was looking back to an idealised age of local community and townships. However, this description does capture the importance of civic space, urban expansion and the transformation of town centres into commercial and recreational spaces that had occurred by the end of the century. Important scholarship by Simon Gunn and other historians has demonstrated how the use of social space is an important factor for understanding the changes from the more rowdy street culture of the previous century to the civilising rational recreational model of the mid-nineteenth century.[2] The image of the industrial city at the start of the Victorian era was markedly different by the end of the century.[3] The last years of the nineteenth century brought the dawning of a new age and a different attitude towards life. It was an era when social differences dissipated, and the mores, customs and expectations of the middle-class citizenry became apparent in national and local government. The wonders of the modern world, accelerated by technology and progress in the 1880s and 1890s, increased the rewards of modern industrialisation and mass-produced abundance. The Edwardian era was a period of tremendous social and political change, an age of innovative scientific and technological advances, where the sound

of progress was heard in the jingle of the telephone, the clatter of the telegraph and the first mass-produced typewriters. It saw the emergence of the age of material novelties, where the public first experienced the mobility of the motorcar and were dazzled in the glare of electric light. By the start of the Edwardian period, the forces of modernity, which had emerged in the previous century, became increasingly apparent in transport, civic and urban planning and the growth of the consumer society.[4]

The transformation of town centres into commercial and recreational spaces by the Edwardian era is vitally apparent in *Leeds Street Scenes* (1902)

Louis Lumière claimed that the cinematic apparatus could 'represent the movement of the streets, of public places, with truly astonishing fidelity'.[5] When we examine the films of street life and urban centres produced by Mitchell & Kenyon, this observation appears uncannily prophetic. The company filmed from the front of trains, trams and aeroplanes so that their audience could partake of the shared experience of virtual travel, and there are over forty phantom journey films in the collection. They also captured street parades, local processions, military marches and the great Victorian municipal parks, which, by the early twentieth century, had become a feature of nearly every town and city in the UK. The films reveal the contrast between the densely concentrated urban centres and the parks and emerging suburbs that offered a retreat from the noise and bustle of the industrial town and city. They show the vibrancy and energy of street life in the early 1900s and demonstrate how parades and processions were manifestations of local and community pride.

The rough physicality of street life in the 1900s is reflected in *Darwen Street Scenes* (1901)

Manchester Band of Hope Procession (1901) reveals the vibrancy and energy of street life in the early 1900s, and demonstrates how parades and processions were notable manifestations of community pride

Procession in Accrington Park (1900). The parks offered a retreat from the bustle and activity of urban dwelling

The Edwardian City

> The Edwardian era was short by comparison with the Victorian . . . Nevertheless, during these Edwardian years the city, in both actuality and perception, took on a recognisably modern form . . . Partly because of a new reign and a new century and partly because of the particular stage which urbanisation had reached, there was a collective stocktaking of what urban meant and how far the city had come to represent society as a whole.[6]

Although a new, more intensive phase of urban growth had begun in earnest during the first part of the nineteenth century, it was only in the second half of the century that the majority of people lived and worked in the city. When Edward ascended the throne, he was truly the first monarch of a fully urbanised society, which had risen from 77 per cent of the population in 1901 to 80 per cent by 1911. These figures marked the culmination of a century of continuous population growth, and by the end of the Edwardian era, the rapid rate of expansion was considerably less than in the 1890s.[7] A change in perception of the city itself was required, as suburban regions, historically on the outskirts of the city, became part of the city-region. In the Victorian era, rural residents had migrated to the cities, with migration counting for over 50 per cent of the population increases throughout urban areas. In the Edwardian era, the city expanded into the countryside, the extension of local boundaries made possible by new electric tramway systems, which broadened the concept of locality. The various urban centres ranged in size and population with just under a third of residents living in towns of between

Proclamation of King Edward VII, Market Place, Accrington (1901) heralded a new age, and when Edward ascended the throne he was a monarch of a fully urbanised society

ORS 23
MOSS & SON.

BELLE VUE HYDE Rd
TEA

Urban centres were places of commerce, with many retail outlets as *Manchester Street Scenes* (1901), previous pages, and *Liverpool Street Scenes* (1901) demonstrate

10,000 and 50,000 people.[8] The social critic Charles Masterman described the new urban populace as the '"Multitude" . . . a new race, hitherto unreckoned and of incalculable importance is entering the sphere of practical importance – the "City" type of the coming years; the "street bred" people of the twentieth century; the "new generation knocking on our doors"'.[9] The emergence of the new urban centres throughout the decades of social and municipal reform was manifest in Leeds, Manchester, Liverpool and Birmingham, in particular. Municipal reforming movements started by charitable and prosperous middle-class Unitarian reformers in the 1840s and 1850s were then underpinned by changes in, and the strengthening of, local government authority in the 1870s.[10]

The reforming message of the civic fathers was part of an attempt to change the image of the industrial city, which by the mid-Victorian era was one of dark satanic mills, populated by sprawling slums, a view that was only underlined by Charles Dickens's depiction of Coketown in *Hard Times*. In the first years of Victoria's reign, the rapidly expanding industrial centres of Manchester and Birmingham, as well as other cities, became objects of fascination and disgust.[11] In an attempt to alter this image of the industrial heartlands, local civic authorities concentrated on the streets and central marketplaces, transforming these social and urban spaces into symbols of civic pride.[12] From the mid-1850s onwards, the town centres became areas of retail economies, in which shopping and professional services replaced the rowdier elements, which were driven underground or out of sight.[13] Libraries and art galleries became symbols of civic pride and responsibility, with town halls taking on the appearance of municipal palaces, reflecting the aspirations and status of the cities from which they sprang.[14] Manchester's town hall, designed by Alfred Waterhouse and opened in 1878 amid civic rejoicing and a 45,000-strong procession of local tradesmen, can be seen in *Lord Roberts's Visit to Manchester* (1901).[15] From the 1850s onwards, the cities and towns of the industrial heartlands underwent dramatic changes, with Manchester developing at faster rate than Birmingham, which needed greater changes in local authority and the growing influence of Joseph Chamberlain to kickstart its urban regeneration.[16] 'Bromagen has altered so. There's scarce a place in it I know', sang a local comedian, and the changes wrought by interventional policies at local levels are apparent in *The Return of the Warwickshire Volunteers* (1901).[17] The large civic square where the soldiers were greeted by a patriotic crowd and local dignitaries was filmed at the height of Birmingham's civic splendour and pride.[18]

> New Year's Day 1901, finds Birmingham vastly altered. It is in all respects a striking contrast for the city . . . of a hundred years ago. Now it is a great industrial city . . . It is a city of broad and for the most part well laid out streets, although opinions differ on the quality of the paving. It has numerous public buildings of imposing appearance, handsome shops and commercial houses, with, in the suburbs numerous mansions and villa residences . . .[19]

The same writer praised the city as the 'best governed in the world' and, indeed, it was local governance that had been responsible for the transformation. Greater interventional policies were ratified and carried out at local levels in cities and towns throughout the country. For example, once Leeds purchased Roundhay Park in 1874 for the recreational benefits of its citizens, it then assumed the responsibility of investing in the latest electric tramway system in 1891, which would enable access to the park for all of

A process of municipal responsibility and greater control, which grew from the mid-nineteenth century onwards, reached its peak during the Edwardian decade with its links to Christian piety reflected in *Congregation at Preston Parish Church* (c. 1901)

Manchester Street Scenes (1901), filmed in the city centre on the intersection of Cross Street and Corporation Street – the frame is filled with rapid movement of traffic and people

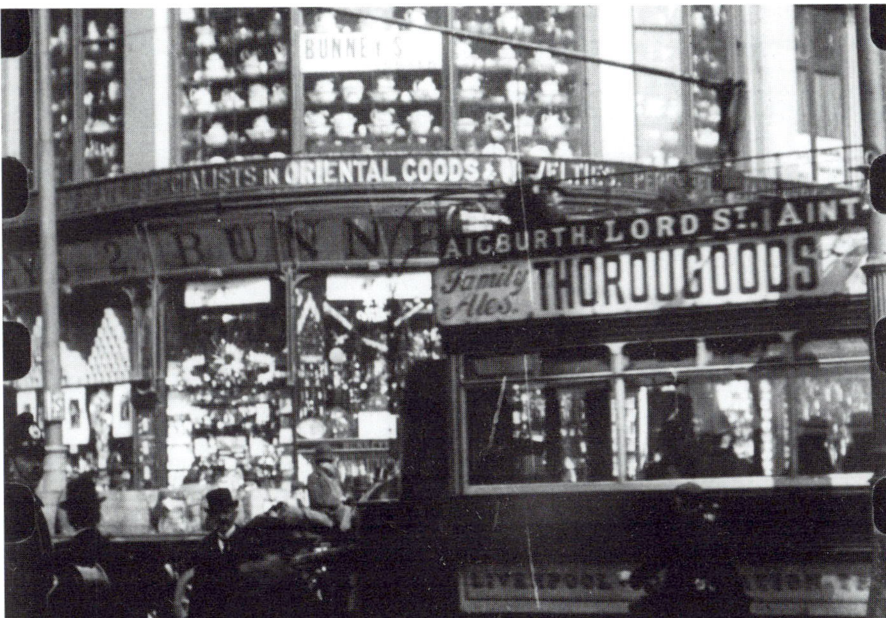

Liverpool Street Scenes (1901) including a shot of Bunney's famous department store – a cathedral of consumption

their ratepayers.[20] A process of municipal responsibility and greater control, which grew from the mid-nineteenth century onwards, reached its peak during the Edwardian decade, as the populations of towns and cities in the industrial heartlands received the benefits of previous decades of municipal reform and change.[21] Municipal developments were linked to aspects of social control, as it was felt that a cleaner, healthier and better-organised society would lead to more industrious and respectable citizens.[22] As Simon Gunn writes: 'Moral, sanitary and social prescriptions were conflated in the drive to render the city centre an uninhabited, sanitised space, enabling the visual power of buildings and monuments, squares and widened streets to achieve its full effect.'[23] The impact of half a century of urban improvement can be seen in the street scenes in the Mitchell & Kenyon Collection, in particular the phantom ride films taken from the fronts of the electric trams. Sheffield, Leeds and Bradford city centres appear modern in concept and design, as the tram aids the flow of traffic in and out and around the civic centres.

The films encapsulate the energy and vibrancy of the street life they record. The urban centres depicted in titles such as *Liverpool Street Scenes* (1901), filmed on the intersection of Holy Corner, are 'busy, jostling and full of a rough physicality which makes modern streets seem sanitised'.[24] This is also apparent in *Manchester Street Scenes* (1901). Filmed in the city centre on the intersection of Cross Street and Corporation Street, it shows the rapid movement of traffic and people.[25] This title was part of a season of films, 'Life in Manchester', shown daily at St James Hall during the summer months by the showman exhibitor A. D. Thomas. The development of commercial centres at the heart of the industrial cities is evident in the parade of shops, and in the scenes of women walking up and down the thoroughfares, getting on and off trams and visiting stores such as Bunny's in *Liverpool Street Scenes*, the department stores captured in *Sheffield Street Accident* (1902) and the array of small local shops that line the streets of the Bradford suburbs.[26] The culmination of this revolution in nineteenth-century consumerism was the growth of the

Jamaica Street Glasgow (1901) – a women pedestrian carrying new purchases – shopping became one of the pleasures of urbanity

large-scale city-centre department store, which developed rapidly from the 1860s onwards, with David Lewis's opening new branches in Manchester and Birmingham in 1880 and 1885.[27] Shopping became one of the pleasures of urbanity, as middle-class women utilised horse-drawn and electric trams and the omnibus to visit the city centre for recreational purposes.[28] 'The changing social geography of the urban middle class transformed parts of the central business district into temples of consumerism', as women felt increasingly secure in better policed and move civilised areas.[29] The freedom to travel on public transport, shop in the new centres or enjoy visiting the city or town centre as a leisure activity can be seen in the variety of street scenes in the Mitchell & Kenyon Collection. In *Manchester Street Scenes*, women can be seen entering the various stores on Market Street and looking in shop windows, and views of *Jamaica Street Glasgow* (1901) reveal women pedestrians carrying shopping bags, while others nimbly hold their skirts and bags as they ride on the back of a tram in Leeds. Department stores have been described as 'cathedrals of consumption', which reached a pinnacle of consumer delights from the 1880s onwards, grounded on the premise that shopping was an important component of middle-class culture, particularly for women.[30] These films and other scenes of bustling street life not only demonstrate the importance of commercial expansion in urban centres but also that the streets were used as arenas for parades and demonstrations.

Civic Centres and Parades

Street processions have been described as 'a living breathing music-playing representation of the social order itself'.[31] Processions in the Victorian and Edwardian periods were outward expressions of the rich social mix of the populace that made up the urban centre. The streets were used by friendly societies, churches, schools, temperance groups and trade unions. There were parades celebrating royal visits, and military parades remembering Trafalgar Day. People practically lived on the streets, which became an extension of locality and neighbourhood and offered a cheaper form of entertainment than more commercial venues such as music halls and theatres where an entrance fee was payable. Parades became important vehicles for demonstrations of political allegiances, as in the *Miners' Demonstration at Wakefield* (1908), religious and community affirmation, as in the Manchester and Warrington Whit walks in particular, and civic celebrations.[32] The films reflect the underlying tensions between urbanisation and respectability, the social tensions that were increasingly prevalent leading up to the First World War and the religious sectarianism that was commonplace in the major northern cities.[33] This is the case with *Manchester Band of Hope Procession* (1901), filmed by the Thomas-Edison Animated Photo Company in June 1901.[34] The Band of Hope was a temperance society founded in the 1840s to combat the evils of drink. Its target audience were children and the Band of Hope used the latest technologies, such as the magic lantern in the 1840s and the cinematograph from 1896 onwards, as an instrument of education in their fight against the perils of alcohol. The importance of youth to the organisation is apparent in the shots of well-dressed groups of children holding banners that declare 'Bread not Beer in this House', one example of many such messages on display. Although there are fundamental similarities in many of the parades, differences are manifest in the way the processions are organised and presented in the streets and urban centres. For example, Andrew Prescott has compared the organised military precision of the *Visit of HRH Princess Louise to Blackburn* (1905) with the informal, rowdy chaos of *Miners' Demonstration at Wakefield*.[35] The Mitchell & Kenyon Collection includes a wide range of processions from towns and cities throughout the UK and Ireland. These parades, which were associated with local carnivals and charitable fund-raising events, have been examined in previous chapters. Processions by friendly societies, churches, schools, temperance

Parades were expressions of political and religious ideologies with the *Manchester Band of Hope Procession* (1901) of particular importance to the temperance movement

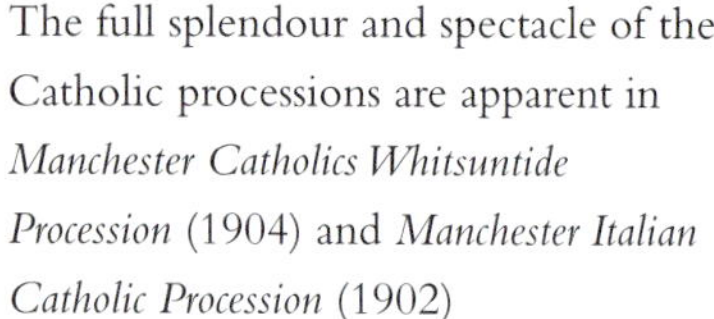

The full splendour and spectacle of the Catholic processions are apparent in *Manchester Catholics Whitsuntide Procession* (1904) and *Manchester Italian Catholic Procession* (1902)

ent Protestant parades on the Monday.[44] The Whit walks also posed domestic and economic problems, as dressing a child for the annual event could exacerbate the poverty of the family.[45] Special clothes and shoes had to be purchased, and the children walking in the *Manchester Catholic Orphanage Boys' Whit Walk* appear clean and 'well scrubbed' despite being orphans. The prosperous and well-dressed children representing all the denominations taking part in the walks in Warrington demonstrate how the event was an 'important index of a working-class family's social standing'.[46]

Warrington Walking Day owes its origins to one individual, the Reverend H. Powys, who, between 1832 and 1834, instituted the anniversary of the Sunday schools. As in Manchester, the event became an occasion on which all the schools would go in procession to the parish church to hear a service and sermon, and afterwards retire for refreshments. The Reverend Quekett, writing in 1865 to the *Warrington Guardian*, infers that the tradition began as a counter to the vice and iniquity of the races held at Newton, which were attended by local parishioners. By 1858, it had become an annual festival, a holiday for the young people of Warrington, 'a day sacred to running and racing, to rollicking and frolicking, to romping, dancing, jumping, riding, climbing – in fact, everything except working' and going to the races. Starting early on the Friday morning, the different church schools walked in procession throughout the town. From 1857, they were joined by the local Roman Catholics, and by 1908 all the different religious denominations in the town took part in the walk but followed different routes.[47] The religious make-up of the walk is apparent in *Warrington Walking Day* (1902), filmed on 27 June, which has survived in six sections. The inscriptions on the negatives reveal that the films are organised according to the religious denomination of the walkers, with one of the reels inscribed 'Warrington Catholics' and the other five 'Warrington Protestants'.[48] The groups process through Victoria Park holding aloft the banners representing their local churches; the scale of the procession equals the 1901 parade from Manchester, which attracted over 22,000 children, and the twelve-minute film is one of the longest in the collection. The final edited version only reflects a fraction of the actual walk itself, which lasted over three hours. Although the films are only a small sample of the overall event, they do reveal the magnificence and splendour of this local tradition, a tradition that still continues in Warrington, Padgate and other Cheshire towns and villages. The Manchester Catholic Whit walk was described as 'in any year no doubt, the biggest spectacle that Manchester affords', and the surviving films are important as expressions of both community and religious identity.[49]

Civic Celebrations

Parades were not only a respectable form of middle-class recreational activity but also a means of displaying pride in the civic achievements of the town or locality. The return of Boer War soldiers, visits of VIPs or commemorations of national events at local level were all ways in which the town or city could celebrate progress and local identity. Liverpool commemorated the coronation of Edward VII and the visit of Lord Roberts and Lord Kitchener to the city in 1902 with a huge civic parade and a celebration of its new electric tramway system, opened in 1901. In Liverpool, the Edwardian era and the years leading up to the Second World War were enlivened by many ceremonial occasions, including elaborate street decorations, fireworks displays in the parks and civic processions reflecting local and regional pride in the city. The collection echoes the fondness of the city fathers for parades and festivities, which range from *Princess Louise at Liverpool* (1906) to *Visit of Earl Roberts and Viscount Kitchener to Receive the Freedom of the City, Liverpool* (1902), and were all marked by large crowds, civic parties and parades through the streets of the city. Liverpool, in 1901, appears to be in a constant state of military and patriotic celebration, with *Trafalgar Day in Liverpool*, *St George's Day in Liverpool* and *Lord Roberts Pre-*

Liverpool was in a constant state of celebration in 1901 with parades marking a host of commemorative events, such as *Trafalgar Day in Liverpool* (1901)

The opening of the new electric tramway system in 1901 marked a period of celebration for the city seen here in *Liverpool as Seen from the Front of an Electric Car from the Pierhead to the Circus* (1901)

senting Medals to Boer War Volunteers in Liverpool just three of the large-scale events filmed by Mitchell & Kenyon.[50] The processions 'were the most spectacular organised manifestations of provincial culture in Victorian industrial cities'.[51]

Liverpool was at its peak of confidence in the Edwardian era, and the new electric tramways were a notable part of its success story in the thriving years up to 1914: 'public transport made the city possible and let it grow'.[52] The electric tramways not only conveyed thousands to and from the various events but, with their decoration and illumination, were an attraction in themselves. The opening of the new system, the commemoration

Liverpool's specially designed tram, built in 1902 and covered in 1,500 electric lights can be seen during the *Visit of Earl Roberts and Viscount Kitchener to Receive the Freedom of the City, Liverpool* (1902)

of local events or national celebrations were often marked in towns by the decorating of the local trams. Liverpool actually used a specially designed tram, built in 1902, and first introduced for the coronation of Edward VII. The car was covered in 1,500 electric lights and yards of bunting, with a bust of Edward mounted on the canopy. The bodywork was re-panelled and picked out in white and gold, and as the tram moved, the many coloured lights were switched on and off in rotation. The Tramway Company Band played popular and patriotic songs from its open top. The tram is clearly visible in *Visit of Earl Roberts and Viscount Kitchener to Receive the Freedom of the City, Liverpool*: 'The illuminated tram was ideally suited to Edwardian times as it symbolised the colourful patriotism of that flamboyant era combined with civic pride in the tramways and the new found achievements of electrical engineering.'[53]

The association of electric tramway systems with celebrations of civic pride reflects their importance in the development of the Edwardian city. Despite the assention by some commentators that the Edwardian period was the era of the motorcar, it was the mass utilisation of the electric tramways that brought dramatic changes in working-class transportation.

Transport and the Development of the Electric Trams

> The narrowest shave of an accident I had was one day when I boarded the electric tram and arranged with the driver to fix my apparatus . . . secured my picture, which was of an exciting nature, as besides the ordinary street traffic, the tram had a desperate shave of running down a butcher's cart! That part of the film is always applauded, as the tram apparently is bound to collide with the cart.[54]

Mitchell & Kenyon were filming during a time of great change when both new developments and existing patterns of transport co-existed for a brief transitory period. The company captured towns and cities throughout the north of England during this ever-evolving period, where modes of urban public transport were changing from horse and steam to electric power. In less than a decade, Patrick Geddes' image of the Victorian

Before the introduction of the electric tramway systems, horse power reigned supreme and *Manchester Street Scenes* (1901) offer the viewer glimpses of the horse tramways in their last years

Horse trams were still a feature of transport in Belfast as apparent from *Ride on a Tramcar Through Belfast* (1901) and (below left) horses were still an important means of road transport overall as reflected in the many horse and carts on *Jamaica Street Glasgow* (1901)

city built around steam and horse power had been transformed into the Edwardian city constructed around electricity and, in the north of England, the electric tramways. Before their introduction in the urban environment, the horse had been the dominant locomotive power. From the 1860s onwards, horse tramways had become a growing urban phenomenon in Britain. By 1901, the number of horses used in road transport overall was an estimated 1,766,000, a figure that declined throughout the decade as steam and then predominantly electrification was utilised for tramway systems.[55] The films offer the viewer glimpses of the horse tramways in their last years, and also an insight into the new and burgeoning technology of electric tramways and the surviving steam trams. *Jamaica Street Glasgow* and *Ride on the Tramcar through Belfast* (1901) reveal a time when the horse reigned supreme, as public transport and work traffic were underpinned by the use of horse power.[56] Within a year, electrification would transform these bustling metropolises, as electric trams replaced horse-drawn transport by 1902 in Glasgow and 1905 in Belfast.[57]

The Electric Tramways

Electric trams were first introduced at Crystal Palace in 1881 by Werner von Siemens, and both Blackpool and Brighton claim to be the first British towns to open a permanent electric tram system, in 1884 and 1885, along the seafronts.[58] However, it was the innovations introduced by Frank Sprague in the United States that ensured the commercial success of electrified tramways, and from 1891 onwards the electric tram spread to Britain. 'Its success rested on proven American technology combined with local coach-building experience to produce the distinctive British double deck tramcar', and its impact was immediate.[59] Steam trams had proved popular in various northern cities, particularly in West Yorkshire and Lancashire, where their continued use is evident in street scenes of Oldham and Wigan.[60] But by 1901, steam trams were seen as antiquated and, according to the *Birmingham Daily Mail*, 'relics of a bygone age which mark our halting in the progressive path'.[61] The opening of electric tramways became linked to civic pride, as new systems were marked by celebrations and public openings. If the Victorian era was the age of the railway, the Edwardian period belonged to the tram.

Steam trams were still a feature of some Northern towns as seen in *Living Wigan* (1902) and (below left) *Wigan Coronation Celebrations and Street Scenes* (1902)

(Above) If the Victorian era was the age of the railway, the Edwardian period belonged to the tram, *Liverpool as Seen from the Front of an Electric Car from the Pierhead to the Circus* (1901); (below) the tram linked the urban and the rural, the town centre and the suburbs. *Tram Ride into Halifax* (1902), with its dramatic scan of the valley and the industrial landscape of towering chimneys

The real boom period of electric tramway growth in Britain was from 1900 to 1903. Although growth continued at a reduced pace throughout the period of Mitchell & Kenyon's activity, by 1912, tram passenger numbers had grown by 150 per cent in ten years. The expansion of the electric tram system continued unabated throughout the early 1900s. In 1898, there were 150 miles of electrified tramways; by 1910, this had increased to over 2,000 miles. By 1900, sixty-one tramway systems were managed by local authorities, and another eighty-nine by private companies.[62] The new electric tram systems brought many advantages and changes, with an unparalleled intrusion into existing urban landscape, to the extent that districts such as Edgbaston in Birmingham and Victoria Park, Manchester, placed an embargo on tramlines to their area. Although tram tracks initially used horse trams, from the 1860s, electrification resulted in a large-scale extension of the system. Bigger cars were constructed to increase capacity, with large double-decker trams able to carry up to seventy people. It was also a more structured system of transport and replaced the previous regime of stopping at public houses and inns along a route with recognised designated tram stops and a formal system of fare stages.

According to John Armstrong, the main advantage of the tram was that it allowed 'a greater dispersal of residential areas from central business areas by providing quick cheap and frequent transport'.[63]

The tram linked the urban and the rural, the town centre and the suburbs. *Tram Ride into Halifax* (1902) opens with a shot of the beautiful snow-covered industrial landscape of Halifax, and was filmed in January on the former tram route towards Keighley (now the A629). With its dramatic scan of the valley and the industrial landscape of towering chimneys, this title stands out as one of only a handful in the collection that focuses purely on the landscape rather than trying to capture Edwardians in their everyday activities.[64] In the Edwardian world of Mitchell & Kenyon, progress in street traffic was represented by the new electric tramways, which offered longer journeys with cheaper fares and at twice the speed of a trotting horse.[65] The tramway could operate on street track in the pre-motor age, affording little danger to passengers boarding and alighting in the roadway. *Tram Ride through the City of Sheffield* (1902) shows several people, includ-

(Left and below) *Electric Tram Rides from Forster Square Bradford* (1902) takes us from the heart of the Edwardian town to the outlying suburbs through Manningham Lane to Lister Park

(Overleaf) An electric tram intersects the swarming crowd – in *Halifax Catholic Procession* (c. 1905)

The electric trams as seen in *Tram Rides Through Nottingham* (1902) became an expression of progress and became an essential part of the modern urban dweller's daily existence

ing women, boarding trams in motion as they are leaving the stops, and there appears to be remarkably little conflict with the general horse-drawn traffic.[66] This is also apparent in a section of *Leeds Lifeboat Procession* (1902), in which the tram is shown leaving the busy city-centre intersection, with passengers getting on and off the vehicle.[67] *Halifax Catholic Procession* (1905) ends with an electric tram cutting across the swarming crowds of the religious parade, and then continuing on its way along the top of the road.[68]

Electric Tram Rides from Forster Square, Bradford (1902) takes us from the heart of the Edwardian town and city, the city of change, of consumer society, where the street was an extension of community life, to the outlying suburbs, through Manningham Lane to Lister Park.[69] Forming part of four sequences, the film was commissioned by Sydney Carter of New Century Pictures and shown at the St George's Hall in Bradford in April 1902.[70] The title is fascinating on many levels, illustrating not only the tram journey from the heart of the city to the suburbs but also other forms of Edwardian street traffic, such as the horse and carts and bicycles. These changes in Bradford illustrate how the transition to electric tramways produced the greatest impact on locality and modernity in the north of England in particular. In Sheffield, in 1898–9, the original horse depots in Tinsley (built in 1874 for the Sheffield Tramways Company) were converted for the use of the electric tramways. Shot in September 1902, *Tram Ride through the City of Sheffield* reveals outlying districts such as the London Road area, three to four miles from the city centre, and ends in the heart of Sheffield as it rides through the two main shopping centres of the Moor and Fargate to Ponds Forge.[71] The thoroughfares are wide and spacious, the flow of traffic seemingly uninterrupted by the criss-crossing of the electric tram system. Other northern cities made the transition to electrification at different rates: Leeds in 1894, Halifax in 1898, Oldham in 1900, Bradford initially in 1892, but only fully in 1898. The trams became an expression of progress and an essential part of the modern urban dweller's daily existence.[72] For tramway historian Ian Yearsley, the Mitchell & Kenyon films reveal 'the new electric tramway in all its glory during the brief years when it was the undisputed monarch of the road', and highlight the contrast between the old and the new forms of transport systems in the Edwardian era.[73] The electric tram system opened in Manchester in August 1901, and by 1906 its importance to the people of Manchester was celebrated in the *Manchester Alphabet*: 'The Tram Cars glide about the streets as if they were alive and men and women fight for seats each night at half past five.'[74]

Although the Edwardian age is marked by other changes in the transport system, such as the introduction of the motorcar and the new motorised buses, these are not apparent in the Mitchell & Kenyon films. The street scenes are filmed at a time when the tram reigned supreme and the company was at its financial height, and it is only at the end of the decade that motorised buses became part of the urban landscape. Although motorcars had been emancipated by legislation of 1896, in 1904, for example, only 8,465 were in private ownership, a figure that rose to 132,015 by 1914.[75] Rare examples of the motorcar in the collection can be found in *Liverpool Street Scenes*, in which a motor vehicle leaves Rochet Cars of Rochet-Schneider, a Lyon-based car manufacturer, with three male passengers.[76] The return of Clive Wilson, the son of an important Hull family, from the Boer War was captured in a sequence entitled *Lieutenant Clive Wilson and Tranby Croft Party* (1902) where the party drive up and down the driveway at the infamous Tranby Croft residence in a motorcar.[77] Yet to intrude on the Edwardian city transport system, in the early 1900s the motorcar remained the preserve of the rich and privileged and was only suitable for short journeys.

Sagar Mitchell can be seen in a motor car leaving Rochet-Schneider's showroom in *Liverpool Street Scenes* (1901)

Motor-car ownership grew throughout the 1900s but in 1904 only 8,465 were in private ownership and were mostly the preserve of the privileged, as seen in *Lieutenant Clive Wilson And Tranby Croft Party* (1902), where the family drive around the grounds of Tranby Croft in a motorcar

As we have seen, electric tramways were linked to progress and modernity and were introduced by local authorities from the 1890s. The success of Roundhay Park in Leeds was due to an enhanced public transport system, based on the existing horse-drawn transport routes, which allowed greater access to the surroundings and to another aspect of Victorian municipal life, the public park.[78]

Municipal Parks

> If people will understand that the more recreation grounds there are the quieter and less crowded each will be then the cities of the future would no longer be vast accumulations of monotonous rows of houses.[79]

The need for parks grew out of the sprawling urban development of the first part of the nineteenth century, which necessitated the management and control the working-class population as it expanded in urban centres. As the Victorian city expanded and populations increased, parks became identified as a counter-balance to growing social unrest and the divide that was seen to be emerging between the working populace and their employers.[80] The reforming concerns, reflected in the Select Committee on Public Walks (1833), arose out of a disquiet that rapid urban growth was creating a dense environment that isolated the slum dwellers from pure air, healthy recreation and other moral and physical benefits associated with access to the countryside.[81] It was believed that the construction of parks would attract the working class away from cruder and rowdier pleasures, such as the taverns, music halls and dancing saloons that were largely available to adult members of the community. Park reformers believed that such recreational activities were morally and physically reprehensible and lacked any spiritual and social foundation.[82]

The Police Annual Inspection at Birchfields Park, Manchester (1901) – parks were places for rational recreation as well and social and civic occasions

Sunday Parade in East Park in Hull (1904) shows families and children enjoying the green open spaces, newly created for the working classes

As Hazel Conway, historian of British parks has demonstrated, the history of parks goes back further than their expansion and development in the nineteenth century, with royal parks in London, in particular, having their origins in the seventeenth century.[83] However, it is the municipal parks, largely constructed during the nineteenth century, that were captured on film by Mitchell & Kenyon. The control of these public parks lay with

Preston Egg Rolling (c. 1901) was one of the many activities that took place in Avenham Park

Parks were also used for community events and the finale and crowning of the May Queen seen in *Bootle May Day Demonstration and Crowning of the May Queen* (1903) took place in North Park

the local authority, and as the century progressed, their powers became more extensive through local by-laws. It was believed that only through proximity to their social betters would in the uncivilised working class benefit, through cultural osmosis, from the model of good behaviour offered by the middle class. Parks were primarily intended for the working class, 'for the enjoyment of those who, in crowded districts, have no other outlet'.[84] Particular attention was paid by the Select Committee on the need for fresh air, enhancement of family togetherness and exercise through public games.[85] These civilising influences would be enabled by providing an arena where both the working and middle classes could meet and mix through rational recreation. This ideology of greater assimilation between two distinct social groups can also be found in other nineteenth-century reforming institutions aimed at educating the working class: in particular the rise of the mechanics institutes, which used education and debate as a moralising influence on the working classes.[86] Reactions to these moralising forces was mixed and regionally diverse.[87] Moreover, the Committee's recommendations were motivated by a mixture of charity and self-interest, as one of the underlying aims was to negate the power of the unruly mob and to safeguard the property and the security of the rich.[88] The park was seen as a 'machine for promoting Civilization and exciting Industry'.[89]

Although by the 1880s, most towns had at least one park, the public park movement was at its height between 1885 and 1914, a period when more parks were built than at any other time before or since.[90] While there is no common pattern of park development, with local and regional issues determining the location, position and name of the park, the underlying ideology was the same: namely, that to provide arenas for healthy exercise and fresh air. By the early 1900s, the parks filmed by Mitchell & Kenyon reflected many of these underlying ideologies, revealing them not only as venues for physical exercise and recreation but as arenas of social and civic pride, where all aspects of Edwardian society converged. Eleven parks are featured in the collection, demonstrating the wide range of activities that took place in these arenas at the time. Children are seen skipping in Avenham Park, Preston, gentlemen play bowls at New Brighton, and carnivals and civic parades reach their finale in the local parks in Bootle, Crewe and Accrington. All these aspects will be covered in the following sections, where the films will be analysed in the context of the changing leisure patterns and growing municipal control exerted by local authorities from the mid-nineteenth century onwards.[91]

Parks as Symbols of Civic Pride

> (Parks) offered a metaphor for an ideal and rational society . . . a society which combined the order and civility of the polite urban community with the scientific detail, managed beauty and spiritual resonance of the native countryside . . .[92]

East Park, featured in *Sunday Parade in East Park in Hull* (1902), was opened to the public on 21 June 1887, the day of Queen Victoria's Golden Jubilee and was the largest park in Hull

The urban park, perhaps more than any other landscape, is redolent of the aspirations of its time. The creation of public parks in the northern industrial heartlands and the Midlands began in the 1840s and continued throughout the nineteenth century, forming part of the civic developments outlined earlier. From the mid-nineteenth century, the civic authorities extended their authority even further, looking beyond the centre to the outskirts of the town or city. Legislation gave local authorities greater power to control the excesses of urban living, as well as the funds to buy and develop land for the good of their community. The excitement and publicity generated by the public parks movements in the 1830s had in many ways faded from public attention by the end of the century. Parks were seen as a necessity, not something to be fought over or campaigned for, and it became accepted that major industrial centres or towns with civic pride and aspirations had at least one area of public recreation that catered for the moral and physical well-being of its urban population. The Public Health Act (1875) made loans available from central government for the purchase of land, while the Public Parks Act (1871) allowed land to be donated for use as a public park. Parks were created in a variety of ways: private individuals or local wealthy families might sponsor the landscaping of the grounds, while celebrations of national events such as the Queen's Jubilee or coronation events attracted local subscription appeals. East Park, featured in *Sunday Parade in East Park in Hull* (1902), was opened to the public on 21 June 1887, the day of Queen Victoria's Golden Jubilee. Designed by Joseph Fox Sharp, it covered a site of fifty-two acres, expanding to 120 acres by the 1930s, making it the largest public park in Hull.[93] Between 1885 and 1914, most of the land for these new parks was purchased by town councils rather than donated by generous benefactors. The 1880s were just the beginning of the great wave in public acquisition of open space and these new parks equalled those they followed, and averaged between ten and fifty acres.[94]

'A well organised park is one of the most important, as it is one of the most virtuous, in the Unitarian sense of our public institutions,' reported the *Gardeners' Chronicle* in 1910.[95] Parks were the physical manifestation on the landscape of great local pride, intended not only to shape the way in which the 'local populace related to the landscape but as a place to define and cement community pride and values':[96]

> If there are any still among us who doubt the educational, social and sanitary advantage of such fine open spaces as this park and the adjourning commons affords, one visit on a Saturday would surely suffice for their conversion. The ample open spaces, the well furnished parks and gardens, with their supply of seats, are crowded with their thousands of happy men, women and children, in search of health, happiness, and the higher education of sweetness and light which close fellowship with Nature at her best cannot fail to impart.[97]

Along with the streets and the urban centres, the parks became popular venues for civic parades and local celebrations. *Bootle May Day Demonstration and Crowning of the May Queen* (1903) links both arenas. Filmed on 9 May, due to the cancellation of the original event a week earlier, it starts with the local trades procession and May Queen celebrations promenading through the spectator-lined streets of Bootle and finishes in North Park.[98] Maypole dancing and a horse and pony race are just two of the events that

are captured, while the landscaped environment of the municipal park, along with a travelling fair, is visible in the background.[99] Other aspects of civic pride are demonstrated in *The Police Annual Inspection at Birchfields Park* (1901), filmed in Manchester on 23 May.[100] The annual inspection took place in one of the many parks that had been built in Manchester in the nineteenth century.[101] Birch Fields Park was one of the last municipal parks to be opened in Manchester (in 1885), and the annual parade demonstrated the importance of the local constabulary and its position in the community. The police are shown parading, with scenes of the mounted police, displays of first-aid skills, followed by the civic inspection by the local dignitaries and officials. Birchfields Park was utilised as not only a recreational arena but also to demonstrate the importance of the local services, cementing 'local pride' in all aspects of the facilities offered by its municipal authority. Parks were not only venues for civic occasions but were also linked to recreational events such as carnivals, shows and local calendar customs. As the local authorities assumed control of the organisation and landscaping of the parks, the type of activities that took place in them became more regulated, with particular emphasis on local by-laws pro-

The Police Annual Inspection at Birch Fields Park (1901 took place in one of the last municipal parks to be opened in Manchester in 1885. The annual parade demonstrated the importance of the local constabulary and demonstrates the importance of the local services and all aspects of the facilities of its municipal authority

Local school events and sporting days were held in the local parks and children can be seen competing in *Day School Sports at Park Avenue in Bradford* (1902)

hibiting public meetings.[102] The need for rational recreation space for the working class was an important aspect of the nineteenth-century reforming movements, and this also impacted on the park movement from the 1830s onwards. 'The Victorian park developed in the context of an ever expanding population a changing economy and the growth of transport facilities.'[103]

Rational Recreational Playgrounds

> The reformers, like other reformers, thought that working class recreations were physically, socially and morally reprehensible. If they were replaced by 'suitable' recreations then many of the 'problems' of working class behaviour would be solved.[104]

Parks were a manifestation of the rise of modern institutions and their attempts to control the physical and social processes of urbanisation, and they complemented the streets, which continued to be used for special occasions as the recreation area of the poor. The Select Committee on Public Walks referred to earlier, while concerned with the physi-

More leisurely activities were encouraged in the newly built civic parks, and groups of smartly dressed children play in front of the camera

cal need for open spaces in urban areas, was also worried about the problem of working-class recreation.[105] Although areas of green land and common land existed around urban settlements, many originated on the outskirts of towns and were owned by private landowners. Some of these areas were converted into public parks, such as Avenham Park, the venue for *Preston Egg Rolling*, created in 1847, and already an area of common use for recreation and civic protests.[106]

Local authorities also saw it as their duty not only to provide and build the parks but to attract people to them with the kinds of events and facilities that could be controlled. By the 1830s, recreational needs began to be associated with educational and physical improvements, and the move towards rational recreational activities involving sport and leisure also impacted on the park movement. The encouragement of rational recreation was designed to negate the impact of the preferred recreations of the working classes, including 'sexual license and its evil consequences', 'excessive alcoholism' and 'the delight in immoral exhibitions', all of which were seen by the moral reformers as encouraging revolutionary activity and antisocial behaviour.[107]

The expansion in the population of the large urban centres provided the audience and venues for these new leisure and sporting industries. These events developed or relied on a large urban community, as well as a good transportation system, and were linked to earlier recreational and sporting traditions. As sporting events became more tightly regulated and professional, amateur and less rowdy recreational activities were pursued in the parks and all were available to women. Although sober in comparison with the pleasure gardens, which continued to flourish, they were free, open to all and offered an opportunity to mix with a fraternity that in most areas of recreation was divided on class and economic grounds. The recreational facilities encouraged within parks were in line with these more leisurely, civilised pursuits. Certain types of games were permitted and bowling greens and tennis courts were allowed but not the more physical team games (with the exception of cricket). Bowling greens became synonymous with the smaller recreation areas found by the seaside, as can be seen in *New Brighton, Egremont and Seacombe Promenade*, which shows holiday-makers playing bowls on a green attached to a local pub.[108]

Parks became used as venues not only for civic events, but also festivals and shows. Roundhay Park, which opened in 1872 was the venue for the *Great Yorkshire Show in Leeds* (1902) – a lavish social occasion

Bandstands and pavilions for musical performances were seen as an opportunity for revenue, and lakes supported fishing and boating. The Public Health Act (1907) legitimised many of the activities that were already commonplace, making it legal, for example, to charge for the hire of bowling greens, the opening of refreshment grounds and the payment of bands, as long as it was under a penny. By the end of the Edwardian period, summer musical performances had become an essential feature of the public park life, and bandstands, such as those in West Park in Hull and Corporation Park in Blackburn, were an integral part of the design and architecture.[109]

Parks were used not only for civic events but also festivals and shows. Roundhay Park, which opened in 1872, was the venue for the *Great Yorkshire Show in Leeds* (1902), while Blackburn Corporation Park, founded in 1857, provides the backdrop for *Blackburn Plant Growing Competition* (1905), its marquees, refreshment tents and other facilities illustrating a more formal recreational use of the park.[110]

Parading in the Park

> The Park rose in terraces from the railway station to a street of small villas almost on the ridge of the hill. From its gilded gates to its smallest geranium-slips it was brand-new, and most of it was red . . . The immense crowd, in order to circulate, moved along in tight processions, inspecting one after another the various features of which they had read full descriptions in the Staffordshire Signal . . .[111]

Public walks in the eighteenth century were scenes of social privilege and took place in areas where society's elite were guaranteed exclusivity due to high admission prices and regulations imposed by the gatekeepers. This is in marked contrast to the social inclusion message that underpinned the development of public parks in the Victorian era.[112] Contact between different social classes, it was believed, would reduce misconception and social unrest through shared recreational experiences and activities: 'The more they mix the more they will understand each other.' Additionally, the more amusements on offer to the people, the more contented and industrious they would be, with parks providing a safety valve for the causes of social unrest. The importance of the Sunday promenade as a means by which the various classes could share a social place was one of the underlying messages inherent in park design. Further contact between the classes would also improve their appearance, with dress code and conduct in public being emphasised by the Committee, who believed that they would be 'desirous to be properly clothed'.[113]

> The richer have never, to my knowledge, openly objected to the invasion of the spaces and parks they themselves use by the poorer . . . the workaday world can . . . don their best clothes and disport themselves in a becoming manner . . . the majority of the more favoured will be pleased to see them there, so long as their behaviour is such as it should be.[114]

These factors had an impact on the design of the parks, with walkways and elaborate paths being an essential aspect of their landscaping. Recreational events were also governed by the local authorities, who frowned on football and contact sports but encour-

Sunday Parade in East Park in Hull (1904) with groups of young men and boys enjoying a stroll

aged the more genteel recreations such as walking. By the 1870s and 1880s, the parks had become more elaborate, with complex circular and serpentine walkways, the formation of grand terraces that commanded fine views over the landscape and stately avenues to be traversed in leisure and harmony. By the early 1900s, the impact of the decades of park developments and recreational changes can be seen in the scenes captured on film by Mitchell & Kenyon:

> The best Victorian public parks, like the science and art museums which were also so distinctly a product of this society, were intended to instruct and delight. They were, in effect, gigantic stage-sets, in which the design facilitated the appropriate comportments and responses of the players.[115]

These players are evident in the films taken of Weston Park, Sheffield, East and West Park in Hull and Abington Park in Northampton. Filmed on late Sunday morning or early afternoon, they are the most family orientated representations in the collection, and show the full spectrum of Edwardian society. Top-hatted gentlemen in formal dress walk

Sunday Promenade of Spectators in West Park Hull (1902). Parading in the park on a Sunday afternoon became a regular fixture in the Edwardian weekly calendar and an essential part of maintaining one's position in the local community

alongside men in bowler hats, flat caps and straw boaters in *Sunday Promenade of Spectators in West Park, Hull* (1902), as all aspects of the local community commingle in the park. The family groups promenade along broad and spacious avenues, and their Sunday best formality reminiscent of the scenes from seaside resorts, with their promenades and piers. Similar scenes are captured in East Park, which, interestingly, does not appear to attract such a broad cross-section of the public. Instead, the films are populated by groups of young men, and there are fewer family groups on show. Also, in contrast to West Park, the landscape is more diverse, including a large lake, a Japanese-style bridge and more assorted walkways.[116] West Park was opened in 1885 and East Park in 1887, and both were part of the later municipal park movement. People visited the park to see and be seen, and a whole cross-section of the local society utilised the park as gigantic stage-sets for their weekly performances. Parading in the park on a Sunday afternoon became a regular occurrence in the Edwardian weekly calendar and was an essential part of maintaining one's position in the local community.

Abington Park, the first public park in Northampton, was established in 1897, and, as captured on film by Mitchell & Kenyon in 1902, shows how effectively it operated as a social space. *Scenes in Abington Park, Northampton* (1902) reveals a developed social and recreational space, complete with well-designed paths and a museum for educational pursuits, all set in beautiful landscaped surroundings. The audience are as formally attired as their counterparts in Hull and Sheffield. *Spectators in Weston Park, Sheffield* (1902) was also filmed on a Sunday afternoon (7 September) after the local church service,[117] and focuses purely on the spectators in their Sunday best as they parade along the main pathway around the park. Weston Park was built on the west side of the city in 1874, away from the industrial centre of the factories and steelworks. Not as socially elite as the earlier

Botanical Gardens situated less than a mile away, this five-hectare site, by the early 1900s, had incorporated additional facilities, including a museum, a bandstand for musical performances and tennis courts.

The original Select Committee Report of 1833 had called for a better use of the Sabbath, maintaining that the provision of a safe and family-centred arena for the working man and his family would have an impact not only on his conduct and dress but also his aspirations and work ethic.[118] The importance of Sunday for the family is clearly apparent in the Mitchell & Kenyon views of the parks and recreational spaces in Sheffield, Northampton, Hull, Manchester, Blackburn and Leeds. The parks made available an elevated social space for urban dwellers away from the dirt and bustle of the urban centres. They offered an idealised countryside, where you were never too far away from local transport amenities, or educational and recreational facilities, while providing a clean and safe environment, all within the confines of the locality. The spectators in the Mitchell & Kenyon films were on display both for the cinematograph camera and their fellow park-goers. The representations captured on film reveal an oasis of calm and tranquillity in stark contrast to the busy towns in which they were constructed:

> The other elevating influence of the park must by degrees train and educate the people in neatness in dress, habit of order and respectability of conduct and behaviour. It is remarkable how the very perfection of order and condition to which the park is kept influences the manner and conduct of those who hitherto have been unaccustomed to the sphere of such examples. It is one secret of its success in training the unruly.[119]

The parks filmed by Mitchell & Kenyon developed at different stages throughout the nineteenth century, with Abington in Northampton the last in the collection to be opened as a public arena. The films captured them at the height of their glories, with views of the promenading public, the stratified landscape and the recreational activities enjoyed by all classes. The films also include scenes that demonstrate the various forms of transport that made many of the parks fully accessible to a wide and diverse public: the horse-drawn and then electrified tramway systems. The development of urban parks in the

Spectators in Weston Park, Sheffield (1902). Filmed on Sunday, 7 September, after the local church service – the camera focuses on the spectators in their Sunday-best, parading the main pathway as it circulates around the park

As this extravagantly dressed group of women at the *Great Yorkshire Show at Leeds* (1902) demonstrate, the spectators in the Mitchell & Kenyon films were on display both for the cinematograph camera and their fellow park-goers

nineteenth century allowed access to a new landscape for a large percentage of city dwellers. The parks were created for the people, used by the people and became a yard-stick of local pride. The city metropolis expanded geographically in size and scope, with 'Mr Oakroyd's tram' taking the residents on a journey through parklands, civic avenues and squares, industrial quarters, suburban residents and the commercial centre.

Case Study: Bradford Coronation Procession – A Study in Locality

> At a time when British historians are increasingly preoccupied with the breadth of imperial consciousness at the end of the nineteenth century, it is worth remembering the Edwardian preoccupation with the local.[120]

The impact of transport technology on the demography of towns and cities, and the move from a rural to industrial economy, dramatically changed the concept of the locality in the mid- to late nineteenth century and particularly in the first decade of the twen-tieth century. The films in the Mitchell & Kenyon Collection record a time of increased mobility, with a fourfold increase in travel, much of it made possible by the new electric tramcars. By the mid-1900s, the rapid modernisation of modes of transportation extended people's range of activity. In 1891, the average person travelled no more than one-and-a-quarter miles a day; by 1911 this had increased to five miles a day. Compare this to today's individual daily average of twenty-eight miles, of which nine is abroad by air. This extension of boundaries affected the concept of locality, with a gradual widening of the distance between workplace and living quarters. The electric tram systems extended this concept of locality, as speeds increased from twelve to twenty miles an hour and travel became cheaper and faster at a time of continuing population growth, and 'electric trams were crucial to this extension of the urban area without overcrowding'.[121] Local governance transformed urban centres, a revolution, as Philip Harling writes, 'that was carried out through local means and chiefly for local reasons'.[122] This consciousness extended to local pride and feeling, as national events were commemorated at local levels with the returning volunteers of each individual city and township being marked by large gatherings and crowds. While boundaries may have become extended, the urban dwellers also became defined by their perception of belonging to their particular town or city.[123] The concept of locality was not only extended geographically but also in the minds and emotions of its citizens. The reporter for the *Manchester Evening News*, reporting on the small crowds who attended the return of the Imperial Yeomanry, believed that this was due to the fact 'that it was recognised that the regiment had not a very close connection with Manchester, and that comparatively few of the returned men belonged to the city'.[124]

Key national celebrations were commemorated at both the national and local level, but local celebrations often emphasised the connection of the city or town to the national

Bradford Coronation Procession (1902), which tells the tell the story of Bradford's historical industries – concentrating on the story of the woolen industry and how it had contributed to both the power of Bradford and the Empire

Bradford Coronation Procession (1902)

cause and made that the centre of their celebrations. Edward's coronation in September 1902 was the rationale behind street parades and local pageants in towns and cities throughout the UK. However, the theme of many of the parades was one of local prowess and how local industries had added to the might of the Empire that Edward was to rule. This is demonstrated in *Bradford Coronation Procession* (1902), where the lavishly decorated floats tell the story of Bradford's historical industries, and in particular the story of the woollen industry and how it had contributed to both the power of Bradford and the Empire.[125] The film itself is filmed in three separate sequences and was shown as a film of 1,000 feet in length. Three sections of the parade are filmed, with particular emphasis placed on the series of floats that relate the history of Bradford. The parade tells the story of 'Bradford's Industries Illustrated in Historic Tableaux', with the wool industry taking centre stage. Tableaux illustrating ancient methods of manufacturing, such as 'wool growing and shearing', 'wool combing', 'worsted spinning', hand dyeing' and 'piece dying', are displayed in a series of floats, with the Bradford Dyers Association section requiring over ten separate wagons.[126] Although a set of floats dedicated to the reigns of the seven Edwards is included in the pageant, a theme also utilised by Leeds for their coronation procession, it is the floats that reflect the history of the city that are the most lavishly decorated.[127] As well as this part of the two-hour procession, the film-makers chose to illustrate other aspects of civic pride on display, including the Chamber of Commerce, the Municipal Technical College and a multitude of brass bands from the different parts of Bradford, such as Bowling, Morley, Cleckheaton, Pudsey and Great Horton. *Bradford Coronation Procession* appears to be the most complete of the many coronation celebrations filmed by Mitchell & Kenyon. The size and scale of the event, and its emphasis on the city's history and industries, is not only reflected in the detailed report in *The Bradford Daily Telegraph* but also in Sydney Carter's film exhibition later that week.[128] The procession lasted for many hours but the final film was a twelve-minute selection of the aspects of the procession that would appeal to the local spectators: the floats celebrating the city of Bradford and its local industries.[129]

The decision by Mitchell & Kenyon to film civic celebrations reveals their business acumen, as these films remained popular long after the event. They served as a visual reminder of the power of the city, and various examples can be found in the film programme of repeat performances a year or more later.[130] Although military processions, coronation celebrations and events of national importance emphasised the centrality of the Empire for the Edwardian town dwellers, 'that experience was intensely local as Edwardian working class life was bounded by the neighbourhood'.[131]

Conclusion

The industrial towns and cities filmed by Mitchell & Kenyon developed in the wake of the expansion of the Victorian industries that underpinned their financial and economic development. By the Edwardian era, towns and cities in the UK had benefited from nearly half a century of urbanisation brought about by strong local governance and issues of civic responsibility, as the city fathers became determined to provide a fitting testament of their importance to the national economy. However, as Philip J. Waller has emphasised, they remained foremost places of work 'as all improvements . . . advanced the faster for serving the end'.[132] Factories provided the goods that the Edwardian consumers required and as recreational time expanded and goods became mass-produced, the modern consumer society developed. The main industries that underpinned the Victorian economy – cotton, coal, steel and shipbuilding – also continued to flourish throughout the Edwardian era. The centrality of these industries to the local, national and international economy is apparent in the most frequently filmed subject in the Mitchell & Kenyon Collection, workers leaving the factories at lunchtime.

Notes

1 J. B. Priestley, *The Good Companions* (London: Heinemann, 1929; Granada edn, 1981), p. 19.

2 M. Golby and A.W. Purdue, *The Civilisation of the Crowd: Popular Culture in England, 1750–1900* (London: Batsford Academic and Educational Press, 1984). For more recent scholarship see Simon Gunn, *The Public Culture of the Victorian Middle Class: Ritual and Authority and the English Industrial City 1840–1914* (Manchester: Manchester University Press, 2000), and Andy Croll, *Civilizing the Urban: Popular Culture and Public Space in Merthyr, c. 1870–1914* (Cardiff: University of Wales Press, 2000).

3 There are numerous influential studies on the Victorian City, and many of these will be referred to in the chapter. For a more visual approach see H. J. Dyos and Michael Wolff (eds), *The Victorian City: Images and Realities* (London: Routledge, Kegan and Paul, 1973), and

39 See John K. Walton, *Lancashire: A Social History, 1558–1939* (Manchester: Manchester University Press, 1987), p. 184. Walton does make the point that also at this time only five English counties had lower figures of church attendance than Lancashire.

40 M&K 617: *Halifax Street Scenes* (c. 1905).

41 Steve Fielding, 'The Catholic Whit-Walk in Manchester and Salford 1890–1939', *Manchester Region History Review*, Vol. 1 No. 1 (1987), pp. 3–10.

42 M&K 452–4, 797: *Manchester Catholics Whitsuntide Processions*; and see also M&K 444: *Manchester Italian Catholic Procession* and M&K 448: *Manchester Catholic Orphanage Boys'*.

43 Andrew Davies, *Leisure, Gender and Poverty: Working-Class Culture in Salford and Manchester, 1900–1939* (Buckingham: Open University Press, 1992), pp. 124–5.

44 See *Manchester Evening News*, 28 May 1904, for a description of the Catholic Whit Friday Parade and the Oddfellows Church Parade on Whit Monday.

45 Davies, *Leisure, Gender and Poverty*, p. 125, for an account by Mrs Phelan and others of the Whit walks and how parents bought special shoes and clothes for the event.

46 Fielding, 'The Catholic Whit-Walk in Manchester and Salford 1890–1939', p. 4.

47 For the history of Warrington Walking Day see Vanessa Toulmin, 'Going Walking: Warrington Walking Day and its fair', *World's Fair*, 24 July 1997, p. 11. Available at <www.nfa.dept.shef.ac.uk/history/worlds_fair/articles/warrington.php> (accessed 2 January 2006).

48 M&K 375–80: *Warrington Walking Day*.

49 Fielding, 'The Catholic Whit-Walk in Manchester and Salford 1890–1939', p. 3.

50 M&K 404, 423: *Trafalgar Day in Liverpool*; M&K 410: *Princess Louise at Liverpool*; M&K 416–17: *Visit of Earl Roberts and Viscount Kitchener to Receive the Freedom of the City, Liverpool*.

51 Gunn, *The Public Culture of the Victorian Middle Class*, p. 163.

52 J. B. Horne and T. B. Maud, *Liverpool Transport Volume 2 1900–1930* (Glossop: Light Railway Transport Association and Transport Publishing Company, 1982), pp. 208–17.

53 Ibid., p. 209.

54 *The Showman*, 3 January 1902, p. 272.

55 Theo Barker and Dorian Gerhold, *The Rise and Rise of Road Transport 1700–1990* (Cambridge: Cambridge University Press for the Economic History Society, 1993), p. 51.

56 M&K 186: *Jamaica Street* Glasgow; M&K 183: *Ride on the Tramcar through Belfast*.

57 I am indebted to the National Tramway Museum, Winston Bond and Brian Cook for supplying additional information on the history of the electric tramway system and its local development.

58 John Armstrong, 'Transport', in Waller (ed.), *The English Urban Landscape*, pp. 208–33.

59 See Ian Yearsley, 'On the Move in the Streets: Transport Films and the Mitchell and Kenyon Collection', in Toulmin, *et al.* (eds), *The Lost World of Mitchell & Kenyon*, pp. 181–91.

60 M&K 361–2: *Life in Wigan Day by Day* (1902), in particular M&K 361; and M&K 12: *Workmen Leaving Platt's Works, Oldham* (1900).

61 *Birmingham Daily Mail*, 1 January 1901.

62 Waller, *Town, City and Nation*, p. 162.

63 Armstrong, 'Transport', p. 224.

64 M&K 184, 614: *Tram Ride into Halifax*.

65 Ian Yearsley, 'The Tramway World of Mitchell & Kenyon', *Tramway Review: Historical Journal of the Light Railway Transit Association*, Vol. 26 No. 202, July 2005, pp. 52–60.

66 M&K 176–7: *Tram Ride through the City of Sheffield.*

67 There are three films of the Leeds Lifeboat Procession filmed 5 July 1902. M&K 554–7: *Leeds Lifeboat Procession* was shot by one of the Edison companies for R. S. Smethurst and shown at the Queen's Theatre Holbeck, on 7 July, M&K 557, a section of this title also has an inscription of 'Leeds Street Scenes' on the original negative.

68 M&K 616–17: *Halifax Catholic Procession*, in particular M&K 616.

69 M&K 166–9: *Electric Tram Rides from Forster Square, Bradford.*

70 *Bradford Daily Argus*, 19 April 1902.

71 M&K 176–7: *Tram Ride through the City of Sheffield.*

72 M&K 616–17: *Halifax Catholic Procession* shows the tram to Brighouse cutting through the procession.

73 Yearsley, 'The Tramway World of Mitchell & Kenyon', p. 60.

74 Roger Oldham, *Manchester Alphabet*, published in 1906, cited in George Mould, *Manchester Memories* (Lavenham: Terence Dalton, 1972), p. 123.

75 See Waller, *Town City and Nation*, p. 163; William Plowden, *The Motor Car and Politics 1895–1970* (London: Bodley Head, 1971); and Ronald Pearsal, *Edwardian Life and Leisure* (Newton Abbot: David and Charles, 1973), p. 134.

76 M&K 405–6: *Liverpool Street Scenes* in particular M&K 405 for the scene of the three passengers, one of whom might be Sagar Mitchell.

77 M&K 663–6: *Lieutenant Clive Wilson and Tranby Croft Party*, and see M&K 666, in particular, for film of the motorcar. Edward, when Prince of Wales, was staying at Tranby Croft, the residence of Arthur Wilson, when one of his companions, George Gorden Cummings, was accused of cheating at the illegal card game baccarat. In an agreement drawn up and signed by those who witnessed the game, and others including Edward who hadn't, Cummings agreed not to play cards again in return for silence of the affair. However, rumours began to circulate and in an attempt to clear his name Cummings brought a lawsuit against the signatories in June 1891. Edward was obliged to attend the court and was cross-examined by Cummings' lawyer. It caused a minor scandal to have a member of the Royal Family appearing in court and testifying to participating in a game that was illegal in England at that time and became known as the Tranby Croft Affair.

78 See Brian Barber, 'Municipal Government in Leeds 1835–1914', in Fraser (ed.), *Municipal Reform and the Industrial City*, pp. 61–111.

79 'London in May, Saturday Afternoon', *Gardening Chronicles*, No. 19 (1896), p. 671.

80 Hazel Conway, *People's Parks: The Design and Development of Victorian Parks in Britain* (Cambridge: Cambridge University Press, 1991).

81 *Report from the Select Committee on Public Walks, Parliamentary Papers*, 1833 (448, xv), pp. 337–405.

82 Golby and Purdue, *The Civilisation of the Crowd*, pp. 102–4.

83 Hazel Conway, *Public Parks* (Princes Risborough: Shire Publications, 1996).

84 Harriet Jordan, 'Public Parks, 1885–1914', *Garden History*, Vol. 22 No. 1 (Summer 1994), pp. 85–113 (86). There are exceptions: see Hesketh Park in Southport.

85 Conway, *People's Parks*, p. 35.

86 Hunt, *Building Jerusalem: The Rise and Fall of the Victorian City*, pp. 166–7.

87 McMaster, 'The Battle for Mousehold Heath 1857–1884', pp, 117–54.

7
Edwardian Industries and the Workforce

> The Edwardian poor have attracted little attention in imaginative literature and play almost no part in commonly held images of Edwardian England.[1]

Introduction

The late nineteenth and early twentieth centuries saw the gradual erosion of Britain's dominance in the world economy, and although the main staples of the late-Victorian economy – cotton, coal, steel and shipbuilding – continued to flourish throughout the Edwardian era, a subtle downturn in Britain's fortunes was becoming apparent.[2] Although the economy was 'fundamentally sound' and still possessed 'hidden reserves at least the equal' of its international rivals, it was responding less effectively to a changing international market.[3] However, the continued importance of the textile and engineering industries, in particular, to the local, national and international economy is apparent in the most frequently filmed subject in the Mitchell & Kenyon canon, the factory gate exit.

There are more than 124 factory gate films in the collection, illustrating the workforce of approximately a hundred known factories in over sixty-five recognised locations, the majority of which relate to Lancashire, in particular the towns and areas surrounding Manchester and Salford and the industrial areas of eastern and central Lancashire.[4] Although significantly larger than any other body of film from this period, it covers only a very small percentage of the factories that operated in the UK at this time. For example, only one cotton factory is represented in Stockport, *Workers at India Mills, Stockport* (1900), and one hat factory, *Workers Leaving T. & W. Lees of Stockport* (1901).[5] However, over sixty-seven independent textile factories operated in the town, with an additional ten forming part of the Fine Cotton Spinners and Doublers Association Ltd.[6]

The factory gate exits are perhaps some of the most extraordinary films in the collection, exposing a relationship between the camera and its audience that is both intimate and

A cross-section of the British workforce can be found in the Collection. Men on the deck preparing the *S.S. Skirmisher at Liverpool* (1901) as it leaves port

Miners Leaving Pendlebury Colliery (1901) is clearly staged, with the workforce processing or parading in front of the camera

intrusive.[7] As documents of social and filmic history, they are equally fascinating, revealing the dynamics of the crowd, the structure of an apparent surging group of employees and aspects of class and gender in the Edwardian era. The films are clearly staged and reveal the workforce processing or parading in front of the camera, sometimes formally, more often en masse, as the lens struggles to capture the sea of faces that fills the screen. Nevertheless, as snapshots of history they appear at first to be problematic, because, with a few exceptions, it is only the workforce that is shown. Very few of the films reveal the interior of the factories, or even the exterior, but merely the factory exit, and the moment of leaving work is often staged or framed by the camera rather than a snapshot of a spontaneous live event. In order to evaluate the importance of this material, this chapter will examine the factories filmed by Mitchell & Kenyon in the context of both the local and national economic history of the period.

Edwardian Economy and Industries

> Now Bradfield, as everybody knows, is first and foremost in the land as a manufacturing town – that is, in all kinds of hardware. It is, moreover, the metropolis of the Midland Counties, and the men of Bradfield are proud of their birthplace, and hold their own among the magnates of cities still prouder than their own.[8]

When we examine the range of industries filmed by Mitchell & Kenyon, it becomes apparent that they captured the industrial heartlands of the north of England and the Midlands. The company filmed the workers in order that they would pay to see themselves

Employees of Messrs Lumb & Co. Leaving the Works, Huddersfield (1900) filmed in order that the workers would pay to see themselves on the cinematograph screen

Many types of manufacturing and industrial plants were filmed by Mitchell & Kenyon including *Pilkington Glass works in St Helens*, (1901) and the *Co-operative Society Printing Works in Manchester* (1901) and *Blundell's Paint Works in Hull* (1901)

at the cinematograph in the local town hall as in *Messrs Lumb and Co. Leaving the Works, Huddersfield* (1900) or at the annual fair.[9] By the start of Edward's reign, factory workers had benefited from important legislative changes implemented in the late nineteenth century. The Factory Act (1891) had made two important additions to previous legislation. The first prohibited employers from hiring women within four weeks following a confinement; the second raised the minimum age at which a child could be set to work from ten to eleven, with compulsory attendance at school until the age of eleven brought forward in the Education Act (1893). Improved wages and better working conditions led to an increase in trade union membership throughout the decade. Tensions born of disputes over wage demands, workers' rights and hours of work accelerated. From the late 1890s, increasingly powerful trade unions tried to maintain the buying power of wages, and by 1911–12, the return of inflation and the growing self-confidence of the unions resulted in the Great Labour Unrest, with 1,497 strikes in 1913 alone.[10] The trade unions' increased power is manifest in *Wakefield Miners' Demonstration*, which on film appears to be a festive and jolly occasion, with women, children and babes in arms taking part, but is reported by the local press as 'organised rowdyism'.[11] The reporter appears to have found the loosely organised demonstration threatening, even though, on film, it appears informal, akin to a family day out rather than a political demonstration.[12] The unrest that was to come in the years leading up to the Great War occurred after Mitchell & Kenyon's main period of activity, and is not reflected in the filmic record, which is predominantly from 1900 to 1902.

Mitchell & Kenyon filmed many types of manufacturing and industrial plants, including Pilkington Glass Works in St Helens, Carr's Biscuit Works in Carlisle, the Co-operative Society Printing Works in Manchester, Gossage's Soap Works, Widnes, Pollock's Caledonian Cabinet factory, Beith, and Blundell's Paint Works in Hull, to name but a few.[13] Glass, soap and chemical productions were largely concentrated in Merseyside and the factories featured in *Operatives Leaving Messrs Pilkington Bros. Works, St Helens* (1901) and

Miners Leaving Pendlebury Colliery (1901)

Workers Leaving Gossage's Soap Works, Widnes (1901) were part of industries that played important roles in the local and national economy in the later part of the nineteenth century.[14] The factories captured by Mitchell & Kenyon ranged from small- to medium-sized mills with a workforce of between 150 and 450, larger mills with a workforce of over 1,500, to those of the large engineering companies, where the employees were in the thousands. Moreover, the coal industry, that most important resource in terms of economic revenue and size of workforce (and fundamental to the rest of the economy for domestic as well as industrial fuel and power), was also captured on film, with collieries from Pendlebury, Creswell and Tyldesley forming part of the collection.[15] By 1914, Britain's share of world trade in manufacturing remained at 31 per cent, the largest of any country, with the textile industry and engineering playing a particularly important part.[16] Their importance to the national economy is also reflected in the number of films relating to these industries in the collection, and these will be emphasised in the following sections.

Textile Industries

Textile industries, incorporating cotton, wool, jute and lace factories, account for over forty titles in the collection, with another possible twenty unidentified films from Lancashire and the north of England. In Lancashire, for example, the cotton industry was concentrated in definite centres, with east and north-east Lancashire associated with cotton, while it was of minimal importance in the area around Liverpool such as St Helens and Warrington.[17] Nottingham was closely identified with the lace industry, as illustrated in *Workpeople and Girls Leaving Thos. Adams Factory, Nottingham* (1900).[18] The woollen industry is under-represented in the Mitchell & Kenyon Collection despite its importance within the textile industry in West Yorkshire in particular, with only two films of fac-

Towns such as Preston, here captured in *Turn Out of the Preston Fire Brigade* (c. 1901), were heavily associated with the textile industry

tory gate exits. *Messrs Lumb and Co. Leaving the Works, Huddersfield* and *Workers Leaving Oldroyd & Sons Mill, Dewsbury* (1900) are the only indications of the importance of the wool industry on the other side of the Pennines, where the variety of specialist processes created diversification and smaller factory units but not the high-waged, high productivity and highly unionised economies that existed in Lancashire.[19] In Lancashire, cotton factories had increased in size between 1850 and 1890, with the workforce of an average spinning firm rising from 108 to 165, weaving firms from 100 to 188 and a medium-sized company rising from 310 to 429 hands.[20] Large textile companies such as Horrocks of Preston, seen in *Workforce at Horrocks Miller & Co., Preston* (1901), operated a number of mills, employing up to 3,000 people by the 1890s, while Hornby's of Blackburn, also one of the most important and earliest textile companies in Lancashire, engaged up to 1,400 workers at its height.[21] Although certain aspects of the Edwardian textile industry were not responding to technological changes in the same manner as their overseas competitors, textiles still accounted for nearly half of British exports and continued to expand, despite growing competition from America.[22]

From the earliest days of mechanisation, spinning and weaving were undertaken in different centres: for example, spinning was concentrated in Bolton and Oldham, while weaving was the main industry in Blackburn, Burnley and other east Lancashire towns.[23] *Workforce of Ormerod's Mill, Great Moor Street, Bolton* (1900) shows us the workforce leaving a company that specialised in spinning, in particular fine yarns, while *Workpeople Leaving Hornby's Brookhouse Mill, Blackburn* (1900) is an example of one of the few large integrated firms that practised both weaving and spinning in 1900.[24] By the end of the nineteenth century, further specialisation within both spinning and weaving centres was emerging town by town, with Bolton becoming the home of the finest yarns, while Oldham

'Engineering provided the capital goods and the technology for the rest of industry' and *Workmen Leaving Platt's Works, Oldham* (1900) provided employment for 8,000 people

people in one factory block.[37] Platt's Hartford Works in Werneth occupied a site of sixty-five acres and was part of a company that also included East Works, a twenty-acre site at Greenacres Moor, as well as collieries, which brought the total workforce to 15,000.[38] As P. F. Clarke writes when considering the importance of cotton to the Lancashire economy: 'Often the only other industry of at all major proportion was engineering, the presence of which reflected the industry's reliance upon a high degree of mechanisation.'[39]

The productivity and success of Platt's of Oldham was linked to the growth of the textile industry throughout the nineteenth century, as the company produced woollen and worsted machinery for Yorkshire factories, cotton machinery, spindles and spinning machines. To cope with increasing orders from the late nineteenth century onwards, Platt's incorporated a forge and sawmills and acquired Oxford Mill in Oldham in order to demonstrate its new machinery in a working cotton mill.[40] The relationship between the engineering and textile industries is also evident in the films of Manchester and Salford. For example, there is a greater concentration of factory exits from engineering as opposed to textile companies in Manchester: five engineering factories in Manchester and one in Salford are represented in the collection, as opposed to three cotton factories in Manchester and one in Salford. Engineering, which had developed in response to the demand

for machinery for the cotton industry, was a significant part of the productivity and prosperity of both Manchester and Salford. Although 24 per cent of Manchester and Salford's industrial workforce was still employed in the textile industry, by 1914 Manchester was one of the world's foremost engineering centres.[41] The industrial concentration and diversification in the city is apparent in the films of the various engineering works. These include Peacock's Engineering Works, Brooks and Doxey's West Gorton Works, Galloways' Boiler Works on Hyde Road, Crossley's Works in Openshaw and Craven's Ironworks, Ordsall Lane Salford.[42] The 1901 census for Salford, for example, reveals that the dominant male occupation was in engineering and machine-making where 7,464 men and boys were employed, as opposed to 2,376 men and boys in the textile industry.[43] Robert Roberts, in *The Classic Slum* and *A Ragged Schooling*, describes working life in just such a setting.[44] Manchester, in the Edwardian era, was not reliant on one form of industry, despite its historic association with the textile industry, and was diversifying its industrial and trading base. The opening of the Manchester Ship Canal in 1894 saw the city rise to Britain's fourth largest port in terms of trade by the end of the Edwardian era.[45]

Engineering was as important for the economy as the textile industry in the 1900s and factories filmed by Mitchell & Kenyon include *Workers Brooks and Doxey, West Gorton Works, Manchester* (1900), *Employees of Galloways Ltd. Boiler Works, Hyde Road, Manchester* (1900) and *Employees Leaving Crossley's Works, Openshaw* (1900)

Workforce of Parkgate Iron and Steel Co., Rotherham (1901) is unusual for a factory gate film in that it shows not only views of the workforce leaving the factory but also views inside the factory gate itself. The company produced iron and steel and had a workforce of approximately 7,000 with the whole of the neighbouring economy of Rawmarsh directly related to the factory

Royal Visit to Barrow & Launch of H.M.S. Dominion (1903) built by Vickers and Maxim of Barrow-in-Furness

in 1903 by Princess Louise.[54] The might of the Royal Navy was central to all this, as is clear in *Torpedo Flotilla Visit to Manchester* (1901), a filmic record of the flotilla passing through the Manchester Ship Canal.[55] Although Britain was the undisputed ruler of the ocean, Germany had already begun to build up its mercantile and naval fleets, and joined the international race for supremacy in the North Atlantic.

Railways

Although the railway industry does not feature prominently in the Mitchell & Kenyon Collection, the factory gate exits of railway works and the films of phantom rides remind us that the Victorian and Edwardian period was without doubt the age of the railway.[56] The railway-related products produced by the engineering companies filmed by Mitchell & Kenyon ranged from heavy industrial goods, such as cast-iron and steel rails, and, most notably, the roof of St Pancras station, to the steam locomotives produced by Fowler's of Leeds.[57] *Workers Leaving Butterley Ironworks, Ripley* (1900) features one of the most important engineering companies in the UK at the time. The Butterley Forge and Wagon Works was a vast industrial site that followed the course of the Cromford Canal from the village of Stoneyford all the way to Golden Valley in Derbyshire. Founded in 1790 by Benjamin Outram, the company expanded and was responsible for the industrial 'model village' of Ironville, providing workers' cottages, a school, church and even a mechanics institute for their workers.[58] The workforces associated with the railway industry usually dominated the employment of the towns in which they were based, with *Employees Leaving the Midland Railway Loco Works, Derby* (1900) and *Workforce of Crewe Engineering Works* (c. 1901) showing the sheer number of employees.[59] The continued importance of the railway both for transportation and the economy is apparent in *Employees Leaving*

North Eastern Engine Works, Gateshead (1901) and *Great Northern Railway Works at Doncaster* (1901), where an endless sea of workers of all ages pours out of the factories.[60]

The link between the engineering industries and the growth of the railways is further demonstrated elsewhere in the collection. Factories such as Peacock's, as seen in *Workmen Leaving Peacock's Works at Meal Time, Gorton, Manchester* (1900), supplied locomotives for the East Indian Railway, the Royal Swedish Railway, as well as British companies.[61] Another film that demonstrates the link between the growth of engineering and the expansion of the transport network is *Workforce of Brush Electric Co., Falcon Works, Loughborough* (1900), filmed in November for Loughborough Fair. This company manufactured tramcars and, by the twentieth century, locomotives for both the electric tramways and the railways.[62] Although Mitchell & Kenyon predominantly filmed tramways rather than railways, five titles in the collection are of phantom rides filmed from the front of a railway carriage, of views in Ireland, Scotland and the south-west of England.[63]

(Overleaf) *The 'Hands' Leaving Work at North-Street Mills, Chorley* (1900). In the 1900s, the proportion of women workers in the Lancashire textile industry was the highest in the country

Gender and Division of Labour

Perhaps the most striking aspect of the images captured in the factory exits, in particular the textile mills and heavy industry and engineering works, is the division of labour within the workforce by age and gender. Indeed, the gender division in the films is a guide to distinguishing the types of industry on view, with the textile factories revealing a larger percentage of women workers than the engineering films. Gender relations in both the nineteenth and early twentieth centuries were characterised by large local and regional variations, 'with a rich mosaic of experiences across a variety of different communities, labour markets and traditions'.[64]

The employment of women within fishing communities in Scotland and along the North East coastline of England are illustrated in *North Sea Fisheries, North Shields* (1901)

Engineering works seen in *Employees Leaving Messrs Vickers and Maxim's in Barrow* (1901)

The employment of women within fishing communities in Scotland and along the north-east coastline of England is illustrated in *North Sea Fisheries, North Shields* (1901). The film shows the fisherwomen who followed the Scottish fleet down the coast, cleaning and preparing the catch and then selling it at the ports. This work created some measure of economic independence for women from eastern Scotland.

In the 1900s, the proportion of women workers in the Lancashire textile industry was higher than the national average in the rest of the country. Women worked as weavers and ring spinners, as they were excluded from mule spinning (primarily a male preserve), with 90 per cent of women under the age of twenty-five who lived in the cotton towns finding employment in the textile industry. Between 1901 and 1911, three-quarters of unmarried women in weaving and spinning towns were in employment, with a high proportion of married women, more than one-third in certain weaving towns, also forming an essential part of the workforce.[65] The weaving towns of Blackburn and Burnley, for example, were dependent on female labour, and by the Edwardian era over 60 per cent of the operatives employed in cotton factories in Britain were women or girls over the age of thirteen.[66] Weavers were described by Robert Roberts as 'top in their class', enjoying a higher standing within the community than the spinners and dyers.[67] Fanny Hawthorne, the heroine of Stanley Houghton's play *Hindle Wakes*, was a weaver, and the ability to provide an income for the family or to be economically independent is reflected in her response when she chooses to leave her house and family: 'I shan't starve. I'm not without a trade at my finger tips, thou knows. I'm a Lancashire lass, and as long as there's weaving sheds in Lancashire I shall earn enough brass to keep me going.'[68]

The range of work undertaken by women in the factories included weaving, preparation of cotton and, from the 1880s onwards, the new technology of ring spinning. However,

20,000 Employees Entering Lord Armstrong's Elswick Works (1900) shows an almost 100-per-cent male workforce

even within the more lucrative area of weaving, women did not earn as much as their male counterparts and were excluded from positions of authority and supervision within the factory.

According to Robert Roberts, at first clogs and shawls were standard wear for all women workers. This can be clearly seen in the films in the collection relating to the textile industry, where the shawl-covered women exit the factories in droves, some hiding their faces with the shawls to avoid being filmed. By the 1900s, weavers and spinners were starting to wear different clothing, with the better-paid weavers scorning the shawls and clogs in place of a hat and coat. Examples of this in the collection include *The Millhands of Cheetham's Bankwood Mills, Stalybridge* (1900), where, interestingly, the women wear both shawls and hats, and *Workpeople and Girls Leaving Thos. Adams Factory, Nottingham*, where the women are wearing smart coats and hats but no shawls or clogs.[69] This could lead to resentment, as Roberts reveals: 'so clearly in fact did headwear denote class that, in Glasgow, separate clubs existed for "hat" girls and "shawl" girls'.[70] This pattern of female labour was also apparent in other textile regions, where the predominantly female Dundee jute workers captured in *Employees Leaving Baxter's Jute Works, Dundee* (1901) and *Employees Leaving Gilroy's Jute Works, Dundee* (1901) contributed a major part of the family budget.[71] Interestingly, the resentment shown towards the weavers and their attire can be seen in *Employees Leaving Gilroy's Jute Works, Dundee*, where one of the shawl-clad women appears to spit derogatively at another woman wearing a hat.[72]

The gender division in the workforce is again very apparent in a comparison of *Workers Leaving the Jute Works, Barrow* (1902) with *Employees Leaving Furness Railway Works, Barrow* (1901) and *Employees Leaving Messrs Vickers and Maxim's in Barrow* (1901). The workers in the two later titles are overwhelmingly male, while at the jute works, female employees represent a large proportion of the workforce.[73] The workforce in the heavy industries in Sheffield, captured in *Employees Leaving Vickers, Sons and Maxim Works, Sheffield* and *Employees Leaving Brown's Atlas Works, Sheffield*, was predominantly male, with 20,696 men employed in 1891, as opposed to only 688 women in engineering, iron and steel manufacture, and boiler-making, for example.[74] Although there were limited opportunities in Sheffield and South Yorkshire for women workers, in contrast to the textile towns and cities of West Yorkshire, over 9,000 women worked in light industries in Sheffield in 1901, including those employed buffing and burnishing the finished cutlery.[75]

The different types of work undertaken in the factories are not really apparent in the films, showing as they do only the exit of the workforce. This brief overview is really an attempt to place the films in the context of a representative sample of the films in the collection. Perhaps the most striking images in the films are those that relate to the employment of children within the late-Victorian and Edwardian factory systems. Shot during lunchtime, the films reveal scenes of half-timers, children employed as operatives while still attending school, a practice that was particularly prevalent in the textile factories in Lancashire and Yorkshire.

Child Labour

> These were the scrawny, dirty, hungry, ragged, verminous boys and girls who were to grow up into the working classes of twentieth-century England. This was the generation which was to man the armies of the First World War, although they were inches shorter and pounds lighter than they would have been if they had been properly fed and cared for.[76]

Although the practice of employing children to work half-time was prevalent throughout Britain, it was particularly widespread in the cotton mills of Lancashire, and in the West Riding of Yorkshire. Indeed, this practice continued until the 1920s in certain parts of the counties. The debate about the employment of children in the factory continued from the middle decades of the nineteenth century, when proposed legislation to abolish the half-time system was defeated in 1890 and again in 1914.[77] By the end of the nineteenth century and throughout the Edwardian period, there were growing concerns regarding the employment of children and working practices involving child labour. The Employment of Children Act (1903) was an attempt to combat the growing anxieties of Liberals and the medical profession, who feared that excessive use of child labour was impairing physical development. Calls for the system to be abolished grew stronger, as the children were often working a full day before coming into school and complaints that they fell asleep in class were commonplace: 'The healthy, bright child of ten degenerates into the sallow weakling of thirteen and the deterioration of our industrial population, especially in mills, has become a real source of danger to the nation.'[78]

The fear that morally degrading behaviour might affect the young workers was an additional factor in the calls to abolish the half-time system, particularly in Lancashire. Young girls, it was believed, were transformed from 'loveable children' into 'loud-voiced coarse vulgar girls', while boy half-timers tended to become clever at repartee and 'in the

The scenes of child workers captured in *Workforce Leaving Alfred Butterworth and Sons, Glebe Mills, Hollinwood* (1901) employed in the half-time system are some of the most powerful in the Collection

use of mannish phrases'.[79] In 1901, approximately 300,000 children were employed in England and Wales, with a third of them finding work as half-timers.[80] The age at which children worked in the half-time system changed throughout the nineteenth century.[81] The system was first put into legislation in the Factory Act (1833), which enabled children from the age of nine onwards to be employed within the factory system for up to forty-eight hours a week.[82] This was dropped to eight years of age in 1844, increased to ten in 1874, raised to eleven in 1893 and then twelve from 1899.[83] Although the Education Act of 1893 had raised the school-leaving age to eleven, and the 1899 Education Act had extended the age for compulsory schooling to twelve, certain loopholes and exemptions still enabled the employment of children. These loopholes continued after the Education Act of 1902 and the Employment of Children Act (1903), as the half-time system proved too strong to legislate against effectively in certain parts of the country. In 1910, even after the 1902 Education Act, 23 per cent of Liverpool children between eleven and fourteen were working, while in Nottingham the figure was 25 per cent, due in part to the employment of half-timers in the lace industry.[84] Mitchell & Kenyon's *Workpeople and Girls Leaving Thos. Adams Factory, Nottingham*, filmed for Nottingham Goose Fair, shows a workforce of young girls and women, the hierarchy marked by dress: the younger operatives wear shawls, while the older, more experienced and presumably higher-paid women wear straw hats and smarter clothing.[85]

One of the major flaws of the Employment of Children Act (1903) was that it made local authorities responsible for implementing by-laws that prohibited the employment of children in certain occupations and for prescribing working hours and the age threshold. In reality, nearly one-third of local authorities did not adopt the Act and those that did were not terribly effective in policing their own by-laws.[86] The employment of children within theatres perhaps received more effective legislation, with individual cases often highlighted by the entertainment press as theatre and circus proprietors campaigned vigorously for exemptions for their professions.[87] The half-time system resulted in children working four-hour shifts either in the morning or from lunchtime onwards, with an estimated 300,000 children employed while still at school, representing 8 per cent of the total population under the age of fourteen. The system continued in some areas until the First World War, and in some parts of Lancashire and the Midlands until 1921. Nominally, the half-time procedure did involve having to pass an educational test and undergo a physical examination. Additionally, if a child had attended 300 sessions over the previous five years, he or she could combine schooling with the factory system. Inevitably, the system was open to abuse; according to Harry Pollitt in his autobiography, *Serving My Time*: 'The mill-owners who controlled the educational bodies took precious care that the biggest dunce in the school could pass it . . .'.[88]

The half-time system was also utilised by the woollen industry, and examples in the collection include *Messrs Lumb and Co. Leaving the Works, Huddersfield* and *Mill Workers Leaving Oldroyd & Sons Mill, Dewsbury*. Scenes from *Employees Leaving Baxter's Jute Works, Dundee*, also reveal crowds of young boys, many apparently younger than twelve, leaving the factory at lunchtime. However, it is in Lancashire, Mitchell & Kenyon's heartland, where the material capturing child operatives dominates the filmic record.[89]

Lancashire and the Half-time System

> Lancashire cotton mills not only remained the focus of the majority of children employed as half-timers but also . . . they appeared to be relatively impervious to the currents of social change affecting the rest of the nation.[90]

Evidence for the industries where the half-time system was essential to the success of the factory can be found in the factory gate exits filmed by Mitchell & Kenyon between 1900 and 1902. Over forty different factories are represented in the collection, of which twenty-six in Lancashire alone utilised this type of labour.[91] Successive governments took the view that the half-time system was beneficial and various attempts to change it throughout the Edwardian era were met with resistance, in particular from Lancashire and other textile regions, where half-timers remained an important part of the workforce.[92] The strength of support for the half-time system in Lancashire is illustrated by the opposition from Lancashire MPs to R. D. Denman's bill of 1914, which proposed the abolition of the system. This opposition was expressed not only by the textile workers themselves, who voted in 1908 against any changes because of the economic importance of child workers for the family, but also by the local authorities in the towns where the textile factories were located.[93] Any attempts to change the system were campaigned against by the cotton operatives whenever balloted by their unions and the Lancashire fac-

The half-time system, which utilised the employment of children under the age of 12 was more dominant in Lancashire than in any other county. *Workforce Leaving Alfred Butterworth and Sons, Glebe Mills, Hollinwood* (1901) shows young boys and girls leaving work

tory owners, who campaigned vigorously to maintain this system on the grounds that children were needed for the smaller but more technical work that would later be replaced by mule spinners and power-loom weavers.[94] In the 1890s, there were still nearly 100,000 half-timers employed in the mills in Lancashire, although the numbers were beginning to fall.[95] Although half-timers were employed in a wide variety of trades, by the early 1900s the textile industry was still the largest employer, with an estimated 47,360 children nationally in 1906–7, of which 65 per cent were employed in Lancashire and Yorkshire. The concentration of the cotton factories in individual towns resulted in a higher percentage of half-timers: in Bolton, in 1908, for example, the figure was over 70 per cent.[96]

The methods of production utilised by the cotton textile industry and its continued support for the half-time system meant that cotton was the largest single employer of half-timers in the years leading up to the First World War. This was also due to the nature of the subcontract system employed in textile factories, where the children were actually hired by the adult operatives rather than the mill owners.[97] It was the adult operatives who believed that it was better to work in the mills from an early age, as children learned quickly and their fingers were more deft. Although the number employed was in decline, an upsurge in business, first in 1906, then again in 1908, saw a further increase in the use of the half-timers. In the collection, the films that capture the half-time system were filmed between 1900 and 1902, only a year after legislation had raised the age to twelve for half-timers and the Education Act (1902) had raised the age of school leaving to fourteen. In *Alfred Butterworth and Sons, Glebe Mills, Hollinwood* groups of children appear like adults, smiling at the camera and responding to the presence of the showmen. Closer examination of the images reveals children with rickets, as undernourished bodies crowd

Young girls wearing shawls over their heads and boys with flat caps in *Leaving Alfred Butterworth and Sons, Glebe Mills, Hollinwood (*1901), crowd the frame of the film with eyes old beyond their years

the frame of the film staring back at the camera with eyes old beyond their years. Their ill-fitting clothing and shoeless feet add to the picture of poverty and deprivation. The shawl-covered Salford mill girls, clutching their billy-cans as they leave Egerton Mill and Howarth's Mill on Ordsall Lane at lunchtime, are almost indistinguishable from the older workers in dress and bearing, but again appear younger than twelve.[98] The true age of the young workers is difficult to determine. Some of the children, almost certainly sons or daughters of the workers, are taking baskets of food to their parents working in the factory, as in *Workers Leaving Textile Factory in Patricroft* (1901).[99] Certainly, the material from early 1900, a few months after changes to the legislation in 1899, does appear to show half-time operatives younger than twelve in the factories in east Lancashire, in particular Blackburn, Darwen and Nelson. Examples include *Employees Leaving Olive Mill, Darwen* (1900), *Workpeople Leaving Fish's Waterfall Mill, Blackburn* (1900), *Workpeople Leaving Ordnance Mill, Blackburn* (1900) and *Workers at Spring Bank Mill, Nelson* (1900), in which the young operatives of both sexes appear noticeably younger than their fellow workers.[100]

Despite the argument put forward by supporters of the regime about beneficial employment and how it ensured some kind of education for poor children, the real beneficiaries were the children's parents and families. P. Sandiford reported in 1908 that working in the mills was popular with half-timers as it contributed to the family income, helped them learn a trade and gave them some financial independence.[101] George Tomlinson, Minister of Education in 1944, wrote candidly in his autobiography about the reality of the half-time system:

> There was only one reason why I went into the mill at twelve years of age. Make no mistake about it. I know the reason. It meant 2s. 3d. per week in the home, in which, at that time, were seven people with an average wage coming in of 26s. per week.[102]

Employees Leaving Storey's Moor Lane Mill, Lancaster (1902) brings to life the view that 'Lancashire retained the highest proportion of half-timers, working girls, and working women in the whole country'

The young operatives of both sexes appear noticeably younger than their fellow workers in *Workers Leaving Textile Factory in Patricroft* (1901)

The collection captures only a fraction of the actual number of factories located in many of the towns. Films in Chorley, Middleton, Manchester, Colne, Lancaster, Bolton, Clitheroe, Blackburn, Preston and Pendlebury, for example, demonstrate the prevalence of child labour in the factory system at the time.[103] *Operatives of Acme Spinning Company, Pendlebury* (1901), *Workforce of Howorth's Ordsall Mill, Salford* (1900) and *Workpeople Leaving*

Ryland's Mill, Gorton, Manchester (1900) reinforce the view that 'Lancashire retained the highest proportion of half-timers, working girls, and working women in the whole country'.[104] This is underlined through examining the 1901 census returns for Salford, which reveal that 7,774 women and girls aged over ten, who were living in Salford, were employed in cotton manufacture, easily outnumbering the 2,376 men and boys.[105] While the employees appear to be predominantly women and half-timers, of course the one to two minutes captured on film are not fully representative of the workforce as a whole. What is apparent is that Peter Laslett's vivid description of 'scrawny, dirty, hungry, ragged . . . boys and girls' is reflected in the image of child-workers within the half-time system in the factory films of Mitchell & Kenyon.[106]

Education Act (1902)

To prepare for the future, Arthur Balfour, Prime Minister from 1902 to 1905, recognised that Britain needed to update its educational system and strengthen its defences. Concern was also felt that the future generation was physically and mentally ill-equipped to cope with the economic and possibly military challenge of a resurgent Germany. One of the concerns regarding the half-time system was that the children were becoming undernourished and physically weakened, as well as missing out on a good education, by working from such an early age. One of the effects of the Education Act (1902) was the abolition of the school boards, as primary, technical and secondary education was placed directly under the control of local authorities.[107] Physical, spiritual and academic instruction became more disciplined after 1902, and this is apparent in *Audley Range School, Blackburn* (c. 1905), where the children perform exercises for the camera.[108] The regimental structure of

Children at St Barnabas School, Blackburn (1905) shows a different face of childhood as the Education Act 1902 created greater opportunities and placed primary and secondary education directly under the control of local authorities

Special Parade of St Matthew's Pupils and Special March Past of St Joseph's Scholars (1905) demonstrate that the education regime had become more disciplined after 1902

Edwardian schooling is evident in the two schools featured in *Special Parade of St Matthew's Pupils and Special March Past of St Joseph's Scholars, Blackburn* (1905), as they file past the camera in military fashion.[109] From 1902 and the years leading up to the Great War, local authority expenditure on education rose from £9.5 million to £30.6 million, with central government increasing its spending from £12.5 million to £19.5 million.[110]

The emphasis placed on physical education is also apparent in the collection, with *Calisthenics* (1905) and *Day School Sports at Park Avenue, Bradford* (1902) providing wonderful footage of the exercise and sporting regimes of the time.[111] For Mitchell & Kenyon, the films of school processions and displays were almost as popular a subject as the factory gate exit, as they encouraged a wider audience of family members to attend the screenings later that evening. *Love Burn Street School, Dumfries* (c. 1901) and *Scholars Leaving St Andrew's RC School, Dumfries* (c. 1901) reveal a vision of childhood in complete contrast to the life captured in the factory gate exits.[112]

Calisthenics (1905) was a popular exercise regime at the time for children and also for the armed forces

Case Study: Holidays and Wakes Week

Paid holidays were not part of the Victorian or Edwardian economy, but the creation of leisure time and the industries that developed from the mid-nineteenth century onwards were linked to the workers' holidays. The most important of these traditional holidays in Lancashire was the wakes, which had changed from the earlier pre-industrial times to an industrial holiday introduced in the nineteenth century and became an important part of the factory workers' leisure time.[113] As Robert Poole writes, 'the wakes holidays have for a century and more been regarded as the annual closure period of the cotton industry', associated with seaside excursions, the closure of the local factories, and 'are one of the region's best known social customs'.[114] By the 1890s, each specific area took their seasonal holidays at a customary time of year. Starting at the end of May and finishing in mid-September,

> The Lancashire wakes, especially in the areas around Manchester . . . were more than just well established fairs. They remained for most of, if not all, of the nineteenth century, affirmations of community identity, both past and present, in which people expressed themselves through uninhibited pleasure-seeking.[115]

Many of the wakes were an important part of the traditional culture of pre-industrial Lancashire, and were transformed and strengthened throughout the Industrial Revolution, in particular by the railway excursions and the emergence of the seaside holiday.[116] Although wakes survived in parts of Yorkshire and Cheshire, and the custom of closing down factories in rotation for the works' annual holidays was also adopted in the Midlands, it was in the Lancashire cotton-manufacturing district, where the development of the factory sys-

Workers at Yates's Foundry, Blackburn (1900) is one of the many films associated with the holiday season in Lancashire and were filmed predominantly for showing at the local Wakes fairs

Wakes holidays could be enjoyed by the seaside, in particular at Blackpool shown (above) in *Blackpool Victoria Pier* (1904), or by visiting the annual fair – (above left) *Sedgwick's Bioscope Showfront at Pendlebury Wakes* (1901)

tem was so extensive, that it developed into 'a mass industrial holiday faster and further than anywhere else in the country'.[117] Even though a large proportion of Lancashire towns had regular summer holidays by the 1870s, these were often based upon the existing pattern of festivities such as the wakes festivals, which by the end of the nineteenth century had spread to the whole of the county: 'All of the cotton holidays, regardless of their origins, became known as wakes and by the mid-1900s, when even the stragglers were enjoying a full seven days, as wakes weeks.'[118] Wakes holidays were staggered in Lancashire and Cheshire from the period after Whitsuntide to early autumn, with holidays ranging from eight to ten days, and a fortnight becoming more common between 1890 and 1910.[119] The leisure industries that developed out of the increase in recreational time in the nineteenth century, in particular the seaside resorts in the north of England, have been covered in Chapter 4.[120] In the case of travelling exhibitors who commissioned Mitchell & Kenyon to film factory gate films, the immediate impact of the holiday period was the association between wakes week and the visit of the travelling fair, which became an important part of the festivities throughout the nineteenth century. So important were they for the fairground exhibitors that the *Showmen's Year Books* included a separate list for the wakes weeks near to Manchester and the Yorkshire feast dates each year from 1900 onward.[121] The visit of the travelling fair, complete with cinematograph shows for the local wakes festivals, explains why factory gate films dominate the Mitchell & Kenyon Collection, as the majority of the 124 titles were filmed for the annual wakes holidays in Lancashire and Cheshire. The showmen followed the factory closures and hired Mitchell & Kenyon to film the workers leaving the local factories. In addition, Mitchell & Kenyon advertised for sale a stock of factory gate exits, which showmen could use when attending the fairs. When the collection was discovered, it was found that the dates or locations on the negatives on the first fifty-plus reels directly corresponded to these factory holidays in Yorkshire, Lancashire and Cheshire. By utilising the dates from the *Showmen's Year Book*, the films have now been dated in the order they were originally filmed and exhibited, and include *Workforce Leaving Salt's Works in Saltaire* (1900), filmed on 24 July for Shipley Feast; *Operatives Leaving Jubilee Mill, Padiham* (1900), exhibited two days later at the local fair, on 9 August; and *The 'Hands' Leaving Work at North-Street Mills, Chorley* (1900), taken on 30

The 'Hands' Leaving Work at North-Street Mills, Chorley (1900), taken on 30 August for the September holidays

August for the September holidays.[122] This pattern is also apparent in *The Millhands of Cheetham's Bankwood Mills, Stalybridge*, exhibited on 24 July at Stalybridge Wakes, one of the largest of the wakes fairs held in Cheshire.[123] Mossley Wake followed Stalybridge, and the report in *The Herald* includes an account of a cinematograph show depicting scenes of the local employees from Mayall's Mill:

> On the left here is a cinematograph show, the proprietors of which have hit upon the new idea of throwing up views of the employees at local mills leaving work at dinner time. Messrs. Mayall's Mills were chosen for Mossley and a roaring patronage was the result.[124]

Oldham Wakes was one of the largest in Lancashire, and its influence on neighbouring areas was such that by the end of the nineteenth century, towns such as Hollinwood were closing down their factories for the holiday period in line with Oldham: *Alfred Butterworth and Sons, Glebe Mills, Hollinwood* was filmed for showing at Oldham Wakes.[125] *Workmen Leaving Platt's Works, Oldham* was filmed on 20 August 1900 and then exhibited ten days later at the wakes fair.[126] Unlike other parts of Lancashire, Manchester had, by the late nineteenth century, lost most of its traditional wakes festivities, with Gorton

Wakes a rare example of the continuation of a former village custom after the area had become subsumed by the growth of Manchester.[127] In line with their counterparts in other manufacturing centres, the workers' holidays in Manchester followed the pattern of the traditional festivities and different parts of the city closed down their operations for a week during the wakes. Within the collection, for example, there are five titles relating to Gorton, and these films were commissioned and shot in August in anticipation of Gorton Wakes, which was held in early September:

> A great feature in the fair was the prominence given to 'Living Pictures', these being on view at Mr Clark's exhibition, where the great hit was a local picture of the workmen leaving Peacock's at a meal hour: at Sedgewick's menagerie, where the local picture was the workmen leaving Gorton Tank: and at Cordwell's lifeograph establishment where the local picture represented the workpeople leaving Ryland's mill.[128]

The majority of the factory gates commissioned from Mitchell & Kenyon in Yorkshire and the Midlands are also linked to local factory closures or annual fairs, such as Nottingham Goose Fair.[129] In Sheffield and parts of the Midlands, the phenomenon known as 'bull' or 'calf' weeks also occurred, where double time was worked the week before the holidays so that productivity would not drop and the workforce would not necessarily lose any pay.[130] The wakes and holiday weeks continued well into the twentieth century, maintaining the established pattern of time and location over fifty years after the factories had first been filmed by Mitchell & Kenyon.

Some of the attractions of the Edwardian fair that the workers enjoyed during Wakes week – *Sedgwick's Bioscope Showfront at Pendlebury Wakes* (1901)

Conclusion

With the exception of a few titles, the Mitchell & Kenyon Collection only really captured the great industries in the first two years of the twentieth century, where the economy of Edwardian Britain was greatly helped by the continuing Anglo-Boer War, which began in 1899.[131] As Peter Laslett writes: 'the huge coalfields of Yorkshire and Lancashire, the great shipbuilding towns, the acres and acres of factory floor given to textiles, were made busier by the demand for armaments and uniforms and machinery'.[132] The factory gate exits filmed by Mitchell & Kenyon reveal a pattern of industrial life that had continued from the mid-nineteenth century. In contrast to Laski's observation cited at the opening of this chapter on the paucity of images for the Edwardian poor, the collection now provides a rich record with which to study and investigate both the Edwardian working class and the society in which they worked and played. The spirit of optimism and economic power persisted throughout the decade despite labour unrest, downturns in certain aspects of both the engineering and textile industries, and the growing might, both economic and military, of a resurgent Germany. On a political level, Britain in the Edwardian age existed in a twilight zone: the balance of power in so many areas was shifting in a Europe in which the decisive factor was the rise of a united Germany, and in a world in which the United States would soon dominate. However, the fear of being overtaken economically, politically and militarily by its rivals also resulted in a shift towards greater militarism in the early 1900s, as government spending on the army and navy increased. The final group of films in the collection illustrates these changes and shows how the military powers and the public responded both to the impact of the Anglo-Boer War and the need for Britain to strengthen its defences both on land and at sea and build for the future.

Notes

1 M. Laski, cited in Robert Roberts, *The Classic Slum: Salford Life in the First Quarter of the Century* (Manchester: Manchester University Press, 1971).

2 See Sidney Pollard, *Britain's Prime and Britain's Decline: The British Economy, 1870–1914* (London: Edward Arnold, 1989), for an overview of the factors leading to the downturn in British fortunes leading up to the Great War. For an introduction to issues of class and the Victorian and Edwardian workforce see Patrick Joyce, *Visions of the People: Industrial England and the Question of Class, 1848–1914* (Cambridge: Cambridge University Press, 1991).

3 Pollard, *Britain's Prime and Britain's Decline*, pp. 270–1.

4 Sixty-five known locations with an additional thirteen locations still to be identified. See subject listing in the Filmography for further details.

5 M&K 19: *Workers at India Mills, Stockport* (1900) and M&K 91: *Workers Leaving T. & W. Lees of Stockport* (1901).

6 P. J. Waller, *Town, City and Nation 1850–1914* (Oxford: Oxford University Press, 1983), p. 71; M&K 19: *Workers at India Mills, Stockport.*

7 For an evaluation of the factory gate exits as film texts see Tom Gunning, 'Pictures of Crowd Splendour: The Mitchell and Kenyon Factory Gate Films', in Vanessa Toulmin, Simon Popple and Patrick Russell (eds), *The Lost World of Mitchell & Kenyon: Edwardian Britain on Film* (London: BFI, 2004), pp. 49–59.

8 Emma Jane Worboise, *A Woman's Patience* (London: Clarke, 1879).

9 M&K 28: *Messrs Lumb and Co. Leaving the Works, Huddersfield.*

10 G. R. Searle, *A New England? Peace and War 1886–1918* (Oxford: Oxford University Press, 2004), pp. 441–53.

11 *Wakefield Express*, 18 July 1908; M&K 594: *Miners' Demonstration at Wakefield.*

12 Andrew Prescott, '"We Had Fine Banners": Street Processions in the Mitchell and Kenyon Films', in Toulmin *et al.* (eds), *The Lost World of Mitchell & Kenyon*, pp. 125–36.

13 M&K 24: *Workers at Pilkington Glass Works, St Helens (*1900); M&K 25–6: *Operatives Leaving Messrs Pilkington Bros. Works, St Helens* (1901); M&K 56: *Employees of Co-operative Wholesale Society Printing Works, Longsight, Manchester* (1901); M&K 86: *Workers at Carr's Biscuit Works, Carlisle* (1901); M&K 89: *Workforce of Pollock's Caledonian Cabinet Works, Beith* (1901); M&K 79: *Workers Leaving Gossage's Soap Works, Widnes* (1901); and M&K 82: *Employees of Blundell's Paint Works, Hull* (1901). For a complete list of the factories filmed by Mitchell & Kenyon see the Filmography, and for a breakdown of the individual industries these factories represent see Pollard, *Britain's Prime and Britain's Decline*, Ch. 3, pp. 18–49.

14 M&K 79: *Workers Leaving Gossage's Soap Works, Widnes.*

15 M&K 13: *Creswell and Langwith Miners, Mansfield* (1900); M&K 57: *Workers at St George's Colliery, Tyldesley* (1901); and M&K 58: *Miners Leaving Pendlebury Colliery* (1901).

16 Paul Thompson, *The Edwardians: The Remaking of British Society*, 2nd new edn (London: Routledge, 1992), pp. 152–3.

17 P. F. Clarke, *Lancashire and the New Liberalism* (Cambridge: Cambridge University Press, 1971), p. 76.

18 M&K 31: *Workpeople and Girls Leaving Thos. Adams Factory, Nottingham.*

19 Patrick Joyce, *Work, Society and Politics: The Culture of the Factory in later Victorian England* (London: Methuen, 1980), p. 75.

20 Ibid., pp. 158–9.

21 M&K 283: *Workforce at Horrocks Miller & Co., Preston*; for information on Horrocks of Preston see M. Burscough, *The Horrockses: Cotton Kings of Preston* (Lancaster: Carnegie, 2004). For Hornby's importance to Blackburn see Joyce, *Work, Society and Politics*, pp. 189–91; George C. Miller, *Blackburn: The Evolution of a Cotton Town* (Blackburn: Blackburn Town Council, 1951); and M&K 48: *Workpeople Leaving Hornby's Brookhouse Mill, Blackburn* (1900).

22 Pollard, *Britain's Prime and Britain's Decline.*

23 Clarke, *Lancashire and the New Liberalism* p. 77.

24 M&K 39: *Workforce of Ormerod's Mill, Great Moor Street, Bolton* and M&K 48: *Workpeople Leaving Hornby's Brookhouse Mill, Blackburn.* See *The Industries of Lancashire* (Blackburn: Historical Publishing Company, 1889); reprinted as *Blackburn and Darwen a Century Ago* (Nelson: Landy Publishing, 1989), where Hornby's is described as being one of the best combined spinning and weaving mills in England.

25 John K. Walton, *Lancashire, A Social History, 1558–1939* (Manchester: Manchester University Press, 1987), p. 200.

26 Inland Revenue Valuation Office Field Book, The National Archives, IR 58/72845.

27 M&K 20: *Howarth's Egerton Mill, Ordsall Lane, Salford* and M&K 21: *Workforce of Howarth's Ordsall Mill, Salford* (1900).

28 *Kelly's Directory of 1901* lists Alfred Butterworth & Son, Cotton Spinners and Manufacturers, Glebe Mills, Drury Lane, Hollinwood; and see D. Gurr and J. Hunt, *The Cotton Mills of Oldham* (Oldham: Oldham Education and Leisure, 1998).

29 Walton, *Lancashire, A Social History*, p. 201.

30 Ibid.

31 Ibid., p. 206.

32 M&K 570: *Razing of a Mill Chimney in Leeds* and M&K 328: *Felling of Hibson Road Brick Works Chimney in Nelson.*

33 *Burnley Leader*, 1 June 1906.

34 George Falconer, *A Life of Peril: The Lancashire Steeplejack* (Bolton: W. & L. Mappin, 1902). See also *The Lancashire Steeple-jack: A Sketch of His Career and Work by an Outsider* (Bolton: W. & T. R. Morris, 1898).

35 Pollard, *Britain's Prime and Britain's Decline*, p. 20.

36 M&K 38: *Employees at Robey's Works, Lincoln* and M&K 78: *Workers at Messrs. Kynock's Ltd Ammunition Works, Birmingham* (1901).

37 M&K 12: *Workmen Leaving Platt's Works, Oldham.*

38 R. H. Eastham, *Platt's Textile Machinery Makers: Civic Leaders in Oldham, County Squires in North Wales* (Oldham: privately published by R. H. Eastman, 1994), p. 45.

39 Clarke, *Lancashire and the New Liberalism*, p. 77.

40 Eastham, *Platt's Textile Machinery Makers*, pp. 45–6.

41 Waller, *Town, City and Nation*, p. 89.

42 M&K 14: *Workmen Leaving Peacock's Works at Meal Time, Gorton, Manchester* (1900); M&K 17: *Workers at Brooks and Doxey, West Gorton Works, Manchester* (1900); M&K 50: *Workmen Leaving Brooks and Doxey, West Gorton Works* (1900); M&K 18: *Employees of Galloways Ltd Boiler Works, Hyde Road, Manchester* (1900); M&K 762: *Workers Leaving Craven Ironworks, Ordsall Lane, Salford* (1901); M&K 55: *Workers at Berry's Blacking Works, Manchester* (1901); and M&K 60: *Employees Leaving Crossley's Works, Openshaw* (1900).

43 Figures taken from the 1901 census and available on <www.nationalarchives.gov.uk/ pathways/census/pandp/salf.html>, accessed 5 March 2006.

44 Roberts, *The Classic Slum*, and Robert Roberts, *A Ragged Schooling: Growing up in the Classic Slum* (Manchester: Manchester University Press, 1976).

45 Waller, *Town, City and Nation*, pp. 88–9, and see also Douglas Farnie, *The English Cotton Industry and the World Market, 1815–96* (Oxford: Oxford University Press, 1979).

46 Tony Munford, *Iron and Steel Town: An Industrial History of Rotherham* (Stroud: Sutton, 2003).

47 M&K 84: *Employees Leaving Vickers, Sons and Maxim Works, Sheffield* and M&K 77: *Employees Leaving Brown's Atlas Works, Sheffield.*

48 For Brown's Atlas Works and John Brown and Co. of Clydebank see Sir Allan Grant, *Ships & Steel: The History of John Brown's* (London: Michael Joseph, 1950).

49 M&K 37: *Workers Leaving Ropener & Co., Shipbuilders, Stockton-on-Tees* (1900); M&K 35: *20,000 Employees Entering Lord Armstrong's Elswick Works* (1900); M&K 80: *Employees Leaving Messrs Vickers and Maxim's in Barrow* (1901); M&K 409: *Employees Leaving Alexandra Docks, Liverpool* (1901); and M&K 90: *Workforce of Scott & Co., Shipyard, Greenock* (1901).

50 Sidney Pollard and Paul Robertson, *The British Shipbuilding Industry, 1870–1914* (Cambridge, MA: Harvard University Press, 1987).

51 M&K 233: *SS Saxonia in Liverpool* (1901), and Grant, *Ships & Steel*, pp. 39–45.

52 Noel Reginald Pixell Bonsor, *North Atlantic Seaway; An Illustrated History of the Passenger Services Linking the Old World with the New, Vol. 1*, 2nd edn (Jersey, Channel Islands: Brookside Publications, 1975), p. 317.

53 Pollard and Robertson, *The British Shipbuilding Industry*, pp. 54–5.

54 M&K 80: *Employees Leaving Messrs Vickers and Maxim's in Barrow* and M&K 225–7: *Royal Visit to Barrow & Launch of HMS Dominion* (1903).

55 M&K 459–65: *Torpedo Flotilla Visit to Manchester*, and see Gary S. Messinger, *Manchester in the Victorian Age* (Manchester: Manchester University Press, 1985), in particular Ch. 11 for details of the Ship Canal.

56 John R. Kellett, *Railways and Victorian Cities* (London: Routledge, 1979).

57 M&K 42: *Employees Leaving Fowler's Ironworks, Leeds* (1901).

58 M&K 546: *Workers Leaving Butterley Ironworks, Ripley* and M&K 42: *Employees Leaving Fowler's Ironworks, Leeds* (1901).

59 M&K 72: *Employees Leaving the Midland Railway Loco Works, Derby* and M&K 67: *Workforce of Crewe Engineering Works*.

60 E. J. Larkin and J. G. Larkin, *The Railway Workshops of Great Britain 1823–1986* (London: Macmillan Press, 1988); M&K 41: *Employees Leaving North Eastern Engine Works, Gateshead*; and M&K 593: *Great Northern Railway Works at Doncaster*.

61 M&K 14: *Workmen Leaving Peacock's Works at Meal Time, Gorton, Manchester*; the firm is Beyer, Peacock and Co., formed in 1854 in Gorton, Manchester.

62 M&K 36: *Workforce of Brush Electric Co., Falcon Works, Loughborough*.

63 M&K 239, 245: *A Beautiful Panorama of Railway Ride from St German to Milray* (1901); M&K 242: [*Unidentified Railway Journey*]; M&K 241: *Ride over the Tay Bridge* (1901); M&K 243, 723: *Ride from Blarney to Cork on Cork & Muskerry Light Railway* (1902); M&K 244: *Train Arriving at Ilkeston Station* (1900).

64 Arthur J. McIvor, *A History of Work in Britain, 1880–1950* (Houndmills; Palgrave, 2001), p. 177. For regionally specific studies pertaining to women's work see Elizabeth Roberts, *A Woman's Place: An Oral History of Working-Class Women 1890–1940* (Oxford: Blackwell's, 1984).

65 Clarke, *Lancashire and the New Liberalism*, p. 77, and John Walton, 'Factory Work in Victorian Lancashire', <www.bbc.co.uk/legacies/work/england/lancashire>, accessed 11 March 2006.

66 Walton, *Lancashire A Social History*, p. 202.

67 Roberts, *The Classic Slum*, p. 7.

68 Stanley Houghton, *Hindle Wakes*, citation taken from *The Works of Stanley Houghton*, Vol. II (London: Constable and Co. Ltd, 1914), p. 179.

69 M&K 8: *The Millhands of Cheetham's Bankwood Mills, Stalybridge* and M&K 31: *Workpeople and Girls Leaving Thos. Adams Factory, Nottingham*.

70 Roberts, *The Classic Slum*, p. 7.

71 M&K 87: *Employees Leaving Baxter's Jute Works, Dundee*; M&K 88: *Employees Leaving Gilroy's Jute Works, Dundee*. See E. Gordon, *Women and the Labour Movement in Scotland, 1850–1914* (Oxford: Oxford University Press, 1991).

72 M&K 88: *Employees Leaving Gilroy's Jute Works, Dundee*. The spitting incident was first noticed by a member of the audience at one of the Glasgow showings of the films in 2004 who recalled that there was animosity in her day between the weavers and the spinners.

73 M&K 673: *Workers Leaving the Jute Works, Barrow*; M&K 81: *Employees Leaving Furness Railway Works, Barrow*; and M&K 80: *Employees Leaving Messrs Vickers and Maxim's in Barrow*. For gender difference in the Barrow workforce see Roberts, *A Woman's Place*, and Elizabeth Roberts, 'Working Class Standards of Living in Barrow and Lancaster, 1890–1914', *The Economic History Review*, New Series, Vol. 30 No. 2 (May 1977), pp. 306–21.

74 M&K 84: *Employees Leaving Vickers, Sons and Maxim Works, Sheffield* and M&K 77: *Employees Leaving Brown's Atlas Works, Sheffield*. See Sidney Pollard, *History of Labour in Sheffield* (Liverpool: Liverpool University Press, 1959), p. 333.

75 Pollard, *A History of Labour in Sheffield*, pp. 210–11.

76 Peter Laslett, *The World We Have Lost*, 2nd edn. (London: Methuen, 1971), p. 214.

77 Neil Dalglish, 'Education Policy and the Question of Child Labour: The Lancashire Cotton Industry and R. D. Denman's Bill of 1914', *History of Education*, Vol. 30 No. 3 (2001), pp. 291–308.

78 R. Betts, D. T. Macnamara, 1861–1930, cited in Dalglish, 'Education Policy and the Question of Child Labour', p. 293.

79 P. Sandiford, 'The Half-Time System in the Textile Trade', in M. E. Sadler (ed.), *Continuation Schools in England and Elsewhere* (Manchester: Manchester University Press, 2nd Edn, 1908), p. 334.

80 For more information on the history of child labour in the nineteenth century see Hugh Cunningham, *The Children of the Poor: Representations of a Childhood since the Seventeenth Century* (Oxford: Oxford University Press, 1991), and Hugh Cunningham, 'The Employment and Unemployment of Children in England, c. 1680–1851', *Past and Present*, No. 126 (February 1990), pp. 115–50.

81 For an overview of the legislation see Edmund and Ruth Frow, *A Survey of the Half-Time System in Education* (Manchester: E. J. Morten, 1970).

82 The half-time system was officially abolished in the Education Act (1918) and through local by-laws by 1921.

83 Searle, *A New England?* pp. 50–1 and Michael J. Childs, *Labour's Apprentices: Working-Class Lads in Late Victorian and Edwardian England* (London: The Hambledon Press, 1992), p. 74.

84 Childs, *Labour's Apprentices*, pp. 74–5.

85 M&K 31: *Workpeople and Girls Leaving Thos. Adams Factory, Nottingham.*

86 Childs, *Labour's Apprentices*. See also Michael J. Childs, 'Boy Labour in Late Victorian and Edwardian England and the Remaking of the Working Class', *Journal of Social History*, Vol. 23 (1987), pp. 783–802.

87 The Employment of Children Act (1903) raised the age for child employment in the theatre and circus to ten and over and the press and public were largely in favour of the employment of child performers. See M. Sanderson, *From Irvine to Olivier: A Social History of the Acting Profession in England, 1888–1983* (London: Athlone, 1984).

88 Harry Pollitt, *Serving My Time* (London: Lawrence and Wishart, 1940), p. 29.

89 M&K 28: *Messrs Lumb and Co. Leaving the Works, Huddersfield*; M&K 7: *Mill Workers Leaving Oldroyd & Sons Mill, Dewsbury*; M&K 87: *Employees Leaving Baxter's Jute Works, Dundee.*

90 Dalglish, 'Education Policy and the Question of Child Labour', p. 299.

91 See the Filmography for factory gate films listed by subject, but examples outside Lancashire are predominantly from Cheshire, Yorkshire, Staffordshire and Dundee, and all textile factories, such as jute works in M&K 87: *Employees Leaving Baxter's Jute Works, Dundee* and M&K 88: *Employees Leaving Gilroy's Jute Works, Dundee*, and silk factories in M&K 70: *The Employees Leaving Wardle & Davenport Silk Works, Leek* (1901) and M&K 68: *Living Pictures of Leek Brough Nicholson & Hall, Silk Works* (1901), and woollen mills in M&K 28: *Messrs Lumb and Co. Leaving the Works, Huddersfield* and M&K 7: *Mill Workers Leaving Oldroyd & Sons Mill, Dewsbury.*

92 Trevor Griffiths, *The Lancashire Working Classes, c. 1880–1930* (Oxford: Clarendon Press, 2001), pp. 116–17, for a detailed discussion of the opposition by workers in Lancashire to proposals to change the system leading up to the Education Act (1918).

93 Dalglish, 'Education Policy and the Question of Child Labour', p. 300, and see also P. Bolin-Hort, *Work, Family and the State: Child Labour and the Organisation of Production in the British Cotton Industry, 1789–1920* (Lund: Lund University Press, 1989).

94 Alan Fowler, 'Labour in the Lancashire Cotton Industry', *Manchester Region History Review*, Vol. 9 (1995), pp. 3–10.

95 Walton, *Lancashire, a Social History*, p. 288.

96 Griffiths, *The Lancashire Working Classes, c. 1880–1930*, p. 114.

97 See E. and R. Frow, *A Survey of the Half-Time System in Education*, pp. 26–7, for a description of the type of work children were employed to do in the factories.

98 M&K 20: *Howarth's Egerton Mill, Ordsall Lane, Salford* and M&K 21: *Workforce of Howarth's Ordsall Mill, Salford.*

99 M&K 471: *Workers Leaving Textile Factory in Patricroft.*

100 M&K 54: *Workers at Spring Bank Mill, Nelson*; M&K 49: *Workpeople Leaving Fish's Waterfall Mill, Blackburn*; M&K 50: *Workpeople Leaving Ordnance Mill, Blackburn*; M&K 51: *Workpeople Leaving Dugdale's Paradise Mill, Blackburn* (1900); M&K 52: *Employees Leaving Olive Mill, Darwen*; and M&K 48: *Workpeople Leaving Hornby's Brookhouse Mill, Blackburn*, for example.

101 Sandiford, 'The Half-Time System in the Textile Trade', p. 338.

102 George Tomlinson, *Fred Blackburn, MP* (London, 1934), cited in and Frow, *A Survey of the Half-Time System in Education*, p. 31.

103 M&K 760–1: *Workforce of Haslam's Ltd, Colne*; M&K 23: *Employees of J. & E. Waters, Talbot Mills, Ellesmere St, Manchester* (1900); M&K 15: *The 'Hands' Leaving Work at North-Street Mills, Chorley* (1900); M&K 53: *Workers at Bradley Shed, Nelson, Lancashire* (1900); M&K 39: *Workforce of Ormerod's Mill, Great Moor Street, Bolton*; M&K 63: *Employees Leaving Williamson's Factory, Lancaster* (1901); M&K 336–7: *Factory Workers in Clitheroe*; M&K 61: *Operatives of Acme Spinning Company, Pendlebury*; M&K 283: *Workforce at Horrocks Miller & Co, Preston.*

104 Farnie, *The English Cotton Industry and the World Market, 1815–96*, p. 171.

105 <www.nationalarchives.gov.uk/pathways/census/pandp/places/salford>, accessed 18 March 2006.

106 Laslett, *The World We Have Lost*, p. 214.

107 For further information on the Education Act (1902) see Wendy Robinson, 'Historiographical Reflections on the 1902 Education Act', *Oxford Review of Education*, Vol. 28 No. 2–3 (2002), pp. 159–72, and Tony Taylor, 'Arthur Balfour and Educational Change: The Myth Revisited', *British Journal of Educational Studies*, Vol. 42 No. 2 (1994), pp. 133–49.

108 M&K 266: *Audley Range School, Blackburn* (c.1904/5).

109 M&K 269: *Special Parade of St Matthews Pupils and Special March Past of Joseph Scholars, Blackburn.*

110 Donald Read, *Edwardian England 1901–1915: Society and Politics* (London: Harrap, 1972), p. 163.

111 M&K 756: *Calisthenics* and M&K 632–6: *Day School Sports at Park Avenue, Bradford.*

112 M&K 690: *Love Burn Street School, Dumfries* and M&K 289: *Scholars Leaving St Andrew's RC School, Dumfries.*

113 For further information on the Lancashire wakes festivities and their history see John K. Walton and Robert Poole, 'The Lancashire Wakes in the Nineteenth Century', in Robert D. Storch (ed.), *Popular Culture and Custom in Nineteenth Century England* (London: Croom Helm, 1982); pp. 100–24. For a description of a wakes fair in the Edwardian era see *The Worlds Fair*, 24 August 1907, p. 6.

114 Robert Poole, *The Lancashire Wakes Holidays* (Preston: Lancashire County Books, 1994), p. 1.

115 Walton and Poole, 'The Lancashire Wakes in the Nineteenth Century', p. 119.

116 See John K. Walton, *The English Seaside Resort: A Social History, 1750–1914* (Leicester: Leicester University Press, 1983).

117 Robert Poole, 'Oldham Wakes', in John K. Walton and John Walvin, *Leisure in England* (Manchester: Manchester University Press, 1983), pp. 71–90 (72).

118 Poole, *The Lancashire Wakes*, p. 22.

119 Poole, 'Oldham Wakes', p. 89.

120 See Chapter 4 and Walton and Poole, 'The Lancashire Wakes in the Nineteenth Century'.

121 Thomas Horne (ed.), *Showmen's Year Book* (Manchester: UKVDPA, 1900), National Fairground Archive, Showmen's Guild of Great Britain Collection.

122 M&K 9: *Workforce Leaving Salt's Works in Saltaire*. See *Shipley Times*, 28 July 1900, p. 1, for details of the exhibition. M&K 10: *Operatives Leaving Jubilee Mill, Padiham*, see *Nelson Express*, 10 August 1900; and for M&K 15: *The 'Hands' Leaving Work at North-Street Mills, Chorley*, see *Chorley Guardian and Leyland Hundred Advertiser*, 8 September 1900, p. 3.

123 M&K 8: *The Millhands of Cheetham's Bankwood Mills, Stalybridge*, see *The Herald*, Saturday 28 July 1900, p. 8. For details of Stalybridge Wakes see George Shaw's detailed summary and transcripts of news reports from 1830 to 1947 (NFA Q Shaw/1358).

124 *The Herald*, 4 August 1900, p. 3.

125 M&K 12: *Workmen Leaving Platt's Works, Oldham*, and see *The Era*, 1 September 1900, p. 20, for description of local films at Oldham Wakes.

126 M&K 58: *Miners Leaving Pendlebury Colliery* and M&K 59: *Alfred Butterworth and Sons, Glebe Mills, Hollinwood*.

127 *The Gorton Reporter*, 1 September 1900, p. 8.

128 Ibid., 8 September 1900, p. 8. See M&K 16: *Workpeople Leaving Ryland's Mill, Gorton, Manchester*; M&K 14: *Workmen Leaving Peacock's Works at Meal Time, Gorton, Manchester*; M&K 17: *Workers at Brooks and Doxey, West Gorton Works, Manchester*; and M&K 18: *Employees of Galloways Ltd Boiler Works, Hyde Road, Manchester* all marked August 1900 on the negatives as the date of filming and commissioned for Gorton Wakes.

129 For details of factory closures and fairs in Birmingham see Douglas Reid, 'Interpreting the Festival Calendar: Wakes and Fairs as Carnivals', in Storch (ed.), *Popular Culture and Custom in Nineteenth-Century England*, pp. 125–53.

130 Pollard, *A History of Labour in Sheffield*, p. 62.

131 These exceptions are M&K 74–5: *Workers at Barlow and Tweedale Ironworks, Castleton nr Rochdale* (1905) and M&K 45–6: *Employees of Marshall's Engineering Works, Gainsborough* (1908).

132 Laslett, *The World We Have Lost*, p. 213.

8
Militarism in the Edwardian Age

> It is a well known fact that every war that takes place stimulates in a very marked degree the sale of books and maps relating to the countries that are at war . . . What books and maps do for people of leisure, the showman can do in a more realistic and pictorial manner for those whose time will not permit much study of books.[1]

Introduction

The last ten years of the nineteenth century saw the public's fascination with war increase dramatically. Images and stories of exploits in foreign and exotic lands by plucky British 'Tommies' who battled valiantly to secure the Empire against the Queen's enemies proliferated in magazines, serials, juvenilia and newspapers. In addition, a whole variety of new media pandered to this public fascination, including the cinematograph and the rise of the foreign newspaper correspondent. As Michael Paris

Return of the East Lancashire Regiment at Preston (1902). From the late 1890s onwards, the public's fascination with war increase dramatically. The onset of the Anglo-Boer War in 1899 saw the cinematograph become an important means of pandering to the public's increased interest

Morecambe Church Lads' Brigade at Drill (1901). The Collection covers all aspects of increased militarism in the Edwardian period including the rise of military style organisations for boys

writes, 'by the last decades of the nineteenth century popular militarism had became a major strand in the cultural fabric of the nation'.[2] The increase in literacy throughout the nineteenth century created an expanding market for broadsheets, newspapers, serial newspapers aimed at the youth market and, by the 1890s, the rise of popular journals such as *The Strand* and *Pearson's*. Juvenile literature, especially the works of G. A. Henty, proliferated from the 1880s onwards. These publications romanticised war and created the young idealistic boy hero who relied on his wits, greater intelligence and guile to overcome adversity and achieve glory, thus saving the Empire from her enemies. As many historians of the period had demonstrated, war became a means of defining one's character, in which the boy hero could prove his worth to the nation while gaining fame and fortune along the way.[3]

The army at this time was a small specialist military unit swelled by volunteers in times of war, and during the later part of the nineteenth century, the Empire's soldiers were continually engaged in combat. The forces were stretched, and both the government of the day and the military command were uneasy as the rising threat of German militarism, in particular, highlighted the ill-disciplined and physically weaker volunteers that the British Army relied on. The Anglo-Boer War had a significant impact on Edwardian society and its government up to and including the start of the First World War.[4] Various trends have been identified by historians of the period, including the importance of imperialism, the militarisation of all aspects of society, the growth and the expansion of the Edwardian navy, and the impact and dissemination of the conflict in all aspects of popular culture.[5] In relation to early film history, the importance of the Boer War cannot be overerestimated: from the start of the conflict in October 1899 to its cessation on 31 May 1902, films of the war dominate the film programmes in cities and towns throughout the UK. When one examines contemporary newspaper accounts of the material commissioned by the travelling exhibitors from Mitchell & Kenyon and other companies, it becomes apparent that films of the Boer War were an important factor in the success of the cinematograph at this time.[6] Of the 120 towns and cities surveyed for the Filmography from 1900 to 1902, every exhibition between 1899 and 1902 listed a Boer War-related title. However, within the collection itself, only twenty titles have survived that relate directly to the war, along with an additional fifteen films taken during and after the conflict that demonstrate the country's continued fascination with the armed forces and militarism. Therefore, in this instance, the collection does not reflect the large number of films that would have been originally commissioned from Mitchell & Kenyon. Examination of the surviving material reveals that the prevailing trends outlined earlier also dominate the film record: namely, the impact of the Boer War within popular culture, the importance of the Volunteer movement to the armed forces, the rise of the Boys' Brigade, the expansion of the navy and the continued cult of the celebrity generals. In order to evaluate the material in the collection, this chapter will outline the various themes prevalent at the time, including the impact of the conflict on a variety of media and cultural forms, and how the cinematograph benefited from the Anglo-Boer War.

The Anglo-Boer War and the Media

The Anglo-Boer War (1899–1902) has been portrayed by historians as the 'first fully mediated conflict in British imperial history', a distinctly contemporary war in its impact on the media,[7] and a seminal and crucial period in the evolution of the British press.[8] It was a war that became far more significant than originally anticipated, as the might of the British Army was humbled by an enemy that appeared fitter, more manly and better suited to combat than the undernourished, weak volunteers who made up the British forces. What started as an attempt to stop the Boer invasion of Natal with only 75,000 troops gradually became an embattled combat. Forces from Canada, Australia, India and New Zealand swelled the imperial forces to 450,000, as the conflict became a major episode in British history.[9] Its impact can be seen in many arenas, including popular and entertainment genres, newspapers and serials, and, of course, the cinematograph.

Photography was the standard medium for war coverage prior to the Boer War as shown in these images of the British campaign in South Africa taken in Ladysmith, 1900

Edwardian Newspapers and the Depiction of War

Coverage of the war in all the media was intense. This was due partly to a mass readership eager to read daily bulletins from the warfront, partly to the advent of a range of media such as the cinematograph, photography and other means of disseminating visual representations of the war beyond the standard engravings in the newspapers. Coverage of the conflict by the newspaper industry was immense: at the height of the conflict, fifty-eight correspondents were stationed in Africa, of whom between thirteen and sixteen alone worked for *The Times*.[10] Members of the armed forces, such as Winston Churchill, also acted as special correspondents.[11] The visual representation of the war was of paramount importance: not only was it a war that you could read about, but an ever-fascinated public was inundated with a mass saturation of images, whether photographic or cinematographic, on all aspects of the conflict. The development of a more commercial reader-oriented press, 'the New Journalism' typified by the founding of the *Daily Mail* in 1896, saw a rapid expansion in both readership and the number of daily papers, which doubled from 1896 to 1906.[12] The prevailing perception of the use of military force in Edwardian Britain was that war was beneficial and desirable to the societies engaged in it, and the event that crystallised the idea that warfare was a test of national fitness was the Boer War. The 'handful of farmers', as the press initially described them, put up a deter-

Members of local communities, such as those seen in *Comic Pictures in High Street, West Bromwich* (1902), volunteered for action in South Africa, but only one-in-three of the recruits were deemed physically fit for combat

mined fight, with the high number of British casualties and the physical superiority of the enemy demonstrating that the military might of the Empire was built on shaky foundations. Certainly, the Boer fighting men compared well with the often physically feeble recruits to the British Army, whose poor health was later condemned in 1904 by the Committee on Physical Deterioration, which called for a healthier, more efficient population.[13] Moreover, the number of soldiers required and the amount of time taken to subdue what was originally perceived as a local rebellion was an embarrassment to the military establishment and the government.

Although the majority of the press promoted the war in its early stages, by mid-1901 anti-war feelings and concern about the treatment of the Boers in the concentration camps also began to emerge. The representation of the Boer insurgents by the press was also interesting. Unlike previous campaigns, Britain was facing a white, Christian European enemy, and press opinion was often mixed and sometimes confusing: while the Boers were depicted as cunning and sly by some newspapers, they were generally seen as a civilised enemy. Some of the liberal press campaigned actively against the war, including the *Manchester Guardian*, whose anti-war stance was in complete contrast to the nationalistic, jingoistic approach favoured by *The Times*.[14] However, whatever the criticisms levied at the government for the failures of the conflict, the armed forces themselves, both officers and foot soldiers, were universally acclaimed for their heroic and positive character.

Boer War and Popular Culture

> We've songs about Pretoria (which rhymes with Queen Victoria):
> We've patriotic photo-frames and soap and statuettes;
> For war we are all gluttons, e'en to wearing portrait buttons,
> And decking out with tri-colours our harmless household pets;
> But the khaki-covered camera is the latest thing . . .[15]

As the poem *The Photogram* demonstrates, all aspects of popular culture began to reflect and respond to changes and events in the social and cultural fabric of the country (see Plate 16). The start of the Anglo-Boer War in 1899, coupled with the use of troops against the Boxer Rebellion in China in 1900, saw the diffusion of militarism into popular culture. These factors would come to the fore as

> a genuinely popular movement which reflected acceptance of war as a means of achieving national goals, an admiration for and pride in the exploits of the army and its heroes; a belief that military values and attitudes would improve the health of the people, create a more efficient workforce and eliminate social ills.[16]

Popular art, which had been an important means of providing the public with visual representations of conflict since the Crimean War, proliferated throughout the nineteenth century in serials, illustrative newspapers and magazines.[17] Indeed, John Springhall argues that the kind of material published in the *Graphic, Illustrated London News* and other illustrative titles was just as important as war reporting or popular fiction in providing support for imperialist policies.[18] The Anglo-Boer War also was the first instance in which both

Lord Roberts admirably portrayed by a child in the *Manchester and Salford Harriers' Cyclists Procession* (1901)

famous and ordinary soldiers were used to promote and sell products, with Lord Roberts, for example, being used by Ogden's to sell their particular brand of cigarettes.[19] During the conflict, manufacturers of children's toys produced models of the battalions, regiments and irregulars that made up the army, as well as depictions of the enemy, so that boys (both young and old) could re-enact the war at home. This market developed throughout the Edwardian era, as a whole range of war paraphernalia was produced for the expanding juvenile market. Additionally, there was a rapid growth in children's literature promoting, through the pleasure and culture of war, a sense of duty and responsibility that the future of the Empire relied on their courage and spirit.[20] Richard Price believes that the Boer War was mostly supported by a patriotic middle class, and that the working classes were generally politically apathetic about the conflict.[21] However, the films of the fancy-dress parades in the Mitchell & Kenyon Collection reveal that war fever affected all aspects of the population. *Manchester and Salford Harriers' Cyclists' Procession* includes 'Lord "Bobs" admirably portrayed by a little fellow mounted on a big horse'.[22] 'Lord Bobs' also appeared in the later Lifeboat Procession in October. Working-class indifference to the conflict is certainly not apparent when one examines the impact of the war on popular leisure arenas frequented by the working class, such as the fairground and the music hall.

Travelling Fairs and Shows

Fairgrounds have always been an interesting barometer of how trends in popular culture reach working-class society. The Crimean War in the 1850s, for example, had produced a patriotic effect on the showmen, who carved likenesses of leading figures in the conflict onto shooting galleries and Aunt Sallies.[23] The advent of war in 1899 resulted in similar reactions, with loyal showmen such as Professor Wall renaming his fairground cinematograph show the Boer War-o-graph:

The Boer War touched all aspects of popular culture, with a likeness of Lord Roberts here replacing a horse's head on a roundabout horse (1900) (NFA)

> No part of the fair seems to attract more attention than that in which Wall's Boer Warograph is situate. The features shown are an admirable series and meet with general approval. They include representations of incidents which have not previously been seen and which have taken place during the wars in South Africa and China.[24]

Shooting galleries with a nationalistic theme also appeared on the fairground during the South African conflict, which became transformed into a visual representation of the war.[25] A visitor to Stalybridge Wakes in July 1900 commented on 'the long row of Aunt Sally's, which are modernised into Kruger, Steyn and other Boer War leaders'.[26] Rides, shows and stalls participated in this spirit of patriotism, with the reporter for the *Hull News* declaring that 'the number of shows that offer war pictures, both in South Africa and China, are too numerous to count'.[27] People could see war pictures in the cinematograph shows, ride on the Boer War roundabouts and play games on war-themed stalls:

> Another form of ball-throwing largely indulged in was that of shying at card-board masks, the object being to send the missile through the wide-open mouth: the majority bore the name of some prominent Boer, Kruger, Steyn, Cronje, De Wet, Botha, Leyds, and so on, and one could not but notice that the late President of the Transvaal received a greater amount of pelting than the others did collectively.[28]

In June 1900, the reporter for the *Preston Guardian* commented on 'how the public found amusement in shooting and battering for all they were worth' the tin likenesses of Kruger, Steyn and other Boer leaders at the shooting galleries and throwing stalls.[29] In contrast to the unpopularity of the insurgents, the British generals became national

Henry Powell's Boer War roundabout with centaurs instead of horses. Note the horses' heads have been replaced by the carved heads of prominent Boer War generals, c. 1901 (NFA)

heroes. This is apparent on the roundabouts, where the galloping horses were substituted for centaurs representing British generals.[30] The staff on the front of Colonel Clarke's cinematograph wore military uniforms, performed military-themed songs on the lavishly decorated fair organs and draped Union Jacks over the front of the show. Panorama shows of the Boer War were also shown by the Poole family at the Great Barracks Carnival in Glasgow, with scenes of the Battle of the Modder River, Storming of Magersfontein and the Victory of General Roberts proving particularly popular (see Plate 17).[31] The fairground showman George Green went one step further than his rivals by re-enacting the Relief of Mafeking at the Great Barracks carnival in August 1901, advertising it as a 'startling and realistic war production with over 200 performers, armoured trains, machine guns etc'.[32]

These themes continued into other entertainment arenas, where perhaps the most ambitious was Frank Fillis, 'The Barnum of South Africa', and his Savage South Africa Show, which arrived in England in April 1899, six months before the start of the Boer War. This grandiose extravaganza of African history, colonial power and apparent ethnographic reality toured until April 1901 to large crowds. Although the show benefited from the conflict in South Africa, it never really used it as the focus of the entertainment.[33] The real stars of the show were the Zulu warriors, with other circus showmen picking up on both the interest in all things South African and the public's fascination with the African warriors. Zulu warriors had featured in circus and music-hall shows in London from as early as 1890, when in February the Covent Garden Grand Circus featured 'The War in Zululand' or 'The British in South Africa' (see Plate 18). The Anglo-Boer War reignited this interest, and Lord George Sanger incorporated the conflict into his Circus and Hippodrome exhibition in 1902, while the Crystal Palace presented a 'Special Peace Festival' in July 1902 to mark the end of the fighting.[34]

Music Hall

The music hall also reflected this patriotic theme, and a variety of commentators have emphasised its importance in the dissemination of popular and cultural trends in the Victorian era, particularly in relation to imperialism and nationalism.[35] Writers such as J. A. Hobson have blamed the music hall for its excessive jingoism and condemned it for manipulating working-class opinion towards imperial policies, in particular the conflict in South Africa.[36] By the time of the Anglo-Boer War, songs depicting narratives of great heroism and plays featuring storylines incorporating the conflict in South Africa were also an aspect of regional theatre performances. Ilkeston New Theatre Royal, for example, featured the Anglo-African drama 'Briton and Boer' in August 1900, the great patriotic drama 'For the Colours: A Story of the Matabele War with ten Real Zulu Chiefs' three weeks later, and the South African drama 'Under the Red Cross' at the end of September.[37] However, it was in the music hall that the immense popular support for the conflict was most apparent (see Plate 19). The music hall's interest in the army reached its peak between 1880 and 1900, and gradually tailed off after the relief of Mafeking in May–June 1900. Key moments, such as the beginning of the Boer War and of the Great War, for example, produced a resurgence of interest in the army, and any performer/singer on the halls was likely to include material relating to soldiers in their repertoire.[38] Representations of military personnel also changed, as the music-hall soldier, invariably an officer until the 1890s, was later replaced by the discovery of the common soldier, the 'Tommy' character. By the 1890s, the soldier was a fighting man, a lover or a grizzly old veteran; essentially noble and glamorous, his life could be illustrated with tales of heroic deeds, tragedy, pathos and moments of patriotic duty. As Dave Russell states: 'The support for the soldier, the praise of heroism, and so forth is so closely bound up in the lyrics and the performance with general hymns of praise to imperial achievement.'[39]

The army became a popular theme for sketches and songs, with the life of a soldier offering a range of melodramatic opportunities; indeed, there were instances of serving soldiers taking part in drilling displays, and military bands providing musical accompaniment for both the acts and the cinematograph films (see Plate 20). In Birmingham, for example, A. D. Thomas of the Thomas Edison Co., employed the Edgbaston Military Band to 'perform a Grand Fantasia "The Relief of Mafeking"', while the Northumberland Fusiliers ('Fighting Fifth') accompanied Edison's show in Halifax.[40] The music hall also helped present a sanitised view of warfare, promoting an image of Britain engaged in an imperial war to protect the Empire, and taking on the role of peace-maker. War was a just and Christian conflict that personified the ideals of manliness, physical courage, endurance and selflessness: 'It is undeniable that the music hall's projection of the soldier was ultimately a positive one and one which helped to raise the army and the common man in the public esteem.'[41]

Despite the unpopularity of the music hall in some quarters of the Edwardian press and with politicians, 'during the Boer War the halls remained loyal and managed to wrest gentle humour even from the most trying situations'.[42] This loyalty to the imperial cause remained constant throughout the Edwardian era, as the halls were used as recruiting grounds during both the Boer War and the First World War, with official calls being made on stage for men to enlist.[43] The halls were also one of the many venues in which the cinematograph was beginning to make its mark, with films of a Boer War-related theme forming an important part of the programme from late 1899 onwards.

Infantry in Pretoria shows an extensive military parade of soldiers preparing for War in South Africa. Although this film is in the Collection it is not believed to have been made by Mitchell & Kenyon and is more likely to be a Warwick Trading Co. title

The Boer War and the Cinematograph

The cinematograph tapped into this thirst for first-hand material, and films of the major personalities were featured at the music hall, on travelling cinematograph shows and in stand-alone film shows. The films built up patriotic fervour in a number of ways. They elevated the reputation of the commanders-in-chief, combined local loyalty with nationalism by filming volunteers leaving and returning from South Africa, and produced fake war films to show close-ups of valour and heroism that could not be shot in reality due to the limitations of the cinematographic equipment. The war was a popular subject for the cinematograph and, indeed, is seen as an important factor in the increasing popularity of the moving image at this time. Earlier wars had been adapted and incorporated into films by enterprising film-makers before 1899, with the knowledgeable public recognising that the films were not necessarily true records of the event:

> I saw a picture said to have been taken during the Greek and Turkish war – but I much doubt it . . . Several soldiers fell down, apparently dead, and (what made us doubt the truthfulness of the picture) one immediately had his head enveloped in a bandage by some unseen and extraordinarily quick agency.[44]

By the turn of the twentieth century, films of a military theme became an essential feature of the cinematograph programme. Robert W. Paul's series of films, 'Our Army', tapped into this national interest, programming an entire exhibition of 'patriotic entertainment' around the theme of 'Army Life'.[45] The following review of the North American Animated Photo exhibition in Bolton demonstrates the popularity of war in the cinematograph programme at the time, with the audience being treated to films of

> An attack by the Boxers . . . a street scene in Peking, and the bombardment of the Taku Forts by the Allied squadrons, which were rendered startlingly realistic by the aid of gunpowder and various mechanical effects, and the accompaniment of military music . . . fairly took the audience by surprise, and a repetition was demanded.[46]

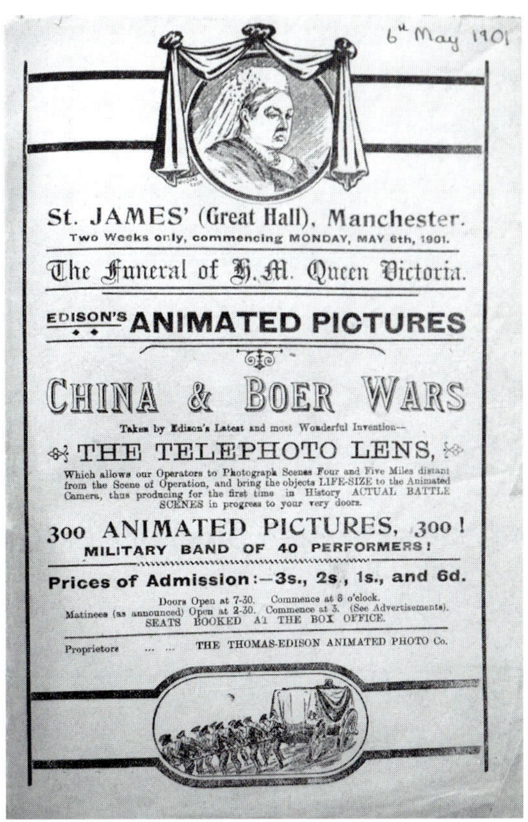

Handbill for Edison's Animated Pictures showing the popularity of war pictures at the St James's Hall, Manchester (1901)

Film-makers responded in a variety of ways to produce material that satisfied the expectations of the public.[47] As Richard Brown states, 'the Anglo-Boer War had a significant, catalytic effect on the early development of the British film business'.[48] The Warwick Trading Company produced a supplementary film catalogue in 1899 of subjects taken 'of the War with the Transvaal' taken by their photographic staff in South Africa.[49] Mitchell & Kenyon, among others, produced fictional titles of events, also referred to as fakes at the time. With the conclusion of the conflict in 1902, they advertised these as a series, 'How Tommy Won South Africa', in which they proclaimed 'the War is over and now the country is eager to know how Tommy won South Africa – Our films touch the spot'.[50]

Film exhibition carried the war theme into the programme material, the style of advertisements used to promote the show and the special effects employed to heighten the effect of reality. 'War Films' featured heavily on the poster for the London Hippodrome in 1900; individual titles highlighting the commanders-in-chief were a popular attraction at the Argyle Theatre in Birkenhead; and travelling exhibitors made war films the highlight of their exhibition.[51] The 'photographs of the stirring events in South Africa and China were received with unbounded delight', wrote one reviewer in Nottingham.[52] A. D. Thomas advertised 'War' in Newcastle, Morecambe, Manchester and Birmingham, to name but a few of the many cities in which his show was presented. Ralph Pringle and The North American Animated Photo Company followed his example with 'War in Liverpool, The Siege of the Circus', and these military-style advertisements were used in other venues.[53]

In March 1901, The North American Animated Photo Company was showing both local films and Boer War material in Newcastle, and there are twelve items listed on the programme, including *Local Animated Pictures of Newcastle* and Boer and China War films.[54] In spite of the popularity of the films, the showman did not necessarily rely on the public's fascination with the war to continue unabated but instead applied tricks of audience recognition to maintain attendance figures, as the following report demonstrates:

> 'HELLO, BILL!' – When showing animated pictures it is said to be no unusual thing for a girl to cry out 'Dada!' on seeing the figure of her father, who is perhaps a soldier in South Africa, walking on the screen, whilst old pals of soldiers can rarely resist the impulse to call out to their pictures in the old terms, 'Hello, Bill!'[55]

QUADRANT CYCLES | Our Chainless Safety with Free Wheel gives the pleasure of Cycling and Motoring combined. 13 GOLD MEDALS. HIGHEST AWARDS. | QUADRANT DEPOT: 13, VICTORIA ST., MANCHESTER.

FINDLATER & MACKIE
Begs to call special attention to their
BLENDS OF
Scotch Whiskies

They have of late years bestowed very great care on this Department, and as they are holders of an immense stock of the highest class of

OLD SCOTCH MALT WHISKIES,
Are confident in inviting comparison between their Blends and any others at present on the market.

	Doz.	Sample Bottle.
Fine Old Islay Blend (5 years old) - - -	37/-	3/1
V.S.O. Highland Blend (8 years old) - - -	43/-	3/7
"Glen Fyne" very choice Blend (8 years old) -	43/-	3/7
Special Liqueur Blend (10 years old) - - -	49/-	4/1

Nothing finer than these can be procured.

CHAMPAGNES
Of the celebrated Vintages of 1889, 1892, and 1893, from the Leading Shippers, at specially cut prices.

WINES & SPIRITS
Of every description, of the finest quality and in perfect condition, at the lowest possible cash prices.

Full Price List forwarded on application.

FINDLATER AND MACKIE,
Wine, Spirit, and Liquer Merchants,
ROYAL EXCHANGE, BANK ST.,
MANCHESTER.
Telephone 922.
Telegrams: "VINTAGE," Manchester.

WAR IN MANCHESTER!
IN GREAT
ST. JAMES'S HALL,
OXFORD STREET, MANCHESTER.
TWICE DAILY at 3 & 8,
AND UNTIL FURTHER NOTICE.
GRAND CHANGE OF PICTURES.
Under the distinguished patronage of The Right Hon. Sir James Ferguson, K.C.S.I., K.C.M.G., M.P., etc., etc.; Sir Henry Houldsworth, M.P.; The Hon. Arthur Wellesley Peel, M.P.; Winston Churchill, Esq., M.P., and other influential Noblemen and Gentlemen.
Visited up to the present time by over 246,000 people.

EDISON'S ANIMATED PICTURES,
CHINA & BOER
WARS.
Taken by the latest and most wonderful invention, the Telephoto Lens, which allows our operators to photograph scenes four and five miles from the scene of operations, and bring the objects life-size to the Animated Camera, and we produce, for the first time in the history of the world, Actual Battle Scenes in progress to your very doors. WONDERFUL SCENES FROM THE
CHINA WAR.
Destruction of Taku Forts by the Fleets of the Allies.
Bluejackets Landing and Capturing Forts. Chinese Chamber of Torture and Death. Prince Tuan, Leader of the Boxers. Flight of the Emperor and Empress. Entry into the Forbidden City, etc., etc.
Thrilling Attack on a MISSION STATION by Boxers.

RETURN OF GENERAL BULLER.
RETURN OF THE MANCHESTER VOLUNTEERS.
THE WHIT-MONDAY PROCESSION AND CATHOLIC PROCESSION.
Ride on an Electric Car, showing the Lord Mayor Opening the NEW ELECTRIC CAR SYSTEM.

Special Engagement of the
Besses-o'-th'-Barn Band,
Who will play each Evening an original Musical Fantasia—
"The Relief of Ladysmith."
Synopsis—The Sleeping Camp. Morning Gun. The Alarm. Camp in Motion. Prayer before Battle. Advance of the Sons of the Empire. Charge. Battle. Victory. Flight of the Boers. Relief and Grand Entry into Ladysmith. Illustrated by appropriate Animated Pictures.

MAGNIFICENT ANIMATED PICTURE OF THE
BRAVE MANCHESTER'S AT WAGON HILL.

The GREAT FIGHT between
JOHN BULL & KRUGER.
Second for John Bull—America.
Seconds for Kruger—France and Russia.

EDISON STANDS ALONE.

Doors open at 2-30 and 7-30. Commence at 3 and 8. Early Doors at 7, 3d. extra to all parts.
Prices - - 3/-, 2/-, 1/-, & 6d.
Proprietors - THE THOMAS-EDISON ANIMATED PHOTO CO.

THE PALATINE RUBBER COMPANY
FOR
Ladies' Waterproofs.
Gents' Waterproofs.
Children's Waterproofs.
Coachmen's Waterproofs.

DRIVING RUGS.
TRAVELLING RUGS.

MECHANICAL RUBBER GOODS.
SURGICAL RUBBER GOODS.
HOT WATER BOTTLES.
WATER BEDS
(ON HIRE OR PURCHASE).
AIR BEDS. AIR CUSHIONS.
GOLOSHES and SNOW BOOTS.
ELASTIC STOCKINGS.
ABDOMINAL BELTS, &c., &c.

Experienced Lady Attendants.

NOTE THE ADDRESSES:
63, MARKET STREET,
Between COOK'S & L.&N.W. EXCURSION OFFICES,
MANCHESTER.

SKIN RUGS & MATS.
BEST VALUE FOR
House, Carriage, Bassinette, and Mail Cart.
CALL OR WRITE,
ALEC TAYLOR,
SHEEP SKIN DRESSER & DYER,
Edmund Street Dye Works,
LOWER OPENSHAW, MANCHESTER.
Rugs and Mats Cleaned and Re-Dyed.

LLANDUDNO.
VINCENT'S
HIGH-CLASS
PRIVATE AND FAMILY HOTEL,
Situated in the
CENTRE OF THE MARINE PARADE,
LLANDUDNO.
Possesses the most extensive sea frontage on the Parade, also an uninterrupted and commanding view of the Carnarvonshire Mountains.
JOHN VINCENT, Proprietor.

6

Thomas-Edison's two-hour film show at the St James's Hall, Manchester, featured the China and Boer War as the main feature of the show in June 1901 (NFA)

Showmen also utilised effects and trickery to heighten public reaction to the films, including hiring an actor to appear in the audience dressed as a soldier who would pretend to recognise his fallen comrades, and the firing of gunshots into the audience whenever rifle fire was shown on screen.[56] Before the discovery of the Peter Worden Collection, Mitchell & Kenyon were only known through their fake Boer War re-enactments, with the Yellow Hills outside Blackburn doubling as areas of the South African Veldt, as well as scenes of the Boxer Rebellion in China.[57] The material in the collection extends their interest in the Boer War and includes military processions and the cult of the war celebrity, in particular the commanding officers.

Mitchell & Kenyon's Treatment of the Boer War

Unlike those of their contemporaries, Mitchell & Kenyon's war films all originated on home soil and were not an attempt to document or cover the conflict. Simon Popple has previously grouped the material into Fakes and Re-enactments, Military Life, Celebrity, and Pageants and Festivals.[58] In order

Clive Wilson a local celebrity and Boer war hero poses for the camera during the filming of *Lieutenant Clive Wilson And Tranby Croft Party* (1902)

Clive Wilson, hailed as a returning hero in *Lieutenant Clive Wilson And Tranby Croft Party* (1902). His family and the community erected banners proclaiming his deeds and thousands turning out for his homecoming

to examine the films as historical documents, the following additional areas will be examined: the role of the volunteer movement and the films of the key military personnel, such as Lord Roberts, General Buller, Lord Kitchener and Robert Baden-Powell. Mitchell & Kenyon, in line with other companies, relied on fake films, staged pageants and the glorification of the military generals to put across the magnificent achievements of the Empire and its soldiers. The reality of war was sanitised, as photographic equipment remained bulky and was unable to convey the full horrors of warfare. Mitchell & Kenyon relied on fakes to re-enact fictional scenes from the Transvaal, such as *A Sneaky Boer*, a short narrative about a British soldier on watch who falls asleep. As he sleeps, the Boers sneak up and wound him, but another soldier intervenes and kills the enemy soldiers before dragging away his wounded comrade.

Mitchell & Kenyon's films of the Anglo-Boer War were commissioned in a similar way to the local films. The local hero returning home from the warfront was a popular subject for the camera, and in April 1902, the company filmed *Lieutenant Clive Wilson and the Tranby Croft Party*.[59] The film illustrates his rapturous homecoming, complete with a commemorative archway, enthusiastic crowds and glowing family scenes at the Tranby Croft residence. Although Clive Wilson was a minor figure in the combat, it was the importance of the family to Hull society and, indeed, for the national consciousness (his family home was the scene of the infamous Tranby Croft Affair in 1890) that ensured both Mitchell & Kenyon and Jasper Redfern were there to film his return home.

On the March with the Bradford Artillery at Buckshaw Brow, Settle (1902) is more in line with Robert Paul's 'Our Army' programme, with its series of tableaux depicting army life:

> Probably the most notable addition this week is a representation of the Bradford Artillery in camp at Morecambe. Following the struggle up Buckhaw Brow with the guns, the onlooker is taken to the camp ground at Batr, where the Bradford lads are seen indulging in the morning shave, the sergeants going for a bathe, and other scenes. A very fine film shows the kit inspection of the battalion.[60]

On the March with the Bradford Artillery at Buckshaw Brow Settle (1902), is one of a series of titles that the company produced with only this section surviving. Mitchell & Kenyon had moved to making small features of military life as well as filming military celebrities and homecomings

The review demonstrates that the title is part of a much larger group, of which only the struggle of Buckshaw Brow survives in the collection.[61] Mitchell & Kenyon's treatment of the Boer War was both local and nationalist in theme and interest, filming as they did the visit of the personalities of the conflict – Kitchener, Buller and Roberts – to cities such as Manchester and Liverpool, as well as the local volunteer brigades leaving or returning from the conflict. As such, the material in the collection demonstrates again how aspects of nationalism and Empire were played out at both local and regional levels.

Volunteer Regiments

> The great majority of the Lancashire soldiers who served in South Africa were not professional soldiers . . . in their thousands they left civilian occupations, families friends and workmates, a local community of interest which followed their progress with a keen sympathy, identifying with triumphs and tribulations alike, in a way which is not so evident when only Regular soldiers are engaged.[62]

The ten volunteer regiments featured in the collection represent only a small percentage of the material that Mitchell & Kenyon actually filmed; many of the titles that were advertised in the newspapers have not survived.[63] In addition, the films of Kitchener and Roberts in Liverpool include scenes of volunteers from the King's Own Regiment receiving commemorative medals from Roberts for their service in the Anglo-Boer War.[64] The films of the volunteers are probably some of the most important filmed by the company, illustrating as they do the important and invaluable contribution made by these regiments in the war. They provide further evidence to reinforce recent scholarship on the impact and effect of the conflict on the working class in Britain at this time.[65] The appearance of volunteer units in the Boer War was a direct consequence of 'Black Week', when, by mid-December 1899, the British Army had suffered three consecutive defeats at Magersfontein, Stormberg and Colenso. As a result of these calamitous defeats, the War Office replaced General Redvers Buller with General Lord Roberts, with Lord

Return of the East Lancashire Regiment at Preston (1902)

Kitchener acting as his Chief of Staff. Additional troops were mobilised and the government engaged volunteers from home to serve overseas in order to solve the pressing manpower problems.

The volunteer regiments were based on the idea of raising self-sufficient forces during crises, and their use dates back to the 1650s. In 1816, all Volunteer units were disbanded, but were reinstated in the 1850s due to a mistrust of revolutionary France and fear of invasion. Between 1860 and 1863 they were organised into administrative battalions and, following the Cardwell reforms of the armed forces in 1881, became attached to specific brigades and regiments in their respective counties.[66] Volunteers were initially set up to support the local civil power, but could occasionally serve outside their locality, in which case they were paid and lodged as regulars. After 'Black Week', the War Office took the decision to allow a contingent of volunteer forces based on the standing yeomanry regiments to participate in the conflict. The first and largest of these units was the Imperial Yeomanry, founded immediately after 'Black Week' and consisting by the end of the conflict of over 35,000 volunteers. The Imperial Yeomanry was established through a Royal Warrant of 24 December 1899, in which the standing yeomanry regiments were asked to provide service companies of around 115 men each. The new Imperial Yeomanry was to be raised on a county basis, with a core of men from the existing volunteer units, the remainder being recruited from individuals who met the

After a series of calamitous defeats in 1899, the War Office allowed volunteer units to serve in the Boer War. Films of local volunteer units leaving or returning from South Africa as in *The Return of the Lancaster Volunteers* (1901) were a popular feature of the cinematograph programme

strict criteria laid down.[67] Interestingly, recent scholarship has testified to the popularity of the Imperial Yeomanry, as illustrated by the press reviews of the large crowds that greeted their departure to and arrival from South Africa.[68] On a more local level, the response to their homecomings was not as overwhelming. Indeed, reaction to the return of the Imperial Yeomanry to Manchester was decidedly mixed, and a variety of letters in the *Manchester Evening News* blame this reaction on the pro-Boer element.[69] The crowds in *Manchester's Welcome to the Imperial Yeomanry* (1901) appear decidedly muted in comparison with other similar occasions filmed by Mitchell & Kenyon.[70] The low turnout was blamed on the fact that the local community had no real identity with the returning troops:

> On the way to the Cathedral there was little or no enthusiasm, a possible explanation being that it was recognised that the regiment had not a very close connection with Manchester, and that comparatively few of the returned men belonged to the city.[71]

Despite the apathy of the spectators at the homecoming, the films of the event resulted in large crowds for A. D. Thomas's show at the St James' Hall. Thomas continued the military theme by advertising that 'the Officers, Non-commissioned Officers, and Troopers of the Imperial Yeomanry will attend by special incitation and witness the portrayal of themselves by Animated Photography'.[72] Although the letter page in the *Manchester Evening News* may have put down the lack of enthusiasm to a pro-Boer element, the scenes that welcomed Manchester's own volunteer regiment back to their home city the previous month reveal the genuine enthusiasm felt by the people.[73] *Return of the Brave Manchester Volunteers* (1901) shows large crowds greeting the volunteers outside Exchange Square and through the streets as they paraded to the cathedral for the civic reception.[74] The Manchester Regiment, established in 1881 through the Cardwell reforms, had six volunteer units at this time.

The overwhelming size of the crowds for these homecomings is testimony to the feelings of local and national patriotism on show. *The Return of the Warwickshire Volunteers*, (1902) warranted a civic reception, a grand parade through the streets of Birmingham and large and enthusiastic crowds for their entrance into Birmingham.[75] The return of local volunteer regiments to their home cities or towns was treated by Mitchell & Kenyon and the exhibitors as an extension of the local film. The regiments became 'a point of community interest and civic pride, an aid to the military authorities and an outlet for entertainment', and they contributed to the successful maintenance of popular support for the Anglo-Boer War.[76] The cinematograph exhibitors commissioned this material and emphasised its paramount importance in their programme, realising, as did the reviewer from Bradford, that 'the most popular item of all was the return of the Active Service Volunteers from South Africa, which was given as a grand finale'.[77]

Return of the East Lancashire Regiment at Preston (1902) is different from the images captured in Manchester and Birmingham, with their cheering crowds and the pageantry of the soldiers marching through the cities.[78] Instead, it concentrates on the soldiers returning to their home barracks to be reunited with family and friends. There are two sets of films of the East Lancashire Regiment in the collection: one illustrates the departure on bicycles of the *1st Volunteer Battalion, East Lancashire Regiment – Blackburn Rifle Volunteers* (1900) on Preston New Road, Blackburn; while the second features the Burnley Militia, who formed part of the 1st Battalion of the East Lancashire Regiment and had been based in Burnley until January 1899.[79] Interestingly, and again reflecting the local

The volunteers homecomings were often greeted by large crowds and civic receptions. *Return of the East Lancashire Regiment at Preston* (1902) is more low key than other titles and instead concentrates on the soldiers returning to their home barracks to be reunited with family and friends

The Return of the Lancaster Volunteers (1902), is similar to the Preston volunteer titles and shows the soldiers drilling, posing for the cameras and joking about with their comrades

bias of the exhibitions, the film appears to have received more coverage in Burnley than in Preston.[80] The film shows the soldiers parading, the medal ceremony and then a more relaxed series of views, where the soldiers are reunited with their families and friends. *Regiments Returned from Boer War to Victoria Barracks, Cork* (1902) is similar in feel to the Lancashire title, as it captures the soldiers in their barracks rather than parading through the streets. Although the regiment remains as yet unidentified, it shows that despite mixed reaction in Ireland to the conflict, Irish soldiers also participated in the war, with over 30,000 Irishmen fighting for the British Army during this time.[81]

The scenes that greeted the departure and return of the volunteer regiments on film echoed the popular sentiments in the streets through which they paraded. In the months during and following the end of the conflict, the various volunteer regiments returned to their home towns, and examples in the collection include *The Return of the Lancaster Volunteers* (1902) and *Parade of the Bolton Artillery Volunteers* (1901).[82] Volunteer regiments from Northampton, Liverpool, Bolton and the Royal Scots Regiment were also filmed by Mitchell & Kenyon, with the latter proudly boasting that none of their troops surrendered on the field of action in the Anglo-Boer War.[83] By the end of the conflict, in May 1902, these volunteer forces, comprising the Militia, the Volunteers and the Imperial Yeomanry, had supplied over 100,000 men, with estimates that over a third who had volunteered had been rejected as unfit for duty. As Stephen Miller writes, 'the British press regardless of their political leanings . . . seemed united in their promotion of the volunteer force'.[84]

The filming of volunteer regiments often coincided with the visit of one of the Boer War commanders for a local award ceremony. The continuing interest in military personnel who were brought to prominence by the cinematograph continued after the ending of hostilities. During the Boer War, there was an unusual degree of interaction between the commanding officers and the gentleman of the press, with all the leading commanders playing a part in the way the war was presented by the media. Lord Roberts, seen in *Lord Roberts Presenting Medals to Boer War Volunteers in Liverpool*, was perhaps the most media aware of all the commanders, and unlike the original Commander-in-Chief, General Redvers Buller, his popularity was enhanced by the conflict.[85]

The filming of volunteer regiments often coincided with the visit of one of the Boer War commanders for a local award ceremony – *Lord Roberts Presenting Medals to Boer War Volunteers in Liverpool* (1901)

Boer War Generals

The Boer War commanders filmed by Mitchell & Kenyon were some of the most famous military personalities of their age, including General Buller, Lord Kitchener and Lord Roberts, all of whom served in different capacities between 1899 and 1902 and were associated with different phases of the conflict.[86] Films of the heroes of the war were advertised as 'portraits of Roberts, Kitchener, Baden-Powell and all the Celebrities of the Day' by the local exhibitors and Mitchell & Kenyon.[87] *Visit of Lord Methuen to Bristol* (1902) reveals the popularity of all the military personnel. Paul Methuen was Commander of the 1st Division, known variously as the Mobile Marvels, the Mudcrushers and the Salvation Army, because of their speed and endurance in relieving garrisons and pursuing the enemy.[88]

The media consciousness reached its height with the hero of Mafeking, Robert Baden-Powell, who achieved 'iconic status with the new cinematography'.[89] Interestingly, Baden-Powell was only filmed by Mitchell & Kenyon two years after the war had ended and not between 1899 and 1902. Although Mitchell & Kenyon only filmed Roberts, Kitchener, Methuen, Buller and Baden-Powell on home soil, the overwhelming feelings of patriotism sometimes resulted in hysterical scenes and overcrowding. One such incident is captured in *Lord Roberts's Visit to Manchester*, in which a woman faints on

Visit of Lord Methuen to Bristol (1902) – another Boer War hero was greeted by a civic reception and cheering crowds

camera and is carried off by the police on duty. 'Dear Old Bobs', as he became affectionately known, was always greeted by 'vast and enthusiastic gatherings', in recognition of his military prowess and role as a saviour of the people.

Lord Roberts

Lord Roberts's Visit to Manchester reveals the popularity of these national heroes at the time.[90] Roberts built up his own image substantially and continued to use his popularity long after he had left South Africa.[91] His was a glittering military career, and one that was carefully enhanced by his friends in the media. Roberts had replaced Redvers Buller as Commander-in-Chief in January 1900, and 'true to his heroic reputation, within five months of arriving stunningly reversed the course of the war'.[92] He had a particularly strong relationship with the media and used his contacts to ensure that he was seen and heard. There are three films of Roberts in the collection, shot in Liverpool and Manchester. *Lord Roberts Presenting Medals to Boer War Volunteers in Liverpool* shows Roberts presenting commemorative bronze shields to each of the local volunteer battalions that sent contingents to the war, as well as reviewing veterans from India, a reflection of his previous role as Commander-in-chief in India. The *Liverpool Daily Post* commented on the large crowds that, despite the terrible weather, came to the presentation. The combination of the local volunteer brigades and Roberts's visit swelled the numbers, with the event combining both local pride with national patriotism: 'All this time every eye of the great multitude was upon "Bobs" for whom the whole British nation has an affectionate regard, and instanced by the familiar appellation by which he is known.'[93]

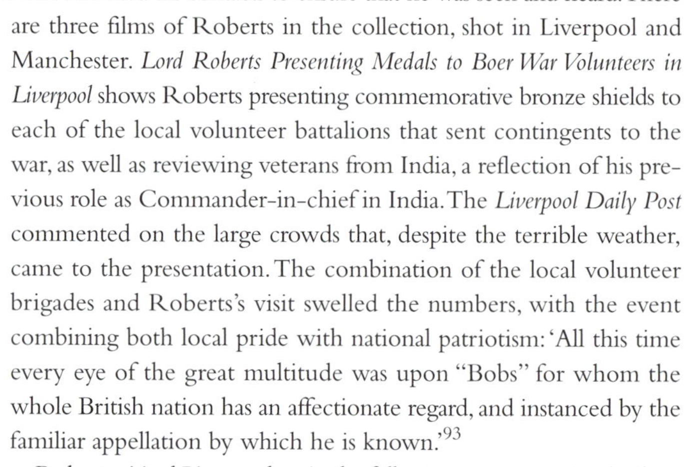

Field Marshal Lord Roberts.
Ogden's Guinea Gold Cigarettes

Roberts visited Liverpool again the following year to receive the freedom of the city with Lord Kitchener for their actions during the Boer War. The *Liverpool Daily Post*'s editorial observes how this honour reflected a 'popular endorsement' of these 'distinguished soldiers', who, in 'difficult circumstances have served their country with devotion and brilliant success'.[94] Vast crowds turned out for the *Visit of Earl Roberts and Viscount Kitchener to Receive the Freedom of the City, Liverpool*, and the film also captures an illuminated tram decorated with bunting proclaiming 'Welcome to our Brave Generals'.[95]

Lord Roberts' Visit to Manchester (1901) reveals the popularity of these national heroes at the time, as cheering crowds in their thousands greeted the arrival of Lord Roberts on 9 October 1901, for the unveiling of the statue to Queen Victoria in Piccadilly

Lord Kitchener

Lord Kitchener served in the Boer War as Chief of Staff to Roberts, replacing him as Commander-in-Chief in mid-1900. Pictorial representations of Lord Kitchener are more recognisable to today's audience due to the appearance of his face in possibly the most famous piece of military propaganda in the First World War, 'Your Country Needs You'.[96] During the Boer War, Kitchener also received the same kind of iconic status given to his former Commander-in-Chief, Lord Roberts. However, Kitchener never inspired the kind of loyalty and devotion accorded to 'Our Bob' either by his troops or the British public. His image was more severe, stern, not lovable like Roberts, and he was revered for his strength and resolution. As Keith Surridge writes:

Lord Kitchener of Khartoum.
Ogden's Guinea Gold Cigarettes

> Kitchener was a colossal figure in an age which looked up to men whose image had been forged in war. His physical appearance belied all that was apparently wrong with the ordinary British population. He was fierce and cruel and therefore a touchstone against the enemies that seemed to be gathering around the frontiers of empire.[97]

The films of Kitchener, both in the Mitchell & Kenyon Collection and those held by the national collections, do not show the intimacy of those taken of Roberts. *Visit of Earl Roberts and Viscount Kitchener to Receive the Freedom of the City, Liverpool* is less personal than the other films of Lord Roberts and reflects a formal civic occasion.[98] The main title featuring Kitchener in the collection is *Return of Kitchener* (1902). This event was filmed by Mitchell & Kenyon in London on 26 July, as well as by other cinematographers, including Robert Paul.[99] In line with the more well-known *Lord Kitchener's Arrival at Southampton* (1902), the film shows the pomp and splendour of the Empire celebrating victory overseas. There is none of the familiarity of the Roberts return, where the crowd overwhelm the victorious hero. Instead, we have the magnificence and formality of a national celebration, including processions of carriages, soldiers lining the roads in salute and the parade of troops.[100]

General Buller

Despite the overwhelming support for Roberts and Kitchener, public reaction to General Redvers Buller was more mixed, perhaps because of the calamitous effects of the disastrous defeats of 'Black Week' referred to earlier.[101] After the defeat of Spion Kop in January, Buller became known as 'Reverse' Buller and suffered the ignominy of being replaced by his bitter rival, Lord Roberts. Despite Buller's unpopularity in some quarters, David Russell emphasises that he too received some of the heroic treatment. Buller was accorded songs of encouragement by the music-hall performers, with 'Cheer Up Buller' by F.V. St Clair being one example.[102] Following his replacement by Roberts, Buller returned to England to assume command at Aldershot, but was eventually sacked following a series of feuds with Lord Roberts in late 1901. However, this did not dissipate the cinematograph's interest in his activities, as the review in the *Liverpool Daily Post* for the Prince of Wales Theatre reveals:

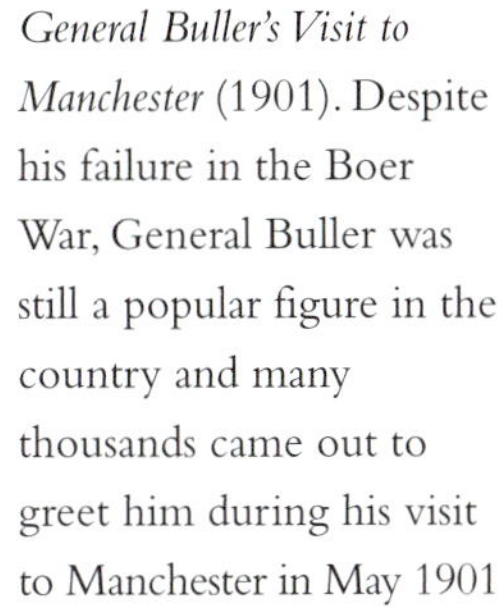

General Buller's Visit to Manchester (1901). Despite his failure in the Boer War, General Buller was still a popular figure in the country and many thousands came out to greet him during his visit to Manchester in May 1901

> For instance, the life story of General Buller, illustrated by many graphic and warlike pictures of his military career, completely carried away the people, Buller's name being cheered again and again to the echo . . . Special efforts have also been taken to get some very effective pictures of the Boer war. Altogether, the show is high class and interesting.[103]

A review of the show in the *Liverpool Mercury* also includes a reference to Lindon Travers's pictorial lecture on 'How Buller Won the Victoria Cross', in which he described in 'a lucid and agreeable style the various incidents in the career of General Buller during his 40 years' service in the army'.[104] Both Roberts and Buller visited Manchester in 1901, and the events were filmed by Mitchell & Kenyon. The exhibitors in Manchester and other locations sometimes combined a screening of the latest films of Lord Roberts with earlier films of Buller.[105] The footage of Buller that survives in the collection relates to his visit to Manchester in May 1901, where he was met with an 'enthusiastic reception on his arrival for the purpose of opening the Victorian Fete' in aid of the Soldiers and Sailors Families Association.[106] The 'inevitable cinematographist' was there, reported the *Manchester Evening News*. *General Buller's Visit to Manchester* (1901), or 'Animated Photography of the Gallant Hero and thousands of spectators', was shown the following evening at the St James Hall.[107]

Gen. Sir Redvers H. Buller, V.C.,
G.C.B., K.C.M.G., P.C.
OGDEN'S
CIGARETTES

Push to Militarism

> In money and lives, no British war since 1815, had been so prodigal. The 'tea-time' war, Milner's little 'Armegeddon', which was expected to be over by Christmas 1899, had cost the British taxpayer more than £200 million. The cost in blood was equally high.[108]

The Boer War began with a spirit of boundless optimism and public displays of popular patriotism, before descending into a protracted guerrilla campaign and the political controversy of British concentration camps. The war undoubtedly delivered a psychological shock, shattering 'national complacency and creating an intensified sense of danger', with Britain being taught a valuable lesson.[109] As Kenneth Morgan writes, 'as soon as the war was over the British media were pivotal in voicing disgust with the concentration camps and the colossal loss of life' (22,000 British soldiers, while the Boers lost 7,000 men in the field and 27,000, many of those women and children, in the concentration camps).[110]

The consequences of the Boer War on the organisation of Britain's military forces were varied and interesting. The fear that the British race was deteriorating became a major concern and led to the creation of the Inter Departmental Committee on Physical Deterioration. The report published in August 1904 was originally intended to allay these fears but actually demonstrated the need for better and healthier soldiers. It highlighted how poverty and the poor health of the volunteers had contributed to the lack of fitness displayed by the British Army.[111] After the end of the Boer War, in May 1902,

Schooling became more regimented, with the increasing use of the military-style discipline apparent in *Special Parade of St Matthews Pupils and Special March Past of St Joseph's Scholars* (1905)

a review of the army took place and a Royal Commission reported on the Militia and Volunteers. The War Office was concerned over the different standards of efficiency, but had to concede that this lay in the hands of individual commanding officers. The newly elected Liberal government passed the Territorial and Reserve Forces Act (1907), which brought together volunteer units to form the Territorial Force. This gave further recognition to the territorial units, which could now act as backup to the Regular Army if the need arose. *Parade of the Blackburn Territorials* (1909) is an example of this reorganisation, with other units, such as the Bradford Artillery, seen in *On the March with the Bradford Artillery at Buckshaw Brow, Settle*, losing their heavy guns and becoming field brigades.[112]

The British newspapers also contrasted the physical prowess of the Boers with the poor showing of the volunteers, with General Sir Frederick Maurice stating in 1902, 'that sixty percent of those who volunteered were unfit for military duty'.[113] The war was seen in some circles as a blessing, highlighting the decaying state of national life, and that only through conflict would the Empire emerge stronger and better equipped to deal with its enemies. In a leading article entitled 'The Blessing of War', the *Daily Mail* described the war as a double blessing, where the redemptive nature of warfare was emphasised.[114] Warfare became linked to the ideas of social Darwinism, and 'the prevailing perception of the use of military force in Edwardian Britain was that war was both beneficial and desirable to the societies engaged in it'.[115] These themes continued during and after the Anglo-Boer War, with the *Daily Mirror*, *News of the World* and the *Daily Mail* just some of the newspapers that believed that warfare demonstrated the good health of the nation.[116] Glenn Wilkinson's work on Edwardian newspapers and their

Working-class war heroes achieved celebrity status and the North American Animated Photo Co., made a film of *Ralph Pringle Interviewing Private Ward, V.C. Hero in Leeds* (1901)

coverage of war demonstrates this link further when he states: 'These articles indicate that war was perceived as an activity which was beneficial to society and the "race", and as an acceptable and necessary antidote to degeneration.'[117]

The link between warfare and the state of the moral, physical and spiritual fabric of the Empire continued throughout the Edwardian era and became linked to increasing militarisation in all other aspects of society. This was particularly apparent in public schools, which channelled their emphasis on athletics and sports to 'training for defence of King and country'.[118] Drills, shooting competitions and the formation of a Cadet Corps all became part of the life of a public schoolboy.[119] Schools were maintained on military models, especially after the 1902 Education Act raised the compulsory age of school leaving.[120] Schooling became more regimented, with the increasing use of the military drill clearly evident in *Audley Range School, Blackburn*.[121] The use of the drill in schools was seen as important in maintaining discipline, responsibility and respect for authority. Military tournaments became a means of attracting better standards of recruits to the army, while ensuring the continued popularity of the armed forces in the eyes of the public through the use of military spectacle. *The Military Tournament at Batley Football Ground* (1901) was just one of many held during this period, and other such events in the collection include *Military Review at Racecourse* (c. 1901).[122]

Working-class heroes also achieved celebrity status, and their patriotism was called upon for matters other than combat in the period leading up to the Great War. Private Charles Ward, who featured in *Ralph Pringle Interviewing Private Ward VC Hero in Leeds* (1901), is an interesting case in point.[123] Ward was the last man to receive a Victoria Cross for his valour in the Anglo-Boer War from Queen Victoria in December 1900. The original film taken by Ralph Pringle shows the 'Tommy' soldier elevated to the status of the more famous military heroes such as Roberts and Baden-Powell. Ward was the guest of honour at the screening in Leeds Coliseum, alongside members of the Leeds Rifles.[124] After the conflict had ended, Private Ward was often called upon to help the army in other capacities, appearing at charitable events for the military. He re-enlisted in 1914 and served as a drill instructor and recruiting officer for other working-class lads like himself in the Great War.[125]

New Navalism

The impact of the Anglo-Boer War on the Edwardian navy is also apparent in the Mitchell & Kenyon Collection. Although Britain was the undisputed ruler of the sea, Germany had already begun to build up its mercantile and naval fleets and joined the international race for the supremacy of the North Atlantic. The campaigns to raise awareness and reform the apparent weakness of the Royal Navy had resulted in the Naval Defence Act (1889), which legislated that naval resources must be equal to the combined strength of its two closest rivals. The might of the new naval forces is apparent in *The Fleet in the Tyne* (1901), which includes images of a variety of warships built from the 1890s onwards, including torpedo boat destroyer the *Peterel*, launched in 1899.[126] An older example of a battleship can be seen in *Panorama of the River Avon to Portishead* (1902), in which HMS *Formidable*, an 84-gun two-decker built in 1825, is visible. The ship had been moored off Portishead since 1869, when it became the 'Formidable Industrial Training Ship for Homeless and Destitute Boys'.[127]

S.S Skirmisher at Liverpool (1901). Investment in both military vessels and commercial ships became more pronounced from the 1900s as Cunard and other companies built luxury liners for transatlantic crossings

Despite increased investment from the 1890s onwards, the nature of the victory in South Africa strengthened the navy's resolve and new battleships continued to be commissioned. One such battleship was HMS *Dominion*, captured on film in *Royal Visit to Barrow & Launch of HMS Dominion* (1903). The *Dominion* was described by the local paper as one of the finest and most effective warships in the world.[128] This 'new navalism', reflected in the formation of the British Navy League in 1894, was an attempt to raise public awareness and resulted in increased expenditure on the navy, which by 1900 exceeded £29 million.[129] Military commandments were increasingly employing spectacle in the forms of the review and the ceremonial parade, with the aim of raising the profile of their units and making them more visually attractive to society. *Trafalgar Day in Liverpool*, (1901) organised by the Liverpool branch of the Navy League, includes a spectacular procession of cadets, serving officers and crew parading in honour of the greatest of all naval victories. Despite the commemorative nature of the occasion, it was in reality a public display of patriotism and imperial might that demonstrated the strength and importance of the navy.[130]

The might of the new naval forces is apparent *in The Fleet in the Tyne* (1901), which includes images of a variety of warships built from the 1890s onwards including torpedo boat destroyer the *Peterel,* launched in 1899

Past naval glories were celebrated and commemorated to raise the profile of the navy. *Trafalgar Day in Liverpool* (1901) organised by the Liverpool branch of the Navy League, shows a magnificent spectacular procession of cadets, serving officers and crew, parading in honour of the greatest of all naval victories

Public fervour for all aspects of the armed forces continued throughout the 1900s. The cinematograph was also utilised, with programmes of a naval and patriotic nature promoted by Alfred John West of 'Our Navy and Our Army' fame, who sometimes appeared under the patronage of the Navy League.[131] West not only presented films promoting and extolling the wonders of the armed forces but he also used a military theme to publicise his events. One of his more extravagant ideas involved towing a large model of a ship around the halls to advertise the show.[132] The pictures, wrote the *Brighton and Hove Guardian* reporter, 'showed almost every aspect of a sailor's life', and 'were watched by a large and appreciative audience who greeted the various scenes with thunders of applause'.[133]

The might of the Royal Navy was central to the British belief that they were still the most important military and political force in the world, as is clear from *Torpedo Boats Passing through the Manchester Ship Canal* (1901).[134] The boats are filmed passing under Barton Bridge, and three cameramen are required to film the lengthy scenes. Four sections of the film are dedicated to the torpedo boats, with only a short sequence recording the civic reception at the town hall in Manchester, and a parade of the seamen coming ashore.[135]

The combination of the most popular officers in the Anglo-Boer war and the new emphasis on physical education up to military standards is demonstrated in *Inspection of the Ambulance Drill Hall in Accrington by Inspector-general Baden Powell* (1904)

(Opposite below) The might of the Royal Navy was central to the British belief that they were still the most important military and political force in the world, as is clear when one sees *Torpedo Boats Passing Through the Manchester Ship Canal* (1901). The boats are filmed passing under Barton Bridge with three cameramen present to film the lengthy scenes

The impact of the Boer War on the militarisation of Edwardian society cannot be overestimated. The feeling of disbelief that had greeted the disastrous campaigns at the start of the conflict were replaced by growing discomfort over the military's ability to combat a stronger and more local force in Europe. The involvement of the British media in propagating the war continued long after its cessation in 1902, with the symbol of a good war hero typified by Baden-Powell. The combination of the most popular officers in the Anglo-Boer War and the new emphasis on a military standard of physical education is further demonstrated in *Inspection of the Ambulance Drill Hall in Accrington by General-Inspector Baden-Powell* (1904).[136] Youth movements, especially those associated with military ideals and organisations, had flourished from the 1880s onwards, but with the onset of war and the nature of the victory, their importance became paramount in preparing the youth of the day for future combat.

Case Study: Boys' Brigade

Before the founding of the Scouts movement in 1908, the most popular form of military-style organisation for boys was the Boys' Brigade. The proliferation and spread of such organisations in the Edwardian era has been identified as one of the consequences of the Boer War. As we have seen, one of the most frightening factors of the conflict for the greater British public and the ruling classes was how it appeared to show the physical decline of society. Physical deterioration was linked to decadence and immorality, with, to some extent, urban living being blamed for this decline in standards. Founded in Glasgow in 1883 by Sir William Alexander Smith, the Boys' Brigade provided a model for these youth organisations, in particular the Scouts, of which Robert Baden-Powell was a former member. Smith's original idea was to use the military training he had learned from his time serving in the Lanarkshire Rifle Volunteers to instil discipline in the children he was

Morecambe Church Lads' Brigade at Drill (1901). The proliferation and spread of military-style organisations for boys in the Edwardian era has been seen as one of the consequences of the Boer War

teaching. The training was originally seen as an extension of the Sunday school, but as the meetings became more popular and attracted more recruits, the cadets were given military-style uniforms and drilled using replica rifles. The movement spread throughout Scotland, its emphasis on true Christian manliness and 'Sure and Steadfast' motto reflecting in some part the message of the public schools but directed at working-class boys in urban neighbourhoods. Membership increased throughout the 1890s, and by 1892, membership in England and Wales was greater than in Scotland. By 1899, the Brigade had risen from an original membership of thirty in 1884 to 35,148, a pattern of uninterrupted expansion that continued throughout the 1900s.[137] The popularity of the movement in England and its links to religion and militarism can be seen in *Church Parade of the Boys' Brigade in Birmingham* (1902).[138] The parade took place the day after the Saturday meeting of the Birmingham Athletics Club at Edgbaston and was filmed and exhibited in a military-themed programme presented by New Century Pictures. The innocent views of the Boys' Brigade was highlighted alongside films of Lord Kitchener's Return, the 1st Volunteer South Staffordshire Regiment and the Champion Athletes at Birmingham.[139]

Scenes from Boys' Brigade inspections in the Collection. The Boys' Brigade founded in Glasgow in 1883 by Sir William Alexander Smith provided a model for these youth organisations in particular the Scouts, with Robert Baden-Powell a former member

The Church Brigade seen in *Morecambe Church Lads' Brigade at Drill (1901)* was formed in England in 1891 by Walter Gee as an Anglican Youth organisation

Despite its appeal throughout the UK, Glasgow remained the headquarters of the Boys' Brigade and the location of its annual inspection. *Boys' Brigade Inspection at Yorkhill, Glasgow* (1906) was one such national inspection and demonstrates how the use of military spectacle in drills, parades and pageantry was also utilised by the youth organisations. The ten minute sequence, one of the longest films in the collection, reveals row after row of uniformed boys marching with military precision across the arena. Crowds of spectators applaud their drills as the camera pans across the playing fields to reveal even more columns of tunic-clad youths. These scenes are also apparent in two other films featuring the Boys' Brigade in the collection, in particular *Boys Brigade Review at Racecourse* (c. 1902), where the scenes are more reminiscent of a commander inspecting his troops for war rather than an organisation keen to instil Christian virtues.[140] However, the association between Christianity, manliness and military strength was part of the founding message. As John Springhall writes: 'Smith also reasoned that a new uniformed organisation appealing to a boy's sense of patriotism and martial spirit would serve as a useful instrument for a primarily religious end.'[141]

Other military-style youth organisations followed William Smith's example. The Church Lads' Brigade, of which *Morecambe Church Lads' Brigade at Drill* is a wonderful illustration, was formed in England in 1891 by Walter Gee as an Anglican youth organisation.[142] He had been impressed with the non-denominational work of the Boys' Brigade and wanted to create a Church of England section within it. When this proposal was rejected, he formed his own separate organisation. The message of the Church Lads, often seen as the main English rival to the Boys' Brigade before the foundation of the Scouts movement, was to maintain a grip on the youth at a critical moment in their development.[143] With its links to the Church of England Temperance Society, its organisers saw unorganised recreation as a danger, and the brigades offered instead structured leisure that contained a strong religious message. Although its stronghold was largely in the south-east of England, the presence of the Church Lads' Brigade in Morecambe is not unusual as membership grew rapidly, and by 1908 there were over 70,000 members in the organisation. Interestingly, despite its religious message and similarity to the Boys' Brigade, the films of the Church Lads in the collection are very informal in style and presentation. The first section of the title the intimate close-ups of the young cadets smiling and fooling around in front of the camera, as they perform their drills. The second section reveals the drill and parade along Morecambe promenade, and is in complete contrast to the military discipline implied in the Boys' Brigade titles.

(Overleaf) *Special Parade of St Matthews Pupils and Special March Past of St Joseph's Scholars* (1905) who attempt to march past the camera with military precision!

JONES BROS
MAKERS OF DOUBLED YARNS
DOBBY & JACQUARD

The creation of the Boy Scouts severely affected the popularity of many of these religious-based brigades, and only the Boys' Brigade managed to maintain membership and support throughout the twentieth century. Ironically, Baden-Powell was a former commander of the Boys' Brigade and his original plan had been to amalgamate the scouting activities outlined in his book *Scouting for Boys* into the brigade.[144] This was not to be, and by 1912 this new organisation had attracted over 130,000 scouts. However, for most of the decade, the organisation founded by William Smith in Glasgow was the most successful youth organisation ever seen, and it is its members that we see parading in racecourses, athletics grounds and other large public arenas in front of thousands of spectators. The Boys' Brigade was referred to by a contemporary commentator as a 'juvenile citizen army' and, eight years later, many of the young boys marching merrily in the films would no longer be playing at war but living the reality.[145]

Conclusion

Despite the patriotism displayed in the Mitchell & Kenyon films, the disastrous nature of the 'victory' in South Africa, and the manner in which it had been achieved, did little to convince the public and the government that Britain could maintain its Empire. The dynamics of politics and warfare was no longer the domain of the printed press. The media expanded and incorporated modern visual forms, as new technology resulted in a greater mass audience who wished to view as well as read about the latest events. As society prospered and leisure and sporting arenas expanded and developed, the growth of militarism became more apparent in society. The cinematograph exhibitions, in line with other forms of popular entertainment, brought the military into the fairground, the music hall and, through popular literature, into the family home. Cinema audiences grew throughout the decade, 'with the cinema far outstripping any previous form of commercial entertainment in its appeal to the young'.[146]

The first decade of the twentieth century brought about dramatic changes in the organisation of the military. Army reforms from 1907 onwards, the rise of the 'new navalism' and a change in government in 1905 saw a shift in emphasis, as Britain prepared to strengthen its military defences. The growth in military-style organisations for boys, the reforms in education and changes to working hours for children were in some ways an attempt to improve the physical and intellectual metal of the future defenders of the Empire. The films in the collection demonstrate how militarism impacted on all aspects of society, as the reality of warfare became diffused into popular culture. The Mitchell &

Parade of the Blackburn Territorials (1909)
Although Mitchell & Kenyon never filmed the Great War, the changes and reorganisation of the military, prevalent throughout the Edwardian era were captured by the company

Kenyon Collection provides us with a window to view how change was effected on the ground, with its images of volunteers marching off to war, young boys drilling with military precision and the might of the Edwardian navy. Although Mitchell & Kenyon never filmed the Great War, the underlying themes in society that were prevalent throughout the Edwardian era were captured by the company. For, as Michael Paris writes:

> August 1914 was simply the fulfilment of the expectations of war. It was what the youth of the nation had been prepared for and as such it was welcomed as an end to uncertainty and the opportunity to take part in the 'great adventure'.[147]

Notes

1 *The Showman*, September 1900, pp. 16–17.

2 Michael Paris, *Warrior Nation: Images of War in British Popular Culture 1850–2000* (London: Reaktion Books, 2000), p. 48.

3 John Springhall, *Youth, Empire and Society* (London: Croom Helm, 1977), and John M. Mackenzie (ed.), *Imperialism and Popular Culture* (Manchester: Manchester University Press, 1986), for two examples; see also Paris, *Warrior Nation*.

4 For an overview of this see G. R. Searle, *A New England: Peace and War, 1886–1918* (Oxford: Oxford University Press, 2004).

5 See, for example, John Gooch (ed.), *The Boer War: Direction, Experience and Image* (London: Frank Cass, 2000); Keith Terrance Surridge, *Managing the South African War: Politicians v. Generals* (London: The Boydell Press, 1998); and Donal Lowry (ed.), *The South African War Reappraised* (Manchester: Manchester University Press, 2000). Also see Neil Parsons, *King Khama, Emperor Joe and the Great White Queen: Victorian Britain through African Eyes* (Chicago: University of Chicago Press, 1998), for African attitudes.

6 For a record of films produced at this time see John Barnes, *The Beginnings of the Cinema in England 1894–1901: Vol. 4 Filming The Boer War* (London: Bishopsgate Press, 1992).

7 See Simon Popple, '"But the Khaki-Covered Camera is the *Latest* Thing": The Boer War Cinema and Visual Culture in Britain', in Andrew Higson (ed.), *Young and Innocent? The Cinema in Britain 1896–1930* (Exeter: Exeter University Press, 2002), pp. 13–27, and Simon Popple, '"Startling, realistic, pathetic": The Mitchell and Kenyon "Boer War" Films', in Vanessa Toulmin, Simon Popple and Patrick Russell (eds), *The Lost World of Mitchell & Kenyon: Edwardian Britiain on Film* (London: BFI, 2004), pp. 150–7.

8 Kenneth O. Morgan, 'The Boer War and the Media (1899–1902)', *Twentieth Century History*, Vol. 13 No. 13, p. 8.

9 The main history of the conflict is Thomas Pakenham, *The Boer War* (London: Weidenfeld and Nicolson, 1979), but see also D. Judd and K. Surridge, *The Boer War* (London: John Murray, 2002). For its importance to the media see Morgan, 'The Boer War and the Media (1899–1902)', pp. 1–16.

10 Jacqueline Beaumont, '*The Times* at War, 1899–1902', in Lowry (ed.) *The South African War Reappraised*, pp. 67–84.

11 Stephen Badsey, 'War Correspondents in the Boer War', in Gooch (ed.), *The Boer War: Direction, Experience and Image*, pp. 187–203.

12 See Glenn Wilkinson, *Depiction and Images of War in Edwardian Newspapers, 1899–1914* (Houndmills: Palgrave, 2003), p. 8.

13 Morgan, 'The Boer War and the Media (1899–1902)', p. 6.

14 Mark Hampton, 'The Press, Patriotism and Public Discussion: C. P. Scott, *The Manchester Guardian*, and the Boer War, 1899–1902', *The Historical Journal*, Vol. 44 No. 1 (2001), pp. 177–97.

15 Ward Muir, 'Photographic Merriment and Songs of the Camera', *The Photogram*, July 1900.

16 Paris, *Warrior Nation*, p. 48.

17 Tim Wilcox, 'Painting and Public, Print and Profit: Lady Butler's Painting "Balaclava" and its Dissemination', in Simon Popple and Vanessa Toulmin (eds), *Visual Delights: Essays on the Popular and Projected Image in the 19th Century* (Trowbridge: Flicks Books, 2000), pp. 127–35.

18 John Springhall, '"Up Guards and at Them": British Imperialism and Popular Art, 1880–1914', in Mackenzie (ed.), *Imperialism and Popular Culture*, pp. 49–72.

19 Glenn R. Wilkinson, '"To the Front": British Newspaper Advertising and the Boer War', in Gooch (ed.), *The Boer War: Direction, Experience and Image*, pp. 203–12.

20 J. S. Bratton, 'Of England, Home and Duty: The Image of England in Victorian and Edwardian Juvenile Fiction', in Mackenzie (ed.), *Imperialism and Popular Culture*, pp. 73–94.

21 Richard Price, *An Imperial War and the British Working Class: Working Class Attitudes and Reactions to the Boer War, 1899–1902* (London: Routledge and Kegan Paul, 1972).

22 M&K 424, 428, 429: *Manchester and Salford Harriers' Cyclists' Procession*, in particular 424; *Manchester Courier*, 24 June 1901, p. 8.

23 See Vanessa Toulmin, *Pleasurelands* (Hastings: The Projection Box, 2003).

24 *Nottingham Evening News*, 4 October 1900, p. 4.

25 *The Showman*, 11 October 1901.

26 'Stalybridge Wakes – A Gloriously Fine Week – In the Fair', *The Reporter*, 28 July 1900. Taken from G. Shaw (compiled) Stalybridge Wakes: News Items 1830–1947 National Fairground Archive Q Shaw/1358.

27 *Hull News*, 13 October 1900, p. 9.

28 *The Banbury Advertiser*, 25 October 1900.

29 *Preston Guardian*, 9 June 1900.

30 John Barker's beautifully illustrated book contains many images of his collection of Boer War centaurs. See John Barker, *Roundabout Relics: English Fairground Carvers and Antique Collectables* (Wokingham: Jumper Books, 2006).

31 *The Glasgow Programme*, 18 June 1900.

32 *The Glasgow Programme*, 5 August 1901, p. 1.

33 Ben Shepherd, *Kitty and the Prince* (London: Profile Books, 2003), and Ben Shepherd, 'Showbiz Imperialism: The Case of Peter Lobengula', in Mackenzie (ed.), *Imperialism and Popular Culture*, pp. 94–112.

34 Programme for Grand Circus at Covent Garden, 19 February 1890, private collection; handbill for Lord George Sanger's Circus and Hippodrome, 1902, Crystal Palace, Peace Festival, 5 July 1902, NFA Ephemera Collection, University of Sheffield Library.

35 See Penelope Summerfield, 'The Effingham Arms and the Empire', in Eileen and Stephen Yeo (eds), *Popular Culture and Class Conflict* (Brighton: The Harvester Press, 1981), pp. 209–41; J. S. Bratton, 'The Theatre of War', in David Bradby *et al.* (eds), *Performance and*

Politics in Popular Drama (Cambridge: Cambridge University Press, 1980); Penny Summerfield, 'Patriotism and Empire: Music Hall Entertainment 1870–1914', in Mackenzie (ed.), *Imperialism and Popular Culture*, pp. 17–48; and Dave Russell, 'We Carved Our Way to Glory: The British Soldiers in Music Hall Song and Sketch, c. 1880–1914', in John McKenzie, *Popular Imperialism and the Military 1850–1950* (Manchester: Manchester University Press, 1992), pp. 50–79.

36 J. A. Hobson, *Psychology of Jingoism* (London: G. Richards, 1901).

37 Information taken from Ilkeston's New Theatre Royal supplied by Dr Ann Featherstone from *Ilkeston Pioneer*, 31 August 1900, 21 and 28 September 1900.

38 Russell, 'We Carved Our Way to Glory', p. 56.

39 Ibid., p. 75.

40 *Birmingham Daily Mail*, 29 May 1901, p. 1, and *Halifax Evening Courier*, 12 March 1901, p. 3.

41 Russell, 'We Carved Our Way to Glory', p. 73.

42 Ibid., p. 74.

43 Ibid.

44 Sydney Race Diaries transcribed by Dr Ann Featherstone, October 1897, Nottingham Archives (M24, 420/A/16).

45 'Advert for Royal Assembly Rooms, Mr R. W. Paul's PATRIOTIC ENTERTAINMENT – ARMY LIFE', *Leamington Spa Courier*, 24 November 1900.

46 *Bolton Chronicle*, 2 February 1901, p. 8.

47 For details of the films produced around the Boer War see Barnes, *The Beginnings of the Cinema in England*.

48 Richard Brown, 'War on the Home Front: The Anglo-Boer War and the Growth of Rental in Britain. An Economic Perspective', *Film History*, Vol. 16 No. 1 (2004), p. 28.

49 Warwick Film Catalogue and Supplementary List No 4 (1899), Science Museum Collection, London, cited in Barnes, *The Beginnings of Cinema in England*, p. 105. See also Stephen Bottomore, 'Joseph Rosenthal: The Most Glorious Profession', *Sight and Sound*, Vol. 54 No. 4 (Autumn 1983), pp. 260–5.

50 *The Era*, 9 August 1902, p. 32.

51 Information taken from the NFA Ephemera Collection, poster for the London Hippodrome, 1900, Argyle Theatre Collection January 1900, for example, has several examples of this.

52 *Nottingham Evening Post*, 19 March 1901, p. 4.

53 *Liverpool Daily Post*, 22 April 1901, p. 1.

54 *The Showman*, 15 March 1901, p. 179, and *The Newcastle Evening Chronicle*, 4 March 1901.

55 *The Photographic Chronicle*, 1 August 1901, p. 61.

56 T. C. Hepworth, 'Music and "Effects" in Cinematography', *The Showman*, 6 September 1901, p. 574, and *The Showman*, 15 November 1901, p. 146, for an account of the fake soldier in the audience.

57 See John Barnes, *The Beginnings of the Cinema in England, 1894–1901, Vols. 1–5* (Exeter: University of Exeter Press, 1997), for further details of this material.

58 Simon Popple, '"Startling, Realistic, Pathetic": The Mitchell and Kenyon Boer War Films', in Toulmin *et al.* (eds), *The Lost World of Mitchell & Kenyon*, pp. 150–8.

59 M&K 663–6: *Lieutenant Clive Wilson and the Tranby Croft Party*.

60 *Bradford Daily Argus*, 29 July 1902.

61 M&K 642–4: *On the March with the Bradford Artillery at Buckshaw Brow, Settle.*

62 John Downham, *Red Roses on the Veldt: Lancashire Regiments in the Boer War, 1899–1902* (Lancaster: Carnegie Publishing, 2002), p. 2.

63 One of the many examples of this include the reference from the *Birmingham Daily Mail*, 4 July 1902, for a film of 'Warwick Yeomanry at Camp', and also *Newcastle upon Tyne Evening Chronicle*, 3 December 1900, for film of the Northumberland Fusiliers.

64 The regiments being Northamptonshire, Warwickshire, Bolton, East Lancashire, Lancaster, King's Own Regiment, Manchesters, Imperial Yeomanry, Bradford Artillery and Royal Scots Regiment.

65 Stephen M. Miller, 'In Support of the "Imperial Mission"? Volunteering for the South African War, 1899–1902', *The Journal of Military History*, No. 69 (July 2005), pp. 691–712.

66 Hugh Cunningham, *The Volunteer Force: a Social and Political History 1859–1908* (Hamden: Archon Books, 1975).

67 For further information on the formation of the volunteers and their individual regimental histories, including the Imperial Yeomanry, see <www.regiments.org/regiments/uk/lists/targts.htm>, accessed 12 April 2006. See also John Stirling, *Our Regiments in South Africa 1899–1902* (London: William Blackwood, 1903).

68 Miller, 'In Support of the "Imperial Mission"?', pp. 691–712.

69 *Manchester Evening News*, 22 June 1902, p. 2.

70 M&K 434, 743: *Manchester's Welcome to the Imperial Yeomanry.*

71 *Manchester Evening News*, 25 June 1901, p. 2.

72 Ibid., p. 1.

73 Ibid., 22 May 1901, p. 4, for a report of the Manchester Volunteers' arrival at Southampton, 23 May 1901; pp. 4–5, for report of the return of the Manchester Volunteers and the arrival of Manchester Regiment; and 24 May 1901, pp. 2–3, for a report of the return of the Manchester Volunteers, including the welcome and service at the cathedral.

74 M&K 431–3: *Return of the Brave Manchester Volunteers.*

75 M&K 520–2, 814–15, 819: *The Return of the Warwickshire Volunteers.*

76 Miller, 'In Support of the "Imperial Mission"?', p. 703.

77 *Bradford Daily Argus*, 29 July 1902.

78 M&K 281–2, 329: *Return of the East Lancashire Regiment at Preston.*

79 M&K 277: *1st Volunteer Battalion, East Lancashire Regiment – Blackburn Rifle Volunteers* and M&K 281–2, 329: *Return of the East Lancashire Regiment at Preston.* For a history of the different brigades of the East Lancashire regiments and their role in the Boer War see Downham, *Red Roses on the Veldt.*

80 See *Burnley Express*, 3 December 1902, for a report of the show held at the mechanics institute for the following two weeks.

81 M&K 713: *Regiments Returned from Boer War to Victoria Barracks, Cork*, and for information on Irish soldiers in the conflict see Keith Jeffery, 'The Irish Soldier in the Boer War', in Gooch (ed.), *The Boer War*, pp. 141–52.

82 M&K 671: *The Return of the Lancaster Volunteers* and M&K 481: *Parade of the Bolton Artillery Volunteers.*

83 M&K 774–5, 811: *Lord Roberts Presenting Medals to Boer War Volunteers in Liverpool*, M&K 481: *Parade of the Bolton Artillery Volunteers*; M&K 507: *All Saints Church with Parade of the Northamptonshire Regiment* (1902); and M&K 792, 798: *Royal Scots Regiment at Edinburgh Castle* (1901).

84 Miller, 'In Support of the "Imperial Mission"?', p. 707.

85 M&K 774–5, 811: *Lord Roberts Presenting Medals to Boer War Volunteers in Liverpool*.

86 For more information see Peter Trew, *The Boer War Generals* (new edn. England: Wrens Park Publishing, 2001; original edn. Stroud: Sutton, 1999).

87 *Leamington Spa Courier*, 24 March 1900.

88 Stephen Miller, 'Lord Methuen and the British Advance to the Modder River', *South African Military Journal Society*, Vol. 10 No. 4 (1996), <rapidttp.com/milhist/journal.html>, accessed on 22 April 2006. See M&K 502–3: *Visit of Lord Methuen to Bristol* (1902).

89 Morgan, 'The Boer War and the Media (1899–1902)', p. 7.

90 M&K 420–2, 430, 777: *Lord Roberts's Visit to Manchester*, in particular M&K 422.

91 Heather Streets, 'Military Influences in Late Victorian and Edwardian Popular Media: The Case of Frederick Roberts', *Journal of Victorian Culture*, Vol. 8 No. 2 (August 2003), pp. 231–56.

92 Ibid., p. 245.

93 *Liverpool Daily Post*, 9 October 1901, p. 7.

94 Ibid., 13 October 1902.

95 M&K 416–17: *Visit of Earl Roberts and Viscount Kitchener to Receive the Freedom of the City, Liverpool*.

96 See Nick Hiley, '"Kitchener Wants You" and "Daddy, What Did YOU Do in the Great War?": The Myth of British Recruiting Posters', *Imperial War Museum Rev.*, Vol. 11 (1997), p. 49.

97 Keith Surridge, 'More than a Great Poster: Lord Kitchener and the Image of the Military Hero', *Historical Research*, Vol. 74 No. 185 (August 2001), pp. 298–313 (307).

98 M&K 416–17: *Visit of Earl Roberts and Viscount Kitchener to Receive the Freedom of the City, Liverpool*.

99 See *London's Reception of Lord Kitchener* (1902) filmed by R. W. Paul, cited in Dennis Gifford, *The British Film Catalogue Volume 2: Non Fiction Films (1888–1994)* (London: Fitzroy Dearborn, 2000), p. 84.

100 Although this film is often cited in the local reports as *Lord Kitchener's Return*, the title is taken from the negative inscription made by Mitchell & Kenyon: 418–19: *Return of Kitchener*.

101 For circumstances of Buller's position as Commander-in-Chief see Ian F. W. Beckett, 'Buller and the Politics of Command', in Gooch (ed.), *The Boer War*, pp. 41–56.

102 Russell, 'We Carved Our Way to Glory', p. 74.

103 *Liverpool Daily Post*, 26 November 1901, p. 5.

104 *The Liverpool Mercury*, 26 November 1901, p. 5.

105 *The Wigan Examiner*, 11 December 1901.

106 *Manchester Evening News*, 22 May 1901, pp. 2–3.

107 M&K 466–9, 779: *General Buller's Visit to Manchester*, and see *Manchester Evening News*, 23 May 1901, p. 1.

108 Pakenham, *The Boer War*, p. 572.

109 Searle, *A New England*, p. 302.

110 Morgan, 'The Boer War and the Media (1899–1902)', p. 1.

111 Glenn R. Wilkinson, '"The Blessings of War": The Depiction of Military Force in Edwardian Newspapers', *Journal of Contemporary History*, Vol. 33 No. 1 (1998), pp. 97–115.

112 M&K 278–9: *Parade of the Blackburn Territorials* and M&K 642–4: *On the March with the Bradford Artillery at Buckshaw Brow, Settle.*

113 Wilkinson, '"The Blessings of War"', and see also Paris, *Warrior Nation*, pp. 85–6, for a discussion on eugenics, the physical inferiority of the volunteers and how this became linked to degeneracy and decadence.

114 *Daily Mail*, 1 January 1900, p. 4, and 24 January 1900, p. 4, cited in Wilkinson, '"The Blessings of War"', p. 100.

115 Wilkinson, '"The Blessings of War"', p. 98.

116 Ibid., p. 101, for the newspapers cited.

117 Ibid.

118 See J. A. Mangan, *Athleticism in the Victorian and Edwardian Public School: The Emergence and Consolidation of an Education Ideology*, new revised edn (London: Frank Cass, 2000 originally published: Cambridge: Syndicate of the University of Cambridge, 1981), and also J. A. Mangan, '"The Grit of Our Forefathers": Invented Traditions, Propaganda and Imperialism', in McKenzie (ed.), *Imperialism and Popular Culture*, pp. 113–40.

119 Mangan, '"The Grit of Our Forefathers"', p. 119.

120 M. D. Blanche, 'British Society and the War', in Peter Warwick (ed.), *The South African War, 1899–1902* (Harlow: Longman, 1980), and for works on the public school system in the Victorian age see Mangan, *Athleticism in the Victorian and Edwardian Public School.*

121 M&K 266: *Audley Range School, Blackburn*; M&K 480: *Procession of Children at Tyldesley Church School* (1901); M&K 382: *Parade of Widnes School Children* (1901); and M&K 583: *York Road Board School Leeds* (1901), for other examples.

122 M&K 787, 796, 800: *Military Review at Racecourse* and M&K 586–7: *The Military Tournament at Batley Football Ground.*

123 M&K 585: *Ralph Pringle Interviewing Private Ward VC Hero in Leeds.*

124 See *Yorkshire Post*, 7 February 1901.

125 Information from the King's Own Yorkshire Light Military Gallery, Doncaster Museum and Art Gallery. The star exhibit in the museum is the tunic worn by Charles Ward when presented with the VC by Queen Victoria.

126 M&K: 683, 684: *The Fleet in the Tyne*, and I am indebted to R. G. Todd, Head of Historic Photographs and Ship Plans Section, National Maritime Museum, for identifying this and other ships in the collection.

127 M&K 497–501: *Panorama of the River Avon to Portishead*, but see M&K 500 for scenes of the boys on the rigging of HMS *Formidable.*

128 *The News,* 29 August 1903, p. 4.

129 Peter Padfield, *Rule Britannia: The Victorian and Edwardian Navy* (original edn. London: Routledge and Kegan Paul, 1981; new edn. London: Pimlico, 2002).

130 M&K 423, 404: *Trafalgar Day in Liverpool.*

131 Handbill and programme for West's Our Navy, Handbill & Programme for Animated Photographs of the Cruise of HMS *Crescent*, St James's Hall, Piccadilly, and Regent Street, November 7, 9, 11, 1899, including A GRAND NAVAL ENTERTAINMENT under the patronage of the Navy League. I am indebted to Tony Fletcher for this information.

132 See Stephen Herbert and Luke McKernan, *Who's Who of Victorian Cinema* (London: BFI, 1996); for further information on A. J. West see <www.ournavy.org.uk>

133 *Brighton and Hove Guardian*, 7 February 1900; see also *The Showman*, 18 January 1901, p. 41.

134 In particular, M&K 461, which shows the torpedo boats passing through the Manchester Ship Canal.

135 M&K 459–65: *Torpedo Flotilla Visit to Manchester* (1901).

136 M&K 310–11, 317–18: *Inspection of the Ambulance Drill Hall in Accrington by Inspector-General Baden Powell.*

137 Springhall, *Youth, Empire and Society*, pp. 26–7.

138 M&K 512, 514: *Church Parade of the Boys' Brigade in Birmingham.*

139 *Birmingham Daily Mail*, 15 July 1902.

140 M&K 787, 796, 800: *Boys' Brigade Review at Racecourse.*

141 Springhall, *Youth, Empire and Society*, p. 24.

142 M&K 248–9: *Morecambe Church Lads' Brigade at Drill.*

143 For information on the Church Lads and other religious brigades such as the Jewish Lads and Catholic Lads, for example, see Springhall, *Youth, Empire and Society*, pp. 37–52.

144 For more information on the Scout movement during this time see John Springhall, 'Baden-Powell and the Scout Movement before 1920: Citizen Training or Soldiers of the Future', *The English Historical Review*, Vol. 102 No. 405 (October 1987), pp. 934–42.

145 *The Thames Valley Times*, 10 April 1889, cited in Springhall, *Youth, Empire and Society*, p. 17.

146 See John Springhall, *Youth, Popular Culture and Moral Panics* (Basingstoke: Macmillan, 1998), p. 99.

147 Paris, *Warrior Nation*, p. 109.

Afterword

The Edwardian era that is reflected and revealed in the films of Mitchell & Kenyon is not the world of political turmoil, dominated by issues of Home Rule for Ireland and the rise of German power. Nor does the collection depict the growth of the trade unions, the rise of the Labour Party, the Liberal government of 1906 or the start of the Women's Social and Political Union or Suffragette movement. The later Edwardian era saw the introduction of the Pension Act of 1909, the People's Budget in 1911 and the transition from the Victorian model of self-help to one of social welfare, pioneered and sponsored by the state. In addition, the two politicians perhaps most associated with the Edwardian era, Winston Churchill and David Lloyd George, do not appear to have been filmed by the company. Events south of Birmingham hardly figure at all, with the excep-

The showmen and spectators waving to the camera in *Rotherham Town v Thornhill* (1902) – the Mitchell & Kenyon Collection offers an unparalleled filmic history tour of everyday life and everyday people

tion of the Boer War, which is played out purely in the local context. Rather, the world that is captured in the collection is based on ephemeral documents of filmic impressions that have survived by chance and have been lovingly restored by the staff at the NFTVA in Berkhamstead.

The films reveal to us the tremendous technological and social changes that occurred during the time that the company were filming. The end of the nineteenth century brought the dawning of a new age and a new attitude towards life. It was an era when social differences dissipated and the mores, customs and expectations of the citizenry came together. The wonders of the modern world, which had sprung into life in the 1880s and 1890s, brought the first rewards of modern industrialisation and mass-produced abundance. From factory gates to football matches, the leaving of Liverpool to the leaving of work, the workers on holiday and at play, the material provides an unparalleled opportunity to see the world through the eyes of the working communities of the time – a filmic history tour of everyday life and everyday people.

Although Mitchell & Kenyon filmed both royalty and the celebrities of their day, the real stars of the films are the people: the men, women and children of the working class (who were filmed for economic reasons for the sake of cinematograph showmen revealing a new novelty – moving pictures). They gaze out to us a century later, revealing the secrets of Edwardian Britain, captured in a celluloid tapestry of smiles, gestures, motion and poetic grace, as they walk across the screen beckoning us into the new world of modernity, the dawn of the twentieth century.

Filmography – Subject

The locations used in the Mitchell Kenyon Collection are based on the historical county boundaries that existed in the years covering the firm's output and refer to the original county palatines of Yorkshire, Lancashire for example. * refers to films that are unprintable with no viewing copies available.

Boer War – See also Military

Military Personalities – See also VIP Events

466–9, 779: General Buller's Visit to Manchester (1901)
420–2, 430, 777: Lord Roberts's Visit to Manchester (1901)
774, 775, 811: Lord Roberts Presenting Medals to Boer War Volunteers in Liverpool (1901)
585: Ralph Pringle Interviewing Private Ward VC Hero in Leeds (1901)
663–6: Lieutenant Clive Wilson and Tranby Croft Party (1902)
418–19: Return of Kitchener (1902)
416–17: Visit of Earl Roberts and Viscount Kitchener to Receive the Freedom of the City, Liverpool (1902)
502–3: Visit of Lord Methuen to Bristol (1902)
310–11: Inspection of the Ambulance Drill Hall in Accrington by Inspector-General Baden-Powell (1904)

Regiments

277: 1st Volunteer Battalion, East Lancashire Regiment – Blackburn Rifle Volunteers (1900)
792, 798: Royal Scots Regiment at Edinburgh Castle (1901)
481: Parade of the Bolton Artillery Volunteers (1901)
738–9: Scenes in a Manchester Park (c. 1901)
434, 743: Manchester's Welcome to the Imperial Yeomanry (1901)
431–3: Return of the Brave Manchester Volunteers (1901)
281–2, 329: Return of the East Lancashire Regiment at Preston (1902)
642–4: On the March with the Bradford Artillery at Buckshaw Brow, Settle (1902)
713: Regiments Returned from Boer War to Victoria Barracks, Cork (1902)
520–2, 814–15, 819: The Return of the Warwickshire Volunteers (1902)
671: The Return of the Lancaster Volunteers (1902)
507: All Saints Church with Parade of the Northamptonshire Regiment (1902)

Boys' Brigade

317–18: Opening of the New Drill Hall in Accrington (1901)
248–9: Morecambe Church Lads' Brigade at Drill (1901)
512, 514: Church Parade of the Boys' Brigade in Birmingham (1902)
787, 796, 800: Boys' Brigade Review at Racecourse (c. 1902)
695–8: Boys' Brigade Inspection at Yorkhill, Glasgow (1906)

Church Exits – See also Processions and Parades – Religious

539: Congregation at Hanley Old Church (c. 1901)
740–1: Scenes Outside a Church in Warley (c. 1901)
287: Congregation at Preston Parish Church (c. 1901)
446: Congregation Leaving Manchester Cathedral (c. 1901)
688: Congregation Leaving St Mary's Church, Dumfries (c. 1901)
538: Congregation Leaving Wesleyan Chapel in Mansfield (c. 1901)
252: Old Poulton Parish Church, Morecambe (1901–2)
657: Congregation Leaving St James's Church, Hessle Road, Hull (1902)
722: Congregation Leaving St Mary's Dominican Church in Cork (1902)
721: Congregation Leaving St Patrick's Church in Cork (1902)
374: Congregation Leaving Warrington Parish Church at 12.00 Noon (1902)

509: Portraits of Well-Known Residents Leaving All Saints Church, Northampton (1902)
604: Congregation Leaving Parish Church, Sheffield (1902)
300: Congregation Leaving New Jerusalem Church in Accrington (1902)
307: Crowds Leaving Park Congregational Church in Accrington (1902)
729: Congregation Leaving St Mary's Pro-Cathedral, Dublin (1902)
730: Congregation Leaving Jesuit Church of St Francis Xavier, Dublin (1902)
735: Congregations Leaving St Hilda's Church, Middlesbrough (1902)
736: Congregations Leaving the Centenary Chapel, Middlesbrough (1902)
273: Congregation Leaving All Saints Church, Blackburn (c. 1903)
272: Congregation Leaving St Mary's Catholic Church, Blackburn (1903)
274: Congregation Leaving St Jospeh's Catholic Church, Blackburn (1911)

Civic Events – See also Processions and Parades – Civic

263: Royal Proclamation of Death of Queen Victoria, Blackburn (1901)
523–6: Birmingham University Procession on Degree Day (1901)
437–40: The Police Annual Inspection at Birchfields Park (1901)
670: His Worship the Mayor Leaving Lancaster Town Hall (1902)
668: Opening of the Blea Tarn Reservoir (1902)
599–600: The Funeral of the Late Captain of the Mexborough Fire Brigade (1902)
325–6: Funeral of Canon Morrissey in Burnley (1903)

Factory Demolitions – See also Factory Gate

570: Razing of a Mill Chimney in Leeds (1901)
328: Felling of Hibson Road Brick Works Chimney in Nelson (1906)

Factory Gate – See also Factory Demolitions

Breweries

264: Workers Leaving Nuttall's Brewery in Blackburn (1900)

Coal mining

13: Creswell and Langwith Miners, Mansfield (1900)
57: Workers at St George's Colliery, Tyldesley (1901)
58: Miners Leaving Pendlebury Colliery (1901)

Engineering

38: Employees at Robey's Works, Lincoln (1900)
47: Workers at Yates's Foundry, Blackburn (1900)
14: Workmen Leaving Peacock's Works at Meal Time, Gorton, Manchester (1900)
17: Workers at Brooks and Doxey, West Gorton Works, Manchester (1900)
43: Workmen Leaving Brooks and Doxey, West Gorton Works, Manchester (1900)
18: Employees of Galloways Ltd, Boiler Works, Hyde Road, Manchester (1900)
60: Employees Leaving Crossley's Works, Openshaw (1900)
83: Workforce at Hornsby and Sons of Grantham (1900)
33: Workforce at Steel & Garland Priory Foundry, Worksop (1900)
30: Employees at Walker Engineering Works, Wigan (1900)
34: Employees at White Cross & Co. Ltd Wire Works, Warrington (1900)
12: Workmen Leaving Platt's Works, Oldham (1900)
27: Amos & Smith Boiler Works, Hull (1900)
29: Workers at Jesse Crossley & Sons Ironworks, Ripley (1900)
546: Workers Leaving Butterley Ironworks, Ripley (1900)
36: Workforce of Brush Electric Co., Falcon Works, Loughborough (1900)
475: Robinson's Iron Foundry Workpeople Leaving for Dinner, Rochdale (1901)
42: Employees Leaving Fowler's Ironworks, Leeds (1901)
55: Workers at Berry's Blacking Works, Manchester (1901)
85: Workforce Leaving Smith & Coventry Works, Ordsall Lane, Salford (c. 1901)
762: Workers Leaving Craven Ironworks, Ordsall Lane, Salford (1901)
84: Employees Leaving Vickers, Sons and Maxim Works, Sheffield (1901)
77: Employees Leaving Brown's Atlas Works, Sheffield (1901)
518: Employees Leaving Tangyes Engineering Works, Smethwick (1901)
763, 78: Workers at Messrs Kynock's Ltd Works, Birmingham (1901)
69: The Workforce Leaving Bradwell & Wild, Forge Mills in Congleton (1901)
603: Employees of Yates Haywood & Co. Foundry, Rotherham (1901)
602: Workforce of Parkgate Iron and Steelworks Co., Rotherham (1901)
601: Workers Leaving Guest and Chrimes Brassworks, Rotherham (1901)
44: Employees of Rylands Bros. Ltd Wire Works, Warrington (1902)
74–5: Workers at Barlow and Tweedale Ironworks, Castleton nr Rochdale (1905)
45–6: Employees of Marshall's Engineering Works, Gainsborough (1908)

Railway Works

72: Employees Leaving the Midland Railway Loco Works, Derby (1900)*
41: Employees Leaving North Eastern Engine Works, Gateshead (1901)
593: Great Northern Railway Works at Doncaster (1901)
81: Employees Leaving Furness Railway Works, Barrow (1901)
67: Workforce of Crewe Engineering Works (c. 1901)
71: Exit of Workers at Kerr Locomotive Works, Stoke (c. 1902)*

Shipbuilding – See also Naval

37: Workers Leaving Ropener & Co., Shipbuilders, Stockton-on-Tees (1900)
35: 20,000 Employees Entering Lord Armstrong's Elswick Works (1900)
80: Employees Leaving Messrs Vickers and Maxim's in Barrow (1901)
409: Employees Leaving Alexandra Docks, Liverpool (1901)
90: Workforce of Scott & Co., Shipyard, Greenock (1901)

Textiles

Cotton

54: Workers at Spring Bank Mill, Nelson (1900)
49: Workpeople Leaving Fish's Waterfall Mill, Blackburn (1900)
50: Workpeople Leaving Ordnance Mill, Blackburn (1900)
51: Workpeople Leaving Dugdale's Paradise Mill, Blackburn (1900)
52: Employees Leaving Olive Mill, Darwen (1900)
48: Workpeople Leaving Hornby's Brookhouse Mill, Blackburn (1900)
473: Workpeople from Messrs Mayall's Mills Emerging on Queen Street, Mossley (1900)
8: The Millhands of Cheetham's Bankwood Mills, Stalybridge (1900)
16: Workpeople Leaving Ryland's Mill, Gorton, Manchester (1900)
10: Operatives Leaving Jubilee Mill, Padiham (1900)
11: Workers at Dickens & Heywood, Middleton (1900)
9: Workforce Leaving Salt's Works in Saltaire (1900)
782: Co-operative Wholesale Society Clothing Factory in Manchester (c. 1900)
19: Workers at India Mills, Stockport (1900)
20: Howarth's Egerton Mill, Ordsall Lane, Salford (1900)
21: Workforce of Howarth's Ordsall Mill, Salford (1900)
6: Workers Leaving Haslam's Ltd, Colne (1900)
760–1: Workforce of Haslam's Ltd, Colne (1900)
23: Employees of J. & E. Waters, Talbot Mills, Ellesmere St, Manchester (1900)
15: The 'Hands' Leaving Work at North-Street Mills, Chorley (1900)
53: Workers at Bradley Shed, Nelson, Lancashire (1900)
76: Employees Leaving Thackeray's Cotton Mill, Nottingham (1900)*
39: Workforce of Ormerod's Mill, Great Moor Street, Bolton (1900)
59: Workforce Leaving Alfred Butterworth and Sons, Glebe Mills, Hollinwood (1901)
63: Employees Leaving Williamson's Factory, Lancaster (1901)
336–7: Factory Workers in Clitheroe (1901)
61: Operatives of Acme Spinning Company, Pendlebury (1901)
283: Workforce at Horrocks Miller & Co., Preston (1901)
471: Workers Leaving Textile Factory in Patricroft (1901)
62: Workforce of Storey's White Cross Mills, Lancaster (1902)
64: Employees Leaving Storey's Moor Lane Mill, Lancaster (1902)

Jute

87: Employees Leaving Baxter's Jute Works, Dundee (1901)
88: Employees Leaving Gilroy's Jute Works, Dundee (1901)
673: Workers Leaving the Jute Works, Barrow (1902)

Silk or Lace

31: Workpeople and Girls Leaving Thos. Adams Factory, Nottingham (1900)
70: The Employees Leaving Wardle & Davenport Silk Works, Leek (1901)*
68: Living Pictures of Leek Brough Nicholson & Hall, Silk Works (1901)*

Wool

28: Employees of Messrs Lumb and Co. Leaving the Works, Huddersfield (1900)
7: Mill Workers Leaving Oldroyd & Sons Mill, Dewsbury (1900)

Various Industries

22: Workers Leaving Bamford's Works, Moseley (1900)
32: Workforce Leaving Cartwright & Warner Hosiery Works, Loughborough (1900)
24: Workers at Pilkington Glass Works, St Helens (1900)
25–6: Operatives Leaving Messrs Pilkington Bros. Works, St Helens (1901)
56: Employees of Co-operative Wholesale Society Printing Works, Longsight, Manchester (1901)
86: Workers at Carr's Biscuit Works, Carlisle (1901)
89: Workforce of Pollock's Caledonian Cabinet Works, Beith (1901)
79: Workers Leaving Gossage's Soap Works, Widnes (1901)
91: Workers Leaving T. & W. Lees of Stockport (1901)
40: Workers at Ross & Hardy Paper Works (1901)
82: Employees of Blundell's Paint Works, Hull (1901)
55: Workers Leaving Steiner's Factory in Church, near Accrington (c. 1901)
66: Workforce of Johnston's Pottery in Hanley (c. 1901)*
711: Workers Leaving Lee Boot Factory – Dwyer & Co. Ltd, Cork (1902)
672: Workers Leaving Factory in Barrow (1902)

Unidentified Factories

504: Factory Exit in Lincoln (1900)
294: [Workers Leaving a Factory in Leyland] (c. 1900)
372: Factory Exit in Wigan (1901)
472: Workers Leaving a Factory in Droylesden (1901)
337: Factory Workers in Clitheroe (1901)
360: Workers Leaving a Factory in Wigan (1902)
73: Workers Leaving a Factory in Chesterfield (1902)

Unidentified

238: [Factory Gate Exit in Lancashire] (c. 1900)
791: [Workers Leaving a Factory] (c. 1900)
767: [Unknown Factory Gate Exit] (c. 1900)
766: [Workforce Leaving a Factory in the North of England] (c. 1900)
773: [Workforce Leaving a Factory] (c. 1900)
93: [Factory Gate Exit] (c. 1901)
94: [Workforce Leaving a Factory at Lunchtime] (c. 1901)

759: [Employees Leaving a Factory] (c. 1901)
764: [Textile Workers Leaving a Factory] (c. 1901)
768: [Lancashire Factory Gate Exit] (c. 1901)
804: [Exit of White Collar Workers] (c. 1901)

Fiction

4: Kidnapping by Indians (1899)
700: The Snowman (1901)
802: The Sporting Colliers and the Bobby (c. 1901)
780: Mr Moon (1901)
757–8: Arrest of Goudie (1901)
825: [Lovers in Country Lane] (c. 1901)
783: [Washing up and Blacking up] (c. 1901)
92, 765: Black Diamonds – The Collier's Daily Life (1904)
692: Lizars Edinburgh (1904)

Fire Brigades

584: Turn Out of the Leeds Fire Brigade (1901)
678: Turn Out of the Newcastle Fire Brigade (1901)
691: Turn Out of the Dundee Fire Brigade (1901)
483: Turn Out of the Winsford Fire Brigade (1901)
476–8: Turn Out of the Rochdale Fire Brigade (1901)
289: Turn Out of the Preston Fire Brigade (c. 1901)
595–6: Turn Out of the Keighley Fire Brigade (1902)
648–9, 667: Turn Out of the Hull Fire Brigade (1902)
718–20: Cork Fire Brigade Turning Out (1902)
363: Turn Out of the Wigan Fire Brigade (1902)

Military – See also Boer War

787, 796, 800: Military Review at Racecourse (c. 1901)
586–7: The Military Tournament at Batley Football Ground (1902)
278–9: Parade of the Blackburn Territorials (1909)

Naval – See also Factory Gate – Shipbuilding

459–65: Torpedo Flotilla Visit to Manchester (1901)
0, 683, 684: The Fleet in the Tyne (1901)
423, 404: Trafalgar Day in Liverpool (1901)
225–7: Royal Visit to Barrow and Launch of HMS Dominion (1903)

Offcuts

816, 821, 824: [Miscellaneous Offcuts] (c. 1902)
823: [Fiction Offcut] (c. 1902)

Phantom Rides

Railways – See also Transport – Railways

239, 245: A Beautiful Panorama of Railway Ride from St German to Milray (1901)
241: Ride over the Tay Bridge (1901)
243, 723: Ride from Blarney to Cork on Cork and Muskerry Light Railway (1902)
242: [Unidentified Railway Journey] (c. 1902)

Ships – See also Transport – Ships

210–12: Snowdrop Ferry at Seacombe (1901) *211
236, 820: Panorama of Queenstown Harbour (1902)
496: North Wales Officers and Crew (c. 1902)*
214–22: A Trip to North Wales on the St Elvies (1902)
497–501: Panorama of the River Avon to Portishead (1902) 497*

Tramway – See also Transport – Tramways

724, 183: Ride on a Tramcar through Belfast (1901)
403: Liverpool as Seen from the Front of an Electric Car from the Pierhead to the Circus (1901)
246, 254, 251: Panoramic View of the Morecambe Seafront (1901)
751: Phantom Ride through Southport (1902)
184, 614: Tram Ride into Halifax (1902)
166–9: Electric Tram Rides from Forster Square, Bradford (1902)
710: Tram Ride from King Street to Patrick's Bridge, Cork (1902)
194: Tram Ride from Port Soderic to Douglas Head (1902)
163–5: Tram Rides through Nottingham (1902)
176–7: Tram Ride through the City of Sheffield (1902)
189, 195–9: Lytham Trams and Views along the Route (1903)
170–1: A Tram Ride through Sunderland (1904)

Processions and Parades – See also Recreation – Public Events

Civic

693–4: Procession in Edinburgh (1901)
381: Oddfellows Procession in St Helens (c. 1901)
412, 812, 813: St George's Day Procession in Liverpool (1901)
702: Arrival of VIPs for Official Opening of Cork Exhibition (1902)
717: Lord Mayor of Cork Arriving for Official Opening of Cork Exhibition (1902)
704–5, 712: Trade Procession at Opening of Cork Exhibition (1902)
810: Procession of Firemen (c. 1902)

Coronations – See also Royal Events

621–5, 626–30, 631: Bradford Coronation Procession (1902)
301, 303, 305, 794: Coronation Festivities at Accrington (1902)
361–2: Wigan Coronation Celebrations and Street Scenes (1902)
301–5, 794: Coronation Festivities at Accrington (1902)
367–8: Wigan Mayoral Coronation Procession (1902)
679–82: Hollow Drift Children's Procession, Durham (1902)
330–5: Clitheroe Coronation Procession (1911)
295–9: Great Harwood Coronation Celebrations (1911)
292: Chorley Coronation Processions (1911)

Local Festivities

308–9: Procession in Accrington Park (1900)
424, 428, 429: Manchester and Salford Harriers' Cyclists' Procession (1901)
558–62, 564, 808: Leeds Lifeboat Procession and Sports at Roundhay Park (1901)
356–9: Lytham Club Day Carnival (1902)

383, 385, 387: Southport Carnival and Trades Procession (1902)
554–6: Leeds Lifeboat Procession (1902)
565–9: Leeds Lifeboat Demonstration (1902)
558–62, 564, 808: Leeds Lifeboat Procession and Sports at Roundhay Park (1902)
597: Skipton Hospital Procession (1902)
531–4: Lady Godiva Procession in Coventry (1902)
528–30: March Past of 20,000 Coventry Children (1902)
581–2: Hunslet Carnival and Gala (1904)
577: Armley and Wortley Carnival (1904)
484: Crewe Hospital Procession and Pageant (1907)
618–19: Royal Halifax Infirmary Annual Street Procession (1908)

Other

519: Blue Coat Children Marching to Curzon Hall in Birmingham (1901)
322–4: Treat to 5,000 Poor Burnley Children (1905)
594: Miners' Demonstration at Wakefield (1908)

Religious

407–8: Liverpool Church Parade and Inspection (1901)
441–2, 173: Manchester Band of Hope Procession (1901)
449–51: Manchester Spiritualists' Procession (1901)
448: Manchester Catholic Orphanage Boys (1901)
375: Warrington Walking Day Catholic Procession (1902)
376–80: Warrington Walking Day Procession (1902)
444: Manchester Italian Catholic Procession (1902)
452–4, 797: Manchester Catholics' Whitsuntide Procession (1904)
455–8: Manchester Sunday Schools' Whit Monday Procession (1904)
470: Oldham Catholic Schools' Procession (1904)
616–17: Halifax Catholic Procession (c. 1905)
275–6: St Joseph's Catholic Whit Procession Blackburn (1911)
313–16: Accrington Catholic Procession (1912)
347–50: Mayor's Sunday at St Mary's Church, Clitheroe (1912)
338–46: Whitsuntide Processions at Clitheroe (1913)

Recreation – See also Sport

Calendar Customs

286: Preston Egg Rolling (c. 1901)
389–96: Bootle May Day Demonstration and Crowning of the May Queen (1903)
482: Knutsford Royal May Day Carnival (1904)
540–2: Buxton Well Dressing (1904)
293: Leyland May Festival (1905)
136, 223–4: Llandudno May Day (1907)

Parks

508: Scenes in Abington Park, Northampton (1902)
509: Portraits of Well-Known Residents Leaving All Saints Church, Northampton (1902)
607: Spectators Promenading in Weston Park, Sheffield (1902)
661–2: Sunday Promenade of Spectators in West Park, Hull (1902)
655–6: Sunday Parade in East Park in Hull (1904)

Popular Entertainment

637: The Crowd Entering St George's Hall, Bradford (1901)
608: Bailey's Royal Buxton Punch and Judy Show in Halifax (1901)
772: Sedgwick's Bioscope Showfront at Pendlebury Wakes (1901)
675, 677: Algie's Circus in Carlisle (1901)
588–90: Trip to Sunny Vale Gardens at Hipperholme (1901)
651–2: Hull Fair (1902)
291: Whitsuntide Fair at Preston (1906)
771: Green's Racing Bantams at Preston Whit Fair (1906)

Public Events – see also Processions and Parades

638–41, 645–7: Magnificent Reproductions of the Great Yorkshire Show in Bradford (1901)
685: Tynemouth Swimming Gala in the Haven, North Shields (1901)
785: Preparation of the Cork Exhibition Grounds and Erection of Buildings (1902)
703: Panorama of Cork Exhibition Grounds (1902)
571–3: Great Yorkshire Show at Leeds (1902)
550–3: Leeds Athletic and Cycling Club Carnival at Headingley (1902)
574–6: Leeds Crossgates Flower Show (1904)
261–2: Blackburn Plant Growing Competition (1905)
756: Calisthenics (c. 1905)

River Scenes

285: Ribble at Preston (c. 1901)
485–8: Scenes at Chester on the River Dee (1901)
536: Scenes on the Trent, Nottingham (1902)
537: Views of the Trent Bridge Boulevard (1902)

Seaside

806, 732: Rough Sea at Roker (1901)
246, 254, 251: Panoramic View of the Morecambe Seafront (1901)
248–9: Morecambe Church Lads' Brigade at Drill (1901)
247, 253: Parade on West End Pier, Morecambe (1901)
252: Old Poulton Parish Church, Morecambe (1901)
250: Parade on Morecambe Central Pier (1902)
754: Scenes by the Stone Jetty, Morecambe (1902)
809, 386: Waves at Southport (1902)
174, 384: Panoramic View of Southport Promenade (1902)
383, 385, 387: Southport Carnival and Trades Procession (1902)
356–9: Lytham Club Day Carnival (1902)
351: Les Montagnes Russes, Blackpool's Latest Attraction (1902)
205: Blackpool North Pier (1903)
206–9: Steamboats at Blackpool North Pier (1903)
189, 195–9: Lytham Trams and Views along the Route (1903)
200–1, 203, 742: Blackpool Victoria Pier (1904)
769, 770, 776: New Brighton, Egremont and Seacombe Promenade (1904)
204: Blackpool Promenade (1904)*
202: Blackpool Promenade Extension (1905)
223–4: Llandudno May Day (1907)

Royal Events – See also Processions and Parades – Coronations

807, 817: Funeral of Queen Victoria (1901)
411: Prince of Siam Aboard the New Ferry (1901)
435–6: Royal Visit to Manchester, Owens College (1902)
494, 737: Royal Visit to Rhyl (1902)
495: Royal Visit to Bangor (1902)
826: Coronation of Edward VII (1902)
193: The King's Ride in the Isle of Man (1902)
256–60, 364: Visit of HRH Princess Louise to Blackburn (1905)
410: Princess Louise at Liverpool (1906)

Schoolchildren

479: Children Leaving Tyldesley Catholic School, Lodge Road (1901)
480: Procession of Children at Tyldesley Church School (1901)
382: Parade of Widnes Schoolchildren (1901)
583: York Road Board School, Leeds (1901)
687: Schoolchildren at Dalbeattie Public School (c. 1901)
686: Public School in Annan (c. 1901)
690: Love Burn Street School, Dumfries (c. 1901)
289: Scholars Leaving St Andrew's RC School, Dumfries (c. 1901)
598: Procession of Rotherham Schoolchildren (1902)
632–6: Day School Sports at Park Avenue, Bradford (1902)
271: Children of Preston St Stephen's Football Club and Moss Street School (1904)
290: Schoolchildren at St Ignatius School, (1904)
266: Audley Range School, Blackburn (1905)
269: Special Parade of St Matthew's Pupils and Special March Past of St Joseph's Scholars (1905)
267: Children at St Barnabas School, Blackburn (1905)
803: Parade of Schoolchildren (n.d.)

Sport – See also Recreation

Athletics

591–2: AAA Championships at Fartown, Huddersfield (6 July 1901)
714: Sports Day at Queen's College Ground, Cork (7 June 1902)
510–11, 513, 515–16: Champion Athletes at Birmingham (12 July 1902)
505–6: Cambridge University Sports Day (14 March 1903)
388, 752: Manchester to Blackpool Road Race (1903)

Cricket

489–93: Arthur Mold Bowling to A. N. Hornby (12 July 1901)
319–21: The Great Local Derby, Accrington v. Church Cricket Match (5 July 1902)

Cycling

425–7: Race for the Muratti Cup at Manchester Wheelers' Annual Race Meet (1901)
744–6, 786, 801: Manchester Wheelers' Annual Race Meet (1901)

Exercise

756: Calisthenics (c. 1905)

Football

112: Liverpool v. Small Heath (28 September 1901)
109, 110, 111, 121: Newcastle United v. Liverpool (23 November 1901)
139, 755: Rotherham Town v. Thornhill (11 February 1902)
134: Stoke v. Grimsby Town (14 April 1902)*
606: Sheffield United v. Bury (6 September 1902)
101–3: Everton v. Newcastle United (13 September 1902)
120, 122–3: Notts County v. Middlesbrough (27 September 1902)
106–8: Everton v. Liverpool (27 September 1902)
327: Burnley v. Manchester United (6 December 1902)
124–8: Bradford City v. Gainsborough Trinity (5 September 1903)
104–5: Everton v. Newcastle United (19 September 1903)
117: Sunderland v. Middlesbrough (9 January 1904)
135: Blackburn Rovers v. … (April 1904)
265: Blackburn Rovers v. Aston Villa (2 April 1904)
129–30: Nottingham Forest v. Stoke (1 October 1904)*
99: Preston North End v. Notts County (17 October 1904)
96–8: Preston North End v. Wolverhampton Wanderers (19 November 1904)
137–8: England v. Ireland at Manchester (14 October 1905)
100: Preston North End v. Aston Villa (11 November 1905)
113, 115: Hull City Football (1905–6)
153–4: Wales v. Ireland at Wrexham (2 April 1906)
118–19, 142, 147: Sunderland v. Leicester Fosse (12 January 1907)
95: Blackburn Rovers v. Sheffield United (29 March 1907)
268: Moss Street v. St Philips Football (30 March 1907)

Undated Football

133: Bolton Football
144: Bolton Football
145: Aston Villa
143, 146: Burnley Football
132: Stoke v. Bury*
140: Bolton v. Burton United (1904–5)

General

790: [Crowds Leaving Sporting Event] (c. 1902)

Horse Racing/Trotting

5, 795: Ambush II at Eyrefield Lodge, Curragh (15 January 1902)
352–5: Haworth's Stud Farm, Blackpool (c. 1903)
369–71: Trotting Match at Springfield Park, Wigan (1904)

Rowing

658–9: Kingston Rowing Club at Practice (3 May 1902)
707: Crews Practising on River Lee at Cork Regatta (20 July 1902)
701: Final of International Cup at Cork Regatta (23 July 1902)

Rugby
116: Oldham v. Swinton (12 January 1901)
161: St Helens v. Swinton (19 January 1901)
160: Runcorn v. St Helens (16 February 1901)
151: Hunslet v. Leeds (16 February 1901)
114: Halifax v. Salford (23 March 1901)
157, 156, 155: Dewsbury v. Manningham (19 October 1901)
159, 158 141, 162: Salford v. Batley (2 November 1901)
373: Warrington v. St Helens (30 November 1901)
150, 131, 660: Hull FC v. Hull Kingston Rovers (26 April 1902)
149: Hull FC v. Wigan (4 October 1902)
148, 653: Hull Kingston Rovers v. Wigan (25 October 1902)
152: Northern Union Challenge Cup Final – Halifax v. Salford (25 April 1903)

Water Polo
748: Water Polo Match (c. 1901)

Street Scenes
535: Workpeople and Girls on Stoney Street, Nottingham (1900)
650: Scenes at Monument Bridge in Hull (1900)
547: Buxton Skyline (1901)
270: King Williams Street and Market Hall, Blackburn (c. 1901)*
312: Proclamation of King Edward VII, Market Place, Accrington (1901)
186: Jamaica Street, Glasgow (1901)
405–6: Liverpool Street Scenes (1901)
674: Scenes of Carlisle (1901)
172, 443: Manchester Street Scenes (1901)
180, 280: Darwen Street Scenes (1901)
654: Scenes in Hull (1901)
474: Scenes of Ashton-under-Lyne (1901)
784: [Street Scenes in North of England] (c. 1902)
781, 753: [Views of Unidentified Town Centre] (c. 1902)
793: [Crowds in Town Centre] (c. 1902)
185: [Unidentified Street Scenes] (c. 1902)
611: Mayor Entering His Carriage Near the Town Hall, Halifax (1902)
728: Panorama of College Green, Dublin (1902)
725: Wexford Railway Station (1902)
726–7: Life in Wexford (1902)
188: Cattle Market in Derry (1902)
609–10, 612–13: Street Scenes in Halifax (1902)
527: Comic Pictures in High Street, West Bromwich (1902)
708: Albert Quay in Cork (1902)
709: Views of the Grand Parade, Cork (1902)
557: Leeds Street Scene (1902)
175: Living Wigan (1902)
605: Sheffield Street Accident (1902)
288: Preston Street Scenes (1904)
615: Views of Halifax (c. 1905)
284: Preston Monday Market (1906)

Transport

Railways – See also Phantom Rides – Railways
244: Train Arriving at Ilkeston Station (1900)*

Ships – See also Phantom Rides – Ships
229, 231–2, 234, 237, 240: Cunard Mail Steamer Lucania Leaving for America (1901)
233: SS Saxonia in Liverpool (1901)
235, 788: SS Skirmisher at Liverpool (1901)
731: North Sea Fisheries, North Shields (1901)
213: Scenes at Egremont Ferry (1901)
818: Ship Departing from Port (c. 1901)
228, 750: Lady Mostyn Discharging Drain at Irvine (c. 1901–2)
206–9: Steamboats at Blackpool North Pier (1903)
230, 699: SS Mongolian Leaving the Clyde (1906)

Tramways – See also Phantom Rides – Tramways
187: Manchester Horse Trams (c. 1901)*
190: Horse Trams in Birmingham (1901)
191: [Tram Terminal]* (c. 1901)
181–2, 543–5: Opening of Accrington Electric Tramways (1907) 543 and 545*

VIP Events – See also Boer War – Military Personalities
676: Lord Roseberry in Carlisle (c. 1901)
733–4: Lord Durham at Sunderland (1901)
715–16: The Visit of the Duke of Connaught C-I-C Forces in Ireland and Prince Henry of Prussia to Cork Exhibition (1902)
517: Joseph Chamberlain at Home (1902)
306: Visit of Sir George Cotton at Accrington (1902)
789: [VIP on Balcony] (c. 1902)

Filmography – Location

ENGLAND

BRISTOL

497–501: Panorama of the River Avon to Portishead (1902) 497*
502–3: Visit of Lord Methuen to Bristol (1902)

CAMBRIDGESHIRE

Cambridge
505–6: Cambridge University Sports Day (1903)

CHESHIRE

Birkenhead
397–402: Carnival Processions in Birkenhead (1902)

Chester
485–8: Scenes at Chester on the River Dee (1901)

Congleton
69: The Workforce Leaving Bradwell & Wild, Forge Mills in Congleton (1901)

Crewe
67: Workforce of Crewe Engineering Works (c. 1907)
484: Crewe Hospital Procession and Pageant (1907)

Egremont
213: Scenes at Egremont Ferry (1901)

Knutsford
482: Knutsford Royal May Day Carnival (1904)

New Brighton
769, 770, 776: New Brighton, Egremont and Seacombe Promenade (1904)

Runcorn
160: Runcorn v. St Helens (1901)

Seacombe
210–12: Snowdrop Ferry at Seacombe (1901) 211*

Stalybridge
8: The Millhands of Cheetham's Bankwood Mills, Stalybridge (1900)

Stockport
19: Workers at India Mills, Stockport (1900)
91: Workers Leaving T. & W. Lees of Stockport (1901)

Winsford
483: Turn Out of the Winsford Fire Brigade (1901)

CUMBERLAND

Carlisle
86: Workers at Carr's Biscuit Works, Carlisle (1901)
674: Scenes of Carlisle (1901)
675, 677: Algie's Circus in Carlisle (1901)
676: Lord Roseberry in Carlisle (c. 1901)

DERBYSHIRE

Buxton
547: Buxton Skyline (1901)
540–2: Buxton Well Dressing (1904)

Chesterfield
73: Workers Leaving a Factory in Chesterfield (1900)

Derby
72: Employees Leaving the Midland Loco Works, Derby (1900)*

Ilkeston
244: Train Arriving at Ilkeston Station (1900)*

Ripley
29: Workers at Jesse Crossley & Sons Ironworks, Ripley (1900)
546: Workers Leaving Butterley Ironworks, Ripley (1900)

DEVON

Plymouth
239: Cinematographic View of the Royal Albert Bridge (1901)
245: A Beautiful Panorama of Railway Ride from St German to Milray (1901)

COUNTY DURHAM

Durham
679–82: Hollow Drift Children's Procession, Durham (1902)

Gateshead
41: Employees Leaving North Eastern Engine Works, Gateshead (1901)

Stockton-on-Tees
37: Workers Leaving Ropener & Co., Shipbuilders, Stockton-on-Tees (1900)

Sunderland
806, 732: Rough Sea at Roker (1901)
733–4: Lord Durham at Sunderland (1901)
170-1: A Tram Ride through Sunderland (1904)
117: Sunderland v. Middlesbrough (1904)
118–19, 142, 147: Sunderland v. Leicester Fosse (1907)

ISLE OF MAN

192: Douglas Harbour Paddle Steamer (1902)
194: Tram Ride from Port Soderic to Douglas Head (1902)
193: The King's Ride in the Isle of Man (1902)

LANCASHIRE

Accrington
308–9: Procession in Accrington Park (1900)
317–18: Opening of the New Drill Hall in Accrington (1901)
312: Proclamation of King Edward VII, Market Place, Accrington (1901)
319–21: The Great Local Derby, Accrington v. Church Cricket Match (1902)
301–5, 794: Coronation Festivities at Accrington (1902)
306: Visit of Sir George Cotton at Accrington (1902)
300: Congregation Leaving New Jerusalem Church in Accrington (1902)
307: Crowds Leaving Park Congregational Church in Accrington (1902)
310–11: Inspection of the Ambulance Drill Hall in Accrington by Inspector-General Baden-Powell (1904)
181–2, 543–5: Opening of Accrington Electric Tramways (1907) 543 and 545*
313–16: Accrington Catholic Procession (1912)

Ashton-under-Lyne
474: Scenes of Ashton-under-Lyne (1901)

Barrow-in-Furness
81: Employees Leaving Furness Railway Works, Barrow (1901)
672: Workers Leaving Factory in Barrow (1901)
80: Employees Leaving Messrs Vickers and Maxim's in Barrow (1901)
673: Workers Leaving the Jute Works, Barrow (1902)
225–7: Royal Visit to Barrow and Launch of HMS Dominion (1903)

Blackburn
277: 1st Volunteer Battalion, East Lancashire Regiment – Blackburn Rifle Volunteers (1900)
264: Workers Leaving Nuttall's Brewery, Blackburn (1900)
47: Workers at Yates's Foundry, Blackburn (1900)
48: Workpeople Leaving Hornby's Brookhouse Mill, Blackburn (1900)
49: Workpeople Leaving Fish's Waterfall Mill, Blackburn (1900)
50: Workpeople Leaving Ordnance Mill, Blackburn (1900)
51: Workpeople Leaving Dugdale's Paradise Mill, Blackburn (1900)
263: Royal Proclamation of Death of Queen Victoria, Blackburn (1901)
272: Congregation Leaving St Mary's Catholic Church, Blackburn (1903)
273: Congregation Leaving All Saints Church, Blackburn (c. 1903)
135: Blackburn Rovers v. … (April 1904)
265: Blackburn Rovers v. Aston Villa (2 April 1904)
271: Children of St Stephen's Football Club and Moss Street School (1904)
266: Audley Range School, Blackburn (c. 1905)
269: Special Parade of St Matthew's Pupils and Special March Past of St Joseph's
Scholars (1905)
261–2: Blackburn Plant Growing Competition (1905)
256–60, 364: Visit of HRH Princess Louise to Blackburn (1905)
267: Children at St Barnabas School, Blackburn (1905)
95: Blackburn Rovers v. Sheffield United (29 March 1907)
268: Moss Street v. St Philips Football (30 March 1907)
278–9: Parade of the Blackburn Territorials (1909)
274: Congregation Leaving St Joseph's Catholic Church, Blackburn (1911)
275–6: St Joseph's Catholic Whit Procession, Blackburn (1911)

Fiction Filmed in Blackburn

4: Kidnapping by Indians (1899)
3: [The Unfaithful Wife] (c. 1900)
802: The Sporting Colliers and the Bobby (c. 1901)
825: [Lovers in Country Lane]
783: [Washing up and Blacking up] (c. 1901)

Blackpool

351: Les Montagnes Russes, Blackpool's Latest Attraction (1902)
352–5: Haworth's Stud Farm, Blackpool (c. 1903)
205: Blackpool North Pier (1903)
206–9: Steamboats at Blackpool North Pier (1903)
189, 195–9: Lytham Trams and Views along the Route (1903)
388, 752: Manchester to Blackpool Road Race (1903)
200–1, 203, 742: Blackpool Victoria Pier (1904)
204: Blackpool Promenade (1904)★
202: Blackpool Promenade Extension (1905)

Bolton

39: Workforce of Ormerod's Mill, Great Moor Street, Bolton (1900)
481: Parade of the Bolton Artillery Volunteers (1901)
144: Bolton Football (c. 1901–2)
140: Bolton v. Burton United (c. 1904–5)

Bootle

389–96: Bootle May Day Demonstration and Crowning of the May Queen (1903)

Burnley

327: Burnley v. Manchester United (1902)
143, 146: Burnley Football (c. 1903)
325–6: Funeral of Canon Morrissey in Burnley (1903)
322–4: Treat to 5,000 Poor Burnley Children (1905)

Bury

606: Sheffield United v. Bury (1902)
132: Stoke v. Bury (n.d.)★

Chorley

15: The 'Hands' Leaving Work at North-Street Mills, Chorley (1900)
292: Chorley Coronation Processions (1911)

Clitheroe

336–7: Factory Workers in Clitheroe (1901)
330–5: Clitheroe Coronation Procession (1911)
347–50: Mayor's Sunday at St Mary's Church, Clitheroe (1912)
338–46: Whitsuntide Processions at Clitheroe (1913)

Colne

6: Workers Leaving Haslam's Ltd, Colne (1900)
760–1: Workforce of Haslam's Ltd, Colne (1900)

Darwen

52: Employees Leaving Olive Mill, Darwen (1900)
180, 280: Darwen Street Scenes (1901)

Droylsden

472: Workers Leaving a Factory in Droylsden (1901)

Great Harwood

295–9: Great Harwood Coronation Celebrations (1911)

Hollinwood

59: Workforce Leaving Alfred Butterworth and Sons, Glebe Mills, Hollinwood (1901)

Lancaster

63: Employees Leaving Williamson's Factory, Lancaster (1901)
671: The Return of the Lancaster Volunteers (1901)
64: Employees Leaving Storey's Moor Lane Mill, Lancaster (1902)
62: Workforce of Storey's White Cross Mills, Lancaster (1902)
670: His Worship the Mayor Leaving Lancaster Town Hall (1902)
668: Opening of the Blea Tarn Reservoir (1902)

Leyland

294: Workers Leaving a Factory in Leyland (c. 1900)
293: Leyland May Festival (1905)

Liverpool

409: Employees Leaving Alexandra Docks, Liverpool (1901)
403: Liverpool as Seen from the Front of an Electric Car from the Pierhead to the Circus (1901)
412, 812, 813: St George's Day Procession in Liverpool (1901)
774, 775, 811: Lord Roberts Presenting Medals to Boer War Volunteers in Liverpool (1901)
See also 805: Visit of Lord Kitchener to Liverpool? Or Lord Roberts in Liverpool (1901)
112: Liverpool v. Small Heath (28 September 1901)
405–6: Liverpool Street Scenes (1901)
423, 404: Trafalgar Day in Liverpool (1901)
411: Prince of Siam Aboard the New Ferry (1901)
407–8: Liverpool Church Parade and Inspection (1901)
109, 110, 111, 121: Newcastle United v. Liverpool (23 November 1901)
229, 231–2, 234, 237, 240: Cunard Mail Steamer Lucania Leaving for America (1901)
233: SS Saxonia in Liverpool (1901)
235, 788: SS Skirmisher at Liverpool (1901)
757–8: Arrest of Goudie (1901)
214–22: A Trip to North Wales on the St Elvies (1902)★★ 214 filmed from the landing stage at Liverpool
416–17: Visit of Earl Roberts and Viscount Kitchener to Receive the Freedom of the City, Liverpool (1902)
101–3: Everton v. Newcastle United (1902)
106–8: Everton v. Liverpool (1902)

104–5: Everton v. Newcastle United (1903)
410: Princess Louise at Liverpool (1906)

Lytham
356–9: Lytham Club Day Carnival (1902)
189, 195–9: Lytham Trams and Views along the Route (1903)

Manchester
60: Employees Leaving Crossley's Works, Openshaw, Manchester (1900)
16: Workpeople Leaving Ryland's Mill, Gorton, Manchester (1900)
18: Employees of Galloways Ltd Boiler Works, Hyde Road, Manchester (1900)
17: Workers at Brooks and Doxey, West Gorton Works, Manchester (1900)
14: Workmen Leaving Peacock's Works at Meal Time, Gorton, Manchester (1900)
23: Employees of J. & E. Waters, Talbot Mills, Ellesmere St, Manchester (1900)
782: Co-operative Wholesale Clothing Factory in Manchester (c. 1900)
187: Manchester Horse Trams (c. 1901)*
459–65: Torpedo Flotilla Visit to Manchester (1901)
437–40: The Police Annual Inspection at Birchfields Park (1901)
434, 743: Manchester's Welcome to the Imperial Yeomanry (1901)
431–3: Return of the Brave Manchester Volunteers (1901)
466–9, 779: General Buller's Visit to Manchester (1901)
448: Manchester Catholic Orphanage Boys (1901)
441–2, 173: Manchester Band of Hope Procession (1901)
172, 443: Manchester Street Scenes (1901)
424, 428, 429: Manchester and Salford Harriers' Cyclists' Procession (1901)
427, 744–6, 786: Manchester Wheelers' Annual Race Meet (1901)
425–6, 801: Race for the Muriatti Cup at Manchester Wheelers' Annual Race Meet (1901)
738–9: Scenes in a Manchester Park (c. 1901)
489–93: Arthur Mold Bowling to A. N. Hornby (1901)
56: Employees of Co-operative Wholesale Society Printing Works, Longsight, Manchester (1901)
43: Workmen Leaving Brooks and Doxey, West Gorton Works, Manchester (1901)
55: Workers at Berry's Blacking Works, Manchester (1901)
446: Congregation Leaving Manchester Cathedral (1901)
420–2, 430, 777: Lord Roberts's Visit to Manchester (1901)
449–51: Manchester Spiritualists' Procession (1901)
445: Manchester Races (1902)
444: Manchester Italian Catholic Procession (1902)
435–6: Royal Visit to Manchester, Owens College (1902)
327: Burnley v. Manchester United (1902)
447: Funeral in Manchester (1904)
452–4, 797: Manchester Catholics' Whitsuntide Procession (1904)
455–8: Manchester Sunday Schools' Whit Monday Procession (1904)
137–8: England v. Ireland at Manchester (1905)

Middleton
11: Workers at Dickens & Heywood, Middleton (1900)

Morecambe
246, 254, 251: Panoramic View of the Morecambe Seafront (1901)
248–9: Morecambe Church Lads' Brigade at Drill (1901)
247, 253: Parade on West End Pier, Morecambe (1901)
252: Old Poulton Parish Church, Morecambe (1901–2)
250: Parade on Morecambe Central Pier (1902)
754: Scenes by the Stone Jetty, Morecambe (1902)

Mossley
473: Workpeople from Messrs Mayall's Mills Emerging on Queen Street, Mossley (1900)

Nelson
53: Workers at Bradley Shed, Nelson (1900)
54: Workers at Spring Bank Mill, Nelson (1900)
328: Felling of Hibson Road Brick Works Chimney in Nelson (1906)

Oldham
12: Workmen Leaving Platt's Works, Oldham (1900)
116: Oldham v. Swinton (1901)
470: Oldham Catholic Schools' Procession (1904)

Padiham
10: Operatives Leaving Jubilee Mill, Padiham (1900)

Patricroft
471: Workers Leaving Textile Factory in Patricroft (1901)

Pendlebury
58: Miners Leaving Pendlebury Colliery (1901)
61: Operatives of Acme Spinning Co., Pendlebury (1901)
772: Sedgwick's Bioscope Showfront at Pendlebury Wakes (1901)

Preston
283: Workforce at Horrocks Miller & Co., Preston (c. 1901)
285: Ribble at Preston (c. 1901)
286: Preston Egg Rolling (c. 1901)
287: Congregation at Preston Parish Church (c. 1901)
289: Turn Out of the Preston Fire Brigade (c. 1901)
281–2, 329: Return of the East Lancashire Regiment at Preston (1902)
99: Preston North End v. Notts County (1904)
96–8: Preston North End v. Wolverhampton Wanderers (1904)
288: Preston Street Scenes (1904)
290: Schoolchildren at St Ignatius School, Preston (1904)
100: Preston North End v. Aston Villa (1905)
284: Preston Monday Market (1906)
291: Whitsuntide Fair at Preston (1906)
771: Green's Racing Bantams at Preston Whit Fair (1906)

Rochdale

475: Workpeople Leaving for Dinner, Robinson's Iron Foundry, Rochdale (1901)
476–8: Turn Out of the Rochdale Fire Brigade (1901)
178–9: Rochdale Tram Ride (1905)
74–5: Workers at Barlow and Tweedale Ironworks, Castleton nr Rochdale (1905)

Salford

20: Howarth's Egerton Mill, Ordsall Lane, Salford (1900)
21: Workforce of Howarth's Ordsall Mill, Salford (1900)
114: Halifax v. Salford (1901)
158, 159, 141, 162: Salford v. Batley (1901)
762: Workers Leaving Craven Ironworks, Ordsall Lane, Salford (1901)
85: Workforce Leaving Smith & Coventry Works, Ordsall Lane, Salford (c. 1901)
152: Northern Union Challenge Cup Final – Halifax v. Salford (1903)

Southport

809, 386: Waves at Southport (1902)
751: Phantom Ride through Southport (1902)
174, 384: Panoramic View of Southport Promenade (1902)
383, 385, 387: Southport Carnival and Trades Procession (1902)

St Helens

24: Workers at Pilkington Glass Works, St Helens (1900)
25–6: Operatives Leaving Messrs Pilkington Bros. Works, St Helens (1901)
160: Runcorn v. St Helens (1901)
161: St Helens v. Swinton (1901)
381: Oddfellows Procession in St Helens (c. 1901)

Tyldesley

479: Children Leaving Tyldesley Catholic School, Lodge Road (1901)
480: Procession of Children, at Tyldesley Church School (1901)
57: Workers at St George's Colliery, Tyldesley (1901)

Warrington

34: Employees at White Cross & Co. Ltd Wire Works, Warrington (1900)
373: Warrington v. St Helens (1901)
44: Employees of Rylands Bros. Ltd Wireworks, Warrington (1902)
374: Congregation Leaving Warrington Parish Church at 12.00 Noon, Sunday August 31st (1902)
375: Warrington Walking Day Catholic Procession (1902)
376–80: Warrington Walking Day Procession (1902)

Widnes

79: Workers Leaving Gossage's Soap Works, Widnes (1901)
382: Parade of Widnes Schoolchildren (1901)

Wigan

30: Employees at Walker Engineering Works, Wigan (1900)
372: Factory Exit in Wigan (1901)
360: Workers Leaving a Factory in Wigan (1902)
363: Turn Out of the Wigan Fire Brigade (1902)
361–2: Wigan Coronation Celebrations and Street Scenes (1902)
367–8: Wigan Mayoral Coronation Procession (1902)
175: Living Wigan (1902)
149: Hull FC v. Wigan (1902)
148, 653: Hull Kingston Rovers v. Wigan (1902)
369–71: Trotting Match at Springfield Park, Wigan (1904)

LEICESTERSHIRE

Leicester

142, 118-19, 147: Sunderland v. Leicester Fosse (1907)

Loughborough

32: Workforce Leaving Cartwright & Warner Hosiery Works, Loughborough (1900)
36: Workforce of Brush Electric Co., Falcon Works, Loughborough (1900)

Lincolnshire

Gainsborough

124–8: Bradford City v. Gainsborough Trinity (1903)
45–6: Employees of Marshall's Engineering Works, Gainsborough (1908)

Grantham

83: Workforce at Hornsby and Sons of Grantham (1900)

Lincoln

38: Employees at Robey's Works, Lincoln (1900)
504: Factory Exit in Lincoln (1900)

LONDON

807, 817: Funeral of Queen Victoria (1901)
826: Coronation of Edward VII (1902)
418–19: Return of Kitchener (1902)

NORTHAMPTONSHIRE

Northampton

507: All Saints Church with Parade of the Northamptonshire Regiment (1902)
508: Scenes in Abington Park, Northampton (1902)
509: Portraits of Well-Known Residents Leaving All Saints Church, Northampton (1902)

NORTHUMBERLAND

Newcastle

35: 20,000 Employees Entering Lord Armstrong's Elswick Works, Newcastle upon Tyne (1900)
683, 684: The Fleet in the Tyne (1901)
678: Turn Out of the Newcastle Fire Brigade (1901)
109–11, 121: Newcastle United v. Liverpool (1901)
101–3, Everton v. Newcastle United (1902)
104–5: Everton v. Newcastle United (1903)

North Shields

685: Tynemouth Swimming Gala in the Haven, North Shields (1901)
731: North Sea Fisheries, North Shields (1901)

NOTTINGHAMSHIRE

Mansfield

13: Creswell and Langwith Miners, Mansfield (1900)
538: Congregation Leaving Wesleyan Chapel in Mansfield (c. 1901)

Nottingham

76: Employees Leaving Thackeray's Cotton Mill (1900)★
31: Workpeople and Girls Leaving Thos. Adams Factory (1900)
535: Workpeople and Girls on Stoney Street, Nottingham (1900)
120, 122, 123: Notts County v. Middlesbrough (1902)
163–5: Tram Rides through Nottingham (1902)
536: Scenes on the Trent, Nottingham (1902)
537: Views of the Trent Bridge Boulevard (1902)
129–30: Nottingham Forest v. Stoke (1904)★

Worksop

33: Workforce at Steel & Garland Priory Foundry, Worksop (1900)

STAFFORDSHIRE

Black Country

92, 765: Black Diamonds – The Collier's Daily Life (1904)

Hanley

539: Congregation at Hanley Old Church (c. 1901)
66: Workforce of Johnston's Pottery in Hanley (c. 1901)★

Leek

70: The Employees Leaving Wardle & Davenport Silk Works, Leek (1901)★
68: Living Pictures of Leek Brough Nicholson & Hall, Silk Works (1901)★

Stoke

71: Exit of Workers at Kerr Locomotive Works, Stoke (c. 1902)★
134: Stoke v. Grimsby Town (1902)★
129–30: Nottingham Forest v. Stoke (1904)★
132: Stoke v. Bury (n.d.)★

Warley

740–1: Scenes Outside a Church in Warley (c. 1901)

West Bromwich

527: Comic Pictures in High Street, West Bromwich (1902)

WARWICKSHIRE

Birmingham

190: Horse Trams in Birmingham (1901)
518: Employees Leaving Tangyes Engineering Works, Smethwick (1901)
763, 78: Workers at Messrs Kynock's Ltd, Ammunition Works, Birmingham (1901)
520, 814–15, 819: The Return of the Royal Warwickshire Regiment (1901)
519: Blue Coat Children Marching to Curzon Hall, Birmingham (1901)
112: Liverpool v. Small Heath (28 September 1901)
523–6: Birmingham University Procession on Degree Day (1901)
510–11, 513, 515–16: The Champion Athletes at Birmingham (1902)
512, 513: Church Parade of the Boys' Brigade in Birmingham (1902)
517: Joseph Chamberlain at Home (1902)
265: Blackburn Rovers v. Aston Villa (1904)
145: Aston Villa (c. 1904)
100: Preston North End v. Aston Villa (1905)

Coventry

531–4: Lady Godiva Procession in Coventry (1902)
528–30: March Past of 20,000 Coventry Children (1902)

Moseley

22: Workers Leaving Bamford's Works, Moseley (1900)

YORKSHIRE

Armley

577: Armley and Wortley Carnival (1904)

Bradford

637: The Crowd Entering St George's Hall, Bradford (1901)
638–41, 645–7: Magnificent Reproductions of the Great Yorkshire Show in Bradford (1901)
155–7: Dewsbury v. Manningham (1901)
166–9: Electric Tram Rides from Forster Square, Bradford (1902)
621–5: Bradford Coronation Procession (1902)
626–30, 631: Bradford Coronation Procession (1902)
632–6: Day School Sports at Park Avenue in Bradford (1902)
124–8: Bradford City v. Gainsborough Trinity (1903)

Dewsbury

7: Workers Leaving Oldroyd & Sons Mill, Dewsbury (1900)
155–7: Dewsbury v. Manningham (1901)

Doncaster

593: Great Northern Railway Works at Doncaster (1901)

Halifax

114: Halifax v. Salford (23 March 1901)
608: Bailey's Royal Buxton Punch and Judy Show in Halifax (1901)
184, 614: Tram Ride into Halifax (1902)
609–10, 612–13: Street Scenes in Halifax (1902)
611: Mayor Entering His Carriage Near the Town Hall, Halifax (1902)
52: Northern Union Challenge Cup Final – Halifax v. Salford (25 April 1903)
615: Views of Halifax (c. 1905)
616–17: Halifax Catholic Procession (c. 1905)
618–19: Royal Halifax Infirmary Annual Street Procession (1908)

Hipperholme

588–90: Trip to Sunny Vale Gardens at Hipperholme (1901)

Huddersfield

28: Employees of Messrs Lumb & Co. Leaving the Works, Huddersfield (1900)
591–2: AAA Championships at Fartown, Huddersfield (1901)

Hull

27: Workers at Amos & Smith Boiler Works, Hull (1900)
650: Scenes at Monument Bridge in Hull (1900)
82: Employees of Blundell's Paint Works, Hull (1901)
654: Scenes in Hull (1901)
648–9, 667: Turn Out of the Hull Fire Brigade (1902)
663–6: Lieutenant Clive Wilson and Tranby Croft Party (1902)
150, 131, 660: Hull FC v. Hull Kingston Rovers (26 April 1902)
657: Congregation Leaving St James's Church, Hessle Road, Hull (1902)
661–2: Sunday Promenade of Spectators in West Park, Hull (1902)
658–9: Kingston Rowing Club at Practice (1902)
149: Hull FC v. Wigan (4 October 1902)
778: General French at Tranby Croft (1902)
651–2: Hull Fair (1902)
148, 653: Hull Kingston Rovers v. Wigan (25 October 1902)
655–6: Sunday Parade in East Park in Hull (1904)
113, 115: Hull City Football (1905–6)

Hunslet

151: Hunslet v. Leeds (1901)
581–2: Hunslet Carnival and Gala (1904)

Keighley

595–6: Turn Out of the Keighley Fire Brigade (1902)

Leeds

42: Workers Leaving Fowler's Ironworks, Leeds (1901)
584: Turn Out of the Leeds Fire Brigade (1901)
583: York Road Board School, Leeds (1901)
570: Demolition of a Mill Chimney in Leeds (1901)
151: Hunslet v. Leeds (1901)
585: Ralph Pringle Interviewing Private Ward VC Hero in Leeds (1901)
571–3: Great Yorkshire Show at Leeds (1902)
563: Leeds Mayoral Procession for the Coronation Celebrations (1902)
554–6: Leeds Lifeboat Procession (1902)
557: Leeds Street Scene (1902)
558–62, 564, 808: Leeds Lifeboat Procession and Sports at Roundhay Park (1902)
550–3: Leeds Athletic and Cycling Club Carnival at Headingley (1902)
565–9: Leeds Lifeboat Demonstration (1902)
152: Northern Union Challenge Cup Final – Halifax v. Salford at Headingley (1903)
574–6: Leeds Crossgates Flower Show (1904)

Middlesbrough

735: Congregations Leaving St Hilda's Church, Middlesbrough (1902)
736: Congregations Leaving the Centenary Chapel, Middlesbrough (1902)
120, 222–3: Notts County v. Middlesbrough (1902)
117: Sunderland v. Middlesbrough (1904)

Rotherham

603: Employees Leaving Yates Haywood & Co. Foundry, Rotherham (1900)
601: Workers Leaving Guest and Chrimes Brassworks, Rotherham (1901)
602: Workforce of Parkgate Iron and Steel Co., Rotherham (1901)
599–600: The Funeral of the Late Captain of the Mexborough Fire Brigade (1902)
598: Procession of Rotherham Schoolchildren (1902)
139, 755: Rotherham Town v. Thornhill (1902)

Saltaire

9: Workforce Leaving Salt's Works in Saltaire (1900)

Settle

642–4: On the March with the Bradford Artillery at Buckshaw Brow, Settle (1902)

Sheffield

84: Employees Leaving Vickers, Sons and Maxim Works, Sheffield (1901)
77: Employees Leaving Brown's Atlas Works, Sheffield (1901)
176–7: Tram Ride through the City of Sheffield (1902)

605: Sheffield Street Accident (1902)
604: Congregation Leaving Parish Church, Sheffield (1902)
607: Spectators Promenading in Weston Park (1902)
606: Sheffield United v. Bury (1902)
95: Blackburn Rovers v. Sheffield United (1907)

Skipton
597: Skipton Hospital Procession (1902)

Wakefield
594: Miners' Demonstration at Wakefield (1908)

IRELAND

Belfast
724, 183: Ride on a Tramcar through Belfast (1901)

Blarney
723, 243: Ride from Blarney to Cork on Cork and Muskerry Light Railway (1902)

Cork
708: Albert Quay in Cork (1902)
710: Tram Ride from King Street to Patrick's Bridge, Cork (1902)
709: Views of the Grand Parade, Cork (1902)
711: Workers Leaving Lee Boot Factory – Dwyer & Co. Ltd (1902)
236, 820: Panorama of Queenstown Harbour (1902)
785: Preparation of the Cork Exhibition Grounds and Erection of Buildings (1902)
703: Panorama of Cork Exhibition Grounds (1902)
704, 705, 712: Trade Procession at Opening of Cork Exhibition (1902)
702: Arrival of VIPs for Official Opening of Cork Exhibition (1902)
717: Lord Mayor of Cork Arriving for Official Opening of Cork Exhibition (1902)
715–16: The Visit of the Duke of Connaught CIC Forces in Ireland and Prince Henry of Prussia to Cork Exhibition (1902)
718–20: Cork Fire Brigade Turning Out (1902)
721: Congregation Leaving St Patrick's Church in Cork (1902)
722: Congregation Leaving St Mary's Dominican Church in Cork (1902)
714: Sports Day at Queen's College Ground, Cork (1902)
706: Two-Oared Boat Race, Sunday's Well, Cork (1902)
713: Regiments Returned from Boer War to Victoria Barracks, Cork (1902)
707: Crews Practising on River Lee at Cork Regatta (1902)
701: Final of International Cup at Cork Regatta between Leander and Berlin (1902)

Curragh
5, 795: Ambush II at Eyrefield Lodge, Curragh (1902)

Derry
188: Cattle Market in Derry (1902)

Dublin
729: Congregation Leaving St Mary's Pro-Cathedral, Dublin (1901)
728: Panorama of College Green, Dublin (1902)
730: Congregation Leaving Jesuit Church of St Francis Xavier, Dublin (1902)

Wexford
725: Wexford Railway Station (1902)
726–7: Life in Wexford (1902)

SCOTLAND

Annan
686: Public School in Annan (c. 1901)

Beith
89: Workforce of Pollock's Caledonian Cabinet Works, Beith (1901)

Dalbeattie
687: Schoolchildren at Dalbeattie Public School (c. 1901)

Dundee
87: Employees Leaving Baxter's Jute Works, Dundee (1901)
88: Employees Leaving Gilroy's Jute Works, Dundee (1901)
691: Turn Out of the Dundee Fire Brigade (1901)
241: Over the Tay Bridge on an Express Train (1901)

Dumfries
688: Congregation Leaving St Mary's Church, Dumfries (c. 1901)
689: Scholars Leaving St Andrew's RC School, Dumfries (c. 1901)
690: Love Burn Street School, Dumfries (c. 1901)

Edinburgh
693–4: Procession in Edinburgh (1901)
792, 798: Royal Scots Regiment at Edinburgh Castle (1901)
692: Lizars Edinburgh (1904)

Glasgow
700: The Snowman (1901)
186: Jamaica Street, Glasgow (1901)
230, 699: SS Mongolian Leaving the Clyde (1906)
695–8: Boys' Brigade Inspection at Yorkhill, Glasgow (1906)

Greenock
90: Workforce of Scott & Co., Shipyard, Greenock (1901)

Irvine
228, 750: Lady Mostyn Discharging Grain at Irvine (c. 1901–2)

WALES

494, 737: Royal Visit to Rhyl (1902)
495: Royal Visit to Bangor (1902)
496: North Wales Officers and Crew (c. 1902)★
214–22: A Trip to North Wales on the St Elvies (1902)
153–4: Wales v. Ireland at Wrexham (1906)
136, 223–4: Llandudno May Day (1907)

Unidentified Locations

238: [Factory Gate Exit in Lancashire] (c. 1900)
791: [Workers Leaving a Factory] (c. 1900)
767: [Unknown Factory Gate Exit] (c. 1900)
773: [Workforce Leaving a Factory] (c. 1900)
766: [Workforce Leaving a Factory in the North of England] (c. 1900)
40: Workers at Ross & Hardy Paper Works (1901)
93: [Factory Gate Exit] (c. 1901)
94: [Workforce Leaving a Factory at Lunchtime] (c. 1901)
759: [Employees Leaving a Factory] (c. 1901)
764: [Textile Workers Leaving a Factory] (c. 1901)
768: [Lancashire Factory Gate Exit] (c. 1901)
804: [Exit of White Collar Workers] (c. 1901)
191: [Tram Terminal]★ (c. 1901)
748: [Water Polo Match] (c. 1901)
818: Ship Departing from Port (c. 1901)
792: [Crowds Leaving Sports Event] (c. 1902)
789: [VIP on Balcony] (n.d.)
793: [Crowds in Town Centre] (c. 1902)
784: [Street Scenes in North of England] (c. 1902)
185: [Unidentified Street Scenes] (c. 1902)
803: [Parade of Schoolchildren] (c. 1902)
810: Procession of Firemen (c. 1902)
781, 753: Views of Unidentified Town Centre (c. 1902)
787, 796, 800: Boys' Brigade Review at Racecourse (c. 1902)
756: Calisthenics (c. 1905)
816, 821, 824: [Miscellaneous Offcuts] (c. 1902)
789: [VIP on balcony] (c. 1902)
242: [Unidentified Railway Journey] (c. 1902)

Further Reading

A large and comprehensive body of literature has been produced on various aspects of Edwardian society, its politics, leisure and the development of the urban community, much of which is published in specialist journals and sometimes obscure but nonetheless important publications. These are cited in the main text. The following publications have been highlighted as a guide for future reading or as titles that are essential for understanding the greater context of the developments in early film, leisure, sport, popular entertainment and military history. For overall background to the Edwardian period see G. R. Searle, *A New England: Peace and War 1886–1918* (Oxford: Oxford University Press, 2004) and Paul Thompson, *The Edwardians: The Remaking of British Society*, 2nd new edn (London: Routledge, 1992).

Chapter 1: The Mitchell & Kenyon Film Company

Very little had been written on Mitchell & Kenyon prior to the discovery of the collection and very little, again, on early film in the Edwardian era. For the latter see Rachael Low and Roger Manvell, *The History of British Film, 1896–1906* (London: George Allen, 1948), and for non-fiction films produced in this period see Denis Gifford, *The British Film Catalogue Volume 2: Non-Fiction Films, 1888–1994* (London: Fitzroy Dearborn Publishers, 2001), and Stephen Herbert and Luke McKernan, *Who's Who of Victorian Cinema* (London: BFI, 1997), for an introduction to some of Mitchell & Kenyon's contemporaries. A large amount of work has been published during the Mitchell & Kenyon research project, and individual titles or articles can be found in the text, but see Vanessa Toulmin, Simon Popple and Patrick Russell (eds), *The Lost World of Mitchell & Kenyon: Edwardian Britain on Film* (London: BFI, 2004).

Chapter 2: The Films

A large body of work has been produced over the past twenty years on early cinema, both nationally and internationally, and on the types of films produced, enabling an examination of the films produced by Mitchell & Kenyon alongside those of their contemparies. For individual companies in the Victorian era onwards see Michelle Aubert, Jean-Claude Seguin (eds), *La Production cinématographique des frères Lumière* (Paris: Bibliothèque du film: Editions Mémoires de cinéma, 1996); Richard Brown and Barry Anthony, *A Victorian Film Enterprise: The History of the British Mutoscope and Biograph Company, 1897–1915* (Trowbridge: Flicks Books, 1999); John Barnes, *The Beginnings of the Cinema in England, 1894–1901, Vols 1–5* (Exeter: Exeter University Press, 1996–8). For information on Edison see Charles Musser, *Edison Motion Pictures, 1890–1900: An Annotated Filmography* (Washington, DC: Smithsonian Institution Press, 1997); and for Pathé see Richard Abel, *The Ciné Goes to Town: French cinema, 1896–1914* (Londonberkeley: University of California Press, 1994).

For an introduction to the issues and history of early cinema see Richard Abel (ed.), *Encyclopedia of Early Cinema* (Oxford: Routledge, 2005), which contains individual biographies of the pioneers in the USA, Europe and the UK in particular, along with a wide range of important essays by leading scholars on various aspects of early film, including distribution, cinema of attractions, genres and exhibition. Other relevant publications include Dave Berry, *Cinema and Wales* (Cardiff: University of Wales Press, 1994); Christopher Williams (ed.), *Cinema: The Beginnings and the Future* (London: University of Westminster Press, 1996); Andrew Higson (ed.), *Young and Innocent? The Cinema in Britain 1896–1930* (Exeter: Exeter University Press, 2002); Simon Popple and Joe Kember, *Early Cinema: From Factory Gate to Dream Factory* (London: Wallflower Press, 2004); Colin Harding and Simon Popple, *In the Kingdom of Shadows: A Companion to Early Cinema* (London: Cygnus Arts, 1996). For local films see Stephen Bottomore, 'From the Factory Gate to the "Home Talent" Drama: An International Overview of Local Films in the Silent Era', in Toulmin *et al.* (eds), *The Lost World of Mitchell & Kenyon*, pp. 33–48 (33); Uli Jung, 'Local Films: A Blind Spot in the Historiography of Early German Cinema', *Historical Journal of Film, Radio and Television*, Vol. 22 No. 3 (2002), p. 255; and also Janet McBain, 'Mitchell and Kenyon's Legacy in Scotland – The Inspiration for a Forgotten Film-Making Genre', in Toulmin *et al.* (eds), *The Lost World of Mitchell & Kenyon*, pp. 113–25, for an introduction to the local material produced by and for cinema owners in Scotland from the 1910s to the 1950s. For Germany see Brigitte Braun and Uli Jung, 'Local Films from Trier, Luxembourg and Metz: A Successful Business Venture of the Marzen Family, Cinema Owners', *Film History*, Vol. 17 No. 1 (2005), pp. 19–29.

For an in-depth study of the Victorian craze for crime reporting see Thomas Boyle, *Black Swine in the Sewers of Hampstead* (London: Viking, 1989); and for information pertaining to the *Illustrated Police News* see Leonard De Vries, *'Orrible Murders: An Anthology of Victorian Crime and Passion Compiled from The Illustrated Police News* (London: Macdonald, 1974). For information about Madame Tussaud see Pauline Chapman, *Madame Tussaud in England: Career Woman Extraordinary* (London: Quiller Press, 1992), and Pauline Chapman, *Madame Tussaud's Chamber of Horrors: Two Hundred Years of Crime* (London: Constable, 1984).

Electric Edwardians: The Films of Mitchell & Kenyon (London: BFI, 2005) contains thirty-five films from the collection, with additional highlights, a feature on the preservation programme and an interview and commentary by Dr Vanessa Toulmin.

Treasures from the American Film Archives and *More Treasures from American Film Archives 1894–1931* are lavishly produced five-DVD box sets of highlights of early cinema.

The Lumière Brothers First Films contains eighty-five films made between 1895 and 1897, which were restored by the Lumière Institute in 1996 and released on DVD in 2003.

The Movies Begin: A Treasury of Early Cinema 1894–1913 is a five-volume set of films from Kino Video featuring work by Méliès and British and American pioneers.

Early Cinema – Primitive and Pioneers (London: BFI, 2005), features a collection of fifty-nine films originating from the pre-1910 era of cinema, including those of Robert Paul, Cecil Hepworth and Mitchell & Kenyon.

Edison: The Invention of the Movies, 1891–1918 (Film Center of the National Museum of Modern Art, Kino Video, Library of Congress) is a four-disc set containing 140 Edison films, an overview by Charles Musser and two hours of interviews with scholars and historians.

Chapter 3: Showmanship

No comprehensive study of late-Victorian and Edwardian shows has yet been published, but information prior to the 1860s can be found in Richard D. Altick, *Shows of London* (London/Cambridge, MA: Belknap Press of Harvard University Press, 1978).

For autobiographical accounts published by showmen see Tom Norman, *The Penny Showman: Memoirs of Tom Norman 'Silver King' with additional writings by his son, George Norman* (London: privately published, 1985); Lord George Sanger, *Seventy Years a Showman* (London: Arthur Pearson, 1908; new edn. London: J. M. Dent and Sons, 1952); W. F. Wallett, *The Public Life of W. F. Wallett* (London: Bemrose and Sons, 1870); Thomas Horne, *Humorous and Tragic Stories of Showman's Life* (London: *The Era*, 1909); E. H. Bostock, *Menageries, Circuses and Theatres* (London: Chapman and Hall, 1927). For secondary sources see John Turner, *Dictionary of Victorian Circus Performers* Vol. 1 (Formby: Lingdale Press, 1995) and Freda Allen and Ned Williams, *Pat Collins, King of Showmen* (Wolverhampton: Uralia Press, 1991).

For the world of the cinematograph exhibitor and showman see Deac Rossell, 'A Slippery Job: Travelling Exhibitors in Early Cinema', in Simon Popple and Vanessa Toulmin (eds), *Visual Delights: Essays on the Popular and Projected Image in the 19th Century* (Trowbridge: Flicks Books, 2000), pp. 50–60; Ivo Blom, *Jean Desmet and the Early Dutch Film* (Amsterdam: Amsterdam University Press, 2003); Charles Musser and Carol Nelson, *High-Class Moving Pictures: Lyman H. Howe and the Forgotten Era of Traveling Exhibition, 1880–1920* (Princeton: University of Princeton Press, 1991); Christopher Dingley, *Waller Jeffs at the Curzon Hall: A Study in Early Film Showmanship* (unpublished MA thesis, University of Derby, 2000); Jon Burrows, 'Waller Jeffs Scrapbooks', *Picture House: Journal of the Cinema Theatre Association*, No. 29 (2004), pp. 44–55; Vanessa Toulmin, 'Telling the Tale: The History of the Fairground Bioscope Show and the Showmen Who Operated Them', *Film History*, Vol. 6 No 2. (Summer 1994), pp. 219–37; Mervyn Heard, '"Come in Please, Come out Pleased": The Development of British Fairground Bioscope Presentation and Performance', in Linda Fitzsimmons and Sarah Street (eds), *Moving Performance: British Stage and Screen, 1890s–1920s* (Trowbridge: Flicks Books, 2000), pp. 101–11; and John H. Bird, *Cinema Parade: Fifty Years of Film Shows* (Birmingham: Cornish Brothers Ltd, 1947). For further information on A. D. Thomas see Stephen Herbert and Luke McKernan, *Who's Who of Victorian Cinema* (London: BFI, 1996), pp. 140–1. See also Vanessa Toulmin, 'The Importance of the Programme in Early Film Presentation', *KINtop 11: Kinematographen-Programme*, edited by Frank Kessler, Sabine Lenk and Martin Loiperdinger (2002), pp. 19–33.

Chapter 4: Leisure and Entertainment

Extensive research in leisure studies has resulted in a large body of work that has examined the role of leisure and the rise of popular entertainments. For the main texts see Robert W. Malcolmson, *Popular Recreations in English Society, 1700–1850* (Cambridge: Cambridge University Press, 1973); Hugh Cunningham, *Leisure in the Industrial Revolution, c. 1780–1880* (London: Croom Helm, 1980); John Walton and James Walvin (eds), *Leisure in England* (Manchester: Manchester University Press, 1983); Robert Storch (ed.), *Popular Culture and Custom in Nineteenth Century England* (London: Croom Helm, 1982); Eileen and Stephen Yeo (eds), *Explorations in the History of Labour and Leisure* (Brighton: The Harvester Press, 1981). For an overview of the vast amount research in this area see Emma Griffin, 'Historiographical Reviews: Popular Culture in Industrializing England', *The Historical Journal*, Vol. 45 No. 3 (2002), pp. 619–35. Manchester University Press Studies in Popular Culture, general editor Jeffrey Richards, although focusing mainly on the twentieth century, does contain important studies on aspects of Victorian and Edwardian popular entertainment. See Andew Horrall, *Popular Culture in London, c. 1890–1918* (Manchester: Manchester University Press, 2001) for example.

For circus see Brenda Assael, *Circus and Victorian Society* (Charlottesville: University of Virginia Press, 2005), in particular the extensive bibliography; for popular music see Dave Russell, *Popular Music in England, 1840–1914* (Manchester: Manchester University Press, 1997); and for music hall see Peter Bailey, *Popular Culture and Performance in the Victorian City* (Cambridge: Cambridge University Press, 1998), Paul Maloney, *Scotland and the Music Hall, 1850–1914* (Manchester: Manchester University Press, 2003) and Jackie Bratton (ed.), *Music Hall: Performance and Style* (Milton Keynes: Open University Press, 1986). Women's leisure is a rapidly expanding area of research. See Catriona M. Parratt, *More Than Mere Amusement: Working Class Women's Leisure in England, 1750–1914* (Boston: Northeastern University Press, 2001) and Rosemary Deem, *All Work and No Play: A Study of Women and Leisure* (Milton Keynes: Open University Press, 1986).

John K. Walton's impressive body of work on the Victorian and Edwardian seaside, with particular reference to Blackpool, is essential reading: in particular, *The Blackpool Landlady: A Social History* (Manchester: Manchester University Press, 1978); *The English Seaside Resort: A Social History, 1750–1914* (Leicester: Leicester University Press, 1983); *The British Seaside: Holidays and Resorts in the Twentieth Century* (Manchester: Manchester University Press, 2000); and *Blackpool* (Edinburgh: Edinburgh University Press, 1998). For particular reference to Mitchell & Kenyon see John K. Walton, 'The Seaside and Holiday Crowd', in Vanessa Toulmin, Simon Popple and Patrick Russell (eds), *The Lost World of Mitchell & Kenyon: Edwardian Britain on Film* (London: BFI, 2004), pp. 158–69.

For travelling fairs see Hugh Cunningham, 'The Metropolitan Fairs: A Case Study in the Social Control of Leisure', in A. P. Donajgrodzki (ed.), *Social Control in Nineteenth-Century Britain* (London: Croom Helm, 1977), pp. 163–84; Alun Howkins, 'The Taming of Whitsun: The Changing Face of a Nineteenth-Century Rural Holiday', in Eileen and Stephen Yeo (eds), *Popular Culture and Class Conflict 1590–1914: Explorations in the History of Labour and Leisure* (Brighton: The Harvester Press, 1981), pp. 187–209; John K. Walton and Robert Poole, 'The Lancashire Wakes in the Nineteenth Century', in Storch (ed.), *Popular Culture and Custom in Nineteenth-Century England*, pp. 100–24; Vanessa Toulmin, *Pleasurelands: 200 Years of Life on the Fair* (Hastings: The Projection Box, 2003); David Braithwaite, *Fairground Architecture* (London: Hugh Evelyn, 1968); and Geoff Weedon and Richard Ward, *Fairground Art: The Art Forms of Travelling Fairs, Carousels and Carnival Midways* (London: White Mouse Publications, 1981).

Minstrel shows in the UK is again an area rich for investigation. For further reading see Simon Featherstone, 'The Blackface Atlantic: Interpreting British Minstrelsy', *Journal of Victorian Culture*, Vol. 3 No. 2 (1998), pp. 234–52; J. S. Bratton, 'English Ethiopians: British Audiences and Black Face Acts, 1835–1865', *Yearbook of English Studies* (1981), pp. 127–42; Michael Pickering, 'White Skin, Black Masks: "Nigger" Minstrelsy in Victorian England', in J. S. Bratton (ed.) *Music Hall: Performance and Style* (Stratford: Open University Press, 1986), pp. 70–92; Theresa Jill Buckland, 'Black Faces, Garlands and Coconuts: Exotic Dances on Street and Stage', *Dance Research Journal*, Vol. 22 No. 2 (Autumn, 1990), pp. 1–12; and for a history of minstrelsy in America see Eric Lott, *Blackface Minstrelsy and the American Working Class* (Oxford: Oxford University Press, 1993).

Chapter 5: Sport in the Edwardian Era

Sports history, like leisure history, has expanded rapidly in the last twenty years. For an overview of the role of sport in British Victorian and Edwardian society, many important articles can be found in the *Journal of Sports History*, *International Journal of the History of Sports*, *Journal of Sport in History*, and these are cited in the text when applicable. For monographs see Richard Holt, *Sport and the British: A Modern History* (Oxford: Oxford University Press, 1989); Derek Birley, *Sport and the Making of Britain* (Manchester: Manchester University Press, 1993), and Derek Birley, *Land of Hope and Glory: Sport and British Society, 1887–1910* (Manchester: Manchester University Press, 1995); J. A. Mangan (ed.), *Pleasure, Profit, Proselytism: British Culture and Sport at Home and Abroad, 1700–1914* (London: Frank Cass, 1988); and Neil Wigglesworth, *The Evolution of English Sport* (London: Frank Cass, 1996). For individual sports see Brian Stoddart and Keith A. P. Sandiford (eds), *The Imperial Game: Cricket, Culture and Society* (Manchester: Manchester University Press, 1998); Keith A. P. Sandiford, *Cricket and the Victorians* (Aldershot: Scolar Press, 1994); Tony Mason, *Association Football and English Society, 1863–1915* (Brighton: The Harvester Press, 1983); Dave Russell, *Football and the English: A Social History of Association Football in England, 1863–1995* (Preston: Carnegie Press, 1997); Wray Vamplew, *Pay up and Play the Game: Professional Sport in Britain* (Cambridge: Cambridge University Press, 1988); and for the role of the public school movement in shaping the history of athletics see J. A. Mangan, *Athleticism in the Victorian and Edwardian Public School: The Emergence and Consolidation of an Education Ideology*, new revised edn (London: Frank Cass, 2000). Rugby League's important history has recently been covered by Tony Collins in *Rugby's Great Split: Class, Culture and the Origins of Rugby League Football* (London: Frank Cass, 1998) and *Rugby League in Twentieth Century Britain* (London: Routledge, 2006). For information on the sporting films in the Mitchell & Kenyon Collection see Dave Berry, 'Mitchell & Kenyon in Wales', in Vanessa Toulmin, Simon Popple and Patrick Russell (eds), *The Lost World of Mitchell & Kenyon: Edwardian Britain on Film* (London: BFI, 2004), pp. 103–12, and Vanessa Toulmin, 'Vivid and Realistic: Edwardian Sport on Film', *Journal of Sport in History*, Vol. 26 No. 1 (2006), pp. 124–9.

Chapter 6: The Edwardian City

There are numerous influential studies of the Victorian city, many of which are referred to in the relevant chapter. See Asa Briggs, *Victorian Cities* (Harmondsworth: Penguin Books, 1963), and Philip Waller (ed.), *The English Urban Landscape* (Oxford: Oxford University Press, 2000). For a more visual approach see H. J. Dyos and Michael Wolff (eds), *The Victorian City: Images and Realities* (London: Routledge, Kegan and Paul, 1973); Tristram Hunt, *Building Jerusalem: The Rise and Fall of the Victorian City* (London: Weidenfeld and Nicolson, 2004); and Simon Gunn, *The Public Culture of the Victorian Middle Class: Ritual and Authority and the English Industrial City 1840–1914* (Manchester: Manchester University Press, 2000). The use and development of urban and social space is outlined also by Stuart Croll in *Civilizing the Urban: Popular Culture and Public Space in Merthyr, c. 1870–1914* (Cardiff: University of Wales Press, 2000). For women's use of social space see Judith Walkowitz, *City of Dreadful Delight: Narratives of Sexual Danger in Late-Victorian London* (London: Virago, 1992); Lynda Nead, *Victorian Babylon: People, Streets and Images in Nineteenth-Century London* (London/New Haven, CT: Yale University Press, 2000); Erika Rappaport, *Shopping for Pleasure: Women in the Making of London's West End* (Princeton: Princeton University Press, 2000). For overall writings on the department store see Geoffrey Crossick and Serge Jaumain, *Cathedrals of Consumption: The European Department Store, 1850–1939* (Aldershot: Ashgate Publishing, 1999) and William Lancaster, *The Department Store: A Social History* (Leicester: Leicester University Press, 1995). See also Martin Daunton (ed.), *Cambridge Urban History of Britain, Vol. III, 1840–1950* (Cambridge: Cambridge University Press, 2000); and for particular emphasis on the Edwardian period see Roy Hattersley, *The Edwardians* (London: Little, Brown, 2004).

For municipal reform and individual cities please see endnotes. For further information on Manchester during this period see Alan J. Kidd and K. W. Roberts, *City, Class and Culture: Studies of Social Policy and Cultural Production in Victorian Manchester* (Manchester: Manchester University Press, 1985); Michael Balfour, *Britain and Joseph Chamberlain* (London: George Allen and Unwin, 1985); David Thornton, *Leeds: The Story of a City* (Ayr: Fort Publishing, 2002); Derek Fraser (ed.), *Municipal Reform and the Industrial City* (Leicester: Leicester University Press, 1982); Derek Fraser (ed.), *A History of Modern Leeds* (Manchester: Manchester University Press, 1980); and R. J. Morris, 'The Middle Class and British Towns and Cities of the Industrial Revolution 1780–1870', in Derek Fraser and Anthony Sutcliffe (eds), *The Pursuit of Urban History* (London: Edward Arnold, 1983), pp. 286–306.

Rational recreation and its importance in the expanding urban setting, including the development of parks and civic centres, is featured in the following publications: Hazel Conway, *People's Parks: The Design and Development of Victorian Parks in Britain* (Cambridge: Cambridge University Press, 1991); Peter Borsay, 'The Rise of the Promenade: The Social and Cultural Use of Space in the English Provincial Town, c. 1660–1800', *British Journal of Eighteenth Century Studies*, Vol. 9 (1986), pp. 125–40; and M. Golby and A. W. Purdue, *The Civilisation of the Crowd: Popular Culture in England, 1750–1900* (London: Batsford Academic and Educational Press, 1984).

Additional sources on transport history can be found William Plowden, *The Motor Car and Politics 1895–1970* (London: Bodley Head, 1971); Ronald Pearsal, *Edwardian Life and Leisure* (Newton Abbot: David and Charles, 1973); J. B. Horne and T. B. Maud, *Liverpool Transport, Volume 2 1900–1930* (Glossop: Light Railway Transport Association and Transport Publishing Company, 1982); Theo Barker and Dorian Gerhold, *The Rise and Rise of Road Transport 1700–1990* (Cambridge: Cambridge University Press for the Economic History Society, 1993). For transport and the Mitchell & Kenyon Collection see Ian Yearsley, 'The Tramway World of Mitchell & Kenyon', *Tramway Review: Historical Journal of the Light Railway Transit Association*, Vol. 26 No. 202, July 2005, pp. 52–60; and Ian Yearsley, 'On the Move in the Streets: Transport Films and the Mitchell and Kenyon Collection', in Vanessa Toulmin, Simon Popple and Patrick Russell (eds), *The Lost World of Mitchell & Kenyon: Edwardian Britain on Film* (London: BFI, 2004), pp. 181–91.

Chapter 7: Edwardian Industries and Workforce

For an overview of the Edwardian economy see Sidney Pollard, *Britain's Prime and Britain's Decline: The British Economy, 1870–1914* (London: Edward Arnold, 1989), still the definitive work in the field for an overview of the factors leading to the downturn in British fortunes in the years up to the Great War. For an introduction to issues of class and the Victorian and Edwardian workforce see Patrick Joyce, *Visions of the People: Industrial England and the Question of Class, 1848–1914* (Cambridge: Cambridge University Press, 1991); Arthur J. McIvor, *A History of Work in Britain, 1880–1950* (Houndmills: Palgrave, 2001); Elizabeth Roberts, *A Woman's Place: An Oral History of Working-Class Women 1890–1940* (Oxford: Blackwell's, 1984); and Paul Thompson, *The Edwardians: The Remaking of British Society*, 2nd new edn (London: Routledge, 1992). The importance of Lancashire in the industrial revolution is covered in John K. Walton, *Lancashire, A Social History, 1558–1939* (Manchester: Manchester University Press, 1987), and P. F. Clarke, *Lancashire and the New Liberalism* (Cambridge: Cambridge University Press, 1971). Individual industries are cited in the main body of the text, but for cotton see Douglas Farnie, *The English Cotton Industry and the World Market, 1815–96* (Oxford: Oxford University Press, 1979); Trevor Griffiths, *The Lancashire Working Classes, c. 1880–1930* (Oxford: Clarendon Press, 2001); and Alan Fowler, 'Labour in the Lancashire Cotton Industry', *Manchester Region History Review*, Vol. 9 (1995), pp. 3–10. Other industries, of which these are a few references, are covered in Sidney Pollard and Paul Robertson, *The British Shipbuilding Industry, 1870–1914* (Cambridge, MA: Harvard University Press, 1987); Tony Munford, *Iron and Steel Town: An Industrial History of Rotherham* (Stroud: Sutton, 2003); John R. Kellett, *Railways and Victorian Cities* (London: Routledge, 1979); and E. J. Larkin and J. G. Larkin, *The Railway Workshops of Great Britain 1823–1986* (London: Macmillan Press, 1988).

For first-hand accounts of the social and working conditions at the time see Robert Roberts, *The Classic Slum: Salford Life in the First Quarter of a Century* (Manchester: Manchester University Press,

1971), and Robert Roberts, *A Ragged Schooling: Growing up in the Classic Slum* (Manchester: Manchester University Press, 1976). For the association between factory hours and recreation see John K. Walton and Robert Poole, 'The Lancashire Wakes in the Nineteenth Century', in Robert D. Storch (ed.), *Popular Culture and Custom in Nineteenth-Century England* (London: Croom Helm, 1982), pp. 100–24; Robert Poole, *The Lancashire Wakes Holidays* (Preston: Lancashire County Books, 1994); Robert Poole, 'Oldham Wakes', in John K. Walton and John Walvin, *Leisure in England* (Manchester: Manchester University Press, 1983), pp. 71–90; and in Birmingham see Douglas Reid, 'Interpreting the Festival Calendar: Wakes and Fairs as Carnivals', in Storch (ed.), *Popular Culture and Custom in Nineteenth-Century England*, pp. 125–53.

For the half-time system see Neil Dalglish, 'Education Policy and the Question of Child Labour: The Lancashire Cotton Industry and R. D. Denman's Bill of 1914', *History of Education*, Vol. 30 No. 3, (2001), pp. 291–308, and P. Sandiford, 'The Half-Time System in the Textile Trade', in M. E. Sadler (ed.), *Continuation Schools in England and Elsewhere* (Manchester: Manchester University Press, 1908), p. 334. For more information on the history of child labour in the nineteenth century see Hugh Cunningham, *The Children of the Poor: Representations of a Childhood since the Seventeenth Century* (Oxford: Oxford University Press, 1991); Hugh Cunningham, 'The Employment and Unemployment of Children in England, c. 1680–1851', *Past and Present*, No. 126 (February 1990), pp. 115–50. For an overview of the legislation see Edmund and Ruth Frow, *A Survey of the Half-Time System in Education* (Manchester: E. J. Morten, 1970), and Michael J. Childs, *Labour's Apprentices: Working-Class Lads in Late Victorian and Edwardian England* (London: The Hambledon Press, 1992). For further information on the Education Act (1902) see Wendy Robinson, 'Historiographical Reflections on the 1902 Education Act', *Oxford Review of Education*, Vol. 28 No. 2–3 (2002), pp. 159–72, and Tony Taylor, 'Arthur Balfour and Educational Change: The Myth Revisited', *British Journal of Educational Studies*, Vol. 42 No. 2 (1994), pp. 133–49.

Chapter 8: Militarism in the Edwardian Age

A good introduction to all aspects of the impact of war on visual culture is Michael Paris, *Warrior Nation: Images of War in British Popular Culture, 1850–2000* (London: Reaktion Books, 2000). For the impact of the Boer War and the media see Kenneth O. Morgan, 'The Boer War and the Media (1899–1902)', *Twentieth Century History*, Vol. 13 No. 13 (2002), pp. 1–16; Jacqueline Beaumont, 'The Times at War, 1899–1902', in Donal Lowry (ed.), *The South African War Reappraised* (Manchester: Manchester University Press, 2000), pp. 67–84; Stephen Badsey, 'War Correspondents in the Boer War', in John Gooch (ed.), *The Boer War: Direction, Experience and Image* (London: Frank Cass, 2000), pp. 187–203; and Glenn Wilkinson, *Depiction and Images of War in Edwardian Newspapers, 1899–1914* (Houndmills: Palgrave, 2003). Morgan's important article on the Boer War and the media concentrates on the impact of all media forms on the dissemination of the war in British popular culture. For early film and the Boer War, John Barnes's *The Beginnings of Cinema in Engand, Vol. 4: Filming the Boer War* (London: Bishopsgate Press, 1992) includes a definitive filmography of the films produced in the UK that relate to the conflict; and see also Simon Popple, '"But the Khaki-Covered Camera is the *Latest* Thing": The Boer War Cinema and Visual Culture in Britain', in Andrew Higson (ed.), *Young and Innocent? The Cinema in Britain 1896–1930* (Exeter: Exeter University Press, 2002), pp. 13–27.

Of the many works cited in this section on the history of the Boer War, Thomas Pakenham, *Boer War* (London: Weidenfeld and Nicolson, 1979), is the main source for the political and military consequences of the war both in the UK and South Africa; but see also Gooch (ed.), *The Boer War*; Keith Terrance Surridge, *Managing the South African War: Politicians v. Generals* (London: The Boydell Press, 1998); Lowry (ed.), *The South African War Reappraised*; D. Judd and K. Surridge, *The Boer War* (London: John Murray, 2002); and Neil Parsons, *King Khama, Emperor Joe and the Great White Queen: Victorian Britain through African Eyes* (Chicago: University of Chicago Press, 1998), for African attitudes. I am also indebted to the Queens Lancashire Regiment Museum in Fulwood Barracks, Preston, for information pertaining to Lancashire regiments during the conflict and to pointing out two important works: John Downham, *Red Roses on the Veldt: Lancashire Regiments in the Boer War, 1899–1902* (Lancaster: Carnegie Publishing, 2002), and the reprint published by the Naval and Military Press of John Stirling's *Our Regiments in South Africa*. For the key figures in the conflict see Peter Trew, *The Boer War Generals* (new edn. England: Wrens Park Publishing, 2001; original edn. Stroud: Sutton, 1999).

John Springhall's body of work on the military-style organisations for boys was the main source used for the section on the Boys' Brigades, but see also John Springhall (ed.), *Sure and Steadfast: A History of the Boys Brigade, 1883–1893* (London: Colllins, 1983). For further reading on the association between youth and moral panic see John Springhall, *Youth, Popular Culture and Moral Panics: Penny Gaffs to Gangsta-Rap, 1830–1996* (Basingstoke: Macmillan, 1998), and John Springhall, *Coming of Age: Adolescence in Britain 1860–1960* (Dublin: Gill and Macmillan, 1986).

Additional Sources

Journals and Newspapers

Accrington Observer and Times
The Ashton-under-Lyne Reporter
Athletic News
The Barrow Herald
Belfast Newsletter
The Blackpool Times and Fylde Observer
The Bioscope
The Birkenhead and Cheshire Advertiser
The Birkenhead News
Birmingham Daily Mail
Birmingham Evening Dispatch
Birmingham Owl
The Blackburn Times
Bolton Chronicle
Bootle Times
Bradford Daily Argus
Bristol Times and Mirror
The British Journal of Photography
Burnley Express
Burnley Express and Avertiser
Burnley Leader
Buxton Advertiser
Carlisle Journal
Chester Chronicle
Chorley Guardian and Leyland Hundred Advertiser
The Chorley Standard
The Chronicle, with the Congleton and Macclesfield Mercury
Cinematography and Bioscope Magazine
The Clitheroe Advertiser
Colne and Nelson Times
Cork Examiner
Coventry Standard
The Craven Herald
The Crewe Chronicle
Daily Recorder and Mail
Derby Daily Telegraph
Derbyshire Times
Dewsbury Reporter
Dundee Programme
Durham Advertiser
Durham Chronicle
Eastern Morning News
Edinburgh Evening News
The Encore
The Era
The Fife Free Press
The Film Renter & Moving Picture News
Freeman's Journal
Gardeners' Chronicle
Gazette & News for Blackpool, Fleetwood, Lytham, St Annes and Fylde District
Glasgow Daily Mail
Glasgow Programme
Halifax Evening Courier
The Herald
High Peak News
The Huddersfield Examiner
Hull Daily Mail
Hull News
Hull Times
Ideas
Illustrated Police News
Keighley News
Kinematograph Weekly
Lancashire Daily Post
Lancaster Guardian
Leeds Daily Mail
Leeds and Yorkshire Mercury
Leek Times
Llandudno Advertiser
Llandudno Directory and Visitor
Liverpool Daily Post
Liverpool Echo
Liverpool Mercury
Loughborough Examiner
Loughborough Herald and North Leicestershire Gazette
Lytham Times
Manchester Evening News
Manchester Guardian
Manchester Programme
Manchester Times
Mexborough and Swinton Times
Morecambe Visitor
The Music Hall and Theatre Review
The Nelson Express
Newcastle upon Tyne Evening Chronicle
The News (Rhyl)
Northampton Mercury
North Eastern Daily Gazette
Northern Daily Post
Northern Daily Telegraph
Nottingham Evening News
Nottingham Evening Post
Optical Lantern and Cinematograph Journal
The Optical Magic Lantern Journal and Photographic Enlarger
The Optician and Photographic Dealer Trade Review
The Optician and Photographic Trade Review
Photography
Preston Guardian
Rochdale Observer
Rochdale Times
Rotherham Advertiser
Salford City Reporter
Sheffield Daily Telegraph
Shetland Life
The Shetland Times
The Shields Daily News
Shipley Times
The Showman
Southport Guardian
Southport Visitor
Staffordshire Advertiser
Staffordshire Sentinel
The St Helens Reporter
Stockport Advertiser
The Strand
Sunderland Daily Echo
The Talking Machine News
The Times
Tom-O'-Dick-O'-Bobs 'Blegburn Dickshonary'
Wakefield Express
Warrington Guardian
West Bromwich & Oldbury Chronicle
Western Evening Herald
Widnes Weekly News
Wigan Examiner
Wigan Observer
The Winsford and Middlewich Guardian
The World's Fair
Wrexham Advertiser
Yorkshire Evening Post
Yorkshire Journal

Index

Notes: Place names are indexed only where there is general information relating to the place in question, not for every reference to films shot or shown there (look under film titles or in the Filmography for these). Page numbers in **bold** indicate detailed analysis; those in *italic* refer to illustrations (or captions). *n* = endnote.